"THE FRANCHISE,"

RESTORE CLEAN ELECTIONS AND GOD'S COUNTRY

Election Cheat History,
Conflict of Interest, ?Justice?, Presidential Immunity
Presidential Powers

By George McCarley

DEDICATED TO:

THE MANY PATRIOTIC AMERICANS WHO HAVE PLACED THEMSELVES IN DANGERS WAY WHILE SERVING AS VOLUNTEERS IN THE ONGOING EFFORT TO CORRECT THE ERRANT OPERATION OF VOTING PRACTICES AND ENFORCEMENT, AS THEY CONTINUE TO TAKE ALL STEPS TO MAKE AMERICA GREAT AGAIN.

THE FRANCHISE is a most important means of communicating all the abuses of voting practice dating back to Civil War Reconstruction Period. This book can guide ongoing efforts to identify election irregularity in any form and is fully applicable to any and all Courts level cases that may be created in future.

WHAT FRANCHISE, you ask? While debating The Voting Rights Act in the 1960's, and many other elections cases that came before the court, Supreme Court of the United States began to apply a term to American Voting and Elections they called "The Franchise." They make many statements related to voting, typically making reference to The Franchise. Their lingering thought is that Voting and Elections are the very fabric that holds Democracies and Democratic Republics together. Therefore, to protect The Franchise, we must constantly ensure that we make every effort to protect a free-flowing democracy exercise that returns a result in the best interest of our favorite franchise, The United States of America.

COPYRIGHT PAGE

ISBN: 979-8-9912575-3-4

TABLE OF CONTENTS

CHAPTER 1. Amicus Curiae Overview

This book was originally authored as an AMICUS CURIAE BRIEF, presented for consideration of the Presidential immunity question before SUPREME COURT OF THE UNITED STATES. The author read all other documents presented, wrote an AMICUS, yet was never successful communicating with Supreme Court to determine deadlines. Considering the weight of materials in the original AMICUS, we produced a full-length book.

This book was prepared for publication in time to influence the 2024 election. Those democrats hidden all over America blocked publication.

We respectfully urge Supreme Court of the United States to Concur that Donald Trump is IMMUNE FROM PROSECUTION on any and all his attempts to reverse the outcome of the 2020 election. Herein we will provide this honorable court the HUGE WEIGHT OF THE EVIDENCE of a badly flawed election that rightfully should have led to election officials JAILED.

Supreme Court of the United States did in fact declare Donald Trump to have immunity, in keeping with the long established US Constitution clauses that will be cited in later chapters. Presidential Immunity is not new. It is a fixture of the US Constitution since the earliest days of our Republic.

This writer can well be called a lifetime veteran of the vote cheater "wars." He was TIP OF THE SPEAR cleaning up elections in State of Alabama, with initial actions about 1968, beginning at a time when the only political party active in Alabama was Democrat. Even then, Democrat party took many means outside the law in order to ensure their preferred democrat candidate won the election, although there were rarely any Republican candidates. In recent days, each and every time we clean up one form of election cheating, they only develop new methods to corrupt the outcome. These points will be explained herein, along with points and evidence indicating even the democrats once followed a limit on the extent of ballot stuffing. Today they have thrown caution to the wind, explained herein.

Prior to the advent of computerized and other digital technology entering the world of voting and elections, we only had to contend with human hand corruption. Now today's election technology has injected new levels of corruption over and above the capability of typical poll watchers to identify, trap and report. Today, it is entirely possible that a "computer hacker" working from a thatch roofed hut in a 3rd world country holds the potential to change the outcome of National elections in United States of America. Indeed, the modern sovereign nations could easily apply their "intelligence" technology to impact outcome of our elections. It has never been more important to resolve, fix, and prevent future "election cheating."

The many problems leading up to this case have roots about 1880 at the end of Civil War Reconstruction down south. Democrats developed these many means to control election outcomes as a means of sending the northern "Carpet Baggers" home. While those methods might have been saluted in 1880, those methods should have ceased and desisted altogether at least 100 years ago.

President Donald Trump, via his Oath of Office has now been beset with an election issue that takes on the face of a multi-headed hydra. At the same time democrats attempt to continually loosen the voting rules and allow non-citizens to vote and remove requirements for proof of residency and proof of registration to vote, we continue beset with an unencumbered ability of poll workers to manipulate the result of their precinct, simultaneous to out of control technology. Presented herein we will provide the court access to the huge weight of evidence of these "monsters" influence upon election outcome.

It is blatantly clear to all fully experienced election day "activists" that huge problems did in fact occur during the election of 2020. Given the present sets of seriously incomplete elections control practices, these very same illegal acts are at present unabated and will continue to occur until official legal acts bring the offenders to justice. Thanks to Donald Trump, we now have a national leader who has proven he will continue to fight this fight, and is in process of factually exposing the many vote/election cheating mechanisms existing today.

While many will argue the methods chosen by Donald Trump to attack this problem, we present, American History precedent by other Presidents of the United States, along with historical examples from ancient democratic Roman Republic in the day of Cicero and Julius Caesar that highlight what can happen as a result of leadership disputes that destroyed democracy and yielded The Roman Empire.

Ongoing attempts to repair and remediate this extreme problem have been slowed by a retarded belief in US Congress and Courts that our US Congress has granted the several states the responsibility to establish election practices and voting enforcement. THAT IS AS WRONG AS WRONG CAN BE. A Constitutional Amendment would be required for such responsibility to be relinquished by the Federal government. Until or unless such amendment is passed, our federal government will always retain responsibility to oversee any and all elections that have federal candidates or national issues on the ballot.

It should be clear to the most casual onlooker; United States of America looks much like a third world country on election day. How and why is it possible that so many ongoing third world countries continue to utilize Americans as election advisors and poll watchers. Unless America can clean up our election cheating practices, we are drifting further and further into the third world abyss.

CHAPTER 2. INTRODUCTION PRESIDENTIAL IMMUNITY ATTACK

This book is written with intent to fully inform all professionals and the general public, regarding the 2024 state of political affairs in America resulting from several national elections. While all voters were there, we all know the details that mass media never publishes are overwhelming in terms of destructive effect. It seems our mass media has no understanding of the reverse direction of America.

Our Judges, Prosecutors and most Lawyers have lost touch with our Founding Fathers Constitutional standards that made America the greatest nation. United States Congress of 2023 may be the least prepared Congress in American history. While many Congressmen are a good fit for the job, the vast majority do not need to be elected to any post large or small.

This book was inspired by the 2023 Supreme Court of the United States (SCOTUS) case requesting Presidential Immunity clarification. The many national and electoral issues that transpired leading up to that case led this Author to draft an AMICUS CURIAE brief (standard SCOTUS case brief) in response to the Presidential Immunity case moving forward. Near the end of research and writing, it was discovered SCOTUS no longer maintains a telephone service providing information to the public or Attorneys. Author McCarley docketed a case at SCOTUS (2005) and at that time, SCOTUS staff had a practice of preparing and updating an expected format in which all submissions must be presented. The author called (2024) almost daily for ten days and received nothing but answering machines and forwarding numbers, submission not possible.

Research for writing the Amicus Curiae led us to read and review all the filings presented to SCOTUS by Prosecution and Defense Attorneys. It is somewhat remarkable that none of those filings cited anything presented in our Amicus Curiae. Therefore, the need for this book appears accented.

This book will present our Amicus Curiae in several chapters, and then extend the Amicus Curiae chapters to present all the necessary supporting detail necessary to understand the cause and effect of a Presidential Immunity question being presented to SCOTUS, along with all the supporting details that indicate a substantial number of failures on the part of Federal and State government, Courts, Political Parties, Universities, and all Mass Media sources.

This book is written to document the totality of illegal vote cheating in these United States. All over America, at the same time we send delegations to serve as election observers in many foreign countries, we in America continue to dream up more new ways to destroy the election integrity of the only continuing successful democratic republic in all history. We should feel eternally sorry for the citizens of Venezuela and other empire-like countries, but we in America are demonstrating the same decline, beginning with our elections.

Atop all the vote cheating which has existed at least since the 1880 end of War of Northern Aggression / Civil War Reconstruction, modern technology continues to provide more and simple means to defraud the outcome of local, state, and national elections.

How is it possible the USA has now utilized two small-population weak democracy countries to develop the computer hardware and software that we utilize in our elections? Was it not America who invented the totality of computers and the internet? It was the work of a Texan scientist who would develop "vacuum tubes" and "silicon chips" that would power and operate mainframe computers and modern desktop computers that drive digital operations.

In 2020 elections, TV and video camera's were a great assist to identify the more sinister, large scale cheating, which did in fact occur in several of the largest and most consequential voting centers in America, namely Maricopa County Arizona with a vote total in the 2 million range, followed by Fulton County, Georgia with more than enough votes cast to control national outcome, followed by Pennsylvania and Michigan, with significant vote totals.

How could it be possible that former President Donald Trump received the highest vote total of any president in election history, yet he lost? Obvious criminal actions were seen on many news casts and internet sources. Televised evidence was so overwhelming that Donald Trump sought many ways to overturn the result. Even more dubious was the US Congress Certification of an election that was so criminal that it made Al Capone look like an Angel.

Public outcry was so intense that by January 06, we saw millions descend on Washington, DC in hopes of convincing US Congress to declare the election invalid. Many of those people have been jailed by misguided courts.

Then we saw Prosecutors begin to file cases against Trump. Those Judges were not compelled to docket rogue cases.

Steele Dossier had played all over the national newscasts for several years, only to be found a set of falsehoods. These were the investigations mounted by Robert Mueller and James Comey, lasting several years. Prosecutors tried many means to make Trump look evil, even with the Steele Dossier proven a great lie. Then our Mainstream Media began to declare any and all suggestions of election cheating to be misinformation, whereas their own newscasts showed the televised unambiguous evidence of wrongdoing.

By this time, Congress certified the election and Trump Republicans began plans to put an end to election cheating. Democrats reacted by filing more baseless charges against Trump than were filed against all Mafia figures.

Only a cursory reading of the United States Constitution section on Executive Powers is required to see that Donald Trump was and is perfectly within his authority to take all steps to prevent a criminal result from becoming law by certification. It is not necessary to read any deeper than the Presidential Oath of Office to realize Trump was constitutionally expected to act.

Many previous Presidents have been faced with issues requiring them to act to prevent many disruptions to America. Unfortunately, we would learn the terrible low level of education and preparation within our legal community, as not a single one of the charges against Trump are legitimate and may well be proven to be outright acts of Treason by prosecutors and judges.

How is it possible those Democrat Prosecutors/Lawyers would file thousands of charges, while Republican Legal Eagles remained silent? Given the baseless charges filed by democrats, why did we not see RNC file even more counter charges against these democrat liars? Our legal industry fears electoral issues.

There is a belief within US Congress that Congressional action has delegated electoral law to the states. The Constitution is clear. Federal government controls any and all elections in which a federal candidate or issue is on the ballot.

If in fact electoral responsibility was truly delegated to the states, then most states are in full violation of constitutional law. The several states have failed to uphold any constitutional standard for elections.

Where do we go from here? It is high time all Americans took time to become educated on these issues so that we never again suffer such terrible elections.

While Supreme Court of the United States has upheld the time-honored principle of Presidential Immunity, it was not at all necessary that they look any further than the Presidential Oath of Office, along with The Take Care Clause, reproduced and annotated throughout this book. The Presidential Oath of Office obligates a sitting President to exercise the fullest extent of his power in order to protect and defend America. Then the seldom heard Take Care Clause further empowers our President to be very sure he has in fact taken all due care to safeguard and protect our country. Within this book, we will provide a huge listing demonstrating the extent to which many earlier Presidents have exercised their oath of office along with the Take Care Clause.

This book will provide the key constitutional Articles and Sections that apply to the voting and electoral issues we face, along with a huge indication of prima facie evidence produced by the many television camera's that were heavily deployed around most polling places during the 2024 election. We will also provide chapters detailing the history of Vote Cheating, along with the progression of changes within the vote cheat sector.

CHAPTER 3. EXECUTIVE BRANCH, OATH OF OFFICE, TAKE CARE CLAUSE

Browse the Constitution Annotated
https://constitution.congress.gov/browse/article-2/section-1/

Within this book, the author presents many excerpts of The US Constitution, in a format linked to internet legal resources in order to ease the readers' research. All these points apply to the ongoing analysis of elections and the Donald J. Trump cases.

EXECUTIVE BRANCH AND PRESIDENTIAL POWERS.

This chapter provides verbatim wording of an essential element of the US Constitution in support of Donald Trump.

Article II Executive Branch
S1.C1.1 Overview of Executive Vesting Clause (Powers of the President)
Article II, Section 1, Clause 1:

The executive Power shall be vested in a President of the United States of America. He shall hold his Office during the Term of four Years, and, together with the Vice President, chosen for the same Term, be elected, as follows:

Under Article II, Section 1, Clause 1, the executive power is vested in a single person—the President of the United States. The nature and extent of the executive power is less clear.[1] Article II identifies exclusive powers of the President, including the President's authority as Commander in Chief and the power to pardon;[2] powers the President shares with the Senate, including the appointments and treaty-making powers;[3] and the President's duties, the most important of which is the duty to take Care that the Laws be faithfully executed.[4] Moreover, the Supreme Court has recognized that because no single person could fulfill that responsibility, the *Take Care Clause implicitly provides the President with authority to supervise subordinate officers assisting with this responsibility*.[5] Likewise, Article I provides the President a role in the legislative process, including authority to veto legislation, subject to potential override by a two-thirds vote of both Houses of Congress.[6] It is less clear from the Constitution whether the executive powers expressly identified in the Constitution are exclusive or illustrative. Whereas the Article I Legislative Vesting Clause provides that All legislative Powers *herein granted* shall be vested in a Congress,[7] thereby distinguishing the powers granted by states from those they retained, the Article II Executive Vesting Clause does not limit the executive Power in any way.[8]

Consequently, since earliest days of the Republic, parameters of executive power and, in particular, what implicit or residual powers such executive power encompasses have been the subject of debate.

Footnote

1. 1U.S. CONST. art. II, § 1, cl. 1.
2. 2*Id.* art. II, § 2, cl. 1. *See* ArtII.S2.C1.1.1 Historical Background on Commander in Chief Clause.
3. 3*Id.* art. II, § 2, cl. 2. *See* ArtII.S2.C1.3.1 Overview of Pardon Power.
4. 4*Id.* art. II, § 3. *See* ArtII.S3.3.1 Overview of Take Care Clause.
5. 5Seila Law LLC v. Consumer Fin. Protection Bureau, No. 19-7, slip op. at 2 (U.S. June 29, 2020). *See also* Free Enter. Fund v. Pub. Co. Acct. Oversight Bd., 561 U.S. 477, 492–93 (2010).
6. 6U.S. CONST. art. I, § 7, cl. 2. *See* ArtI.S7.C2.1 Overview of Presidential Approval or Veto of Bills.
7. 7*Id.* art. I, § 1, cl. 1 (emphasis added). *See* ArtI.S1.1 Overview of Legislative Vesting Clause.
8. 8*Id.* art. II, § 1, cl. 1.

Art II.S1.C8.1.2 Oath of Office for Presidency

Article II, Section 1, Clause 8.1.2:
Before he enter on the Execution of his Office, he shall take the following Oath or Affirmation:–I do solemnly swear (or affirm) that I will faithfully execute the Office of President of the United States, and will to the best of my Ability, preserve, protect, and defend the Constitution of the United States.

Several Presidents relied on the oath, alone or in conjunction with the Take Care Clause,[1] for authority to take actions necessary to preserve, protect and defend the Constitution. President Thomas Jefferson contended the oath obligated him to suspend prosecutions under the Sedition Act, which Jefferson repeatedly claimed was unconstitutional.[2] President Andrew Jackson relied in part on the presidential oath in vetoing a bill rechartering the Second Bank of the United States.[3] He advanced the view that the presidential oath, as well as the general oath provision in Article VI,[4] grants each branch of government independent power to interpret the Constitution.[5] Partially repudiating the Supreme Court's decision in *McCulloch v. Maryland*,[6] which upheld the constitutionality of the national bank, President Jackson suggested he authority of the Supreme Court must not . . . be permitted to control Congress or the Executive when acting in their legislative capacities . . .[7] President Lincoln relied on the oath to defend his decision to suspend the privilege of the writ of habeas corpus,[8] claiming that the presidential oath required the President to disregard a single law if doing so would preserve the Union.[9] President Lincoln similarly justified his position on emancipation of enslaved persons during the Civil War by invoking the presidential oath:[10]

During President Andrew Johnson's impeachment trial, his counsel alluded to the theory that the oath might grant the President power, but only in passing.[11] President Johnson's lawyers argued that the oath might allow or obligate the President to disregard an unconstitutional law.[12]

Oaths of Office in most offices remain in effect for life. This is most noted and applied by the U.S. Military. The massive weight of evidence documented herein makes clear that the most guilty party on Jan 06 was the United States Congress election certification. President Trump upheld his Oath of Office. United States Congress wholly failed to uphold their Oath of Office. No single element of the US Constitution calls for Congress to ignore criminal cheating practices in order to meet a deadline to certify an election.

1. U.S. Const. art. II, § 3.
2. Letter from T. Jefferson to Abigail Adams (July 22, 1804), in 1 Adams-Jefferson Letters 274, 275–76 (Lester J. Cappon ed., 1959) (suggesting obligations of oath to protect the constitution, violated by an unauthorized act of Congress, compelled Jefferson to arrest the execution at every stage of the Sedition Act).
3. Veto Message (July 10, 1832), in 3 A Compilation of the Messages and Papers of the Presidents 1139 (James D. Richardson ed., 1897) [hereinafter Messages and Papers].
4. U.S. Const. art. VI, cl. 3.
5. Messages and Papers, *supra* note 3, at 1145 (Each public officer who takes an oath to support the Constitution swears that he will support it as he understands it, and not as it is understood by others.).
6. 17 U.S. (4 Wheat.) 316 (1819).
7. Messages and Papers, *supra* note 3, at 1145.
8. The writ of habeas corpus, which allows detained individuals to challenge their detention in court, is protected from suspension by the Constitution. U.S. Const. art. I, § 9, cl. 2; *see* ArtI.S9.C2.1 Suspension Clause and Writ of Habeas Corpus.
9. Abraham Lincoln, Message to Congress in Special Session (July 4, 1861), Abraham Lincoln's Speeches and Letters, 1832–1865, at 173 (Paul M. Angle ed., 1957) (Would not the official oath be broken if the government should be overthrown, when believed disregarding [a] single law would tend to preserve it?).
10. Letter from Abraham Lincoln to Albert G. Hodges, editor of the Frankfort, Kentucky 'Commonwealth' (Apr. 4, 1864), *in* Abraham Lincoln's Speeches and Letters, *supra* note 9, at 264.
11. Cong. Globe Supp., 40th Cong., 2d Sess. 314 (1868) (suggesting that a President is bound by oath to disregard a law that upon its very face [is] in flat contradiction to express provisions of the Constitution).
12. *Id.*

The plain and simple wording of Presidential Oath of Office and Take Care Clause constitutional Articles and Sections requires little if any additional comment. Donald Trump was fully within the parameters of his Oath of Office and the Take Care Clause in his actions to overturn the 2020 election. The 2020 election is a prime example of WHY Oaths of Office and Take Care Clause are so essential to the continuing freedom of American.

CHAPTER 4. TIP OF THE SPEAR, EXPOSE DIRTY ELECTIONS

We will commence an overview of the history of vote cheating since 1880. Even President Jimmy Carter was forced to overturn illegal democrat voting actions in court to win his first election.

1. Author McCarley was "tip of the spear" cleaning up elections in Alabama. Beginning as a teenager, about 1968, the first time he ever walked into a voting location it was clear we had a huge problem. Twenty-five percent of his small home county votes in a single location, even in 2024. In 1968 they were breaking all the rules, unallowed politicking all the way to the voting machine, hundreds of people in the building. The only thing they were not doing was cooking barbeque. I was 15 years of age at the time and I said to my mother, "I expected a solemn occasion."

Following University graduation in 1975, I continued the effort to seek answers and solutions. In 1980, I wrote a letter to Alabama Secretary of State Billy Jo Camp presenting 12 election questions. I received a quick response that identified 12 different state offices responsible for each of the 12 issues. In the next election, I spoke with a small market TV station in LaGrange, Georgia (range 1 million people in Georgia and Alabama). I explained the situation and they suggested a TV camera outside the voting location and an interview late in the election day to describe the issues and if improvement or more negatives were recognized. No improvement was noted. The interview was televised several days.

Perhaps the greatest issue was the huge mechanical voting machines of the day. Those machines were problematic and failed with regularity throughout the voting day. Poll workers could fix the problem, which leads to questions regarding poll workers tampering with votes being cast. We discovered from continued questions of people who realized their vote had been compromised, that each compromise reported always failed to count a republican vote, likely switching votes to the democrat. Voters could see how their vote had been counted by checking the vote counter on the machine. Those voting machines were so simple that any auto-mechanic could set up the mechanical counters to produce a false result.

The second greatest problem is Voter Registration rules violations by the states creating problems that poll watching cannot remedy. Counties appoint voter registration officials, yet no law exists to ensure registration officials maintain lists of living voters truly residing in a city or county. A prime example was my home county. Once we seated dependable registration officials, we removed several hundred deceased or relocated voter registrations in a county casting 5,000 votes.

2. About 1990, Alabama Republicans (huge minority in 1990) activated a poll watcher system allowed by law. After my first poll watcher duty, my home county, Randolph County, Alabama became the first in Alabama to remove the mechanical voting monsters. Seeing our progress, Tuscaloosa County quickly followed.

The employee responsible for Voting Machine maintenance took a non-compos-mentis early retirement once the change was made to computerized machines, obviously concerned about legal actions.

Within the next two election cycles, all other counties in Alabama switched to computerized election gear, and Alabama became a Red State, (Republican) for the first time since the Civil War. Prior to cleaning up elections, Democrats controlled and won all Alabama elections. Following cleanup, Republicans have continued to win a heavy majority of elected offices at State and National level.

3. Even with computer gear, we experienced cheating such as continues today. The following numbered points will indicate the cheating methods.

4. The lead clerk (retired) would review auto-counted results, complete an audit, and reverse enough results for a Democrat win. Poll Watcher audits later reversed elections by proving changed vote totals by falsely claimed "transcription errors."

5. Alabama's longest serving Republican Judge Perry Hooper had announced his final run prior to retirement, a run for Chief Justice of the Alabama Supreme Court. The initial statewide count showed Judge Hooper losing by some 50 votes. In the initial vote count in my home county of Randolph, Alabama, Hooper lost by 9 votes. There were no automatic recounts in those days. The ongoing audit of election results found transcription errors in the handwritten vote summary that switched the vote count in favor of democrats.

6. Reporting the issue to CJ Perry's Camp, they reviewed all counties, and discovered illegal absentee ballots were counted. We reversed that action and returned a victory for CJ Perry Hooper, upheld by SCOTUS. The chief clerk retired as a result of the transcription discovery.

"In 1994, Hooper was narrowly elected Chief Justice of the Alabama Supreme Court, with a margin of 262 votes. He was not sworn in until October 20, 1995, nine months after his term had begun.[1] Allies of sitting Democratic Chief Justice, Ernest C. Hornsby, challenged the result, seeking to count 2,000 absentee ballots, unwitnessed and unsigned. In September 1995, U.S. District Judge Alex T. Howard Jr. decided they should not be counted.

His decision was upheld by 11th Circuit Court of Appeals and a stay granted by U.S. Supreme Court Justice Anthony Kennedy expired October 14. The full court declined to hear the case on October 19, 1995, Hooper won.[2]"

1. *Johnson, Winthrop (1999). Courting Votes in Alabama. Lafayette, Louisiana: Prescott Press, Inc. p. 250. ISBN 0-933451-41-5.*
2. *"Chief Justice Takes Office In Alabama." New York Times. October 22, 1995.*

The following are links to news stories regarding illegal ballots and the Chief Justice Perry Hooper slim statewide win by 262 votes.

- https://www.alreporter.com/2016/05/25/remembering-chief-justice-perry-o-hooper-sr/
- https://www.nytimes.com/1995/10/22/us/chief-justice-takes-office-in-alabama.html

7. In many elections, poll workers stockpile uncounted ballots and engage in sham recounts, adding votes to democrats, as did happen in Fulton County, Ga. 2020.

8. Republicans in Fulton County, Atlanta, Georgia, (highest county population in Georgia) in 2020 assembled a small army of poll watchers. Fulton Police then improperly ordered a great distance between the poll watchers and voting locations thus preventing the oversight process. That was a serious enough issue to default the election nationally, especially given the size of Fulton County. Poll Watchers are fully granted the authority to observe and review and challenge all actions by poll workers (impossible with binoculars, as was the result in Fulton County). It is essential that Poll Watchers can view the process of balloting closely enough to recognize improper acts in process.

9. Someone created a false story about a water pipe break that night and all poll watchers and workers were allegedly sent home. TV and Security Video proved the election workers returned to their tables and began pulling boxes out from under tables, counting with no poll watchers present. Again, this error was sufficient to invalidate the election. Given proper and authenticated voting machines, there is no justification for stockpiling ballots. The machines count the ballots automatically in line with the flow of voters, with machine maximum capacity stated at 3500 ballots per hour. Many counting machines reside at large voting locations. Some require the issuance of written ballots, the voter marks his ballot and feeds his ballot into a scanner which runs the ballot through the scanner immediately, and the scanned ballot is auto counted. Given truly functional machines, there is ZERO need to store ballots and feed the scanners later. Such activity will only attract suspicion and legal challenges. When storing to count later, an "allegation" of possible double counting of votes and inflating vote count, appears in favor of one party.

One vitally important job of the Secretary of State (chief voting official in most states) is to ensure sufficient voting equipment is in place in each and every county so that there will be no glitches. In the case of Fulton County, it seems clear that more vote counting machines were required at any voting location that had to stockpile ballots, thus a failure of the Secretary of State.

If in fact, the machines are not able to keep up with the flow of voters, we have a condition of failed machines that demand review and recertification of machines, meaning Dominion equipment is a failure, as Texas Secretary of State office has proven since 2012.

The following links provide video of machine counting and other failures in Fulton County, Georgia, and Pennsylvania, sufficient to decertify the 2020 election.

- https://www.foxnews.com/politics/fulton-county-georgia-no-mystery-ballots-under-table-investigator-affidavit
- https://www.hollywoodlanews.com/georgia-video-poll-workers-ballots/
- https://metrovoicenews.com/pennsylvania-senate-testimony-includes-47-missing-usb-devices/
- https://theconservativetreehouse.com/blog/2020/12/03/stunning-cctv-video-from-fulton-county-georgia-shows-workers-unloading-suitcases-of-ballots-after-monitors-told-to-leave-for-night/
- https://www.youtube.com/watch?v=nVP_60Hm4P8

10. Arizona failed to test all equipment prior to the election, as DOMINION VOTING MACHINES requires. Result was ongoing problems at reportedly 50% of voting locations, and that was enough to decertify the election.

Computer equipment has known/recognized failure points. If a computer is allowed to sit for prolonged periods without operation, startup failures may occur. Modern Printer failure is even more problematic if allowed to sit without usage. The ink wells will solidify or dry up. The laser toner cartridges will firm up requiring replacement at an advanced rate. In many computerized voting applications, a computer logs the voter and executes signature and voter registration particulars, then prints a ballot -- the voter marks his ballot and then feeds the ballot into a scanner.

In this example, either the computer, the printer, or the scanner can create a stoppage of voting. Any failure to start up and operate the computer gear prior to election is almost an intentional act of sabotage. That election cannot be certified.

Within point 10., we can see State of Arizona was guilty of two instances of failure, and just a single failure will create problematic conditions on voting day.

The following links will take you to online news stories illustrating the great failure rate of voting machines in a voting district of some 2 million in Maricopa County, Arizona. Links indicate extreme problems in Arizona in which problems strongly identified in the 2020 election were never resolved and continue to plague the 2022 midterm elections.

- https://www.nbcnews.com/politics/2022-election/vote-machine-glitch-roils-arizonas-maricopa-county-fuels-false-stateme-rcna56261
- https://apnews.com/article/maricopa-county-ballot-printers-mcgregor-kari-lake-9edeef525b8afacb767a4960bf951ea1
- https://azmirror.com/2022/12/09/too-big-of-a-job-why-maricopa-countys-ballot-printers-failed-on-election-day/

This story immediately above should demonstrate to anyone with computer printers at home that the Arizona Secretary of State office is not at all prepared to deal with computers or computer problems. "Everyone knows" that computer printers are designed to utilize a common paper thickness as thin as 18 lb. and as thick as 40 lb. Anything more and you will experience many printer problems. WHY DID ARIZONA UTILIZE A PAPER THICKNESS OF 100 lb.?

11. DOMINION Systems (voting hardware) and Smartmatic (voting software) continue to prove the inability of officials who approve machine purchase. Texas Secretary of State shows leadership and applies a system of testing of all equipment submitted prior to purchase for voting. Dominion first submitted machines to Texas Secretary of State for testing in 2012. Archived records at TX SOS prove the state declared Dominion equipment failed to meet requirements. In 2012, Dominion was just another company seeking to sell equipment. There was no drama with Dominion in 2012. Dominion continues to submit their machines yet have never remediated the failed components identified by Texas, yet most blue and some red states use Dominion equipment. Where is the sanity?

Understand that Texas was a founder of the digital revolution. The Vacuum Tube that powered Mainframe computers, and early televisions was the forerunner of Silicon Chips. Both were created by a Texan at laboratories in Texas. Dell Computer of Texas is one of the world's leading Computer suppliers.

Texas Secretary of State Archive of this data is at the following URL's:

- https://www.sos.state.tx.us/...orms/sysexam/2012aug_huff.pdf
- https://www.sos.state.tx.us/...s/sysexam/oct2019-mechler.pdf

12. Executives of major computer security companies posted videos on YouTube demonstrating a purchase of Dominion gear and within 15 minutes, opened the computer and demonstrated means of manipulation, via (1) cable connections and (2) Wi-Fi and radio inputs to system and storage, to change outcome of elections passing through that machine- - "rigged"-altered - hacked to create a false result.

Video indicated may be accessed online at the following URL's:

- https://www.youtube.com/watch?v=CShvCFzjD
  UU Black Hat Security
- https://www.youtube.com/watch?v=q7Oty69m
  Q80 Argonne National Labs
- https://www.youtube.com/watch?v=wmoxE1sJ
  c1c Symantec (Inspect machine, bad)
- https://www.youtube.com/watch?v=BLtHW0G7
  Dls 1 minute vote machine hack
- https://www.youtube.com/watch?v=HA2DWMHg
  Lnc CNN Tech (Watch Hackers do it)
- https://www.youtube.com/watch?v=QtWP0KDx2
  hA NBC (Hacker targets machine)

Given a single discrepancy of any of these points at voting location, YOU CANNOT CERTIFY THE ELECTION. CERTIFICATION MAKES THOSE ALLOWING CERTIFICATION GUILTY OF AN EXTREME OFFENSE.

Televised recordings of these criminal acts by voting officials at either Fulton County, Georgia or State of Arizona was all that was required to refuse to certify the national election. Some may argue the vote total difference between Democrats and Republicans was not sufficient to overturn a national election. However, given your total understanding of the problem, you will know that the total reported vote count from Arizona and Fulton County was unreliable, and a closely supervised repeat of those elections would be the only way to ensure an accurate vote count. Therefore again, sufficient to prevent Congressional certification.

In further chapters, you will learn the extent to which some national politicians were awarded a follow-up election, due to failures and cheating within their respective elections.

CHAPTER 5. VOTE CHEAT METHODS AND SOLUTIONS

NEXT NUMBERED POINTS IDENTIFY SPECIFIC ELECTIONS CHEATING METHODS AND POSSIBLE SOLUTIONS.

1. There are no uniform rules between the states to enforce a review and authentication of new voter registrations. There are no rules to enforce removal of names of voters who have relocated or died.

   SOLUTION
   Enact or uphold laws to annually review and validate voter registrations, adjust, and/or remove relocated or deceased voters no longer present in a jurisdiction. Laws must enforce a review of voter identification documents, current address, and rules to ensure voter has been removed from previous address.

2. Registration on election day shall not be allowed, as no time is available to validate residence or citizenship or possible registration in multiple states.

   SOLUTION
   Enact laws to enforce all new registrations be reviewed and logged months prior to the election. Those rules must enforce a review of voter identification documents, current address to ensure voter does not have multi-registrations.

3. Ballot Harvesting is an act by which an individual knocks on doors and announces he/she has arrived to allow the resident to cast a ballot. We cannot allow such, unless returned a minimum week prior to election and voter credentials are validated. Ballot Harvesting was initiated as a means of assisting the general public to vote safely during the Covid Lockdown. Now that covid danger has ceased, there is no justification for ballot harvesting.

   SOLUTION
   Immediately outlaw ballot harvesting. Due to the points displayed above, voter registration officials must and shall be afforded calendar time to review and accept or deny those credentials of Harvested Ballots. It has never been easier to register to vote and cast your vote, given a plethora of early and absentee voting and laws. Therefore, Ballot Harvesting was never required.

4. CONFLICT OF INTEREST. Greatest case was the 2020 Arizona election in which an incumbent Secretary of State ran for Governor of Arizona, while continuing to lead the Elections function of SOS office. The outgoing SOS was elected Governor and benefited from failures of 50% of polling places.

   SOLUTION
   Enact laws to be heavily enforced that prevent any semblance of CONFLICT OF INTEREST throughout the voting and legal system of these United States. At any time an incumbent chooses to seek re-election or higher office, they must immediately recuse from the Secretary of State function.

5. Disallow foreign owned or produced voting machines or software; by foreign countries and owned by foreign nationals or co-owned by American citizens.

   SOLUTION
   Outlaw the usage of foreign owned, operated, managed, or produced hardware or software for any election in these United States. Why would we dare to allow such, regardless of the presence or absence of applicable laws? This may be the greatest single CONFLICT OF INTEREST in American History. DOMINION IS A CANADIAN CORPORATION. SMARTMATIC IS OWNED AND OPERATED BY A VENEZUELAN, OPERATING IN VENEZUELA.

   Further, no company shall be allowed to create, develop, or represent a voting machine company if they are foreign nationals that divested their Corporation to an American owned company or hold stock or serve as leaders in those firms.

6. Troublesome reports in recent elections insist a late-night phenomenon exists where state and national vote totals are electronically exchanged with foreign countries, with subsequent vote total changes, allegedly flagged by "national security intelligence" resources. In early months of 2024, reports allege a foreign entity, operating in a foreign country purchased ownership and rights to be exercised in that foreign country, setting up two foreign companies, operating in foreign countries, to receive and exchange American vote totals.

   SOLUTION
   We must enact laws to maintain all vote totals, calculations, and/or related efforts within these United States. Transporting vote totals to a foreign country by any means appears an act of TREASON. Further, we must enact laws to ensure those who summarize or calculate results of an election, equally represent all American political parties.

7. Major Media bias must be eliminated. Nearly all Major Mainstream Media sources act in favor of a single political party. In the process, they fail to provide information about the other political parties. This bias extends fully into the Social Media world, where a detestable trick is being called FACT-CHECK. With any brainpower, it is all too easy to see the bias of one party versus the other. Social Media companies have been proven to apply government ordered bias to the political process. This takes us fully within the sphere of Communist propaganda, into real acts of TREASON.

   SOLUTION
   It is far too simple to apply word counts to ensure major media, and Social Media provide middle of the road reporting. No blocking of content shall be allowed unless content violates moral expectations.

8. Weaponization of Government resources (DOJ, FBI, IRS) to support one party and attack the other has been discussed-debated-exposed by whistleblowers.

   SOLUTION
   We must enact laws to prevent this type of TREASON. Such weaponization has been inspired by Soviet style communist takeovers around the world.

9. Those charged with upholding the law seem to "bury their collective heads in the sand" each and every election day. Police, Lawyers, Prosecutors, Judges, the elected, appear to require additional training and schooling in election law, as they never take the lead in investigation of election day or related problems. Might this be another CONFLICT OF INTEREST due to many of those legal officials requiring elections or re-election?

   SOLUTION
   All Police, Lawyers, Prosecutors, Judges, the elected, shall be fully trained in the fullest extent of election problems as they compromise entirety of "THE FRANCHISE" (American voting process). (Phrase attributed to former SCOTUS Justice Byron "Whizzer" White).

10. We refer to in-process review of elections as POLL WATCHING. It should be clear from information herein that enormous election violations can occur within the planning phase for that election and within problems of hardware and software. Poll watching on election day may only identify 20% of infractions.

SOLUTION

Election "poll watching" effort must and shall commence within the office of Secretary of State of each state and continue throughout . It is essential to ensure all necessary election planning actions have been completed and executed properly at state and local level.

11. Uniformly apply actions below, as these are granted to poll watchers:

a. Army of poll watchers in all blue states, probably 500,000;
b. Fully educate all Election Officials, police, prosecutors judges;
c. Poll watcher presence anytime a machine is touched or reviewed between elections;
d. Poll watchers to verify equipment testing 6 months prior to election;
e. Poll watcher presence when voting machines are programmed, setup, tested;
f. Ensure enough poll watchers onsite, start to close, all locations;
g. Document/protest out of order conditions or challenged ballots;
h. Report out of order problem conditions to AG immediately;
i. Monitor ballot storage boxes, location, inventory, marking;
j. Accompany return of ballots/boxes/summaries to county HQ;
k. Prevent TRANSCRIPTION HANDWRITING ERRORS;
l. Audit that all early vote ballots are counted;
m. Audit that all absentee votes are counted;
n. Audit that all military votes are counted;
o. Audit provisional and/or challenged ballots status;
p. All boxes/ballots are inventoried, counted, identified, present and accounted for.
q. Travel along with election data transferred from voting locations to custody of commensurate County level officials.
r. Observe any and all vote counting, result summarization, vote total transfer into Secretary of State offices.
s. Declare an act of TREASON to exist with any act of Weaponization of government resources or departments.
t. DISBAR Prosecutor or Judge that fails to take proper action.
u. If any of these points are violated, THAT ELECTION CANNOT BE CERTIFIED.

12. Ensure the following steps have been mandated by law and fully enforced by all officers of the law and by the courts.
a) Outlaw utilization of foreign owned or produced voting equipment.
b) Outlaw any possibility that vote totals are transferred by any means to another country for any purpose.
c) Remove any possibility of Ballot Harvesting.
d) Ensure Secretaries of State take actions to ensure proper levels of equipment are allocated to each and every voting location statewide.
e) Ensure Secretaries of State enforce startup and testing of all voting equipment a minimum of 6 months prior to elections.
f) Establish uniform national hardware/ software testing and ensure verification is established within the Laws of America and the States, to ensure all equipment works per law.
g) Media bias must be effectively prevented permanently. In 2024, that bias is a result of loyalty to a single party, may be the result of participation between media and government, and that party, that media outlet no longer qualifies for legal protections extended to media.
h) Ensure major political parties are equally represented throughout the holistic sequence of events leading to certification of an election.
i) Establish a national database of officers of the law and courts who completed a review of voting violations and laws.
j) CONFLICT OF INTEREST situations shall result in the violator being prohibited from holding office, and otherwise prosecuted to the fullest extent of the law.
k) If any of these foregoing points are violated, THAT ELECTION CANNOT BE CERTIFIED.

Without these steps, Democrats will once again stuff extra ballots by any means required to ensure democrat victory, just as they have since 1880. Unless we fix this ongoing problem, freedom and democracy die in future elections.

The ancient Romans experimented with voting methodology. Intent of ancient Rome was to improve voter turnout, just as we attempt today. They experimented with more liberal practices, and in each case, they returned to more rigidly controlled practices.

CHAPTER 6. VOTE CHEATING OVERVIEW SINCE 1880

Author George McCarley has developed a seniority of 55 years in poll watching, politics and elections. He is descended from one of America's oldest families. Our family history of 4 centuries in America provides background, history, and launches this book.

History represented by the McCarley Family Tree serves as this book becoming a huge cause of action, if not a mission to ensure acts of election sabotage cease.

- 4 branches of McCarley were there at Jamestown, Plymouth Rock and both Roanoke Island (crewed ships) Colonies
- One of the first to file Property Records in Boston about 1640.
- Recruited by William Penn, 1720, to go to America, defend Penn's Frontier.
- We paid William Penn's rent in Pennsylvania, 1740, (Gettys Tavern).
- We moved to Seneca, SC., in 1769, a McCarley Will was probated, we were second closest homestead to COWPENS battlefield.
- We were on both sides of the Boston Massacre.
- Fought battles of Kings Mountain and Cowpens, our backyard.
- Twelve family branches fought in American Revolution
- College Prep Professor for James Madison is in this extended Family, (Fessor Robertson)
- 2 family branches were with Andrew Jackson, including Battle of New Orleans.
- Brigadier Generals North/South at Gettysburg in family,(Robertson, Barnes)
- 13 family branches paroled at Appomattox
- We beat Stephen Austin to Texas.
- We fed Sam Houston' Army 4 days prior to San Jacinto.
- 1 at San Juan Hill with Rough Riders and Teddy Roosevelt.
- 1 chased Pancho Villa with Blackjack Pershing, then off to WW I.
- Many Branches deployed in World War I and II.
- Deployed in WW II, Battle of the Bulge, death Camps, South Pacific.
- Some deployed in Korean Conflict.
- Mission accomplished with no major conflicts since.
- Family has been involved in all war missions since Korea.
- George McCarley was Captain of Combat Engineers,
- George McCarley in 4 war Zones since leaving Military.
- Missionary duty in Albania/Kosovo during height of Kosovo War.

George McCarley began attempting to discuss politics with family as a young adult. Persistence directed George to an uncle that was Principal of one of Alabama's finest performing High Schools at the same time that he was elected President of the Alabama Education Association. He would only tell me two things. There were three levels of political payoff for voting, and that the payoff money was stored in a safe in my grandfather's home. I was college classmates with many of his students at Jacksonville State University and they were all high performing citizens, and all produced a positive effect on all they touched.

There were no Republicans in Alabama at this time. Republicans held Caucus in a Telephone booth. Democrats simply controlled who got elected as Democrats for there were no other parties. I would learn that as a part of AEA Presidential duties, my Uncle had to take charge of Democrat money distribution in Alabama. He retired about the time Alabama elections were cleansed.

McCarley has developed firsthand knowledge of vote cheating practices of democrats in all states. While widely practiced, you will not find documentation.

PRIOR TO 1880

There is much US History that is not being taught today. Much of that deals with many terrible situations between the writing of the US Constitution and the end of Civil War Reconstruction in 1880. Between 1865 and 1880, there were far too many rules governing who was allowed to vote. Writers of the day continue to try and "write" these events as racial. They rarely discuss the fact that Northern interlopers called "carpet baggers" were allowed to take government roles down south until 1880. Regardless of causation, the Southern population was beyond ready to adopt many means in a continued attempt to protect their time-honored lifestyles. Understand that the true cause of the Civil War was Northern Congressmen and Senators attempting to over-tax the greatest monetary wealth of America which was down south prior to 1860. In fact, 75% of the export volume of America passed through the port of Charleston South Carolina, until 1861. Northern states had only developed two ultra wealthy individuals and needed much added federal tax revenue in order to develop northern states. By 1859, Congress was openly debating an extensive over-taxation plan that was directed at Southern Plantations. Once Civil War commenced, there were draft riots in Appalachia, rioters called it "THE RICH MANS WAR," including my home county.

SINCE 1880

Since 1880, the greatest legal emphasis on voting controls has been many different plans for voter registration. Recently, we have an attempted move to expand voter roles to non-citizens. There have been several different methods to "stuff the ballot box" in the past 2 election cycles, such as BALLOT HARVESTING, by which individuals are rightly or wrongfully allowed to knock on doors and assist voters to cast their votes, with assistance of the "harvester" and then that harvester returns the ballots to a pre-arranged location. The largest case delivered 282,000 New York State ballots to Pennsylvania, by a USPS truckload.

Example: Media Reports harvested votes shipped to Pennsylvania:

- https://headlineusa.com/usps-confirm-ballots-ny-pa-2020/
- https://cleverjourneys.com/2021/07/12/testimony-of-truck-driver-who-delivered-ballots-from-new-york-to-pennsylvania-wont-go-away/comment-page-1/
- https://www.rt.com/usa/508397-truckload-ballots-missing-pennsylvania/
- https://rpwmedia.com/2023/06/06/postal-service-releases-final-report-contract-driver-vindicated-confirms-he-hauled-trailer-of-ballots-from-ny-to-pa-in-late-october-2020/

"The 8% rule."

The greatest corrupt cheating method may be called "The 8% rule."

Across a few decades I had been given information that the democrats applied an 8% maximum guideline to be followed on ballot stuffing, meaning that if their candidate was within 8% of victory, the election workers were coached to stuff the ballot box with enough ballots to insure victory. If the democrat was not within 8%, they did not attempt illegal means to win.

Just how was the 8% determined and implemented?

A detailed poll of each and every voting precinct had to be completed short days before an election, as most undecided voters make up their mind at the last minute. Why is it that the general public has never seen these polls? They are completed by heavily networked individuals residing in each and every precinct. Those people interact and speak with everyone in the precinct on a regular basis.

They will know the election leanings of their precinct, plus added facts of deaths or surgeries or unavoidable travel and other situations that might remove reliable votes on election day, thus a highly predictable result can be determined, given benefit of 140 years practice since 1880.

Once the poll is complete, other workers are comparing the numbers of votes they expect for the opponent. Then the 8% factor is determined thus informing the poll worker cheaters how many votes they need to salt-in to insure the victory. Given nearly all precincts practice this method, cheating wins.

We see in recent 2-3 election cycles; Democrats throw caution and the 8% rule to the wind. They allow illegal votes, from multi-votes to ballot harvesting, to allowing non-citizens to vote

VERIFICATION OF ABOVE

I grew up in the same neighborhood with a career elected state politician. Richard Laird was the son of a preacher with a church in our neighborhood. I often ran his store on Sunday's so that he could be in his dad's Church. He was elected a democrat during the Newt Gingrich sea change that favored Republicans. He remained democrat until his final term. I argued with him many times to change parties and become a conservative Republican. Each time he would argue he was more conservative than any Republican, why convert?

We planned to meet at the local office of Representative Laird one day in 2007. When I arrived, I found two childhood playmates also in his office. They were active doing things for Legislator Laird in our home county. They began to discuss voting habits, discussing this person or this family was infirmed and not likely to go vote. The discussion continued across several precincts. Now for the first time, I had come face to face with those who apply the 8% margin. Several times, they said they could help me get elected, although I did not understand what they were discussing at the time. Now two of the four in that meeting are deceased; prima facie verification evades us.

PRESIDENT JIMMY CARTER writes on his first Election Debacle, "TURNING POINT" by James Earl Carter

President Carter, in his first book, writes widely on the extensive voting abuses against him in his first run for office, which he initially lost. His cousin Hugh Carter was an Appellate Judge and interceded and assisted Jimmy Carter to win a special election, defeating election practices that prevented the Carter win.

The future President of the United States was personally exposed to voting booths in tiny structures, wherein the poll workers would routinely quiz a voter on his preference and take many efforts to influence a voter to cast his vote in a manner consistent with the wishes of the poll workers at the location.

Georgia state senator (1963–1967)

In 1962, Carter announced his campaign for an open Georgia State Senate seat fifteen days before the election.[1] Rosalynn, who had an instinct for politics and organization, was instrumental to his campaign. While early counting of the ballots showed Carter trailing his opponent Homer Moore, this was later proven to be the result of fraudulent voting. The fraud was found to have been orchestrated by Joe Hurst, chairman of the Democratic Party in Quitman County.[54] Carter challenged the outcome, which was confirmed fraudulent in an investigation. A special election was held, Carter won against Moore as the sole Democratic candidate, with a vote margin of 3,013 to 2,182.[2]

Footnotes

[1] Carter, Jimmy (1992). *Turning Point: A Candidate, a State, and a Nation Come of Age*. New York, NY: Three Rivers Press. pp. 83–87. ISBN 978-0-8129-2299-8.
[2] Bourne, Peter (1997).*Jimmy Carter: Comprehensive Bio, Plains to Post-Presidency.* pp. 108–132Scribner. ISBN 978-0-684-195438 LCC 96048593 OL 2233 9703M

CHAPTER 7. EVIDENCE OF 2020 ELECTION CHEATING

BALLOTS SHIPPED IN, NEW YORK TO PENNSYLVANIA, 288,000 REPORTEDLY INPUT TO PENNSYLVANIA VOTE COUNT

HEADLINE USA

USPS Confirms Truckload, 288K Completed Ballots Went from N.Y. to Pa., 2020.

'All the envelopes were the same size. I saw the envelopes had return addresses. ... They were complete ballots...'
https://headlineusa.com/usps-confirm-ballots-ny-pa-2020/ Posted by Jacob Bruns June 6, 2023

(Jacob Bruns, Headline USA) A US Postal Service whistleblower who admitted to shipping hundreds of hundreds of thousands of ballots from New York to Pennsylvania during the 2020 election has finally been validated by a USPS report, the Gateway Pundit reported.

In December 2020, USPS employee Jesse Morgan testified in a sworn affidavit, he personally transferred thousands of ballots across state lines as part of his job in weeks leading to the 2020 election.

"In total I saw 24 gaylords, or large cardboard containers of ballots, loaded into my trailer," he said at the time.

He also said he saw mass numbers of completed ballots in the trailer, which would later disappear without explanation.

"These gaylords contained plastic trays, ballots stacked on top of each other," he said.

"All envelopes were the same size," he added. "I saw the envelopes had return addresses. . .They were complete ballots."

After waiting nearly six hours for someone to process this cargo, Morgan was given none of the usual paperwork. Instead, in an unprecedented step, a self-styled "transportation supervisor" ordered Morgan to drive that shipment to Lancaster, Pennsylvania. Morgan dropped off his rig, whereupon it vanished.

The storyline about the suspicious interstate transport of up to 288,000 completed ballots was one of many irregularities that skeptics pointed to as evidence of the widespread and systemic fraud that Democrats had used to tip the election's balance in favor of Joe Biden over then-President Donald Trump.

Pennsylvania's secretary of state at the time, Kathy Boockvar, was later found by courts to have violated the law by ignoring state legislature directives for mail-in / absentee ballots.

However, then-U.S. Attorney General William Barr refused to investigate the dubious shipment of ballots from New York.

Despite Trump having enjoyed a healthy lead in the state on election night, Biden ultimately flipped Pennsylvania via mail-in ballots with an 81,660-vote margin of victory.

But after years of being threatened, Morgan's claims have been proved true by no less than the USPS itself.

In its recent release of an April 2022 "Closing Memorandum," the USPS recognized that Morgan did indeed drive the large trailer of mail across the border to Pennsylvania.

The heavily redacted memorandum had been withheld by USPS for a substantial period, on grounds they needed to protect "witnesses, victims, subjects, and law enforcement personnel from harassment and intimidation as a result of their association with a criminal matter."

At other times, USPS has given investigative journalist Joe Fried at the *American Thinker* a different story, suggesting the memo contained "trade secrets or privileged or confidential commercial or financial information... that could constitute an unwarranted invasion of personal privacy of third parties."

https://cleverjourneys.com/2021/07/12/testimony-of-truck-driver-who-delivered-ballots-from-new-york-to-pennsylvania-wont-go-away/comment-page-1/

CLEVER JOURNEYS

July 12, 2021, Texans Jack & Dodie
Testimony of Truck Driver Who Delivered Ballots From New York to Pennsylvania Won't Go Away

"All of this was weird."

On December 1, 2020, truck driver Jesse Morgan was ridiculed by corporate media for his account of hauling thousands of ballots from New York to Pennsylvania prior to Election Day.

As with so many other truths that were initially attacked by the press or slanted by the media, Morgan's story has stood the test of time, investigation, and corroboration.

Morgan told America he delivered ballots from Bethpage, N.Y., to Lancaster, Pa., two weeks before Election Day.

Phill Kline, a former attorney general of Kansas and director of The Amistad Project of the Thomas More Society, said The Amistad Project has corroborated the truck driver's story. "Evidence demonstrates, through eyewitness testimony that's been corroborated by others by their eyewitness testimony" that 144,000 to 281,000 completed ballots for the 2020 general election were in Morgan's haul.

TESTIMONY OF TRUCK DRIVER WHO DELIVERED BALLOTS

July 12, 2021, Texans Jack & Dodie Testimony of Truck Driver Who Delivered Ballots From New York to Pennsylvania Won't Go Away

"All of this was weird."

On December 1, 2020, truck driver Morgan was ridiculed by corporate media for his account of hauling thousands of ballots from New York to Pennsylvania prior to Election Day 2020.

As with so many other truths initially attacked by the press or slanted by media, Morgan's story has stood the test of time, investigation, and corroboration. Morgan told America he delivered ballots from Bethpage, N.Y., to Lancaster, Pa., two weeks before Election Day.

Phill Kline, a former attorney general of Kansas and director of The Amistad Project of the Thomas More Society, said The Amistad Project has corroborated the truck driver's story.

"The evidence demonstrates, and it's through eyewitness testimony that's been corroborated by others by their eyewitness testimony" that 144,000 to 281,000 completed ballots for the 2020 general election were in Morgan's haul.

Morgan's Story

Morgan told his story at a press conference. *"I drive a tractor-trailer for U.S. postal service, a subcontractor. I drive a route from Lancaster, Pennsylvania, to Bethpage, New York, to Harrisburg, Pennsylvania, back to Lancaster," he explained.*

"On October 21, when I arrived for my usual route for Bethpage, an expeditor made three references to ballots to be loaded into my trailer, including saying, 'Hey, you have ballots today,'" Morgan noted.

He received 24 Gaylord boxes of ballots, stacked on top of each other, the "envelopes had handwritten return addresses."

"They were complete ballots. I didn't think much of it at the time," Morgan said, but when he arrived in Harrisburg, he was not permitted to offload the mail.

Forced to Wait

"I was made to wait for roughly 6 hours, from 9:15 a.m. to nearly 3 p.m.," he said. "All of this was weird," Morgan recalled. After waiting for six hours, he went inside and asked to see the expeditor.

"I was told to wait for the transportation supervisor," an official Morgan had never dealt with. "He's a top guy; he's the kind of guy that would speak to my boss." "The supervisor told me to drive to Lancaster without being unloaded in Harrisburg," Morgan said. "I knew the ballots were loaded for Harrisburg."

When Morgan asked for his ticket slips that showed he arrival, and a late slip to prove he had been delayed, the supervisor refused.

"I wanted proof I was there," Morgan said. "I wanted proof that I wasn't the one who screwed all this up."

"Since I started driving that Bethpage route, I've always had trailer 10-R-1440". He noticed because it was his favorite trailer to drive.

"What happened on October 21 was a series of unusual events that cannot be a coincidence," Morgan was adamant. "I know I saw ballots with return addresses filled out, thousands of them, thousands. Loaded onto my trailer in New York and headed for Pennsylvania."

"As things became weirder, I got to thinking and wondered why I was driving complete ballots from New York to Pennsylvania. I didn't know why, so I decided to speak up," he said.

He was Refused His Tickets

"The transportation supervisor refused to give me a ticket and told me to leave. I demanded he give me a late slip, since I wanted to get paid for the time I was sitting there waiting for them to off-load me." "He refused to give me that too." "He was kind of rude and wouldn't explain anything to me. He just told me to go to Lancaster."

"I then drove to Lancaster, unhooked my trailer in its normal place, and then drove my truck to where I always park it in a nearby lot. And then I went home." "The next day it just got weirder."

"As I arrived at Lancaster's United States Postal Service facility (in) my tractor, I went to hook up to my trailer and my trailer was gone. Not there no more."

At the same conference, whistleblowers said postal workers delivered Biden campaign mail, discarded Trump campaign mail.

Dominion Voting Machines

Gregory Stenstrom saw a Dominion Voting Systems vendor inserting flash drives into voting aggregation machines in Delaware County, and that election officials mingled various drives from aggregation machines, making auditing problematic.

Ethan Pease, a US Postal Service subcontractor from Wisconsin, testified he was told of plans to backdate tens of thousands of mail-in ballots, to circumvent the legal deadline. Col. Tony Schaeffer, of The Amistad Project, said the organization backed Morgan's story.

Kline said sources told him Morgan's story "matched up perfectly on how to insert fraudulent mail into the stream."

Zuckerberg Bought Elections

"We are fighting Mark Zuckerberg (Facebook) around the country where he is using CTCL, a nonprofit founded and managed by Obama-affiliated operatives, to funnel hundreds of millions of dollars to leftist strongholds in battleground states to determine the outcome of the election," Kline revealed on November 6, two days after the election.

"This is a scheme engineered by partisan activists under the guise of COVID-related support," Kline noted. Privatization of the election undermines the integrity of the election."

Voting Days After

"They are still voting in Pennsylvania," Washington Times reporter Rowan Scarborough said at the time. "Three days after Nov. 3. Dems tried that in other states, but judges said no. Continued voting after election day would be considered fraud by UN observers. News reports said more ballots coming in. No post mark required, no matching signature. UN observers would consider that evidence of fraud."

Commentator Mark Steyn noted: "Swing-state elections are now a subsidiary of Facebook: Votebook. What could go wrong?"

"Just a general observation from a foreigner feeling ever more foreign since Wednesday morning: I have spent election night in many countries over the years, and have never seen what I saw on Tuesday night," Steyn said. *"I am amazed that even the brain-dead American legacy media could pass off what happened in Philadelphia as normal."*

"Everywhere else the polls close and votes are counted until they're all done, and they have a final 100 percent result – by 9pm, 11.30pm, 3am, however long it takes. But, in Philadelphia and elsewhere, they suddenly stop counting and everyone goes home until the following morning, then count boxes that have shown up under cover of darkness."

"But with every couple of hours it's clear that Fox News called Arizona way too early, and that, if it's an honest count, the probability is that that state will fall back into the Trump column – which, with Georgia, NC and Penn, would be enough to get him past 270," Steyn commented. *"That's a very big 'if,' but it would seem more likely than any beneficial result from state judges, even those not cashing a Zuckerberg check."*

https://www.rt.com/usa/508397-truckload-ballots-missing-pennsylvania/

AMISTAD PROJECT

Amistad Project Director Phill Kline says his group has collected sworn expert testimony alleging that *"over 300,000 ballots are at issue in Arizona, 548,000 in Michigan, 204,000 in Georgia, and over 121,000 in Pennsylvania."* The FBI has requested access to their data analysis, Kline noted previously.

Kline's claims received little media attention, unlike the statement of US Attorney General Bill Barr to AP earlier that Department of Justice has *"not seen fraud on a scale that could have affected a different outcome in the election."*

Trump's legal team quickly countered that the DOJ hasn't actually bothered to look into any evidence they've presented so far. They are challenging election results in Georgia, Michigan, Wisconsin, and Pennsylvania, where vast quantities of mail-in ballots allowed this year on the pretext of the pandemic enabled Democrat Joe Biden to claim victory.

Democrats, the US mainstream media and Silicon Valley social platforms have been united insisting there had been no *"widespread"* fraud in the election, labeling Trump's claims to the contrary as *"baseless," "disputed" or misinformation.*

ARIZONA VOTING PROBLEMS IN 2020 ELECTION

- https://www.nbcnews.com/politics/2022-election/vote-machine-glitch-roils-arizonas-maricopa-county-fuels-false-stateme-rcna56261
- https://apnews.com/article/maricopa-county-ballot-printers-mcgregor-kari-lake-9edeef525b8afacb767a4960bf951ea1

Links above will take you to online news stories illustrating the great failure rate of voting machines in a voting district of 2 million in Maricopa County, Arizona. Both links indicate extreme problems in which problems strongly identified in the 2020 election were never resolved and continue to plague the 2022 midterm elections.

NBC NEWS   Decision 2022

By Erik Ortiz, Allie Raffa, Jonathan Allen, and Brandy Zadrozny

PHOENIX — Maricopa County has emerged as a flashpoint in the midterm elections after a state judge declined a last-minute effort to extend voting hours following widespread issues that led officials to use secure ballot boxes.

Technicians were dispatched to polling sites across Arizona's largest county on Election Day to fix dozens of malfunctioning vote tabulation machines, a widespread issue that frustrated voters and led GOP politicians and pundits to spread misleading or false information.

Election officials stressed that the machines were "not inaccurately" reading ballots, but not accepting them at all.

While Maricopa County election officials initially categorized the problem as a "hiccup," it took hours before a solution was identified early Tuesday afternoon. Fallout over the course of the day forced officials to scramble on messaging and push back on claims that questioned the integrity of the election.

"Everyone is still getting to vote. No one has been disenfranchised," Bill Gates, chair of the Maricopa County board of supervisors, a Republican, told reporters in Phoenix following reports of equipment problems Tuesday morning. *"When we test these machines, that's part of the process. We go through it for every election," he added. "And in this instance, this is something we didn't anticipate."* About 60 of the county's 223 voting locations reported problems. Gates said technicians were *"doing what they can to get these back online."*

The Republican National Committee filed an emergency request to extend voting hours just ahead of the closing of state polls at 9 p.m. ET. Judge Timothy Ryan, who was appointed by Democratic Gov. Janet Napolitano (another Conflict of Interest) in 2005, denied the request, saying that GOP failed to show anyone was prevented from voting.

Ryan said, “there might have been some confusion” but there was not any evidence that anyone was “precluded the right to vote.” He added that even if there were such evidence that he would have “no way to communicate” with the polling places given the late time, with polls just about to close.

Matthew Sanderson, co-leader of political law group at law firm Caplin & Drysdale, said, *these are common problems.*

“Some tabulator machines in Maricopa County, Arizona, have malfunctioned, and some commentators on the right have tried to paint that as part of a sinister plot,” Sanderson, a Republican and an NBC News and MSNBC election law analyst, wrote. “The reality is that equipment malfunctions have always been a part of Election Day, Maricopa election officials have had contingency plans to make sure voters can cast their ballots without interruption.”

Sanderson said the judge's *decision "was in line with past decisions by Arizona courts, historically hesitant to extend poll hours."*

"The judge seemed to focus in this case on the Republicans' delay in filing the complaint until late on Election Day and on voters' ability to cast ballots that would be counted through alternative means," he added.

Maricopa, the fourth most populous county in the USA, home to Phoenix and Tempe, is widely considered the key to Arizona elections. Most of the state's ballots are cast there and the results typically match the outcome statewide.

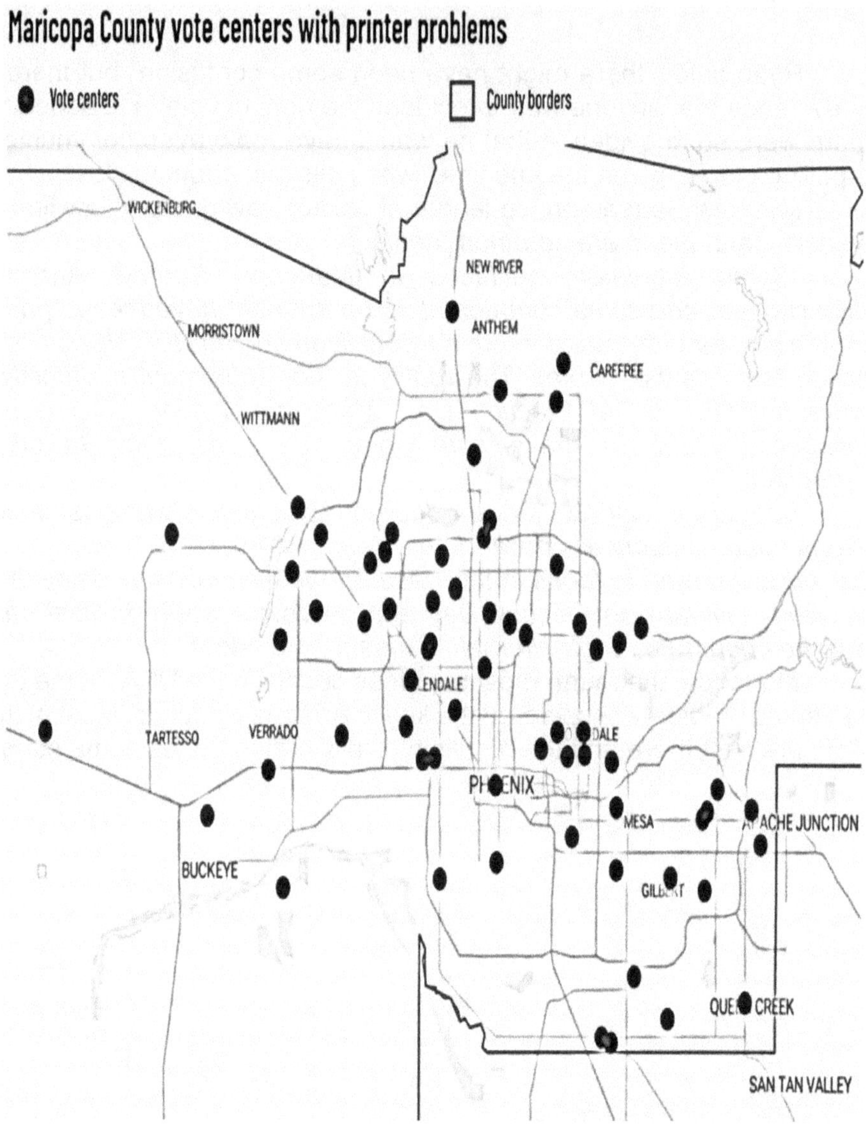

United States Census Bureau, says the county area is 9,224 sq miles. Maricopa County is one of the largest counties in the United States, with a land area greater than four other US states. From west to east, it stretches 132 miles, and 103 miles from north to south.

CHAPTER 8. 2022 ELECTION

Vote machine glitch roils Arizona's Maricopa County and fuels false statements

"Everyone is still getting to vote. No one has been disenfranchised," one county official said in an attempt to push back against claims from some GOP politicians and commentators.

Arizona County Experiences issues with vote tabulators - 02:47
Nov. 8, 2022, 5:55 PM CST / Updated Nov. 8, 2022, 8:54 PM
By Erik Ortiz, Allie Raffa, Jonathan Allen, and Brandy Zadrozny

PHOENIX — Maricopa County has emerged as a flashpoint in the midterm elections after a state judge declined a last-minute effort to extend voting hours following widespread issues that led officials to use secure ballot boxes.

Technicians were dispatched to polling sites across Arizona's largest county on Election Day to fix dozens of malfunctioning vote tabulation machines, a widespread issue that frustrated voters and led some politicians and pundits to spread misleading or false information.

Election officials stressed that the machines were "not inaccurately" reading ballots, but rather, not accepting them at all.

Arizona ballots still being counted for Senate and governor races.01:17

"Everyone is still getting to vote. No one has been disenfranchised," Bill Gates, chairman of the Maricopa County board of supervisors and a Republican, told reporters in downtown Phoenix following reports of equipment problems Tuesday morning.

"When we test these machines, that's part of the process. We go through it for every election," he added. "And in this particular instance, this is something we didn't anticipate."

About 60 of the county's 223 voting locations reported related problems. Gates said technicians were *"doing what they can to get these back online."*

The Republican National Committee filed an emergency request to extend voting hours just ahead of the closing of state polls at 9 p.m. ET. Judge Timothy Ryan, who was appointed by Democratic Gov. Janet Napolitano in 2005, denied the request, saying that GOP failed to show anyone was prevented from voting.

-Ryan said, *"there might have been some confusion" but there was not any evidence that anyone was "precluded the right to vote." He added that even if there were such evidence that he would have "no way to communicate"* with the polling places given the late time, with polls just about to close.

Matthew Sanderson, co-leader of the political law group at the law firm Caplin & Drysdale, said that these are common problems.

"Some tabulator machines in Maricopa County, Arizona, have malfunctioned, and some commentators on the right have tried to paint that as part of a sinister plot," Sanderson, a Republican and an NBC News and MSNBC election law analyst, wrote. *"The reality, though, is that equipment malfunctions have always been a part of Election Day, and Maricopa election officials have had contingency plans in place to make sure that voters can cast their ballots without interruption."*

Sanderson said the judge's decision "*was in line with past decisions by Arizona courts, which have historically been hesitant to extend polling place hours.*" "*The judge seemed to focus in this case on the Republicans' delay in filing the complaint until late on Election Day and on voters' ability to cast ballots that would be counted through alternative means,*" he added.

Maricopa, the fourth-largest county in the country, home to Phoenix and Tempe, is widely considered the key to Arizona elections. Most of the state's ballots are cast there and the results typically match the outcome statewide.

In 2020, Joe Biden won Maricopa County by about 6,000 of the more than 2 million votes cast there. Statewide, he won by less than 12,000 votes out of more than 3.3 million cast.

The dynamics have been similar in midterm elections. When Democrat Sen. Kyrsten Sinema won her seat in 2018, she won with 50% of the statewide vote, including the 51% she took in Maricopa County. About 2.4 million people voted in that race statewide, with 1.4 million ballots cast in Maricopa.

Election officials urged voters at polling sites where machines had malfunctioned to exercise other options, including either dropping their ballots in a secure box to be counted later in the day or going to another location to vote.

https://apnews.com/article/maricopa-county-ballot-printers-mcgregor-kari-lake-9edeef525b8afacb767a4960bf951ea1

"PAPER GLITCH CAUSED THE PROBLEM" as reported.

By JONATHAN J. COOPER
Published 6:08 PM CDT, April 10, 2023

PHOENIX (AP) Problems with ballot printers that caused lines to back up at some Phoenix polling places last year were not caused by malicious actions but by changes to the paper, a retired Arizona Supreme Court justice concluded Monday. County officials used longer ballots on thicker paper than had been used previously, changes that were made in part to respond to unfounded conspiracy theories, but which pushed the printers to the edge of their capabilities, former Justice Ruth McGregor wrote.

She added, pre-election testing may not have caught the problem because the test didn't properly mimic the stresses printers experience on Election Day.

"*Nothing we learned in our interviews or document reviews gave any indication that the problems should have been anticipated*," McGregor wrote.

McGregor's findings show the challenges confronting election officials as they respond to concerns spread by election deniers with changes that carry their own unforeseen consequences that raise further doubts among voters skeptical of election procedures.

Clint Hickman, Republican chair, county board of supervisors, said they will "*make changes to best serve voters, starting with replacing some equipment.*"

Republican Kari Lake, who lost the race for governor, along with the GOP candidates for attorney general and secretary of state have pointed to the printer issues as a reason for their losses. Lake's campaign Twitter account called the McGregor report a "farce."

McGregor's team printed and counted 9,100 ballots, concluding the issue could be traced to a part known as the fuser on Oki B432 printers.

For some printers, the fuser failed to consistently maintain the proper temperature to bond toner to the paper, resulting in ballots that could not be read by precinct-based tabulators. On Election Day, thousands of ballots from problematic printers were counted on more sophisticated scanners at the county's election headquarters in downtown Phoenix. Officials say all voters had a chance to cast a ballot and all legal ballots were counted.

McGregor, who was appointed to the state's high court by former Rep. Gov. Jane Hull, said the problem was more pronounced because of two changes made for the 2022 election.

Ballot length increased from 19 inches to 20 to accommodate more than 70 contests. And the paper thickness was increased after some voters in 2020 complained that the Sharpie brand markers used in polling places caused ink to bleed from one side of the paper to the other. The issue does not affect the ballot count but claims that it was evidence of fraud were widespread among supporters of former President Trump, who narrowly lost in Arizona.

In McGregor's tests, thicker paper led to higher failure rates, adding an extra inch to the ballot length and increased the problems.

McGregor suggested a number of potential fixes for future elections, such as ditching the Oki printers or more aggressively testing to find the ones with problems. She said thicker paper and precinct-based tabulators both increased problems. About half of Arizona's counties count all their ballots at a central location. "You can be sure our board will take any steps necessary to ensure in-person voters have the experience they deserve in 2024," Jack Sellers, a Republican County supervisor, said in a statement.

Storylines immediately above and below demonstrate to anyone with computer printers at home that the Arizona Secretary of State office is not at all prepared to deal with computers or computer problems. "Everyone knows" that computer printers are designed to utilize a common paper thickness of as thin as 18 lb. and as thick as 40 lb. Anything more and you will experience printer problems. SO WHY DID ARIZONA ATTEMPT TO USE PAPER THICKNESS OF 100 lb.?

America has seen many calls for all new Constitutional Conventions in recent years. One point clearly demanding scrutiny as an outgrowth of the failed 2020 election is clearly a need to review any and all qualifications of candidates for elected offices. We must cease the practice of allowing people to be elected for positions in which they have zero functional or educational qualifications, as is the case for many years, all over America.

Too big a job:

Why Maricopa County's ballot printers failed on Election Day
Votebeat analysis finds the county's heavier paper combined with high voter turnout likely pushed aging printers past their limits.
By: Jen Fifield/Votebeat - December 9, 2022, 8:07 am

This article was originally published by Votebeat, a nonprofit news organization covering local election administration and voting access.

As Maricopa County investigates what caused machines to reject thousands of ballots on Election Day, Votebeat analysis of technical evidence found that local officials may have pushed the county's ballot printers past their limits.

The thickness of the ballot paper the county used, the need to print on both sides, and the high volume of in-person voting are all likely to have contributed to poor print quality on ballots, according to Votebeat's review of printer specifications, turnout, and interviews with eight ballot-printing and election technology experts.

"It was a cascade of events, and once the first domino fell, they were setting the dominos back up while rearranging the deck chairs on the Titanic," said Genya Coulter, a senior election analyst and director of relations for election technology security nonprofit OSET Institute.

The poor print quality caused machines to then reject thousands of ballots across the county, forcing voters to instead place their ballots in a secure box to be tallied later. Two technical experts closely familiar with the county's equipment, who did not want to be named because they didn't want to get ahead of the county's public statements, said that the paper thickness was likely a major factor in why the toner — the powder laser and LED printers use to make images on paper — did not properly adhere to both sides of the paper.

The county used thicker ballot paper than the printer supports when printing on both sides of the page, according to the user manual for the OKI B432dn LED printers. Paper weight of up to 80 pounds is supported, but the county's ballots were printed on 100-pound paper.

"To perform high-quality printing, be sure to use the supported paper types that satisfy requirements, such as material, weight, or paper surface finishing," the manual specifies.

The printers' fusers, which melt the toner onto the paper, could have degraded by Election Day, said Coulter, who along with them working for OSET, advises and trains election workers on technology.

One month after the midterm, Maricopa County election officials have yet to provide a full account of the problem. A detailed explanation could help address claims circulating from GOP leaders, including from Republican gubernatorial candidate Kari Lake, that the problems were somehow intentional and aimed at disenfranchising Republican voters. Analysis by numerous media outlets found the problem did not disproportionately impact Republican areas.

At least 30% of vote centers had problems scanning ballots on Election Day, which forced about 17,000 voters to put their ballots in the secure box, known as "door 3," for later counting. The county emphasized repeatedly, everyone was able to cast ballots. Problems exacerbated lines in some locations, said poll workers.

OKI Data Americas spokesperson Lou Stricklin told Votebeat in an email that it is "*up to the elections services provider to test their systems (including the printer) to ensure that the ballot material being used is appropriate for the printer and printing accurately.*"

"*The Oki B432 printers have been a very reliable printer for the Election Department,*" Gilbertson wrote in an email. "*Our stress tests performed before and after the election show that printing on 100lb ballot paper in quick succession does not result in lower print quality.*"

Maricopa's testing did not capture the problem. California is the only state with a state certification program for printers that requires rigorous testing before a county can use a printer, spurring election officials such as Kelley to use a comprehensive process to understand a printer's capacity before buying them.

County officials first used the printers in 2020 and again in this year's primary, and they didn't know what difference could have triggered the problems in the general election. But in 2020, the county used 80-pound paper. And in the primary, the vast majority of ballots, or about 80% of ballot styles, were one-sided, according to Gilbertson. When only printing on one side, up to 110-pound paper is supported, according to the OKI manual.

Why some printers had problems and others didn't is unclear. It could have to do with the age of the printers or the fusers. *The county has only used the printers to print ballots since 2020 but was using them to print ballot envelopes during early voting before that. Of the fewer than 600 OKI printers the county currently has, 20 were purchased in 2017, the rest were purchased in 2018,* Gilbertson said.

Maricopa County officials declined a request for an in-person or phone interview for this story, and instead asked that Votebeat send questions in writing, with Gilbertson citing "lawsuits" as the reason.

"Maricopa County is continuing its root cause analysis to identify why Oki printers did not print the timing marks dark enough," Gilbertson wrote. "This is being done while we have been completing the canvass, recount and responding to public records requests and elections."

Supervisors Chairman Bill Gates, a Republican, has apologized on behalf of the county and said the problems cannot happen again. He has also acknowledged the importance of conducting smooth elections, especially since the 2020 election brought so much scrutiny.

CHAPTER 9. JIMMY CARTER STRUCK WITH MASSIVE VOTER FRAUD IN HIS FIRST RUN FOR GEORGIA STATE SENATE.

The First Campaign:
Excerpt from Jimmy Carter's new memoir, A Full Life.

The book offers a frank look back at Carter's public and private life. Here is the story of his contentious race for state Senate in 1962, in which he was defeated by the democrat cheating machine, was able to bring court attention, then won on a called special election. Yes, this book proves the democrats often used their methods to control which democrats win elections.

By Jimmy Carter August 13, 2015

Although my father had served in the state legislature and our family members were loyal Democrats and publicly supported local and state candidates, I had never had interest in seeking public office and took no part in politics except to join mother—and most Georgians—in supporting Adlai Stevenson and John Kennedy. I decided to run for office in 1962, after the Supreme Court ruled in Baker
v. Carr that all votes had to be weighted as equally as possible. This resulted in the termination of Georgia's "county unit" system, where some rural votes equaled 100 votes in urban areas. As part of the state's response, seats in Georgia Senate that rotated every two years were replaced by permanent ones, with more power and prestige. I decided, somewhat quixotically, to help save the state's public school system—threatened with closure if racially integrated—by becoming a Senate candidate. I was changing from my khakis into a coat and tie when Rosalynn asked if I was going to a funeral. It seems inconceivable to me now, but I had not consulted her about my plans and replied that I was going to the courthouse to qualify as a senatorial candidate and to place an announcement in the local newspaper. Rosalynn was pleased and excited by my decision, which she did not question.

The general presumption was that candidates elected under the old system would be chosen, so only 10 days were allowed for campaigning before the special election. Our new Senate district comprises seven counties, with a total population of about 75,000. I had some posters and calling cards printed and began to go from one county seat to another, visiting the newspaper offices and radio stations in the area and speaking to any civic club that would accept my request.

We were having a one-week revival at our church, and the visiting pastor was staying with my mother. When I stopped by to tell her of my plans, the preacher asked, "Why in the world would you want to become involved in the dirty game of politics?" After thinking for a few moments, I responded, "How would you like to be pastor of a church with 75,000 members?"

My opponent was Homer Moore, a warehouseman and peanut buyer from my mother's hometown whom I knew and respected as an honest business competitor. Each of us had a natural advantage in our home community, and I already knew a lot of farmers and Lions Club members. Another key factor that helped me overcome my late decision was that members of our square-dancing group came from the senatorial district covered, and gave me strong support.

On Election Day I was rushing from one polling place to another when I called in to Rosalynn and she informed me that a cousin of hers had reported a serious problem in Georgetown, the county seat of Quitman County, one of the smallest in Georgia. We asked John Pope, a friend of ours, to go to the courthouse to represent me. When he arrived, he was dismayed to see the local political boss, Joe Hurst, ostentatiously helping my opponent. He was requiring all voters to mark their ballots on a table in front of him and telling them to vote for Homer Moore. The ballots were then dropped through a large hole in a pasteboard box, and John watched Hurst reach into the box several times, remove ballots, and discard them. I called the newspaper in Columbus, Georgia, the largest city in Southwest Georgia, and told their political reporter what was happening. His name was Luke Teasley, and he had interviewed me after I became a candidate. I drove to Georgetown. Hurst did not seem disturbed that he was being observed, even when I demanded that he cease his illegal tampering with the election. He responded this was his county, he was chairman of the Quitman County Democratic Party, and this was the way elections were always conducted. As the candidate, I was free to talk to his friend the sheriff if I had a legal complaint to register. After Hurst discounted my complaints, Teasley arrived in Georgetown, and his attitude was primarily amusement that "Old Joe" was still up to his normal tricks. John Pope stayed and recorded what was happening during the day, and I left to visit the other counties.

I was ahead by 75 votes when the returns were received from the other six counties, but in Quitman County the vote was 360 to 136 for my opponent, although only 333 people had voted. Homer Moore was declared to be elected by the news media. The state Democratic Convention was meeting in Macon that same week, and I went there to register my complaint, which was ignored.

Even some of my closest friends thought I was just a sore loser and advised me to drop the issue and decide if I wanted to run in two years. I heard my mother say to my sister, "Jimmy is so naive, so naive." If I had understood the strange election laws, I may have withdrawn, but I was angry.

I had envisioned recent Supreme Court rulings to be opening a new era in Georgia, based on value of individual votes instead of votes by county, and perhaps involving a new legislators who could ease the way toward racial conciliation.

I went to the law office of Warren Fortson, the county attorney, and he and I examined the statutes relating to contested elections. They were almost exclusively devoted to a mathematical recount of ballots and not to fraud. In such a rare case, the appeal should be made within five days to the county Democratic Committee, of which Joe Hurst was chairman and had handpicked all the members. Our only recourse was to present the necessary appeal and then file for a recount, which would be conducted by a regional trial judge. We had a meeting in the home of my first cousin Hugh Carter, and he suggested we call his older brother, Don, who had been city editor of the Atlanta Journal. The newspaper soon assigned a skeptical reporter, John Pennington, to the story, and he came by to see me, then went to Georgetown, where he had a highly publicized confrontation with Joe Hurst. A series of vivid front-page articles swept the state.

Pennington learned that 117 voters had allegedly lined up in exact alphabetical order to cast their ballots. Many were dead, in prison, or living in distant places. Cartoons in the Journal showed graveyard voting precincts with caskets open while their inhabitants exercised their rights as citizens. We found many Quitman County residents willing to confront Hurst, and we worked day and night to accumulate a stack of sworn affidavits confirming our case. The county courthouse was packed when we appeared before the Democratic Executive Committee, but the first order of business was a motion made by my opponent's attorney that the charges be rejected, and Hurst and his committee voted unanimously to agree with the motion. No evidence was accepted. This left us with the possibility of a simple recount of ballots that were cast, and a conservative judge, Carl Crow, was designated to preside.

Since Fortson was known to be my personal friend and was quite liberal on the racial issue, he decided not to represent me at this hearing. Instead, he introduced me to Charles Kirbo, originally from South Georgia but now practicing in the large Atlanta firm of King & Spalding, and he agreed to take my case. All we knew in advance was that a total of 496 votes had been reported (360–136) but only 333 people had cast a ballot when the polls closed. Even Joe Hurst had stated that there were no absentee ballots. Those who had conducted the election all stated that no voters had been influenced during the day, everything had been done properly, and all ballots, stubs, and voters' lists were in the box. The big question was, where was the box and what was in it? When the cardboard container was finally found (under the bed of Joe Hurst's daughter) and placed on the table, it was seen that the flaps were unsealed and that no documents were there—only a pile of ballots. More than 100 were rolled up together on top and encircled by a rubber band. In a lengthy statement, speaking slowly and with long pauses, Kirbo described what had been revealed and compared the situation to an account of a chicken thief who dragged a broom behind him to conceal his tracks from the sheriff. With no ballot stubs or voters' lists, Hurst had left no way to determine how many ballots should be in the box. The opposing attorneys decided not to respond, and Judge Crow adjourned the session without comment, except that he would announce his decision the next Friday, November 2, in Albany. The Columbus newspaper reported on page 13 that "Jerry Carter from Plains, who lost to Homer Moore," would lose a recount petition.

On Friday, Judge Crow described the disparity in votes cast in Georgetown, stated that there had been no voting booths and no secret ballot, and that there was no way to determine the result of the election. All the Georgetown ballots were nullified, and the three small county precincts had voted 43 for Moore and 33 for me. This made the district total 2,811 to 2,746, in my favor. If implemented, his decision meant that I was the nominee of the Democratic Party, with no Republican opposition! We all pledged to drink only Old Crow whiskey in the future.

The state party and secretary of state ruled that my name should be on the general election ballot the following Tuesday, but Homer Moore appealed to our local superior court judge, Tom Marshall, and he ruled late Monday night that names should be stricken from all the ballots and that the election be decided solely by new votes to be cast throughout the district the following day—beginning in about six hours. I hadn't been to bed for several days and had lost 11 pounds, but I continued to campaign during election day as much as possible. Two county ordinaries did not remove all names as directed, and in most counties the result was similar to the first one. In Quitman County, however, the voters felt for the first time in many years that they were free from oppression, and there were 448 to 23 votes in my favor. The overall tally in the district was 3,013 to 2,182.

Homer decided to appeal directly to the members of the Georgia Senate, whose presiding officer was Lieutenant Governor Peter Zack Geer, a close friend of Homer and Joe Hurst who had always carried Quitman County by 10-to-1 margins. There was another contested election in Savannah, Georgia, and the lieutenant governor refused to discuss either one before the legislature convened. We knew he had absolute control over the Senate and would be assigning the newly elected members to committees and other posts. In effect, Peter Zack would decide between Homer and me. The issue was still in doubt.

I notified my fellow school board members that I would resign as chairman if elected and would concentrate on educational matters as a senator. After sleeping for a full day, I began studying the Senate rules and procedures and other issues of importance in the district.

I went to Atlanta in late November to meet the lieutenant governor, and Peter Zack received me politely. He said he couldn't discuss any possible contest, noted that I was about the last one to come to see him, and asked for my committee preference. Homer Moore had already made his requests. I said my only preference was the education committee, and he was surprised that I didn't ask for rules, appropriations, judiciary, or industry and trade. He said there should be no problem. The top positions were filled, but if I liked to write, he might make me secretary. I accepted and started to leave, then asked if there was a subcommittee on the university system. There was none, and I asked if one could be formed. He called the committee chairman, who had no objection to my being head of the new subcommittee on higher education—if I should be a senator.

It is the custom in Georgia to have a wild hog supper the night before the legislature convenes, and Rosalynn and I went to the affair in the old Biltmore Hotel in Atlanta. As we approached Peter Zack's suite, we met Homer Moore and his attorneys leaving, with broad smiles on their faces. We hoped that the lieutenant governor had just told a joke. The next day we were nervous and discouraged when the Senate was called to order, but I was sworn in without question. I was also on the agriculture committee and, after a few weeks, on appropriations. I worked hard, read all the bills, and enjoyed the few weeks each year when we were in session. I authored a book later called Turning Point to describe this entire event, which was my introduction to politics. I learned a lot in just a few weeks.

My two personal legislative goals were to improve election procedures and to secure a four-year college in Southwest Georgia. Now, having a lot of experience on the voting issue, I worked with a small group of lawyers from the judiciary committee to draft a comprehensive reform package that incorporated effects of recent Supreme Court decisions and clarified procedures to follow in cases of fraud. I remember that one floor amendment was proposed by a senator from Enigma (I envied his hometown's name) that would "prohibit any citizen from casting a ballot in a primary or general election who has been dead more than three years." A good-spirited debate included claims that wives or children could decide fairly accurately how their deceased loved one would still vote after such a brief time. The reforms were overwhelmingly approved, without the proposed amendment.

The other issue was much more important in my district, because the nearest senior college was Auburn University in Alabama, where our students had to pay out-of-state fees. The two junior colleges eligible for promotion were Georgia Southwestern in Americus (my county seat) and a larger institution in Columbus. The elected governor, Carl Sanders, had promised the people of Americus that he would support their request but had backed down under pressure from Columbus.

Their supporter, Bo Callaway, was our district representative on the Board of Regents. He was wealthy, politically influential, and chairman of the committee that decided on academic status of colleges. I was at a great disadvantage, except that I was chairman of the subcommittee that would have to approve any funding for the university system. The governor wanted a new dental school in his hometown, and I had the proposed legislation in my pocket. Following quiet but intense negotiations between me and the governor, he used his influence among the regents, the dental school was funded, and Georgia Southwestern became a senior college. Primarily because of this achievement, I was reelected in 1964 without opposition. But it left some bad feelings between me and Callaway.

The author now repeats the theme of this book indicating the vast numbers of vote cheating methods, and that it sometimes traps democrats who may be at odds with their political party. We have provided evidence that the Democrat party originally commenced vote cheating following the end of Civil War Reconstruction in 1880. Purpose of that cheating was to be sure only the Southern politicians would be elected and that the "Carpet Baggers" would not get elected. Such vote cheating might have been due a salute in that day as it allowed a quicker return to normalcy down south.

While the practice began down south, even the superbly educated Jimmy Carter, a long established son of the southern democrats was beaten by democrat cheaters. Carter succeeded in overturning that bad election and taking his first elected office.

CHAPTER 10. HISTORY OF VOTER REGISTRATION IN AMERICA

In 1800, Massachusetts was the first state to require voter registration as a prerequisite for voting statewide,[6] followed by Maine (1821), Pennsylvania (1836), and Connecticut (1839). During the 19th century, and after the Civil War, more states and cities would establish voter registration as a prerequisite to voting, partially to prevent voting by immigrants. In 1913, Nebraska was first to establish a permanent statewide voter register, overseen by an election commissioner.

According to a 2020 study, voter registration laws adopted from 1880–1916 reduced turnout as much as 19 percentage points.[7]

North Dakota abolished voter registration in 1951 for state and federal elections, the only state to do so.[1] It has since 2004 required voters to produce ID at time of casting a vote. North Dakota was accused of voter suppression as many Native Americans were denied a vote because the address on their tribal IDs had a post office box address, which continues in practice.[8]

In 2002, Arizona made online voter registration available. In 2016, Oregon became the first state to implement a fully automatic (opt-out) voter registration system tied to issuing driver licenses and ID cards.

Federal jurisdiction

While the United States Congress has jurisdiction over laws applying to federal elections, it has deferred most aspects of election law to the states. The US Constitution prohibits states from restricting voting rights in ways that infringe on a person's right to equal protection under the law (14th Amendment), basis of race (15th Amendment), basis of sex (19th Amendment), basis of having failed to pay poll tax or any tax (24th Amendment), basis of age for persons 18 and older (26th Amendment). Administration of elections vary widely across jurisdictions.

In general, US citizens over 18 have a right to vote in federal elections.[12] Permanent residents ("green card" holders) have registered to vote without realizing it was illegal. Non-citizens convicted in criminal court of having made a false claim of citizenship for the purpose of registering to vote in a federal election can be fined and imprisoned up to a year. Deportation/removal actions resulted from several cases.[13] Some municipalities allow non-citizen residents to vote in municipal or school district elections.

1. "The Voter's Self Defense System". Vote Smart. Retr Aug 31, 2017.
2. Common Myths About Voter Registration, Debunked lifehacker.com
3. "Inaccurate, Costly, and Inefficient: Evidence That America's Voter Registration System Needs an Upgrade" Pew Charitable Trusts. Feb 2012. Retr Feb16, 2015.
4. "Make It Easy: Automatic Registration". Democracy. 2013. Retr Feb 16, 2015.
5. Cook, Rhodes (July 12, 2018). "Registering By Party: Where the Democrats and Republicans Are Ahead – Sabato's Crystal Ball". Retrieved January 21, 2022.
6. "Acts, 1800. Chapter 74" Arch Dec 5, 2020. Retr May 7, 2020.
7. Perez, Vanessa M. (Feb 1, 2021). "America's first voter identification laws: effects of personal registration, declining political party competition on presidential election turnout, 1880–1916". Electoral Studies. **69**: 102263. doi:10.1016/j.electstud.2020.102263. ISSN 0261-3794.
8. "North Dakota, native tribes agree to settle voter ID lawsuits". NBC News. Sec. of State North Dakota. "Voter Registration in North Dakota". Retrieved Aug 4, 2010.
9. NBC News. North Dakota, native tribes agree to settle voter ID lawsuits to combat voter suppression. February 14, 2020.
10. "As November Approaches, Courts Deal Blows To Voter ID". NPR. Aug 2, 2016.
11. "The Right to Vote". United States Citizenship and Immigration Services. Archived on October 17, 2011. Retrieved October 25, 2011.
12. Kirk Semple, ""Immigrants Find Voting Can Come At a Cost". NYT Oct 15, 2010.
13. "Felon Voting Rights". ncsl.org. Oct 1, 2020. Retr October 30, 2020.

It is the research discoveries that makes it clear, we in America have much work to do to ensure we bring our elections fully within the Rule of Law, and that the many abuses and illegal acts documented, are never again allowed to repeat.

Blockage Preventing uniform acceptable Voter Registration.

- Non citizens allowed to vote in some states.
- Registration offices not given time to investigate new registrations.
- No uniform laws requiring maintaining clean voter registry's.
- Dead Men voting - - due to failure to remove deceased from voter registry.
- People may register, due to no standard means of investigation.
- Establishing residence in several states may allow multi-state voting.
- Registration allowed up to day of voting, thus no time to investigate.
- Advocacy groups allowed to take voter registration and deliver to registration offices.

The fix for these problems is surprisingly simple. Proper registration procedures might be little more complicated than going into the County Courthouse to obtain your auto license plate. This is a primary reason the sentiment to allow the states to handle such issues is an abysmal failure. The democrat states do not care to acknowledge the relative simplicity of this element of modern elections.

CHAPTER 11. STEELE DOSSIER SERVED AS LAUNCH POINT FOR ALL ACTIONS AND COURT CASES AGAINST DONALD TRUMP

We first saw fabricated questions surrounding Donald Trump in the 2016 election cycle. Most troublesome was the STEELE DOSSIER.

The Steele Dosier was produced by a British Intel analyst charged with Russia analysis. As the following pages will demonstrate, Steele passed his information around the intelligence community in Britian and America. NONE IN THE INTEL COMMUNITY FELT THERE WERE ANY ISSUES WORTHY OF FOLLOW-UP WITHIN THE STEELE REPORT.

If a single issue contained in the Steele report could be considered illegal, then several Agencies could exercise their jurisdiction and begin investigations. IRS, DOJ, Federal Election Commission, Homeland Security, FBI, CIA, and others. NONE FELT THERE WERE ANY INVESTIGATIVE ISSUES.

Politics of the election season crept in and several companies who thrive on politics pushed the issue and found sponsors, many stated dislike for Trump.

Ultimately, Steele Dossier was fully discredited. Then, “bad actors” in the US Legal System began to pile on Donald Trump by filing cases that were stated as “joke level novel cases” by established leaders in the Legal community.

This chapter will provide a documented review of specifics of the STEELE DOSSIER so readers may understand what took place, the “bad actors” within our legal system and MSM mainstream media who push this unfounded issue.

The Steele dossier, also known as the Trump–Russia dossier,[1] is a controversial political opposition research report compiled by Christopher Steele, published without permission as an unfinished 35-page compilation of "unverified, and potentially unverifiable" raw intelligence reports—"not established facts, but a starting point for further investigation".[3][4][5] Written from June to December 2016, contains allegations (never proven) of conspiracy, and cooperation between Trump's campaign and government of Russia during 2016 election campaign.[6]

1. Allen, Nick (March 7, 2020). "Christopher Steele breaks silence over Trump-Russia dossier, says Mueller report 'too narrow'". Daily Telegraph. Retr August 1, 2020.
2. Bensinger, Ken; Elder, Miriam; Schoofs, Mark (January 10, 2017). "These Reports Allege Trump Has Deep Ties To Russia". BuzzFeed News. Retr Dec 24, 2017.
3. Shane, Scott; Goldman, Adam; Rosenberg, Matthew (April 19, 2019). "Mueller Report Likely to Renew Scrutiny of Steele Dossier". NYT. Retrieved April 20, 2019.
4. Gross, Terry; Simpson, Glenn; Fritsch, Peter (Nov 26, 2019). "Fusion GPS On Russian Efforts To Sow Discord: 'They Have Succeeded'". NPR. Fresh Air
5. Kessler, Glenn (Oct 29, 2017). "Analysis – dossier' uranium deal: guide to latest allegations". Washington Post. Retr Oct 27, 2021. Raw intelligence essentially high-grade gossip, without expectation it would be made public unless further verified.
6. Lucas, Ryan (Aug 23, 2017). "Researcher Behind Unverified Trump Dossier Meets Senate Investigators". NPR. Retr Aug 12, 2021.

It was based on information from initially anonymous sources known to, British counterintelligence specialist[14] Christopher Steele.[15] Steele, a former head of Russia Desk for British intelligence (MI6), was writing the report for the private investigative firm Fusion GPS, that was paid by Hillary Clinton's campaign and the Democratic National Committee (DNC).[16] The dossier's 17 reports ALLEGE that Trump campaign members and Russian operatives had conspired to cooperate in Russia's election interference to benefit Trump.[17] It also ALLEGES that Russia sought to damage Hillary Clinton's candidacy.[18]

It was published by BuzzFeed News on January 10, 2017, without Steele's permission.[2] Their decision to publish reports without verifying ALLEGATIONS was criticized by journalists.[19][20] Federal Judge Ursula Ungaro defended BuzzFeed's action as the public has a right to know so it can "exercise effective oversight of the government".[21] For purposes of this book, the reader must remember all these points came to Steele in his capacity as a highly confidential intel analyst. Upon considering none of the points were deemed worthy of further investigation by the many agencies in England and USA, then the so-called Steele Dossier should have gone no further than the desk of intelligence service agents.

While Steele's documents played a significant role, the veracity of specific ALLEGATIONS is highly variable. Some have been publicly confirmed,[10][25][9][11] others are not specifically confirmed,[26][27] and some are dubious in Retrospect but not strictly disproven.[28][29][30] While the dossier played a central and essential role in seeking FISA warrants on Carter Page,[31] it did not play any role in the intelligence community's assessment of Russian actions in the 2016 election,[32] and it was not the trigger for the opening of the Russia investigation into whether the Trump campaign was coordinating with the Russian government's interference in the 2016 presidential election.[33]

Footnote

10. Sciutto, Jim; Perez, Evan (Feb 10, 2017). "US investigators corroborate some aspects of Russia dossier". CNN. Retrieved February 10, 2017.
11. Levine, Mike (Jan 12, 2018). "FBI vets: What many are missing about the infamous 'dossier' amid Russia probe". ABC News. Retr Feb 26, 2018. some of the dossier's implications — that Russian President Putin launched an operation to boost Trump and sow discord in U.S. and abroad — now ring true and were embedded in memo Steele shared with FBI before agency decided to open an investigation.
12. Yourish, Karen; Buchanan, Larry (Jan 26, 2019). "Mueller Report Shows Connections Between Trump Campaign and Russians". NYT. Retr Oct 24, 2019.
13. Leonnig, Carol D.; Helderman, Rosalind S. (May 17, 2019). "Judge orders release what Flynn said to Russian ambassador". Washington Post. Retr May 17, 2019.
14. Harding, Luke; Sabbagh, Dan (Nov 1,2019). "Trump–Russia dossier author gave evidence to UK inquiry". The Guardian. Retr Nov1,2019.
15. Shane, Scott; Confessore, Nicholas; Rosenberg, Matthew (Jan 12, 2017). "How a Sensational, Unverified Dossier Became Crisis for Trump". NYT. Retr Feb 11, 2018.

16. Entous, Adam; Barrett, Devlin; Helderman, Rosalind (Oct 24,2017). "Clinton campaign, DNC paid for research, Russia dossier". Washington Post. Oct 25, 2017.
17. Sumter, Kyler (11/16/2017). "five most interesting claims in the Trump dossier". The Week. Retr Dec 24, 2017.
18. Sipher, John (January 11, 2018). "What Should We Make of The Dirty Dossier at the Heart of the Mueller Investigation?". Newsweek. Retrieved May 11, 2018.
19. Bump, Philip (January 11, 2017). "BuzzFeed, the Russia dossier and the problem of too much information". The Washington Post. Retrieved July 29, 2017.
20. Zurawik, David (Jan 11, 2017). "BuzzFeed undermines all journalists with Trump 'dossier'". The Baltimore Sun. Arch January 7, 2018. Retr Jan 10, 2018.
21. Johnson, Ted (December 19, 2018). "Judge Sides With BuzzFeed Over Publication of Steele Dossier". Variety. Retr March 26, 2019.
22. Breuninger, Kevin (Jan 13, 2018). "Fusion GPS testimony on infamous dossier shines new light on Trump's perilous financial ties". CNBC. Retr Jan 18, 2018.
23. Sengupta, Kim (Jan13, 2017). "Ex-MI6 agent so worried by his Donald Trump discoveries, started working without pay". The Independent. Retr March 3, 2018.
24. Chait, Jonathan (Dec 7, 2017). "Steele Dossier on Trump and Russia Is Looking More and More Real". New York. Retr Dec 28, 2017.
25. Cullison, Alan; Volz, Dustin (April 19, 2019). "Mueller Report Dismisses Many Steele Dossier Claims". The Wall Street Journal. Retrieved August 7, 2019.
26. Lee, Michelle Ye Hee (Dec 26, 2017). "Trump slams FBI, Obamacare in post-Christmas tweets". Washington Post. Retr January 11, 2018.
27. Farhi, Paul (November 12, 2021). "The Washington Post corrects, removes parts of two stories regarding the Steele dossier". The Washington Post. Retrieved November 13, 2021. The Washington Post on Friday took the unusual step of correcting and removing large portions of two articles 'Steele dossier,' a collection of largely unverified reports [that] had identified businessman Sergei Millian as "Source D," the unnamed figure who passed on the most salacious allegation in the dossier to its principal author Steele.
28. "Manafort accuses Mueller deputy of leaking to press. Transcript: 05/22/2018. The Rachel Maddow Show". MSNBC. May 22, 2018. Retrieved September 26, 2018.
29. Hutzler, Alexandra (Aug 16, 2018). "Fox Host Contradicts Hannity, Trump Over Dossier Claims". Newsweek. Retr August 18, 2018.
30. Grant, Sarah; Rosenberg, Chuck (Dec 14, 2018). "The Steele Dossier: A Retrospective". Lawfare. Retrieved Dec 29, 2019. Schiff describes the FBI's wholly independent basis for investigating Page's long-established connections to Russia, aside from the Steele dossier, and emphasizes the Justice Department possessed information 'obtained through multiple independent sources that corroborated Steele's reporting' Re: Page.
31. Sanchez, Julian (Dec 11, 2019). "The Crossfire Hurricane Report's Inconvenient Findings". Just Security. Retrieved December 23, 2019.
32. Benner, Katie; Barnes, Julian E. (Dec19, 2019). "Durham Is Scrutinizing Ex-C.I.A. Director's Role in Russian Interference Findings". NYT. Retr Dec 22, 2019.
33. Goldman, Adam; Savage, Charlie (Nov22, 2019). "Russia Inquiry Review Is Said to Criticize F.B.I. but Rebuff Claims of Biased Acts". NYT. Retr Nov 23, 2019.

History of two research operations and confusion between them

The opposition research conducted by Fusion GPS on Donald Trump was in two distinct operations, each with a different client. First were the Republicans, funded by The Washington Free Beacon. Then came the Democrats, funded by the DNC and the Clinton campaign.

- The Republican operation, from October 2015 to May 2016, focused on Trump's domestic business and entertainment activities; was performed by Fusion GPS; used Wayne Barrett's files and public sources. Immediately after publication of the dossier, the media sometimes falsely assumed the dossier started as a product of research, so the Free Beacon released statement: "none of the work product the Free Beacon received appears in Steele dossier".[36][37]
- The Democratic operation, from April 2016 to Dec 2016, was focused on Trump's Russian connections; was subcontracted to Steele/Orbis; and used Steele's own source network and public sources. Only this second operation produced the dossier.[38][39]

From April to early May 2016, The Washington Free Beacon and the DNC/Clinton Campaign were independently both clients of Fusion GPS. This overlap contributed to media confusion.

Republican operation did not produce dossier

In October 2015, before the official start of the 2016 Republican primary, the founders of Fusion GPS were seeking political work and sent an email to "a big conservative donor who disliked Trump, and they were hired". He arranged for them to use The Washington Free Beacon, an American conservative political journalism website, for their general opposition research on several Republican presidential candidates, and Trump.[40][41] It is primarily funded by Republican donor Paul Singer.[41] The Free Beacon and Singer were "part of the conservative never-Trump movement".[42] Although Singer was a big supporter of Marco Rubio, Rubio denied any involvement in Fusion GPS's initial research and hiring.[36]

36. Leary, Alex (Oct 28, 2017). "Marco Rubio backer's money initially funded anti-Trump research". Tampa Bay Times. Retr Sept 16, 2021.
37. Permanent Select Committee on Intelligence, U.S. House of Representatives (Dec 12, 2017). "Interview of Michael Goldfarb, Dec 12, 2017" (PDF). Office of the Director of National Intelligence. pp. 39, 44. Retrieved March 27, 2023. I've read the dossier. I feel very confident that no material produced and delivered to us appears in that dossier. It was all new information to me when I read it.

And beyond that, I think the dossier itself makes clear that the information was gathered after the time that we ceased working with Fusion on matters related to Donald Trump, to my recollection. There's markers in the dossier about when meetings happened, and when information was gathered and this kind of thing that post-dates our Trump research. And I personally see zero overlap in the work product In my view, I feel confident saying there is no overlap between the work provided and the
work that appears in that document. Searchable version

38. Borger, Julian (January 11, 2017). "John McCain passes dossier alleging secret Trump–Russia contacts to FBI". The Guardian. Retr February 26, 2018.
39. Lima, Cristiano (Oct 27, 2017). "Conservative Free Beacon originally funded firm that created Trump–Russia dossier". Politico. Retr Feb 11, 2018.
40. Mayer, Jane (11/25/19). "Inside Story of Christopher Steele's Trump Dossier". The New Yorker. Retr 11/27/19.
41. Vogel, Kenneth P.; Haberman, Maggie (Oct 27, 2017). " Website Funded Anti-Trump Research by Firm That Produced Dossier". NYT Retr April 1, 2018.
42. Isikoff, Michael; Corn, David (March 17, 2018). "Russian Roulette: real story of Steele dossier on Trump". Australian Financial Review. Retr May 10, 2018.

Democratic operation produces dossier

Hiring and initial reports

The second operation of opposition research was indirectly funded by the DNC and the Clinton campaign, working through their attorney of record, Marc Elias of Perkins Coie.[16] In an October 2017 letter, Perkins Coie general counsel Matthew Gehringer described how, in March 2016, Fusion GPS approached Perkins Coie and, knowing the Clinton campaign and the DNC were its clients, inquired whether its clients wished to pay Fusion GPS "to continue research regarding then-presidential candidate Donald Trump, research that Fusion GPS had conducted for one or more other clients during the Republican primary contest."[48] In April 2016, Elias hired Fusion GPS to perform opposition research on Trump.[16][48]

Fusion GPS co-founder Glenn Simpson had reservations, he did not like the idea of helping Hillary Clinton. In an email, Simpson said, "The only way I could see working for HRC is if it is against Trump."[49]

In June 2016,[15] as part of its work for Perkins Coie, Fusion GPS hired Orbis Business Intelligence, a private British intelligence firm, to look into connections between Trump and Russia. Orbis co-founder Christopher Steele, a retired British MI6 officer with expertise in Russian matters,[15] was hired as a subcontractor.[50]

Prior to his work on the dossier, Steele had been a paid FBI informant[51] for information unrelated to the Russia investigation.[52]

The DNC and Clinton campaign treasurers reported they paid Perkins Coie a total of $12.4 million for legal and compliance services during the 2016 campaign.[53][54]

This led Trump to claim the dossier had cost $12 million,[55] although the actual cost was far less.[56] According to Fusion GPS, Perkins Coie paid them $1.02 million in fees and expenses, and Fusion GPS paid $168,000 to Steele's firm, Orbis Business Intelligence, to produce the dossier.[55][57] Despite that, Trump and his son Donald Trump Jr. continued to claim for more than a year that Steele was paid "millions of dollars" for his work.[58] (Given monetary amounts reported in this documented paragraph, it is clear someone paid many millions for a false report.)

48. Watkins, Eli; Merica, Dan; Polantz, Katelyn (Oct 25, 2017). "Clinton campaign, DNC helped fund dossier research". CNN. Retr Sept 9, 2018.
49. Walsh, James D. (November 22, 2019). "Fusion GPS Lights a Candle for the 'Pee Tape'". New York. Retrieved November 24, 2019.
50. Johnson, Kevin; Kelly, Erin (Jan 9, 2018). "Dossier author was told FBI had source inside Trump Org". USA Today. Retr Jan 10, 2018.
51. Winter, Tom (8/3/18). "FBI documents show payments to Trump dossier author Steele". NBC. Retr 4/18/19.
52. Philips, Amber (February 24, 2018). "Read the Democratic rebuttal to the Nunes memo, annotated". The Washington Post. Retr April 3, 2019.
53. Johnson, Ted (Sept 10, 2018). "Omarosa Reveals New Recording of Trump Blaming Hillary Clinton for Collusion". Variety. Retr Sept 11, 2018.
54. Ballhaus, Rebecca (Oct 25, 2017). "Clinton Campaign, DNC Helped Fund Trump–Russia Dossier". Wall Street Journal. Retr Dec 9, 2018.
55. Hosenball, Mark (November 1, 2017). "Ex-British spy paid $168,000 for Trump dossier, U.S. firm discloses". Reuters. Retr November 7, 2017.
56. Price, Greg (Nov 2, 2017). "Trump's Dossier Cost Nowhere Near as Much as He Claimed on Twitter". Newsweek. Retr September 9, 2018
57. Khan, Shehab (11/2/17). "Former British spy paid £125,000 to detail Trump Russia links". MSN. Retr 9/9/18.
58. Edelman, Adam (October 12, 2018). "Clinton strikes back at Trump for saying she colluded with Russia". NBC News. Retr Oct 13, 2018.

Steele passes reports to Intel agencies

In July 2016, Steele called seasoned FBI agent Michael Gaeta, in Rome.

Shortly after, in July, the report was sent to an agent with expertise in criminal organizations and organized crime at the FBI's New York field office—essentially, the wrong person to handle a counterintelligence investigation.[74][73]

According to Nancy LeTourneau, political writer for the Washington Monthly, the report "was languishing in the FBI's New York field office" for two months, and "was finally sent to the counterintelligence team investigating Russia at FBI headquarters in Washington, D.C." in mid-September 2016.[75][76]

In August 2016, FBI asked Steele for "all information in his possession and to explain how the material had been gathered and identify sources".[63][64]

In October 2016, Steele "described sources' access, but not names" to FBI.[76] By August 22, 2017, Steele provided names of sources for allegations in the dossier.[77] During its intense questioning of Steele, the FBI mentioned their own discoveries of connections between the Trump campaign and Russia[79] and asked Steele about Papadopoulos, but he said he knew nothing about him.[62] The agents "raised the prospect of paying Steele to continue gathering intelligence after Election Day",[79] but Steele "ultimately never received payment from the FBI for any 'dossier'-related information".[52] In October 2022, during questioning from Special Counsel John Durham, Brian Auten, a supervisory counterintelligence analyst with the FBI, testified that, shortly before the 2016 election, the FBI offered Steele "up to $1 million" if he could corroborate allegations in the dossier, but that Steele could not do so.[80][81] Steele has disputed this description: "And to correct the Danchenko trial record, we were not offered $1 million by the FBI to 'prove up' our Trump-Russia reporting. Rather, we were told there were substantial funds to resettle sources in the US if prepared to testify. Understandably they were not."[82]

73. Isikoff, Michael; Corn, David (2018). Russian Roulette: Inside Story Putin's War on America, Election of Trump. Grand Central Publishing. ISBN 978-1-5387-2874-1.
74. Levine, Mike (September 18, 2018). "Trump 'dossier' stuck in New York, didn't trigger Russia investigation, sources say". ABC News. Retr Jan 13, 2019.
75. LeTourneau, Nancy (9/19/18). "Trump should be worried, Brennan dossier". Washington Monthly. Retr 9/22/18.
76. "Volume 5: Counterintel Threats and Vulnerabilities" (PDF). intelligence.senate.gov. Senate Intelligence Committee (SIC). Aug 18, 2020. Jan 22, 2021. Retr Dec 27, 2023.
77. Ross, Brian; Mosk, Matthew; Schwartz, Rhonda (August 22, 2017). "Glenn Simpson key figure behind million-dollar dossier". ABC News. Retr August 23, 2017.
78. Scheuermann, Christoph; Schmitt, Jörg (Feb 7, 2019). "Much Has Been Confirmed in Dossier at Heart of Trump Scandal". Der Spiegel. Retr Nov 22, 2019.
79. Hamburger, Tom; Helderman, Rosalind S. (Feb 6, 2018). "Hero or hired gun? How a British former spy became flash point in Russia investigation". The Washington Post. Retr March 10, 2018.
80. Cohen, Marshall (Oct 11, 2022). "FBI offered Steele $1 million to prove dossier claims, senior FBI analyst testifies". Retr Oct 13, 2022.
81. Rizzo, Salvador (October 12, 2022). "FBI supervisor describes learning he was in crosshairs of Durham probe". Washington Post. Retr Oct 13, 2022.
82. Steele, Christopher [@Chris_D_Steele] (Oct 19, 2022). "Steele tweet". Retrieved Oct29, 2022 – via Twitter.

After public release

The subsequent public release of the dossier in January 2017 stopped discussions between Steele and the FBI.[68] The Inspector General's report later confirmed that the FBI had initially offered to pay Steele $15,000 for his trip to Rome, but when the FBI dropped Steele as a confidential human source because he had shared information with a third party "in late October 2016" (Mother Jones magazine), the payment was halted.[71], [45]

Peter Strzok reported that:[71]

> *FBI closed Steele "because he was a control problem. We did not close him because we thought him [a] fabricator." According to Strzok, Steele's decisions to discuss his reporting with media and to disclose his relationship with the FBI were "horrible and it hurt what we were doing, and no question, he shouldn't have done it."*

In September, Steele met with Jonathan Winer, who was then the U.S. deputy assistant secretary of state for international law enforcement, whom he had known since 2009. In a 2018 editorial for The Washington Post,[83] Winer recounted that during their meeting in Washington, he was allowed to review Steele's reports, but not to keep a copy: "I prepared a two-page summary and shared it with [Victoria] Nuland, who indicated that, like me, she felt that the secretary of state needed to be made aware of this material," he wrote. Later in September, Winer discussed the report with Sidney Blumenthal, who revealed he had received similar information from Cody Shearer, a controversial political activist and former journalist who was close to the Clinton White House in the 1990s. Winer met with Steele again in late September and gave him a copy of Shearer's report, later known as the "second dossier".[84]

On September 19, 2016, after the report had been "languishing in the FBI's New York field office" for two months,[75][76][74] Steele's handling agent sent six of Steele's reports (80, 94, 95, 100, 101, and 102) to the Crossfire Hurricane team, that had been operational since July 31, 2016. This was the first time they and their leader, Deputy Assistant Director of the FBI's Counterespionage Section, Peter Strzok, received any of Steele's reporting.[71][85][76] Strzok cautioned his colleagues: "[The dossier] 'should be viewed as intended to influence as well as to inform' and whoever commissioned it was 'presumed to be connected to the [Clinton] campaign in some way.'"[86] Some reports referred to Trump's inner circle. After that point, he continued to share information with the FBI.[64][63] The IG Report says this material "became an important part of the Crossfire Hurricane investigation and the FBI seeking FISA authority targeting Crossfire Hurricane subjects, Carter Page."[71]:80

On October 28, 2016, days before the election, Director Comey notified Congress that the FBI had started looking into newly discovered Hillary Clinton emails. Simpson and Fritsch described their reaction: "Comey's bombshell prompted the Fusion partners to decide they needed to do what they could to expose the FBI's probe of Trump and Russia. It was Hail Mary time."[70] The founders of Fusion GPS were upset by a misleading November 1, 2016, New York Times article "published a week before the election with the headline: 'Investigating Donald Trump, FBI Sees No Clear Link to Russia'.[47]

Simpson later said, "Steele severed his contacts with FBI before the election following public statements by the FBI that it had found no connection between the Trump campaign and Russia and concerns FBI was being 'manipulated for political ends by the Trump people'."[87] Steele was frustrated with FBI, whom he believed failed to investigate his reports, choosing to focus on the Clinton's emails.

According to The Independent, Steele came to believe there was a "cabal" inside FBI, particularly its New York field office linked to Trump advisor Rudy Giuliani, because it blocked attempts to investigate links between Trump and Russia.[23] He "grew concerned there was a cover-up in progress".[44]

Footnotes (most footnotes for this subsection are in sections above)

83. Winer, Jonathan M. (2/9/18). "Devin Nunes investigating me. Here's the truth". Washington Post. Retr 1/13/19.
84. Multiple sources:
- Siegel, Benjamin; Karl, Jonathan; Turner, Trish (Feb9, 2018). "Congressional Russia investigators interested 2nd Trump–Russia dossier". ABC News. Retr 3/7/19
- Ward, Alex (Jan 30, 2018). second Trump–Russia dossier". Vox. Retr 3/7/19.
- Herb, Jeremy; Borger, Gloria; Gaouette, Nicole (Feb 7, 2018). "GOP puts Sidney Blumenthal in spotlight". CNN. Retrieved March 7, 2019.

85. Levine, Mike (8/29/18). "Russia probe: A timeline, Moscow to Mueller". ABC News. Retr 8/30/18.
86. Savage, Charlie (May 17, 2023). "Analysis: Durham Report Failed to Deliver After Years Political Hype". New York Times. Retr May 19, 2023.
87. Jalonick, Mary (Jan 9, 2018). "Democrat report warns of Russian meddling in Europe, US". Washington Post. Archived Jan 23, 2018. Retr Jan 22, 2018.

Denials of specific accusations

Cohen's attorney, Lanny Davis, says (at 8:50) Cohen was "never, ever" in Prague. Dossier source(s) allege that Cohen and three colleagues met Kremlin officials in the Prague offices of Rossotrudnichestvo (sic) in August 2016,[248][223][109] to arrange for payments to the hackers, cover up the hack,[108][59] and "cover up ties between Trump and Russia, including Manafort's involvement in Ukraine".[17]

Cohen's passport showed that he entered Italy in early July 2016, and that he left Italy in mid-July 2016, from Rome, Italy.[109] Buzzfeed News in May 2017 reported Cohen telling them that he was in Capri, Italy, for the time period in question with his family, friends, and musician and actor Steven van Zandt, and that receipts would prove he had been on Capri, but he declined to provide them.[109] Roger Friedman reported sources quoting van Zandt's wife, Maureen, as saying that she and Steven were in Rome, and never traveled to Capri.[468] From this, Nancy LeTourneau of Washington Monthly commented that Cohen may have "lost his alibi", and thus doubted if he had really not traveled to Prague.[468] A December 2018 statement from Steven van Zandt's Twitter said that he had met Cohen in Rome and not traveled together.[469]

In March 2019, The Washington Post reported that Cohen had been in Capri and Rome during his Italy trip, and that Cohen said he met Steven van Zandt in Rome.[470] Cohen also stated that he was in Los Angeles between August 23 and 29, and in New York the entire month of September.[471]

108. Harding, Luke (May 10, 2017). "What do we know about alleged links between Trump and Russia?". The Guardian. Retr Dec 26, 2017.
109. Cormier, Anthony (May 5, 2017). "This Is The Inside Of Trump's Lawyer's Passport". BuzzFeed News. Retrieved December 24, 2017.
223. Withnall, Adam; Sengupta, Kim (Jan 12, 2017). "10 key Trump allegations from classified Russia memos". The Independent. Retr Dec 29, 2017.
224. Beauchamp, Zack (March 22, 2017). "What we know about evidence of coordination between Russia and the Trump campaign". Vox. Retr Aug 3, 2019.
468. LeTourneau, Nancy (12/18/18). "Cohen may have lost alibi on Prague trip". Washington Monthly. Retr 12/18/18.
469. Friedman, Roger (Dec 27, 2018). "Rocker Steve van Zandt Clears Up Trump Lawyer Michael Cohen's Claim of Hanging Out in Capri, Summer 2016". Showbiz411. Retr Sept 16, 2021. Haha not exactly. Ran into him in courtyard of Rome hotel. Wanted me to meet his wife. Very nice. That was it. We've never gone anywhere together.
470. Helderman, Rosalind; Roig-Franzia, Manuel (March 1, 2019). "Two days in July: As Republicans convened in Cleveland, did Trump receive a heads-up about WikiLeaks?". The Washington Post. Retr Sept 4, 2021.
471. Gray, Rosie (Jan 10, 2017). "Michael Cohen: 'It Is Fake News Meant to Malign Mr. Trump'". The Atlantic. Retr Dec 24, 2017. I'm telling you emphatically I've not been to Prague, never been to Czech, not been to Russia.

In 2016, Cohen told Mother Jones he had visited Prague briefly 14 years before.[463] Wall Street Journal reported Cohen telling them (at an unspecified date) that he had been in Prague in 2001.[464] Following the dossier's publication, as well as after subsequent reports, Cohen repeatedly denied he had ever been to Prague.[109][464][465][466] Cohen's attorney Lanny Davis said Cohen was "never, ever" in Prague, and all allegations mentioning Cohen in the Steele dossier were false.[467]

Cohen's passport showed that he entered Italy in early July 2016, and that he left Italy in mid-July 2016, from Rome, Italy.[109] Buzzfeed News in May 2017 reported Cohen telling them that he was in Capri, Italy, for the time period in question with his family, friends, and musician and actor Steven van Zandt, and that receipts would prove he had been on Capri, but he declined to provide them.[109] Roger Friedman reported sources quoting van Zandt's wife, Maureen, as saying that she and Steven were in Rome, and never traveled to Capri.[468] From this, Nancy LeTourneau of Washington Monthly commented that Cohen may have "lost his alibi", and thus doubted if he had really not traveled to Prague.[468] A December 2018 statement from Steven van Zandt's Twitter said that he had met Cohen in Rome and not traveled together.[469] In March 2019, The Washington Post reported that Cohen had been in Capri and Rome during his Italy trip, and that Cohen said he met Steven van Zandt in Rome.[470]

Cohen has also stated he was in Los Angeles, August 23 and 29, and New York in September.[471]

110. Donn, Jeff (June 29, 2018). "Some questions in Trump–Russia dossier now finding answers". Associated Press. Retr June 29, 2018.

464. Berzon, Alexandra; Maremont, Mark; Rothfeld, Michael (Jan 11, 2017). "Intelligence Dossier Puts Longtime Trump Fixer in Spotlight". Wall Street Journal. Retr Sept 4, 2021.
465. Boboltz, Sara (Dec 28, 2018). "Michael Cohen Denies Report Tying Him To Infamous Prague Trip". HuffPost. Retr Dec 29, 2018.
466. Bump, Philip (April 14, 2018). "Cohen's visiting Prague would be a huge development in the Russia investigation". Washington Post. Retr July 4, 2018.

Aleksej Gubarev

Gubarev has denied all accusations made in the dossier.[254][255] The accusations are twofold, as they mention Gubarev and his companies. While it has been proven that his companies were used to facilitate cybercrimes,[8][392][393] Andrew Weisburd has said that "Neither BuzzFeed nor Steele have accused Gubarev of being a willing participant in wrongdoing."[255]

392. Hall, Kevin G. (March 14, 2019). "Expert in Trump dossier trial says tech firm's services used in hack of Democrats". McClatchy DC Bureau. Retr March 15, 2019.
393. Helderman, Rosalind S.; Hamburger, Tom; Nakashima, Ellen (March 15, 2019). "Documents shed light on Russian hacking of Democratic Party leaders". Washington Post. Retr March 15, 2019.
254. Goldstein, David; Hall, Kevin G.; Gordon, Greg (Feb 3, 2017). "BuzzFeed sued over publication of uncorroborated Trump dossier". McClatchy DC Bureau. Retr 4/1/18.
255. Hall, Kevin G. (Sept 21, 2018). "Cloak-and-dagger saga over cybercrime, Trump dossier plays out in Miami courtroom". McClatchy DC Bureau. Retr Sept 22, 2018.

Paul Manafort

Manafort has "denied taking part in collusion with Russia but registered himself as a foreign agent Retroactively after it was revealed his firm received more than $17m working as a lobbyist for a pro-Russian Ukrainian party."[167]

167. Borger, Julian (October 7, 2017). "The Trump–Russia dossier: why its findings grow more significant by the day". The Guardian. Retrieved December 28, 2017.

Carter Page

Page originally denied meeting Russian officials, but his later testimony, acknowledging he met with senior Russian officials at Rosneft, has been interpreted as corroboration of the dossier.[344][345][346] On February 11, 2021, Page lost a defamation suit he had filed against Yahoo! News and HuffPost for their articles describing his activities in Steele dossier. The judge said Page admitted articles about his contacts with Russian officials were essentially true.[354]

344. Raju, Manu; Herb, Jeremy; Polantz, Katelyn (Nov 8, 2017). "Carter Page reveals new contacts with Trump campaign, Russians". CNN. Retr April 1, 2018.
345. Lanktree, Graham (Nov 7, 2017). "Carter Page Attacked Christopher Steele's Trump Dossier, Testimony Raised Questions Over Russian Meetings". Newsweek. Retrieved April 2, 2018.
346. Kelly, Erin (Nov 6, 2017). "Trump campaign adviser Carter Page acknowledges meeting senior Russian officials: transcript". USA Today. Retrieved April 2, 2018.
354. Multiple sources:

- Leonard, Mike (February 11, 2021). "Carter Page Loses Libel Case Over 'Steele Dossier,' Russia Probe". Bloomberg Law. Retr Feb 13, 2021.
- Leonard, Mike (Mar 16, 2021). "Carter Page to Revive Defamation Case Over Russia Ties". Bloomberg Law. Retr March 17, 2021.
- Montgomery, Jeff (February 11, 2021). "Del. Judge Nixes Carter Page Yahoo, HuffPost Defamation Suit". Law360. Retr Feb 13, 2021.

Others

Russia has backed Trump by attacking the dossier and denying its allegations, calling it an "absolute fabrication" and "a hoax intended to further damage U.S.–Russian relations".[478]

As Putin's press secretary, Peskov insisted in an interview that the dossier is a fraud, saying "I can assure you that the allegations in this funny paper, in this so-called report, are untrue. They are all fake."[483] Putin called the people who leaked the dossier "worse than prostitutes"[484] and referred to the dossier itself as "rubbish".[485] Putin went on to state he believed the dossier was "clearly fake",[486] fabricated as a plot against the legitimacy of President-elect Trump.[487]

Some of Steele's former colleagues expressed support for his character, saying "The idea his work is fake or a cowboy operation is false—completely untrue. Chris is an experienced and highly regarded professional. He's not the sort of person who will pass on gossip."[488]

Bob Woodward called the dossier a "garbage document".[489]

Chuck Todd of CBS News labeled the report "fake news".[143]

143. Shafer, Jack (December 22, 2018). "Week 83: BuzzFeed Takes a Victory Lap". Politico. Retrieved December 23, 2018.

January 2, 2018, Simpson and Fritsch authored an op-ed in The NYT, requesting Republicans "release full transcripts of our firm's testimony" and further wrote, "the Steele dossier was not the trigger for FBI's investigation into Russian meddling. As we told Senate Judiciary Committee in August, our sources said the dossier was taken so seriously because it corroborated reports the bureau had received from other sources, including one inside the Trump camp."[88] Ken Dilanian of NBC News said a "source close to Fusion GPS" told him FBI had not planted anyone in the Trump camp, Simpson was referring to Papadopoulos.[492][87]

On January 5, 2018, in the first known Congressional criminal referral resulting from investigations related to the Russian interference in the 2016 U.S. election, Grassley made a referral to the Justice Department suggesting that they investigate possible criminal charges against Steele[494][495] for allegedly making false statements to the FBI about the distribution of the dossier's claims,[496] specifically possible "inconsistencies" in what Steele told authorities and "possibly lying to FBI officials".[497] Senator Lindsey Graham also signed the letter.[498][499] Both Grassley and Graham declared they were not alleging that Steele "had committed any crime. Rather, they had passed on the information for 'further investigation only'."[500] The referral was met with skepticism from legal experts, as well as Republicans and Democrats on Judiciary committee, reportedly not consulted.[498]

On January 8, 2018, a spokesman for Grassley said he did not plan to release the transcript of Simpson's August 22, 2017, testimony before Senate Judiciary Committee.[501] The next day, ranking committee member Feinstein unilaterally released the transcript.[104][502]

On January 10, 2018, Fox News host Sean Hannity had advance information on the forthcoming release of the Nunes memo and assertions about the dossier, saying "shocking information will be coming out in days that will show systemic FISA abuse". Hannity's new information revealed "a phony document full of Russian lies and propaganda used by the Obama administration to surveil members of an opposition party and incoming president," adding this was "the real Russia collusion story" that represented "one of the largest abuses of power in U.S. history. I'm talking about the shredding of the U.S. Constitution."[503]

483. Neely, Bill (Jan 21, 2017). "Kremlin Spokesman: U.S. Intel Report on Russian Hacking 'Ridiculous'". NBC News. Retr January 15, 2017.

484. Walker, Shaun (Jan 17, 2017). "Putin says those behind Trump dossier 'worse than prostitutes'". The Guardian. Retr February 21, 2020.

485. Dewan, Angela; Veselinovic, Milena (January 17, 2017). "Putin on Trump dossier claims: 'Rubbish'". CNN. Retrieved January 17, 2017.

486. Macfarquhar, Neil (January 17, 2017). "Putin Says Accusations in Trump Dossier Are 'Clearly Fake'". New York Times. Retr Jan 18, 2017.

487. Roth, Andrew; Filipov, David (Jan 17, 2017). "Russia's Putin rejects Trump dossier report as plot against 'legitimacy' of president-elect". Washington Post. Feb 19, 2018.

488. Harding, Luke; Hopkins, Nick (Jan 12, 2017). "Donald Trump dossier: intel sources vouch for author's credibility". The Guardian. Retr Jan 23, 2018.

489. Mahtani, Melissa (Jan 17, 2017). "Woodward: The CNN story was 'exactly right'". CNN. Retr Feb 21, 2020. Asked by CNN's Alisyn Camerota to explain his position, Woodward said, 'I read those 35 pages, quality not good.'

490. "Woodward: Intel Dossier on Trump is "Garbage"". KABC (AM). Jan16, 2017. RetrFeb20,2020.

491. Greenwood, Max (Jan 10, 2018). "BuzzFeed editor defends publication of dossier". The Hill. Retr 3/31/18.

492. Shafer, Jack (Jan 13, 2018). "Week 34: Dossier Strikes Back". Politico.

493. Gerstein, Josh (January 4, 2018). "Judge: Trump tweets don't require more disclosure on dossier". Politico. Retrieved August 18, 2018.

494. Stanglin, Doug (January 5, 2018). "GOP senators recommend criminal probe of 'Steele dossier' author". USA Today. Retr Jan 7, 2018.
495. Fandos, Nicholas; Rosenberg, Matthew (Dec 15, 2017). "Republican Senators Raise Possible Charges Against Author of Trump Dossier". NYT. Retrieved Jan 6, 2018.
496. Sheth, Sonam (Feb 7, 2018). "Congress just declassified a letter that offers critical clues about the Steele dossier and the Nunes memo". Business Insider. Retr 2/8/18.
497. Price, Greg (Jan 5, 2018). "Trump–Russia Dossier Author Should Face Criminal Investigation for Lying to FBI, Top Republicans Recommend". Newsweek. Retr 2/19/18.
498. Barrett, Devlin; Hamburger, Tom (Jan 5, 2018). "Senior Republican refers Trump dossier author for possible charges". Washington Post. Retr Jan 5, 2018.
499. Tau, Byron (Jan 5, 2018). "Senators Ask Justice Department to Open Criminal Probe Into Trump Dossier Author". Wall Street Journal. Retr Jan 5, 2018.
500. "Republicans urge investigation into Trump dossier author". BBC News. January 5, 2018. Retr Jan 7, 2018.
501. Dennis, Steven T. (Jan 8, 2017). "Grassley Won't Release Fusion GPS Transcript From Russia Probe". Bloomberg. Retr Jan 9, 2018.
502. Barrett, Devlin; Hamburger, Tom (Jan 9, 2018). "Fusion GPS founder told Senate investigators FBI had a whistleblower in Trump's network". The Washington Post. Retrieved January 9, 2018.
503. Fernandez, Nick (Feb 5, 2018). "The Nunes memo perfectly lined up with what Hannity has been hyping for weeks". Media Matters for America. Retrieved 4/25/18.

Litigation involving Steele dossier

Multiple lawsuits were filed in connection with the Steele dossier, primarily involving defamation claims by plaintiffs such as Aleksej Gubarev, the three owners of Alfa-Bank (Mikhail Fridman, Petr Aven, and German Khan), Michael Cohen, Devin Nunes, Giorgi Rtskhiladze and Carter Page against Christopher Steele, BuzzFeed, Oath, Orbis, Democratic National Committee and others. All of these cases, except one, were dismissed or withdrawn by the plaintiffs.

Carter Page unsuccessfully sought damages in a lawsuit against US Dept. of Justice, FBI, and several former U.S. government officials, alleging violations of his constitutional rights. Donald Trump also filed unsuccessful lawsuits against Hilary Clinton, Steele, Orbis, and others.

Once again, the Author is obliged to point out all the continuing reports and public statements that are now documented as false.

CHAPTER 12. ELECTION INTERFERENCE AGAINST TRUMP

The following list is a summary of the many, countless, and continuing court actions lodged against Donald Trump. The simple points of the countless falsehoods reported and documented by many outside reports should make clear to the reader that none of these charges can be substantiated, that all the legal practitioners involved are guilty of violating canons of ethics in the legal profession.

1. Trump attempted to enter politics 30 years ago as Democrat, 1990
2. Democrats never accepted him.
3. Democrats threw false cases against him such as Stormy Daniel
4. Just look at Trumps wives to see he never had to chase bad girls.
5. Steele Dossier
6. Mueller Investigation
7. Comey Investigation
8. Russia Hoax 2016
9. Dems claimed Saudi/Egypt money donated to Trump Campaign.
10. Two False, Trump impeachments.
11. 2020 Election Steal and continuing MSM lies 2020
    a. Over 1 million illegal votes documented as being counted by four states to benefit of democrats
    b. Arizona problems with election day 50% equipment failure to benefit of democrats
    c. Fulton County issues in benefit of democrats
        d. Police ordered poll watchers far away from voting location.
        e. Sent Poll Watchers home
        f. Continued counting votes after poll watchers sent home
        g. Lied about broken water line endangering vote counting.
        h. Filed dubious RICO case against Trump
        i. Prosecutor kicked off case
        j. Fanni Willis, now in legal trouble (Judge Scott McAfee)
12. Pennsylvania election day fiasco that would benefit democrats
    a. 288,000 absentees sent to one Pa. county from NYC alone
    b. No follow-up reports of votes sent to other Pa. counties
    c. 46 vote machine devices capable of manipulating vote count not returned to Pa. vote headquarters, endangering future elections
13. Jan 06 false claims, just a democrat setup.
14. False electors claim, yet Trump was upholding his oath of office.
15. Criminal cases falsely filed against Trump White House Officials.

16. Criminal cases falsely filed against Trump Lawyers.
17. Jack Smith files Election Violation case with (Judge Chutkan).
18. Jack Smith files Mar a Lago case.
19. NY state files claim false finance and tax reporting.
20. (NY Judge Merchan) accused of Conflict of Interest due to daughter raising money for democrats. ($500 million)
21. Judge Merchan, Alvin Bragg allow Stormy Daniels and others to repeat a second case barred by Statute of Limitations.
22. House Judiciary committee accuses Judge Merchan and Alvin Bragg of violating the Constitution.
23. Judge Aileen Canon dismisses Mar a Lago case against Trump.

SUMMARY OF COURT ACTIONS AGAINST TRUMP
https://www.pbs.org/wgbh/frontline/article/a-guide-to-the-criminal-cases-against-donald-trump/

January 30, 2024, by Kaela Malig
This story was updated on July 16, 2024, to reflect new developments.

A federal judge dismissed one of three remaining criminal cases against former President Donald Trump in mid-July, ruling that the special counsel who filed the charges was not properly appointed.

This latest legal victory for Trump came after the U.S. Supreme Court ruled in a 6-3 decision earlier in July that the former president had immunity from prosecution for some actions taken while in office. That ruling had major implications for the criminal case against Trump on charges he plotted to overturn the 2020 election and was expected to further delay that trial.

Trump, the presumed 2024 Republican presidential nominee, in late May became the first former president of the United States to be convicted of a felony. The historic conviction came after the jury in a New York trial found Trump guilty on 34 felony counts of falsifying business records to conceal a "hush money" payment made to an adult film star to prevent a scandal from circulating during 2016 presidential campaign.

With one conviction and one case's dismissal — which is likely to be appealed — Trump now faces two remaining criminal cases, in which he has been charged on a total of 14 felony counts.

As FRONTLINE examines in the documentary Democracy on Trial, some of those charges against Trump stem from his election loss in 2020 and his role in widespread efforts to overturn the results.

The former president has pleaded not guilty to the remaining charges. Trump insisted that the cases are politically motivated, and his lawyers argued that presidents have absolute immunity from prosecution for actions taken in office.

"Trump's best strategy right now is delay," David French, a conservative columnist for The New York Times told FRONTLINE in the documentary. "Because he's a very unusual defendant in terms of his potential power. If he wins the election, he can just order the DOJ to drop the case entirely. So he has an enormous personal incentive to win the presidency just to get himself out of legal jeopardy."

Here are key details of criminal cases against the former president.

- The New York State, "Hush Money" Case
- The Federal Classified Documents Case
- The Federal Election Interference Case
- The Georgia Election Interference Case

The New York State, "Hush Money" Case

Date Indicted March 30, 2023
Scheduled Trial Date The trial was scheduled to begin on March 25, 2024, but was moved to April 15.

New York State Supreme Court,
Judge Overseeing New York Supreme Court Judge Juan Merchan,
Person Leading the Investigation Manhattan District Attorney Alvin L.

Bragg Charges 34 counts of falsifying business records in first degree.

What Is the Case About? A grand jury voted to indict Trump, making him the first former U.S. president to be criminally charged and marking the beginning of indictments against the former president.

The indictment accuses Trump of falsifying business records in connection to a payment made during the final weeks of the 2016 presidential campaign to adult film star Stormy Daniels, who had threatened to reveal what she said was a 2006 sexual encounter with Trump. The case alleges that Daniels was paid $130,000 by Trump's personal lawyer Michael Cohen in October 2016 in exchange for her silence. According to prosecutors, Trump then reimbursed Cohen in installment payments through his company, the Trump Organization, under a false retainer agreement after he won the presidency.

In addition to "hush money" payments to Daniels, Trump is charged in connection with payments made to Playboy model Karen McDougal and a doorman to prevent scandals from circulating during the 2016 campaign.

In New York, falsifying business records counts as a felony, rather than a misdemeanor, if the defendant had an intent of committing or concealing a separate underlying crime. The Manhattan district office charged the former president with a low-level felony, which carries a maximum of four years in prison for each count. The indictment alleged that Trump falsified business records to "conceal criminal activity, including attempts to violate state and federal election laws," but did not specify a particular underlying crime. In recent interviews, Manhattan District Attorney Alvin L. Bragg has described the case as an "election interference case" that is about "conspiring to corrupt a presidential election" by concealing damaging information ahead of the vote.

Trump has denied having an affair with Daniels and said that the payment to her was not campaign related, has pleaded not guilty. He accused Bragg of being a "racist" and conducting a "witch hunt" against him. Trump's legal team sought to have the judge on the case removed, alleging a conflict of interest; the judge declined to recuse himself, saying "this Court ... is certain in its ability to be fair and impartial." Trump's legal team dropped an appeal to move the case from state court Trump says is "very unfair" to him to federal court. The Verdict on May 30, 2024, found Trump guilty on 34 felony counts. Trump denounced the trial as a "disgrace" after the verdict and said he's a "very innocent man." Following the Supreme Court's July 2024 ruling on presidential immunity, Trump's lawyers asked the judge for a delay in sentencing, which was granted, urged the judge to vacate the jury verdict and dismiss the case.

The Federal Classified Documents Case

Date Indicted June 8, 2023, and July 27, 2023, when special counsel Jack Smith's team charged Trump with three more counts. The trial was initially scheduled to begin on May 20, 2024. After a hearing in March 2024 to pick a new trial date, the judge overseeing the case has yet to make a decision.

U.S. District Court for the Southern District of Florida
Judge Overseeing U.S. District Judge Aileen Cannon
Person Leading the Investigation Special counsel Jack Smith

Charges 32 counts, willful retention of national defense information, 1 count, conspiracy to obstruct justice, 3 counts, withholding or concealing a document, 2 counts, false statements, 2 counts, altering, destroying, mutilating, concealing an object or record.

What Is the Case About? Trump was indicted by a federal grand jury, making him the first former president to face federal charges. The indictment accuses Trump of taking highly sensitive national security documents when he left the White House in January 2021, resisting government's repeated attempts to retrieve them.

According to the indictment, National Archives and Records Admin repeatedly demanded that the former president return all missing presidential records, which prosecutors allege Trump refused to do. In August 2022, FBI agents recovered more than 100 classified documents from Trump's Florida estate at Mar-a-Lago. In addition to showing classified documents to people who didn't have clearance, the former president — federal prosecutors alleged — stashed the papers in improper locations throughout his Mar-a-Lago resort, including in a "ballroom, a bathroom and shower, and office space, his bedroom, and a storage room." The documents, prosecutors say, include sensitive information on the country's nuclear programs, potential vulnerabilities to a military attack, and plans for possible retaliation in case of foreign attacks. Trump's aide Walt Nauta and his property manager Carlos De Oliveira were named as co-conspirators and charged in the case.

The indictment alleges that the disclosure of these documents could have put the country's safety and national security at risk. Each count of making false statements can lead to five years in prison, while each count of willful retention of national defense information is punishable by up to 10 years. Each count of conspiracy to obstruct justice, withholding documents, and altering, destroying, or concealing records could result in 20 years imprisonment.

Trump, as well as his associates Nauta and De Oliveira, have pleaded not guilty. In a motion filed in January 2024, Trump's lawyers said that they intend to prove the records were stored in secure locations at the Mar-a-Lago estate and that the case was "politically motivated and biased" and intended to harm Trump's 2024 presidential campaign. In March 2024, a federal judge rejected a motion by Trump to throw out the case.

In a decision likely to be appealed, Judge Cannon dismissed the classified documents case, on July 15, 2024, ruling Smith's appointment as special counsel violated the Constitution.

The Federal Election Interference
Case Date Indicted August 1, 2023

The trial was initially scheduled for March 4, 2024, but was postponed while Trump appealed a decision on immunity claims. The Supreme Court's July 2024 ruling on the former president's immunity is likely to delay the trial further. While the majority's opinion stated that Trump was "absolutely immune" from prosecution for his conversations with officials at the Justice Department, the district court judge in charge of the case must now evaluate which of Trump's other alleged actions described in the indictment were official and which were not and might still be subject to prosecution. The three liberal justices dissented, and Justice Sonia Sotomayor wrote, "The relationship between the President and the people he serves has shifted irrevocably. In every use of official power, the President is now a king above the law."

U.S. District Court for the District of Columbia
Judge Overseeing U.S. District Judge Tanya S. Chutkan
Person Leading Investigation Special counsel Jack Smith

Charges 2 counts, obstructing an official proceeding, conspiring to obstruct an official proceeding, 1 count, conspiracy to defraud the United States government, 1 count, conspiracy to violate rights.

What Is the Case About? More than two-and-a-half years after violence erupted at the Capitol on Jan. 6, 2021, special counsel Jack Smith indicted Trump for his alleged efforts to overturn the results of the 2020 election and disrupt certification of the electoral vote so he could remain in power. Prosecutors argued Trump's actions were an attack on American democracy's tradition of peaceful transfer of power.

Among the charges Trump faces, the count of conspiracy to defraud the U.S. government refers to the alleged undermining of the government's counting of the votes, the count of obstructing an "official proceeding" refers to the disruption of the Jan. 6 election certification at the Capitol, and the count of conspiracy to violate rights refers to the allegation that Trump denied voters right to have their votes counted.

The indictment alleges that, in the two months between the November 2020 election and Jan. 6, Trump spread claims of electoral fraud that he knew were false, having been told by multiple officials, both from the Justice Department and his campaign team, that he in fact lost the election. He is accused of pressuring the Justice Department to support false claims.

The indictment also alleges he took part in a scheme involving false slates of electors and pressured Republican state officials, as well as Vice President Mike Pence, to overturn the electoral results. Although federal prosecutors didn't charge Trump with directly inciting the pro-Trump attack at the capitol, they said Trump exploited the violence to try to subvert Biden's victory. Six co-conspirators were referenced in the indictment, Trump is the only person charged.

Trump has pleaded not guilty. Trump said it was his decision to believe the election was "rigged," and that he did not respect the lawyers on his team who told him he had lost the election. The trial court judge in Washington, D.C., threw out a motion by Trump's lawyers to dismiss on grounds that presidents should have absolute immunity from prosecution for actions taken while in office. On Feb. 6, a federal appeals court rejected Trump's claim and said he could be prosecuted. The former president appealed to U.S. Supreme Court.

Last October, the judge overseeing the case imposed a gag order on Trump banning him from making public statements attacking witnesses and officials involved in the case, citing concerns that his comments could spur violence from his supporters. Trump argued that the order violated his First Amendment rights. An appeals court panel in December upheld the order but revised it to allow statements critical of Smith, as well as witnesses in some contexts. In January 2024, the full federal appeals court rejected Trump's bid to lift the order, leaving appeal to the U.S. Supreme Court his last option.

The Georgia Election Interference
Case Date Indicted August 14, 2023

Scheduled Trial Date The case was halted by the Georgia Court of Appeals on June 5 while the appeals court considers a ruling that allows Fulton County District Attorney Fani Willis to stay on the case.
Court Fulton County Superior Court
Fulton County Superior Court Judge Scott McAfee
Leading Investigation Fulton County District Attorney Fani Willis

Charges 1 count related to violating the Racketeer Influenced and Corrupt Organizations Act, 6 counts related to false statements and documents, 2 counts of conspiracy to commit forgery in the first degree, 4 counts related to soliciting or impersonating public officers.

What Is the Case About? The indictment lists 41 charges — 13 of which are against Trump — and 18 other defendants, alleging that they attempted to unlawfully overturn the 2020 election results in Georgia and subvert the voters' will. The indictment charges Trump and his associates with a violation of the state's Racketeer Influenced and Corrupt Organizations Act, a law that allows prosecutors to link different crimes by various people if those crimes were carried out for one corrupt enterprise. The Georgia indictment also accuses Trump of being at the top of the alleged racketeering activity.

The indictment alleges Trump and associates spread false claims about voter fraud, plotted to create fake pro-Trump electors, and urged Georgia officials to overturn Biden's win. One of the key incidents referenced is a recorded phone call with Brad Raffensperger, Georgia's secretary of state, in which Trump can be heard asking the official to "find 11,780 votes," the number needed to defeat Biden in Georgia.

In March 2024, a judge threw out six of the original 41 charges against Trump and others, bringing charges to 10 instead of 13.

Trump's Defense Trump has pleaded not guilty. He has described the phone call with Raffensperger as "perfect." Like the federal election interference case, Trump has sought presidential immunity and asked the Georgia court to dismiss the charges in a motion filed in January 2024. In the same month, Michael Roman, one of Trump's co-defendants, filed a motion accusing Willis of having a romantic relationship with Nathan Wade, the case's lead prosecutor. In a court filing on Feb. 2, Willis acknowledged a "personal relationship" with Wade, but argued that there were no grounds to remove her from the case. In response to claims of a conflict of interest, Wade said none of the money he made on the job was shared with Willis. Trump responded to Willis' acknowledgement of the relationship, posting on the platform Truth Social that the case was a "hoax" so Willis and Wade could interfere in the 2024 election. Trump's lead attorney, Steve Sadow, said that although Willis has admitted to the relationship, she failed to provide "full transparency and necessary financial details."

In mid-March, Wade resigned as special prosecutor to "move this case forward as quickly as possible" after Judge McAfee said Willis and her office could only keep the case if he stepped down. Judge McAfee gave Trump and the other defendants permission to appeal the ruling allowing Willis to remain on the case.

Four of the 18 other defendants have already pleaded guilty. If Trump were found guilty in this case, he would not be able to pardon himself if re-elected as president since he would have violated a Georgia state law, not a federal law.

Priyanka Boghani and Patrice Taddonio contributed updates to story.

NEW YORK CASES AGAINST DONALD TRUMP

https://ag.ny.gov/press-release/2024/attorney-general-james-wins-landmark-victory-case-against-donald-trump

Attorney General James Wins Landmark Victory Against Donald Trump

- Donald Trump, Adult Sons, and Former Executives Ordered to Pay More Than $450 Million They Fraudulently and Illegally Obtained.
- Donald Trump Banned from Serving as an Officer or Director of Any New York Company for Three Years

February 16, 2024

NEW YORK – New York Attorney General Letitia James today released the following statement after Justice Arthur F. Engoron of New York State Supreme Court ruled in her favor in her office's civil fraud case against Donald Trump, the other individual defendants, and the Trump Organization entities, ordering the defendants to pay more than $450 million in total, which represents $363.8 million in disgorgement and pre-judgment interest: *"Today, justice has been served. This is a tremendous victory for this state, this nation, and for everyone who believes that we all must play by the same rules — even former presidents.*

"For years, Donald Trump engaged in massive fraud to falsely inflate his net worth and unjustly enrich himself, his family, and his organization. While he may have authored the 'Art of the Deal,' our case revealed that his business was based on the art of the steal.

"When powerful people cheat to get better loans, it comes at the expense of honest and hardworking people. Everyday Americans cannot lie to a bank to get a mortgage to buy a home, and if they did, our government would throw the book at them. There simply cannot be different rules for different people.

"Now, Donald Trump is finally facing accountability for his lying, cheating, and staggering fraud. Because no matter how big, rich, or powerful you think you are, no one is above the law."

The decision issued by Justice Arthur F. Engoron grants the following:

- Donald Trump and other defendants are ordered to pay $450 million, representing $363.8 million in disgorgement and judgment interest;
- Donald Trump, Allen Weisselberg, Jeffrey McConney are banned from serving as officer or director of a NY company for 3 years;
- Allen Weisselberg, Jeffrey McConney additionally banned from a financial management role in a New York company for life;

- Donald Trump, Jr., and Eric Trump are banned from serving as an officer or director of any New York company for two years;
- Donald Trump and his companies are banned from applying for loans from any NY bank or financial institution for three years;
- A new, Independent Director of Compliance role will be created at the Trump Organization to ensure the company establishes internal protocols and meets financial reporting obligations; and
- The current independent, external monitor will continue to oversee the company's financial dealings to ensure fraud cannot continue.

Following a three-year investigation, in September 2022 Attorney General James filed a lawsuit against Donald Trump, a number of Trump Organization companies, and senior executives for engaging in years of financial fraud and illegal conduct. In Sept 2023, before this trial began, Justice Engoron issued a ruling granting AG James' motion for partial summary judgment, finding that Donald Trump and the defendants committed fraud by falsely inflating the value of his assets. Today's decision and order that Trump and the other individual defendants also engaged in illegal conduct and that relief against the defendants is necessary to prevent further fraudulent and illegal conduct comes after 11 weeks of trial, which concluded with closing arguments last month.

The investigation and subsequent legal action were conducted by the following Army of democrat conflicted investigators;
Senior Enforcement Counsel Kevin Wallace, Special Counsel Andrew Amer, Assistant Attorney General Colleen K. Faherty, Assistant Attorney General Alex Finkelstein, Assistant Attorney General Wil Handley, Assistant Attorney General Stephanie Torre, Assistant Attorney General Sherief Gaber, Special Counsel Eric R. Haren, Real Estate Finance Enforcement Section Chief Louis M. Solomon, former Assistant Attorney General Mark Ladov, former Assistant Attorney General Austin Thompson, and Legal Support Analysts Samantha Stern and Labiba Hasan. Additional support was provided by Data Analyst Anushua Choudhury, Senior Data Analyst Akram Hasanov, Data Analyst Blake Rubey, former Data Scientist Chansoo Song, former Deputy Director of Research and Analytics Megan Thorsfeldt, and former Director of Research and Analytics Jonathan Werberg; as well as Information Technology Specialist Hewson Chen, Information Technology Specialist Paige Podolny, and Information Technology Specialist John Roach. Appellate support was provided by Deputy Solicitor General Judith Vale, Deputy Solicitor General Ester Murdukhayeva, Senior Assistant Solicitor General Dennis Fan, Assistant Solicitor General Cleland Welton, Assistant Solicitor General Daniel Magy, and former Assistant Solicitor General Eric Del Pozo. The investigation was overseen by First Deputy Attorney General Jennifer Levy.

A copy of the decision is available for download.
Letitia James, New York State Attorney General

CHAPTER 13. JUDGES AND PROSECUTORS IN TRUMP CASES, ASSOCIATED CONFLICT OF INTEREST

Factors revolving around the Judges charged with the Trump cases suggests more sinister actions being activated against Donald Trump. One by one, the cases do not give the appearance of extraneous influence. We will display information regarding the life and Professional actions of the judges and prosecutors.

Listing of the Judges and Prosecutors acting against Donald Trump

Ursula Ungaro, Steele Dossier allowed to print
Judge Lewis Kaplan, case of E. Jean Carrol against Trump
Linda Vivienne Parker (A case to overturn Michigan
election) Judge Emmett Sullivan A case against General
Flynn Judge Amit Mehta Jan 06 cases
ALVIN BRAGG and the Trump Cases
Judge Juan Merchan NY cases against Trump
Judge Arthur F. Engoron NY Civil cases on
Trump Judge Aileen Canon Mar a Lago cases

Merrick Garland Appoints Jack Smith

Jack Smith, Prosecutor appointed by DOJ for the Trump
Cases Judge Tanya Chutkan, DC Jan 06 against Trump
Fani Willis, Fulton County DA prosecuting Trump
Nathan Wade Prosecutor in Fulton Co cases against
Trump Judge Scott McAfee Fulton County Cases
Beryl A. Howell, Appellate Judge in Giuliani Defamation Case
Judge William Pryor 11th Circuit US Court of Appeals

Dominion and Smartmatic

Cases Troy Webber
Peter H. Moulton
Martin
Shulman
John Higgitt
Eric Davis

THE JUDGES AND BIO'S

Ursula Ungaro and Steele Dossier publication

Ursula Mancusi Ungaro (formerly Ungaro-Benages; born January 29, 1951) is a former US district judge of the United States District Court for the Southern District of Florida.

Ungaro was born in 1951 in Miami Beach, Florida. She graduated from the University of Miami with a Bachelor of Arts degree in 1973 and from the University of Florida College of Law with a Juris Doctor in 1975.[1]

Career

Ungaro was in private practice in Miami from 1976-1987. Ungaro practiced at Frates Floyd Pearson Stewart Richman & Greer from 1976-1978, Blackwell Walker Gray Powers Flick & Hoehl from 1978-1980, Finley Kumble Heine Underberg Manley & Casey from 1980-1985, and a shareholder at Sparber Shevin Shapo Heilbronner & Book, P.A. from 1985-1987.[2] Ungaro was a judge of Eleventh Judicial Circuit of Florida from 1987 to 1992.[1]

President George H. W. Bush nominated Ungaro-Benages to the U.S. District Court for the Southern District of Florida, November 26, 1991, to a new seat created by 104 Stat. 5089. She was confirmed on October 8, 1992.[1] She assumed senior status on May 2, 2021, and retired[3] May 31, 2021, to join Boies Schiller law firm. Daily Business Review presented her a Lifetime Achievement award.[4]

Notable cases

On September 10, 1998, Judge Ungaro-Benages (presiding in the U.S. District Court for the Southern District of Florida) ruled that an Establishment Clause challenge to Congress's 1954 addition of the words "under God" in the Pledge of Allegiance was "so patently lacking in merit as to be frivolous." The plaintiff in that case subsequently filed a similar lawsuit in California, where the 9th Circuit Court of Appeals eventually ruled in the plaintiff's favor.

On April 26, 2012, Ungaro ruled that an order issued by Florida Governor Rick Scott to random drug test 80,000 Florida state workers was unconstitutional. Ungaro found Scott had not demonstrated a compelling reason for the tests and as a result, they were an unreasonable search in violation of the Constitution.[5]

On December 19, 2018, Ungaro ruled, in Gubarev v. Buzzfeed, that Buzzfeed had not committed defamation in printing, in full, the Steele dossier. The claim was brought by Aleksej Gubarev, a Russian internet entrepreneur, who claimed to have been defamed by the publishing of the dossier by the media company, Buzzfeed.[6] In part, Ungaro ruled the law of defamation does not equally apply to media institutions and does not require institutions to spend considerable resources to go line by line and determine the veracity of every claim in news reports. Ruling "Such a line-by-line review would curtail the scope of the privilege and thus restrict the press's ability to serve its basic function." For Buzzfeed, the use of a hyperlink citing a CNN article which contained a two-page synopsis of the report was sufficient to allow Buzzfeed to publish the report. The lawyers for Gubarev vowed to appeal the decision to the 11th Circuit Court of Appeals and specifically intend to argue the hyperlink to the original CNN article was insufficient. Buzzfeed's counsel praised the ruling "We are extremely pleased that Judge Ungaro affirmed our client's First Amendment rights in this matter. Fighting against restraints on reporting and maintaining public confidence in the constitutionally mandated right to a free and unfettered press is vitally important, perhaps more so now than ever. The ruling is a strong affirmation of the First Amendment. It is more important that the public know what is being discussed at the highest levels of government than anything else. If BuzzFeed had not published, citizens would not understand the current conflict between the president and the other branches of government, as well as the conflict between the president and the special counsel."

1. "Ungaro, Ursula - Federal Judicial Center". www.fjc.gov.
2. "Biographies of Federal Court Judges Sitting in Florida" (PDF).
3. "Why U.S. Judge Ursula Ungaro quit the bench for Boies Schiller partnership". Reuters. 2021-05-14. Retrieved 2021-06-04.
4. "Lifetime Achievement: Federal Judge Ungaro Became a Pillar of Florida's Legal Community". Daily Business Review. Retr 2022-08-22.
5. Alvarez, Lizette (26 April 2012). "State Worker Drug Tests Struck Down in Florida". The New York Times. Retr 27 April 2012.
6. Gerstein, Josh (4 Jan 2019). "Libel suit against BuzzFeed thrown out". Politico.

Lewis Kaplan

Lewis Avins Kaplan (born December 23, 1944)[1] is an American lawyer and jurist who serves as a senior US district judge of the US District Court for the Southern District of New York.[2] He was the presiding judge in high-profile cases, including E. Jean Carroll v. Donald J. Trump, Virginia Giuffre v. Prince Andrew, United States v. Bankman-Fried, and trials of Al Qaeda terrorists such as Ahmed Ghailani.

Kaplan was born to a Jewish family in 1944 in Staten Island, New York. He received a Bachelor of Arts degree from Univ of Rochester in 1966 and J.D. from Harvard Law 1969.[3]

After law school, Kaplan was a law clerk for Judge Edward McEntee of the US Court of Appeals for the First Circuit, from 1969 to 1970. He then entered private practice at the law firm Paul, Weiss, Rifkind, Wharton & Garrison, becoming a partner in 1977. From 1982 to 1983, he served as a Special Master for the US District Court for the Southern District of New York. During his time in the private sector, Kaplan represented Phillip Morris.[4]

He married former New York Times reporter and former VP of Random House Lesley Oelsner, Feb 29, 2004.[5]

Federal judicial service

On May 5, 1994, Kaplan was nominated by President Bill Clinton to a seat on the US District Court for the Southern District of New York vacated by Gerard Louis Goettel. He was confirmed by the US Senate on August 9, 1994, and received his commission on August 10, 1994. He took senior status on February 1, 2011.[3]

Notable cases

From 2021 to 2022, Kaplan was presiding judge on Virginia Giuffre v. Prince Andrew over allegations of sexual assault.[30]

In 2023 Judge Kaplan presided over the civil trial by E. Jean Carroll against Donald Trump for sexual assault and defamation.[31] Kaplan found Trump liable on September 6, 2023, and set the matter for a damages only trial.[32]

1. Hearings before Committee on the Judiciary, US Senate, 103rd Congress, Second Session, Confirmations of Appointees to Federal Judiciary, June 21, 29, 30; July 21; August 3 and 11, 1994. U.S. Gov Printing Office. 1996. p. 81.
2. "Government Gave Big Oil Power to Prosecute Its Biggest Critic". July 14, 2020.
3. Lewis A. Kaplan, Biographical Directory of Federal Judges, a publication of the Federal Judicial Center.
4. Frankel, Alison (Jan 1, 2006). "The LifeSavers." American Lawyer.
5. "Weddings/Celebrations; Lesley Oelsner, Lewis Kaplan". The NYT. Feb 29, 2004. Retr Nov 25, 2019.
30. Pavia, Will; Low, Valentine (Jan 4, 2022). "Prince Andrew hearing: Kaplan deals blow to duke's hopes of Giuffre case dismissed". The Times. ISSN 0140-0460.
31. Shapero, Julia (March 10, 2023). "Judge in E. Jean Carroll's suit against Trump says jury can hear other accusers, 'Access Hollywood'. The Hill. Retr 5/4/23.
32. "Trump suffers big loss in E. Jean Carroll defamation case, judge says he's liable". CNBC. Sept 6, 2023.

Linda Vivienne Parker (A case to overturn Michigan general election Dec. 2020)

Judge Linda V. Parker was nominated by President Obama to the US District Court for the Eastern District of Michigan on July 25, 2013, confirmed by the United States Senate on March 12, 2014.

Judge Parker served on the Third Judicial Circuit Court in the County of Wayne from December 2008 until her appointment.

A native Detroiter, Judge Parker is a former director of the Michigan Department of Civil Rights, a position in which she served from 2003 until 2008. Judge Parker is a former partner of the Detroit-based law firm, Dickinson Wright, PLC, and served as the first Executive Assistant U.S. Attorney for the Eastern District of Michigan in the US Attorney's Office from 1994-2000.

Judge Parker is a University of Michigan graduate and received her law degree from George Washington University.

Source of above
https://www.mied.uscourts.gov/index.cfm?pageFunction=chambers&judgeid=46)

Parker received a Bachelor of Arts degree in 1980 from the University of Michigan. She received a Juris Doctor in 1983 from George Washington University Law School. From 1983 to 1985, she served as a law clerk to the District of Columbia Superior Court. She worked as a staff attorney at the United States Environmental Protection Agency from 1985 to 1989. From 1989 to 1994, she worked at the Detroit law firm of Dickinson Wright, becoming a partner in 1992. From 1994 to 2000, she served as an executive assistant United States attorney, Eastern District of Michigan. She served as director of the Michigan Department of Civil Rights from 2003 to 2008. From 2009 to 2014, she served as a judge of the Third Judicial Circuit Court of Michigan.[1][2]

Federal judicial service

On July 25, 2013, President Obama nominated Parker to serve as a United States District Judge of the United States District Court for the Eastern District of Michigan, to the seat vacated by Judge Robert Hardy Cleland, who assumed senior status on March 1, 2013.[1] On January 16, 2014, her nomination was reported out of committee by a 14–3 vote.[3] On March 11, 2014, the US Senate invoked cloture on her nomination by a 56–42 vote.[4] On March 12, 2014, her nomination was confirmed by a 60–37 vote.[5] She received her judicial commission on March 17, 2014,[2] primary chambers are in Detroit.[6]

Notable rulings

In December 2020, Parker heard a lawsuit brought by attorneys for then-president Trump, to reverse Michigan results for the 2020 U.S. election, one of the so-called "Kraken" suits. She dismissed the suit, saying it was full of "theories, conjecture and speculation" adding "the people of Michigan have spoken."[7]

In July 2021, Parker ordered all the attorneys who had argued Trump's case to appear before her, as she considered motions filed to impose sanctions on the attorneys for arguing that Trump had won the election and presenting evidence that she said they had not evaluated for accuracy.[8] On August 25, 2021, Parker ruled that "Plaintiffs' counsel filed this lawsuit in bad faith and for an improper purpose", demanding that the attorneys, including Sidney Powell and Lin Wood, pay the legal fees of some of the defendants in the suit, and that they be referred to their respective state bars for disciplinary action.[9]

1. "President Obama Nominates Six to Serve on US District Court". whitehouse.gov. White House Office of Press Secretary. July 25, 2013 – NARA.
2. Linda Vivienne Parker at the Bio Directory of Federal Judges, a publication of the Federal Judicial Center.
3. "Executive Business Meeting". Committee on Judiciary. US Senate. Retr 1/16/14
4. "(Motion to Invoke Cloture on Nomination of Linda Vivienne Parker, of Michigan, to be U.S. District Judge)". US Senate. March 12, 2014. Retr Nov 5, 2022.
5. "(Confirmation Linda Vivienne Parker, of Michigan, to be U.S. District Judge for the Eastern District of Michigan)". US Senate. March 12, 2014. Retr Jan 30, 2015.
6. "Judge Linda V. Parker". US District Court – Eastern Michigan District. United States District Court for the Eastern District of Michigan. Retr March 29, 2018.
7. Brown, Bria (December 7, 2021). "Federal Judge Upholds Michigan Election Results Saying, 'The People Have Spoken'". CBS Detroit. Retrieved July 14, 2021.
8. Helderman, Rosalind A. (July 12, 2021). "'This is really fantastical': Federal judge in Michigan presses Trump-allied lawyers on 2020 election fraud claims in sanctions hearing". Washington Post. Retr July 14, 2021.
9. Sneed, Tierney (Aug 25, 2021). "Judge sanctions pro-Trump lawyers who brought 'frivolous' election fraud lawsuits". CNN.

Judge Emmett Sullivan   A case against General Flynn

Emmet Gael Sullivan (June 4, 1947)[2] is serving as senior US district judge, US District Court for the District of Columbia.[3] He earned his undergraduate and law degrees from Howard University. He worked in private practice more than a decade at Houston & Gardner, becoming a partner in 1980. He was appointed to the Superior Court of the District of Columbia in 1984 by President Reagan, to the District of Columbia Court of Appeals as an Associate Judge in 1992 by President George H. W. Bush, and to the federal bench in 1994 by President Bill Clinton.[4]

Sullivan was born in Washington, D.C., in 1947 and attended local schools. He graduated McKinley Technology High School in 1964. In 1968, he received a Bachelor of Arts in political science from Howard University, a historically black university, and in 1971 a Juris Doctor from the Howard University School of Law.[5]

2. Affairs, United States Congress Senate Committee on Governmental (1984). Nominations for Superior Court of the District of Columbia: Hearing Before the Committee on Governmental Affairs, United States Senate, Ninety-eighth Congress, Second Session, on the Nominations of Emmet G. Sullivan, Colleen C. Kollar-Kotelly, Rufus G. King III, Susan R. Holmes, Noel A. Kramer, Robert I. Richter, and Robert S. Tignor, to be Associate Judges of the Superior Court of the District of Columbia, Sept 11, 1984. U.S. Government Printing Office. p. 10.
3. "Emmet G. Sullivan". US District Court. Arch June 18, Retr June 28, 2008.
4. "Report of District of Columbia Judicial Nomination Commission" (PDF).
5. Hsu, Spencer S.; Marimow, Ann E. (Feb 4, 2021). "U.S. judge in Flynn case takes senior status, joining jurists allowing Biden to name successors". Washington Post. Retrieved February 4, 2021.

Blumenthal v Trump

Judge Sullivan presided over a lawsuit involving President Trump, which challenged payments by foreign governments to Trump-owned hotels.[22] Sullivan granted in part and denied in part the Trump team's motion to dismiss for lack of standing;[23] denied the motion to dismiss for failure to state claim;[24] and certified interlocutory appeal.[25] On February 7, 2020, in a per curia decision, the US Court of Appeals for the District of Columbia Circuit held that individual members of Congress lacked standing to bring action against the president.[25][26] The court, finding in favor of Trump, reversed and remanded Sullivan's holding that members of Congress had standing to sue and instructed him to dismiss.[27]

22. Fahrenthold, David A.; Marimow, Ann E. August 21, 2019. "Federal judge allows Trump to appeal over foreign payments accepted by hotels". The Washington Post.
23. 335 F.Supp.3d 45
24. 373 F.Supp.3d 191
25. Blumenthal v. Trump, 19-5237, 2020 WL 593891 (D.C. Cir. 2/7/20) (No. 1:17-cv-01154)
26. US Court of Appeals for District of Columbia, opinion PER CURIAM, Feb 7, 2020, https://www.cadc.uscourts.gov/internet/opinions.nsf/2EFD382E65E33B3C852585070055D091/$file/19-5237-1827549.pdf
27. Blumenthal v. Trump, 19-5237, 2020 WL 593891, at *5 (D.C. Cir. Feb. 7, 2020)

US v Flynn

The case of United States of America v. Michael T. Flynn, the former national security adviser to Donald Trump, was randomly assigned to District Court Judge Rudolph Contreras.[28] On December 1, 2017, Flynn and special counsel Robert Mueller agreed to a plea bargain in the D.C. court.

In the plea bargain, Flynn admitted to one count of lying to the FBI and said he was cooperating with the Mueller investigation. [29][30] On December 7, Contreras recused himself from the case,[31] which was randomly reassigned to Sullivan.[32] After questioning Flynn about his reasons for pleading guilty, Sullivan accepted Flynn's guilty plea.[33] Sullivan deferred sentencing Flynn because prosecutors indicated he was cooperating.[34][35][36][37][38][39]

In June 2019 Flynn changed attorneys, retaining controversial Texas attorney Sidney Powell to head his legal team,[40][41] and began to assert that investigators and prosecutors had acted improperly.[41] On December 16, 2019, Sullivan rejected Flynn's claims of entrapment by the FBI and malfeasance by prosecutors, and set sentencing for January 28, 2020.[42] On January 14, 2020, Flynn filed a motion to withdraw his guilty plea "because of the government's bad faith, vindictiveness, and breach of the plea agreement."[43] On January 16, Sullivan postponed Flynn's sentencing date to February 27.[44]

On May 7, 2020, the Department of Justice (DOJ) said it would move to drop all charges against Flynn.[45] It was left to Sullivan to determine whether to dismiss the charges and, if so, whether to do it "with prejudice" to prevent a Retrial.[46] On May 11, 2020, former federal judge and prosecutor John Gleeson co-authored with other former law enforcement officials an op-ed encouraging Judge Sullivan to scrutinize the DOJ's motion.[47] On May 12, Sullivan announced that he would place a hold on the DOJ's move to drop charges against Flynn, and would consider a hearing involving "friend of the court" (amicus curiae) input from outside parties with interests and perspectives.[48] On May 13, Sullivan appointed Gleeson as amicus to formally oppose the DOJ's attempt to drop charges, and to look into whether Flynn committed perjury when he twice told the court under oath that he was guilty.[47] Sullivan said "at the appropriate time" he would set a schedule for outside parties to argue against DOJ's claims as it moves to drop charges.[48]

On May 19, Flynn's post-conviction attorney Powell filed a writ of mandamus appeal with the D.C. Circuit Court of Appeals, asking that Sullivan be ordered to drop the charges, challenging his decision to appoint Gleeson, and asking that he be removed from the case.[49][50] On May 21, citing US v Fokker Servs, BV, 818 F.3d 733 (DC Cir 2016), the D.C. Circuit ordered Sullivan to respond to the writ of mandamus by June 1, 2020, and invited the government to respond within the same 10-day period.[51] On June 1, as part of his response,[52][53][54] Sullivan argued that the Fokker decision does not apply because it did not consider a situation where the defendant pleaded guilty twice and the prosecutor changed course; Sullivan moved to dismiss.[54] Oral arguments before a D.C. Circuit Court of Appeals panel were held on June 12, 2020.[55] Sullivan was due to hear the case July 16, 2020.[56]

On June 24, 2020, in a 2-1 decision, the D.C. Circuit Court of Appeals panel granted Flynn's petition for a writ of mandamus, ordering Judge Sullivan to dismiss the case. "In this case, the district court's actions will result in specific harms to the exercise of the Executive Branch's exclusive prosecutorial power. The contemplated proceedings would likely require the Executive to reveal the internal deliberative process behind its exercise of prosecutorial discretion, interfering with the Article II charging authority." The decision also vacated Judge Sullivan's amicus appointment on mootness grounds.[57] In response to the higher court ruling, Judge Sullivan issued an order canceling the July 16 hearing date but did not address the DOJ's motion further. Judge Sullivan's options were either to request the full appellate court to review the case or to grant the DOJ's motion to dismiss the charges in accordance with the writ of mandamus.[58]

On July 9, Judge Sullivan asked the entire U.S. Court of Appeals for the District of Columbia Circuit to review the June 24 decision, saying the panel's decision represented a "dramatic break from precedent".[59] On July 20, 2020, Flynn filed his response to Judge Sullivan's request for the full court to review the panel decision to order the criminal charges dismissed.[60] By Order dated July 30, 2020, the full court granted Judge Sullivan's request and scheduled oral argument for August 11, 2020.[61] In addition to vacating the June 24, 2020 panel decision, the Order directs all parties to be prepared to "address whether there are 'no other adequate means to attain the relief' desired" (citation omitted).[61] On August 11, the full appeals court heard arguments from the DOJ and from Flynn's attorney.[62] On August 31, the appeals court declined to order dismissal of Flynn's prosecution.[63] In an en banc hearing, eight of the D.C. Circuit judges ruled in favor of allowing Sullivan to adjudicate the case. Only the two judges who ruled in favor of Flynn in June 2020, appointed by George W. Bush and Trump ruled against the decision. In dissent, they reversed their earlier position that the case should not be taken from Sullivan and assigned another judge.[64]

On November 25, 2020, Trump issued Flynn a full presidential pardon.[65] On December 8, 2020, Judge Sullivan dismissed the case as moot because of the presidential pardon. In his 43-page opinion he commented that the pardon was "extraordinarily broad", noting such a pardon does not render the recipient "innocent", pointed out that acceptance of a pardon implies admission of guilt.[66] (Once again, the Author points out the sheer politics involved in the Flynn case of a highly decorated Army General who receives strong backing from Republican Judges and is convicted by Democrat Judges.)

28. "Flynn Pleads Guilty, Lying to FBI in Russia Probe". Dec 1, 2017. Retr Dec 8, 2017.

29. Sullivan, Eileen; Goldman, Adam; Shear, Michael D. (Dec 1, 2017). "Flynn Pleads Guilty to Lying to the F.B.I." The New York Times. Retr Dec 1, 2017.

30. Ross, Brian et al. "Flynn promised special counsel 'full cooperation' in Russia probe: Source", ABC 12/1/17.

31. "Judge recuses in Flynn case". POLITICO. Retr Dec 8, 2017.
32. "Judge presiding Michael Flynn criminal case recused: court". Reuters. Dec 8, 2017.
33. Rosenberg, Chuck (5/10/20). "list of people who thought Flynn's lies were material". Wash Post. Retr 5/22/20.
34. Bowden, John. "Mueller, Flynn legal teams not ready". The Hill. Retr Feb 14, 2018.
35. Samuels, Brett (5/1/18). "Mueller requests Flynn's sentencing be delayed two months". The Hill. Retr 8/27/18.
36. "Judge delays sentencing for Flynn". NBC News. Nov 27, 2019. Retr Nov 30, 2019.
37. "Flynn's sentencing delayed after judge tells ex-Trump adviser he might not avoid prison". Washington Post. Dec 18, 2018. Retr Dec 24, 2018.
38. Samuelsohn, Darren; Bertrand, Natasha; Gerstein, Josh (June 24, 2019). "Flynn's sentencing delayed again so new lawyer can study up". Politico. Retr July 3, 2019.
39. Kruzel, John (2/10/20). "Judge delays Flynn sentencing second time". The Hill.
40. Trump considered appointing controversial lawyer Sidney Powell to lead election fraud investigation, Yahoo News, Tim O'Donnell, Dec 19, 2020. Retr May 20, 2021.
41. Mangan, Kevin Breuninger, Dan (June 12, 2019). "Michael Flynn hires Sidney Powell, who urged him to withdraw guilty plea in Mueller case". CNBC.
42 Hsu, Spencer; Leonnig, Carol (Dec 16, 2019). " Flynn's sentencing Jan. 28, judge rejects attacks on FBI, Justice Dept". Washington Post. Arch Dec 16, 2019. Retr 5/8/20
43. Hsu, Spencer (Jan 15, 2020). "Flynn moves to withdraw guilty plea, claiming government 'vindictiveness'". Washington Post. Arch May 5, 2020. Retr May 8, 2020.
44. "Flynn sentencing delayed, seeks to withdraw plea". 1/16/20. Retr May 2, 2020.
45. Balsamo, Michael; Tucker, Eric(5/7/20)."Justice Dept dropping Flynn's Trump-Russia case". AP. Retr 5/8/20.
46. U.S. Drops Flynn Case, Move Backed by Trump, NYT, Adam Goldman and Katie Benner, 5/8/20. Retr 5/8/20.
47. Benner, Katie (May 13, 2020). "Judge Appoints Outsider to Take On Justice Dept. in Flynn Case". New York Times. ISSN 0362-4331. Retr May 14, 2020.
48. Hsu, Spencer; Leonnig, Carol (5/13/20). "U.S. judge puts Justice Department's move to drop charges against Flynn on hold". Washington Post. Retrieved 5/14/20.
49. Re, Gregg (5/20/20). "Flynn attorney appeals to shut down Judge Sullivan's orders, boot from case". Fox News. Retr 5/22/20.
50. "writ of mandamus petition'".
51. "'DC Circuit Court Of Appeals May 21, 2020, Order'" (PDF).
52. "Brief For Judge Emmet G. Sullivan In Response To May 21, 2020, Order". Politico. 6/1/2020. Retr 6/2/20.
53. Cheney, Kyle (6/1/20). "DOJ urges appeals court to force dismissal of Flynn case". Politico. Retrieved 6/2/20
54. Re, Gregg (June 1, 2020). "Judge's lawyers hint at 'reason to question' DOJ's motives in new Michael Flynn case; DOJ fires back". Fox News. Retr June 2, 2020.
55. 'Judges skeptical DOJ move to dismiss Flynn case, lawyer alleges 'government misconduct'; DC Circuit Oral Argument in Michael Flynn Perjury Dismissal Case, C-Span. Retr June 15, 2020.
56. Oral Argument Summary: In re: Michael Flynn, Lawfare, Benjamin Wittes, June 12, 2020. Retr June 15, 2020.
57. "In re Flynn, No. 20-5143, June 24, 2020" CNBC. June 24, 2020. Retr July 9, 2020.
58. Blitzer, Ronn (6/25/20). "Flynn case, deadlines nixed, court ordered to allow dismissal". Fox News. Retr 7/9/20
59. "U.S. Judge Hearing Flynn Case Asks Court to Reconsider Dismissal". NYT. Reuters. 7/9/20. Retr 7/9/20.
60. Flynn's filing, accessed 7-20-2020
61. In re Flynn en banc granted, accessed 7-30-2020
62. Phillips, Kristine (August 11, 2020). "Michael Flynn's efforts to force federal judge to dismiss case faces a skeptical appeals court". USA Today. Retr August 11, 2020.
63. Tucker, Eric (8/31/20). "Appeals court Flynn case alive,". AP. Retr Aug 31, 2020.
64. Appeals court deals setback to Flynn's attempt to end DOJ case, Politico, Josh Gerstein, Aug 31, 2020..
65. "Flynn: Trump pardons ex-national security adviser". BBC News. Nov. 26, 2020. Retr November 28, 2020.
66. Polantz, Katelyn (12/8/20). "Judge formally dismisses Flynn case after Trump pardon". CNN. Retr 12/920.

Amit Mehta

Amit Priyavadan Mehta (born 1971) is an American lawyer who served as US district judge of the US District Court for the District of Columbia since 2014. In 2021, Mehta became a judge on US Foreign Intelligence Surveillance Court.

Mehta has notably presided over cases related to the January 6, 2021, United States Capitol attack[1] and the Google antitrust case[2]. In 2022, he rejected efforts by Donald Trump to dismiss lawsuits accusing the former President of legal responsibility in the attacks.[3]

Childhood and education

Mehta was born in 1971 in Patan, Gujarat, India.[4] At the age of one, Mehta moved with his parents, Priyavadan and Ragini Mehta, to the US.[5] His mother worked as a lab tech, his father was an engineer.[6] Mehta was raised in Reisterstown, Maryland, suburb of Baltimore.[5]

Mehta graduated Franklin High School in 1989. He received a Bachelor of Arts degree in 1993 from Georgetown U, graduating Phi Beta Kappa. From 1993-1994, Mehta worked as a paralegal at law firm Patton Boggs (now Squire Patton Boggs). He attended U of Virginia School of Law, where he was an editor of Virginia Journal of Social Policy & Law. He graduated in 1997 with a Juris Doctor and Order of the Coif honors.

1. Hsu, Spencer S. (Feb 18, 2022). "Oath Keepers leader Stewart Rhodes ordered jailed until trial on seditious conspiracy". Washington Post. Retr 19 Feb 2022.
2. Arbel, Tali (2021-04-21). "Meet Amit Mehta, judge for Google's antitrust case". AP NEWS. Retr 2023-06-02.
3. Cheney, Kyle; Gerstein, Josh (2022-02-18). "Judge rejects Trump effort to toss lawsuits accusing him of Jan. 6 conspiracy". POLITICO. Retr 2023-08-14.
4. Rajghatta, Chidanand (May 21, 2019). "Hip-hop loving Indian-American judge rules against Trump in fight for financial records". Times of India. Retr 5/21/19.
5. Maqsood, Zofeen (2019-05-25). "Newsmaker: Amit Mehta, the Indian American judge who ruled against President Trump - American Bazaar". Retr 2023-06-02.

On July 31, 2014, President Barack Obama nominated Mehta to serve as a United States District Judge of the United States District Court for the District of Columbia, to the seat vacated by Judge Ellen Segal Huvelle, who took senior status on June 3, 2014.[10]

He received a hearing before the United States Senate Committee on the Judiciary on September 17, 2014.[11] On November 20, 2014, his nomination was reported out of committee.[12] On December 13, 2014, Senate Majority Leader Harry Reid filed a motion to invoke cloture on the nomination.

10. "WHITE HOUSE NOMINATIONS SENT TO SENATE: Allison Dale Burroughs, Amit Priyavadan Mehta". Don411.com Media: Performing Arts News. Retr 20 April 2016.
11. "Meeting – Hearings & Meetings – US Senate Committee on Judiciary". 17 Sept 2014. Retr 20 April 2016.
12. "Results Executive Business Meeting 11/20/14, US Senate Committee on Judiciary" (PDF).

In May 2019, Mehta ruled that accounting firm Mazars had to provide its records of Donald Trump's accounts from before his presidency to the House Oversight Committee in response to their subpoena.[14] In a 41-page opinion, he asserted Congress has the right to investigate potential illegal behavior by a president, including actions both before and after the president assumed office.[15] The ruling will be appealed by Trump's legal team.[15]

14. Polantz, Katelyn (5/20/19). "Judge orders Trump accounting firm to hand over records to Congress". CNN.
15. Desiderio, Andrew; Cheney, Kyle (May 20, 2019). "Judge upholds Dem subpoena, Trump financial records". Politico. Retr 21 May 2019.

January 6 Capitol attack-related cases

Mehta has presided several cases related to the January 6 US Capitol attack. He has charge of the criminal prosecution of Oath Keepers founder Stewart Rhodes for seditious conspiracy.[1] He is also presiding over three civil lawsuits against Trump and multiple associates, in which several members of Congress and two police officers are suing for damages for physical and emotional injuries they allegedly incurred during the attacks.

On February 18, 2022, Mehta issued a lengthy opinion that rejected Trump's claim of "absolute immunity" from lawsuits, finding that his actions were not part of his presidential duties, and that there was plausible evidence to suggest he engaged in a conspiracy with organized groups to use any means, including violence, to overturn the results of the 2020 election. The opinion allows the case to proceed, with the plaintiffs' demanding documents, depositions, and other evidence from Trump and members of the Oath Keepers and Proud Boys. Mehta dropped other co-defendants from the suit, including Rudy Giuliani, Donald Trump Jr., and Representative Mo Brooks.[18]

On Jan 25, 2024, Mehta sentenced former Trump adviser, Peter Navarro, to four months in jail for contempt of Congress after defying a subpoena related to the congressional investigation into the Jan 6, 2021, US Capitol attack.[19]

1. Hsu, Spencer S. (Feb 18, 2022). "Oath Keepers leader Stewart Rhodes ordered jailed until trial on seditious conspiracy". Washington Post. Retr 19 Feb 2022.

18. Hsu, Spencer S. (Feb 18, 2022). "U.S. judge rejects Trump claim of 'absolute immunity' from Jan. 6 lawsuits". Washington Post. Retr 19 Feb 2022.

19. Cole, Devan; Lybrand, Holmes (25 Jan 2024). "Trump adviser Navarro sentenced to 4 months in jail, defying congressional subpoena". CNN Retr 25 Jan 2024.

Alvin Bragg and the Trump Cases

https://apnews.com/article/manhattan-district-attorney-alvin-bragg-trump-122d18a4ae43e3190df54a4b7ec297ff

By JAKE OFFENHARTZ, MICHAEL R. SISAK and JENNIFER PELTZ
Updated 6:42 AM CDT, June 1, 2024

NEW YORK (AP) — When Alvin Bragg took office as Manhattan district attorney in 2022, he stunned the public and his own staff by pausing an investigation into former President Trump that appeared hurtling toward an indictment.

Two prosecutors were so upset, they quit. One called Bragg's hesitation against Trump "a failure of justice."

Now, Bragg has cemented his place in history as the first prosecutor to win a criminal conviction of a former U.S. president. Speaking after the verdict Thursday, Bragg summed up his role saying, "I did my job." "Our job is to follow the facts and the law without fear or favor, that's exactly what we did," he told reporters.

Trump and his supporters insist Bragg, a Democrat, had a vendetta against the former president and Republican nominee. He has accused Bragg of manufacturing a baseless case.

Here is Bragg's background, his time in office and history regarding Trump.

Child of Harlem

Bragg, 50, grew up in Harlem when New York City struggled with high crime. He once had a knife held to his throat and has talked about being held at gunpoint six times while growing up, including three times by police officers.

When he was 15, one officer stuck a gun in his face and wrongly accused him of being a drug dealer as the teen walked to buy groceries for his father. Bragg filed a complaint.

Education

Bragg graduated Harvard Law School, began his career as a criminal defense and civil rights lawyer, went on to the U.S. attorney's office in Manhattan then worked at New York AG office, where he had his first legal tussles with Trump.

Suing Trump

Bragg was a senior lawyer in the state AG office in 2018, when it engaged multiple battles with Trump, related both to his White House policies and stewardship of his private charitable foundation. Bragg prosecuted a lawsuit against the foundation. Trump settled, agreeing to the foundation's dissolution, and a judge fined him $2 million.

Campaign for District Attorney

Bragg ran for Manhattan district attorney in 2021, on a platform of "justice and public safety" in a crowded primary. In some ways, he was the perfect candidate for predominantly Democratic Manhattan a year after the Minneapolis police killing of George Floyd started a national reckoning with how the criminal justice system has treated Black people and others of color. Bragg had worked as a prosecutor but had personal experience policing the Black community.

He was well positioned to take the criminal investigation into Trump and company from Cyrus Vance Jr., the outgoing DA.

During the race, Bragg was asked how he would handle the probe. His standard answer was to cite his work on Trump-related lawsuits while he was in the attorney general's office, and his willingness to hold powerful figures accountable.

"I don't know where this investigation will go. I don't want to prejudge it. But these types of investigations - white-collar investigations - I've been involved with for years, doing them myself and supervising," Bragg told The Associated Press.

Vance's investigation focused on whether Trump committed fraud by lying about the value of his assets on financial statements given to banks and others.

After winning the primary, Bragg cruised to victory.

Clashes over Crime

Bragg became Manhattan's first Black DA in January 2022. He was challenged over his approach to the job from the start.

One of his first steps was a memo that, among other things, instructed prosecutors not to seek jail time for some low-level offenses, such as minor marijuana possession and sale (the state later legalized such possession), to charge armed robberies in commercial settings as misdemeanor petit larcenies.

Police leaders, conservative media and centrist Democrats accused him of being soft on crime during a pandemic-era crime spike. Bragg's staff said the memo had been mischaracterized.

During the 2022 governor's race, Republican Lee Zeldin promised, if elected, he would try to remove Bragg from office.

Bragg faced criticism again, declining pretrial detention for men accused of brawling with police in Times Square.

The decision drew criticism from Gov. Kathy Hochul, a fellow Democrat. Bragg told reporters, "the only thing worse than failing to bring perpetrators to justice would be to ensnare innocent people in the criminal justice system."

Investigators later determined several men arrested played only a minor role in the fight or were not even there.

Investigating Trump

Bragg's surprising early move as district attorney was to halt the investigation into whether Trump lied on financial statements.

The lead prosecutor on that, Mark Pomerantz, resigned in anger. But the investigation was not over. It was just changing.

In 2022, Bragg's office persuaded the Trump Organization's longtime chief financial officer, Allen Weisselberg, to plead guilty to evading taxes on fringe benefits, including a luxury car and rent-free apartment. Later that year, the DA's office won a conviction of Trump's company on tax charges.

Emboldened by those victories, Bragg convened another grand jury, which indicted Trump in April of 2023 on charges that he falsified records at his company to conceal a scheme to pay hush money to keep a sex scandal from damaging his run for president in 2016. Trump denied any wrongdoing yet was convicted.

TRUMP'S attack on Bragg

Trump and his allies have slammed Bragg as a partisan in the guise of a prosecutor, claiming he brought the case solely to damage Trump's chances of regaining the White House.

Trump called Bragg an "animal" and a "degenerate psychopath," once made a social media post of himself holding a baseball bat next to a picture of Bragg, and described him as "a failed D.A."

He has shrugged off Trump's accusations. "Many voices out there," Bragg said Thursday. "The only voice that matters is the voice of the jury."

Juan Merchan

Juan Manuel Merchan[1] (born 1962/1963)[2] is a Colombian-born American judge and former prosecutor. He is an acting justice of the New York State Supreme Court in New York County (Manhattan). He presided over the 2024 criminal trial of former US president Donald Trump, in which Trump was convicted. Merchan is the first judge in history to preside over the criminal indictment and conviction of a US President, and the first judge to hold a President in criminal contempt of court.

Merchan was born in Bogotá, Colombia.[3] He immigrated to New York City when six years old, growing up in Jackson Heights, Queens, as the youngest of six children. His father had been a military officer in Colombia.[4] Merchan studied business at Baruch College in Manhattan, graduating in 1990, and earned his Juris Doctor from Hofstra School of Law on Long Island in 1994.[2] He was the first member of his family to go to college.[5]

1. "Judge Profile: Juan Merchan". New York Law Journal. Retr March 31, 2023.
2. Gregorian, Dareh; Reiss, Adam (March 31, 2023). "Who's Judge Juan Merchan? Trump says he 'hates me' but lawyers say he's fair". NBC News. Retr 4/1/23.
3. Sharp, Rachel; Dodds, Io (March 31, 2023). "Juan Merchan: Who is the judge likely to try Trump's criminal case?". The Independent. Retrieved March 31, 2023.
4. Rashbaum, William K.; Bromwich, Jonah E. (Dec 6, 2022). "Judge in Trump Co. Trial Knew How to Read Numbers". New York Times. Retr April 1, 2023.
5. Kashiwagi, Sydney (April 1, 2023). "Meet the judge presiding over Trump's criminal arraignment". CNN. Retrieved 4/1/23.

First criminal trial of an ex-President

Justice Merchan is the judge in The People of the State of New York v. Donald J. Trump, concerning former U.S. president Donald Trump, who was criminally indicted on 34 felony counts, making Merchan the first judge in history to preside in the criminal indictment of a US President.[7] (Again, he was Columbian born, another democrat judge, and this is his very first case.) The indictment of Trump was delivered by a grand jury on March 30, 2023.[8][9] It was unsealed the same day, with Trump pleading not guilty.[7] The jury trial began on April 15, 2024, and on April 30, Merchan held Trump in contempt of court, making him the first judge in history to hold a US President in criminal contempt of court.[10]

During the trial, former President Donald Trump called Merchan's daughter, who heads a digital marketing agency that works with Democratic Party candidates and non-profits,[11][12][13] "a rabid Trump hater, who has admitted to having conversations with her father about me."[12] Trump demanded a new judge, but prosecutors asserted Trump's allegation amounted to a "daisy chain of innuendos a far cry from evidence,"[13] and Merchan did not recuse himself.[14]

Reactions to Merchan's management of this Trump trial have varied. On May 21, 2024, Congresswoman Elise Stefanik of New York filed an ethics complaint against Merchan, alleging a conflict of interest.[15] The attorney and legal commentator Elie Honig wrote that, generally speaking, "Judge Merchan has done an exceptional job running this trial thus far",[16] and is a "thoroughly impressive jurist" but he should nevertheless recuse himself.[17] George Grasso, a retired New York City administrative judge who supervised other judges, wrote, "As a retiree, I was able to attend each day of the Trump trial. What I saw was a master class in what a judge should be - how one can serve fairly and impartially for the prosecution and the defense, and remain a pillar for the rule of law."[18] Merchan received threats for presiding over Trump's arraignment and criminal trial.[19][20][21]

On May 30, the case ended in a conviction on all counts. Trump's sentencing was scheduled to take place on July 11, 2024.[22][23][24] This was delayed to September 18, 2024, following the Supreme Court's ruling in Trump v. US that granted absolute immunity to former presidents for official acts in office.[25]

Merchan is the judge assigned over the criminal trial of Steve Bannon, former Trump adviser who was indicted in September 2022 on charges of fraud and money laundering in connection with fundraising. The case was set for trial in May 2024,[37] postponed until Sept.[38]

6. ......
7. Bromwich, Jonah E.; Rashbaum, William K.; Protess, Ben; Haberman, Maggie (April 4, 2023). "From President to Defendant: Trump Pleads Not Guilty to 34 Felonies". The New York Times. Retr April 5, 2023.
8. Jacobs, Shayna; Dawsey, Josh; Barrett, Devlin; Alemany, Jacqueline (March 30, 2023). "Trump indicted by N.Y. grand jury, first ex-president charged with crime". Washington Post. Retr Mar 31, 2024.
9. Marritz, Ilya; Bernstein, Andrea; Chappell, Bill; Romo, Vanessa (Mar 30, 2023). "Trump has been indicted by a Manhattan grand jury". NPR. Retr March 31, 2024.
10. Aftergut, Dennis; Baron, Frederick (4/30, 2024). "Rule of Law Comes for Trump". Slate. Arch, Retr. 5/1/24.
11. Lizza, Ryan, et al. "POLITICO Playbook: Democracy in Washington,"
12. Bagchi, Aysha. "Trump attacks NY judge's daughter, Manhattan DA Bragg requests court intervene," USA Today (4/1/24).
13. Sisak, Michael. "Trump is demanding a new judge just days before the start of his hush-money criminal trial," Associated Press via ABC News (April 5, 2024),
14. "Judge in Trump's hush money case refuses to recuse," NBC News (8/14/23.
15. Casiano, Louis and Singman, Brooke. "Stefanik files ethics complaint against Trump judge, cites daughter's work for promoting Dems," Fox News 5/21/24.
16. Honig, Elie. "The Slippery Question of Reasonable Doubt at the Trump Trial," New York Magazine (5/17/24).
17. Honig, Elie. "Note from Elie: Judge Merchan Is Admirable – But He Should Recuse," CAFE (April 14, 2023).
18. Grasso, George (June 2, 2024). "I Supervised New York City Judges. Juan Merchan Put On a Master Class in Trump Trial". NYT. Archi, Retr June 5, 2024.
19. Milton, Pat; Kates, Graham (4/7/23). "Judge in Trump criminal case targeted with threats". CBS News. Retrieved 6/12/24.
20. Dienst, Jonathan; Shabad, Rebecca; Kamisar, Ben; Jarrett, Laura (April 5, 2023). "Trump judge and family receive threats after NY arrest". NBC. Retr 6/12/24.
21. Eisler, Peter; Parker, Ned; Tanfani, Joseph (May 15, 2024). "'They should all be executed.' How Trump's attacks on judges are fueling online calls for violence". USA Today. Retrieved June 12,

2024.

22. Sisak, Michael R.; Peltz, Jennifer; Tucker, Eric; Price, Michelle L.; Colvin, Jill (May 31, 2024). "Trump former President convicted of felony". AP. Retr May 31, 2024

23. Berman, Mark; Jacobs, Shayna; Barrett, Devlin; Hawkins, Derek (May 30, 2024). "Donald Trump found guilty on all counts in New York hush money trial". The Washington Post. Retr May 31, 2024.
24. Herb, Jeremy (5/30/2424). "Trump found guilty in hush money trial |CNN Politics". CNN. Retr May 30, 2024.
25. Wilson, Taylor (July 3, 2024). "Trump's sentencing delayed after Supreme Court immunity ruling". USA Today. Retr 7/6/24.

In late 2022, Merchan oversaw the five-week criminal trial of the Trump Organization; the organization was convicted of 17 counts of tax fraud.[33] Merchan presided over the criminal case of Donald Trump's former financial chief Allen Weisselberg, who pleaded guilty to his role in a 15-year-long tax-fraud scheme.[34][35] Weisselberg admitted to evading taxes by accepting $1.7 million in off-the-books compensation and entered a plea, in which he testified against The Trump Organization and helped secure the company's conviction.[36] Merchan sentenced Weisselberg to five months at Rikers Island and said he would have imposed a substantially longer sentence but for the agreement.[35]

Merchan is assigned to preside the criminal trial of Steve Bannon, a former Trump adviser who was indicted in September 2022 on charges of fraud and money laundering in connection with a fundraising scheme. The case was set for trial in May 2024,[37] postponed until September.[38]

33. Hurtado, Patricia; Van Voris, Bob (March 31, 2023). "Donald Trump is already attacking the judge handling his hush-money case and spelling his name incorrectly". Fortune. Bloomberg News. Retrieved March 31, 2023.
34. Protess, Ben; Rashbaum, William K.; Bromwich, Jonah E. (August 15, 2022). "Trump Executive Nears Plea Deal". The New York Times. Retrieved March 15, 2024.
35. Protess, Ben; Bromwich, Jonah E.; Rashbaum, William K. (January 10, 2023). "Trump's Finance Chief Sentenced to 5 Months in Jail". NYT. Retr March 15, 2023.
36. Sisak, Michael R. (August 18, 2022). "Trump executive pleads guilty in tax case, agrees to testify". AP News. Retr 3/15/24.
37. Scannell, Kara (5/25/2323). "Trial date set for Steve Bannon's fundraising fraud case". CNN. Retr 3/5/24.
38. Palmer, Ewan (5/1/24). "Bannon's Trial Postponed". Newsweek. Retr May 29, 2024

By Jon Levine and Rich Calder
Published March 30, 2024, 12:37 p.m. ET.

Two major Democratic clients of the daughter of the judge overseeing Donald Trump's hush-money trial have raised at least $93 million in campaign donations — used the case in their solicitation emails — raising renewed concerns the jurist has a major conflict of interest.

Trump's attorneys are considering filing another motion demanding Manhattan Supreme Court Justice Juan Merchan recuse himself from the trial set to begin April 15, sources said.

The judge's daughter, Loren Merchan, is president of Authentic Campaigns, a Chicago-based progressive political consulting firm whose top clients include Rep. Adam Schiff (D-Calif.), who was the lead prosecutor in Trump's first impeachment trial, and Senate Majority PAC, a major fundraiser.

Team Trump has repeatedly called for Judge Merchan (left) to recuse himself in the case. Flickr Geneseo Alumni

"Authentic Campaigns, and thus the judge's daughter, is actively making money from this sham attack against President Trump, rendering Judge Merchan conflicted out," Trump spokesman Steven Cheung told The Post, adding that evidence of bias is even clearer now than it was in August when Merchan rejected Trump's first recusal motion.

"The judge should do the right thing and recuse himself to show the American people that Democrats have not destroyed our justice system completely ... continuing to be involved in this Crooked Joe Biden-directed Witch Hunt is a complete violation of applicable rules, regulations and ethics."

Adam Schiff's campaign for Senate scored $20 million in aid since he began soliciting donations off the presumptive GOP presidential front-runner's unprecedented 34-count indictment last April, according to Federal Election Commission records.

Trump has pleaded not guilty to felony counts of falsifying business records related to alleged hush-money payments made to porn star Stormy Daniels and Karen McDougal. He has denied having affairs with both women. If convicted, he faces up to four years in prison.

Loren Merchan, the daughter of the judge overseeing the prosecution of Donald Trump, is a prominent Democratic activist.

Rep. Adam Schiff (D-Calif.) was lead prosecutor in Trump's impeachment trial. AP

Schiff's fundraising email began, "It is a somber moment, unprecedented for a former president to be indicted, but his alleged offenses are also unprecedented." "Trump will respond as he always does — playing the victim and blaming others for having the temerity to investigate him in the first place," Schiff continued in the email request to supporters for $10 donations last spring.

Trump's 'hush money' trial to start April 15, judge denies his bid to further delay case — as ex-presidents fraud bond reduced to $175M.

Senate Majority political action committee, supporting Democrat Senate campaigns, pocketed $73.6 million since it also began fundraising emails following the ex-president's indictment.

"BREAKING NEWS: Donald Trump indicted by Manhattan grand jury This is an important moment for our democracy, but our work isn't over," the group said in email, Fox News reported.

"We must continue protecting our Senate majority from GOP extremists. Please, rush $10 (becomes $60) to help Defend the Senate."

The super PAC has done more than $15 million in business with Authentic since 2019, including email fundraising and branding assistance, while Schiff's Senate campaign paid Authentic more than $10 million for digital advertising and other consulting services the past year, records show.

Noted attorney Alan Dershowitz said if the judge's daughter is involved in anti-Trump politics, "there seems to be a basis for recusal of the father." "Under the law, close relationships can constitute a recusal," he told The Post.

Loren Merchan's clients have actively raised money off the trial her father is overseeing. Adam Schiff for Senate. Loren Merchan — who worked for VP Kamala Harris' 2020 presidential campaign as "director of digital persuasion" — has said her father detests politicians using Twitter, a reference to Trump.

"I've had conversations with my dad recently where he's kind of like 'I hate that politicians use Twitter,' and like 'It's so unprofessional' and you know, 'That's not how a politician should behave themselves,' and I explain that like yeah, I think there are a lot of instances where it is not used in, like when our President [Trump] tweets anything that he thinks, and like that's not what he should be using it for," the 34-year-old Merchan offered during a podcast in June 2019.

Justice Merchan, 61, on Tuesday imposed a limited gag order on Trump, prohibiting him from publicly bashing witnesses - such as his fixer-turned-enemy Michael Cohen — as well as prosecutors, court staff, and jurors.

Arthur Engoron

Arthur F. Engoron, born 1949, is a judge serving on the Manhattan Supreme Court since 2013. He presided over the New York civil investigation of the Trump Organization in 2024. Engoron was born in Queens, NYC.[3]

In the late 1960s, Engoron drove a yellow taxi for a year while completing undergraduate studies.[4][2][3] He received his bachelor's degree from Columbia U in 1972.[5] He spent four years as a drummer before enrolling at the New York University School of Law,[3] and received his Juris Doctor in 1979.[2]

1. Bromwich, Jonah E. (Feb 16, 2024). "The Judge Who Dealt a Financial Blow to Trump". New York Times. Retr 2/17/24.
2. Sisak, Michael R. (Oct 1, 2023)."Who is Arthur Engoron? Judge weighing future of Trump empire is Ivy League-educated ex-cabbie". AP. Arch & Retr Nov 2, 2023
3. Charalambous, Peter (Oct 3, 2023). "Meet New York judge deciding the fate of Trump's business empire". ABC News. Archi on Nov 2, 2023. Retr Nov 2, 2023.
4. Ross, Barbara (May 31, 2012). "Jurist Arthur Engoron can hack taxi ruling". New York Daily News. Retrieved 2/17/24.
5. "Alumni in the News: January 8, 2024". Columbia College Today. 1/4/24. Archived on 5/13/24. Retr 1/19/24.

On February 16, Engoron levied a $355 million fine on Trump for civil fraud.[11][12][13] He ruled that Trump is not allowed to run a company in New York state for three years. However, Engoron did not order the dissolution of Trump's company.[14][15] The New York State Commission on Judicial Conduct began an investigation into Engoron after an outside attorney allegedly spoke with Engoron about the fraud statute in the case 3 weeks prior to Engoron's verdict. Engoron denied impropriety and said he was uninfluenced in his decision-making.[16][17]

11. "Trump must pay $355M overstating net worth to lenders, NY judge rules in civil fraud case". CBC News. Feb 16, 2024. Retr Mar 30, 2024.
12. Sisak, Michael R.; Offenhartz, Jake; Peltz, Jennifer (Feb 16, 2024). "Judge orders Trump to pay $355 million for lying about his wealth in staggering civil fraud ruling". AP News. Arch May 13, 2024. Retr March 30, 2024.
13. Bromwich, Jonah E.; Protess, Ben (Feb 16, 2024). "Trump Fraud Trial Penalty Will Exceed $450 Million". The New York Times. ISSN 0362-4331. Retr Feb 18, 2024.
14. Schonfeld, Zach (Feb 16, 2024). "Judge pulls back dissolving Trump's businesses in fraud ruling". The Hill. Archi June 25, 2024. Retr Feb 17, 2024.
15. Picchi, Aimee; Sherter, Alain (2/16/24). "Trump $354 million fraud verdict includes NY business ban 3 years". CBS News. Arch June 25, 2024. Retr Feb 17, 2024.
16. "Trump's fraud trial judge faces probe after attorney claims he tried to advise him in $454m case". The Independent. May 9, 2024. Archi June 25, 2024. Retr May 9, 2024.
17. "New York lawyer advise judge in Trump civil fraud case". NBC New York. 5/8/24. Arch 5/13/24. Retr 5/9/24.

Judge Aileen Cannon

Aileen Mercedes Cannon (born 1981) is a Colombian-born American lawyer who served as a US district judge of the US District Court for Southern District of Florida since 2020. President Trump nominated and appointed Cannon to the federal bench after confirmation by U.S. Senate in Nov 2020. Cannon worked for the corporate law firm Gibson Dunn from 2009-2012 and was a federal prosecutor in Southern District of Florida from 2013 to 2020.

In 2022, Cannon presided over the case of Donald J. Trump v. United States of America. She ordered the U.S. government to pause using materials seized from Trump's private club and residence in its investigation, granted Trump's request for a special master to review material. The U.S. Court of Appeals for the Eleventh Circuit reversed Cannon after it found she wrongly exercised jurisdiction.

Cannon dismissed Trump's lawsuit per orders from the Eleventh Circuit.

Following Trump's indictment in June 2023, Cannon oversaw a federal criminal case against Trump. Legal experts, called for her recusal. Under Cannon, the case was considerably delayed getting to trial, with Cannon granting multiple Trump requests to extend pre-trial motions. In July 2024, she dismissed the case entirely, ruling Jack Smith's appointment unconstitutional.

Cannon graduated from Duke University in 2003 with a Bachelor of Arts. In college, she studied for a semester in Spain and wrote for Miami's Spanish language newspaper El Nuevo Herald; her writings included topics such as flamenco dancing, festivals, and yoga.[1][3][4] Cannon then attended the University of Michigan Law School, where she was an articles editor for the University of Michigan Journal of Law Reform and was a quarter-finalist in the school's moot court competition.[5] She graduated in 2007 with a Juris Doctor, magna cum laude, along with membership in the Order of the Coif.[1][3][5]

1. Schnell, Mychael (Sept 7, 2022). "Five things to know about Aileen M. Cannon, the judge who granted Trump a special master". The Hill. Arch. & Retr 2/11/22.
2. Mazzei, Patricia; Haberman, Maggie; Feuer, Alan (Sept 7, 2022). "Trump Ruling Lifts Profile of Judge, Raises Legal Eyebrows". NYT. Retr Sept 9, 2022.
3. Weaver, Jay; Wilner, Michael (September 12, 2022). "Trump-appointed judge at center of ex-president's FBI fight. Who is Aileen Cannon?". Miami Herald. Archived September 12, 2022. Retrieved Dec 11, 2022.
4. Musgrave, Jane (Sept 8, 2022). "Federal judge now at center of Trump's Mar-a-Lago search 'stickler for procedure'". Palm Beach Post. Arch & Retr Dec 11, 2022.
5. "Questionnaire Judicial Nominees" (PDF). US Senate Committee on Judiciary. Arch 6/22/23. Retr 6/10/23.

United States v. Trump, criminal case

Cannon was assigned in June 2023 to oversee the criminal case against former president Donald Trump. After an inquiry by The New York Times, the Southern District of Florida's chief clerk confirmed that the assignment was random.[86][87][88] Several legal experts called for Cannon to recuse herself.[88] Stephen Gillers, a professor emeritus at the New York University School of Law, opined Cannon should recuse from the criminal case, as "her impartiality might reasonably be questioned", due to her being "partial to Trump as a former President" in the previous civil case.[89] Richard Painter, Norman Eisen and Fred Wertheimer, former White House chief ethics lawyers and a good government advocate respectively, jointly called for Cannon's recusal, citing her conduct in the previous civil case, which they described as "fundamentally erroneous ... went well outside the judicial norm and was roundly criticized by the Court of Appeals".[88]

Laurence Tribe, a professor at Harvard Law School, opined that the "historic trial ... should be seen to be entirely unbiased and legally sound", but Cannon being the judge "would cast a long shadow over" the trial.[88] There was no indication Cannon would recuse, and soon began issuing orders for exam of evidence.[90]

This criminal case arose from the investigation into his handling of government documents, which was the subject of a civil case against Trump that Cannon coincidentally previously presided over.[91] In June 2023, The New York Times analyzed records by Bloomberg Law of Cannon's handling of criminal cases as a federal judge, finding that before Trump's criminal case, she had presided over 224 criminal cases, of which only four went to trial, with a cumulative 14 trial days.[92] Politico noted the ongoing Carver case, slated for trial in July 2023, featured the kinds of pretrial motions and procedures this case expected to see.[34]

In late June 2023, Cannon ruled against the Department of Justice, denying its request to keep the identities of 84 potential witnesses under seal.[93] In August 2023, Cannon ruled in favor of Trump on the issue of potential conflicts of interest regarding co-defendant Walt Nauta's lawyer Stanley Woodward representation of possible witnesses in the case. She rejected the notion that sealed filings were required "to comport with grand jury secrecy", striking two such filings by prosecutors from the court record. Instead, Cannon instructed Woodward and prosecutors to discuss "the legal propriety of using an out-of-district grand jury proceeding" to continue actions in this federal case.[94][95] Several legal experts, including notable constitutional scholar Harvard Professor Laurence Tribe, as well as notable former federal prosecutors Andrew Weissmann and Joyce Vance, indicated that the propriety of the grand jury proceedings were obvious, and that Cannon's questioning of their propriety was alarming.[96]

After Trump's legal team in September 2023 requested an extension to the case, Cannon delayed a crucial pre-trial hearing on the Classified Information Procedures Act (CIPA) from October 2023 to February 2024, while also ruling that she would only ponder on further scheduling in March 2024.[97][98] While prosecutors asked for a CIPA hearing in March and the defense teams requested for June, Cannon decided in April that the new hearing date should be in May, but when that date approached, the defense teams again requested delay, so Cannon in May granted the defense teams' earlier request of June CIPA hearings.[99][100] Politico reported that Cannon "has run the pretrial process at a leisurely pace that will make a postponement almost inevitable, according to experts on criminal prosecutions related to classified information"; Politico further states that if the trial is postponed to after the 2024 United States presidential election, Trump could become president and would then be "expected" to instruct the Justice Department to end the case.[101]

In February 2024, Cannon granted Trump's team's motion for the names of witnesses in this case and their testimony to be publicly revealed; this caused the government's prosecutors to ask Cannon to reconsider, citing "significant and immediate risks of threats, intimidation, and harassment" which has been seen in other Trump cases.[102][103] In March 2024, a witness in the case ("Trump Employee 5") and former Mar-a-Lago employee, Brian Butler, identified himself in a media interview and told his story about the incident, citing in preparation for Cannon's plan to publicize the witness names, he would rather tell his story than "just waiting for it to come out ... I think it's better to at least say what happened than it coming out in the news, people calling me crazy. I'd rather just get it out there."[104] In April 2024, Cannon agreed to censor the potential witnesses' names, but not their statements, from the public; Politico wrote that it was the "latest decision in which Cannon sided with prosecutors in an opinion primarily critical of their tactics", with Cannon criticizing prosecutors' speed, compliance, and basis for arguments.[105]

In March 2024, Cannon denied without prejudice an attempt by Trump to dismiss the case.[106] She wrote that Trump's team had raised "various arguments warranting serious consideration", then indicated that the Trump team's arguments about the Espionage Act being too vague could instead be brought up again later in "connection with jury-instruction briefing".[107] After Trump's team argued that the Presidential Records Act allowed Trump to retain classified documents, Cannon instructed both prosecutors and Trump's team to craft hypothetical jury instructions regarding the Presidential Records Act, in an action that perplexed observing lawyers and former judges.[108] Barbara McQuade, a law professor and former federal prosecutor, opined that the Presidential Records Act "is just not relevant in any way it all; it provides no defense. To even allow it to be argued at trial would create confusion for the jury", while former federal judge Nancy Gertner commented that Cannon's instruction was "very troubling" because it was "giving credence to arguments that are on their face absurd".[108] In April 2024, Cannon denied another motion by Trump to dismiss, stating "the Presidential Records Act does not provide a pre-trial basis to dismiss", while criticizing as "unprecedented and unjust" the prosecutors' request for her to elaborate on whether her jury instructions would include the Presidential Records Act.[109][110]

After the March 2024 hearing on postponing the trial, Cannon took until May 7, 2024, to issue an update.[111] Cannon ruled to indefinitely postpone the trial, citing pre-trial matters to settle.[112][113] She accepted Trump's requests to have pre-trial hearings on the appropriateness of appointment of special counsel and, recognizing more government agencies as part of the prosecution, which would allow Trump to conduct the discovery process on them.[114]

Cannon scheduled pre-trial activities to continue up to July 22, 2024, at the earliest.[115] It is "extraordinarily unlikely that there will be a trial before November", opined former CIA attorney Brian Greer, whose work was on classified material.[99]

The Guardian stated that Cannon has "generally given wide deference to Trump and his legal team, granting nearly all extensions they have requested and entertaining his most brazen defense theories, even if they have been without precedent in Espionage Act cases".[114] The New York Times stated that Cannon has "treated seriously arguments that many, if not most, federal judges would have rejected out of hand. Often, her acceptance of Mr. Trump's unorthodox claims have resulted in significant delays in bringing the charges in the classified documents case in front of a jury.[116] The Washington Post wrote that while "facts of the case do not favor former president Trump", "Cannon has repeatedly accommodated Trump's position", and if "there were a judge who actively wanted to delay Trump's Florida trial ... it's not clear what they might have done much differently".[100]

While Donald Trump has continually denounced many of the judges presiding over his legal cases, including Tanya Chutkan, Arthur Engoron and Juan Merchan, he has not criticized Cannon.[100][117] Instead, Trump has described Cannon as a "highly respected", "very smart", "very strong judge".[118][119] Washington Post stated in May 2024 that Cannon's "rulings are generally hailed as uniquely wise" by Trump supporters, and she has "been celebrated by adherents of the QAnon movement".[100] A Reuters investigation found that while Cannon received public criticism on left-leaning websites, this did not include calls for violence, which is contrasted with Trump supporters' calls for violence or death threats against judges that Trump criticized.[120]

After Trump claimed during the Mar-a-Lago raid, "Biden's DOJ was authorized to shoot me!" and Biden was "locked & loaded ready to take me out", prosecutors requested a gag order on Trump pertaining to law enforcement.[121][122] Cannon in May 2024 responded by denying prosecutors' request and instead accusing the prosecutors of being "wholly lacking in substance and professional courtesy" when discussing the issue with the defense team.[122]

On June 20, 2024, The New York Times reported that shortly after being assigned the case, two federal judges in South Florida, including the chief judge, Cecilia Altonaga, urged Cannon to decline the case and pass it on to other jurists. However, Cannon had not taken their advice.[123][124] Cannon was specifically advised to transfer the case to Miami, where they had a facility to store and review sensitive documents, but she declined, a new facility had to be constructed.[124]

CASE DISMISSED DUE TO SMITH ILLEGAL APPOINTMENT

On July 15, 2024, Cannon dismissed the case against Trump, ruling that "Special Counsel Smith's appointment violates the Appointments Clause of the United States Constitution", with a rationale mirroring that of Supreme Court Justice Clarence Thomas' concurrence in a case involving Trump.[125] Another decision that invited scrutiny from legal commentators and the general public, the dismissal incited calls from Monica Lewinsky for Congress to impeach Cannon.[126][127][128]

86. Savage, Charlie (June 9, 2023). "Judge Aileen Cannon, Who Showed Trump Favor, Gets Documents Case". The NYT. Archi June 10, 2023. Retr June 29, 2023.
87. Bowden, John (June 12, 2023). "Trump-appointed judge will stay on Mar-a-Lago documents case unless she recuses". The Independent. Archi, Retr June 29, 2023.
88. Adler, Ben (June 12, 2023). "Calls grow for Judge Aileen Cannon to recuse herself in Trump documents case". Yahoo News. Archived, Retr June 29, 2023.
89. Chotiner, Isaac (June 12, 2023). "Will the Judge in Trump's Case Recuse Herself—or Be Forced To?". The New Yorker. ISSN 0028-792X. Archi, Retr Oct 13, 2023.
90. Feuer, Alan; Rashbaum, William; Haberman, Maggie (June 15, 2023). "Judge Orders Lawyers in Trump Case to Get Security Clearances". NYT. Arch June 16, 2023.
91. Faulders, Katherine; Mallin, Alexander; Bruggeman, Lucien (June 9, 2023). "Judge Aileen Cannon, Trump appointee, assigned to oversee his case: Sources". ABC News. Arch. June 9, 2023. Retr June 10, 2023.
92. Schmidt, Michael; Savage, Charlie (June 14, 2023). "Judge in Trump Documents Case Has Scant Criminal Trial Experience". NYT. Arch & Retr June 16, 2023.
93. Lowell, Hugo (June 26, 2023)."List of witnesses against Trump cannot be secret in documents case, judge rules". The Guardian. Arch June 27, 2023, Retr 6/26/23
94. Sharp, Rachel August 8, 2023. "Trump-appointed Judge Cannon sides with Trump in classified documents case." The Independent. Archi June 20, 2024. Retr 9/2/23
95. Mallin, Alexander (August 8, 2023). "Judge in Trump's classified documents case questions out-of-district grand jury in probe". ABC News. Archi, Retr Sept 2, 2023
96. Levin, Bess 8/8/23). "'Dopey and Constitutionally Dubious': Legal Experts Blast Judge Cannon's Latest Pro-Trump Rulings". Vanity Fair. Arch Aug 8, Retr 10/17/23.
97. Faulders, Katherine Oct 7, 2023 "Judge pauses litigation in classified docs case while mulling Trump's request for extension". ABC News. Archi Oct 6, Retr Oct 7, 2023
98. Lowell, Hugo (Nov 17, 2023). "Trump classified documents trial running about four months behind schedule". The Guardian. Archi June 20, 2024. Retr Nov 20, 2023.
99. Feuer, Alan (May 8, 2024). "Judge's Decisions in Documents Case Play into Trump's Delay Strategy". The New York Times. Archi May 8, 2024. Retr May 9, 2024.
100. Bump, Philip (May 8, 2024). "Trump's classified documents trial blown apart by Cannon". The Washington Post. Archived May 8, 2024. Retrieved May 8, 2024.
101. Gerstein, Josh (11/22/23). "How one judge is slowing down one of Trump's biggest criminal cases". Politico. Retr 11/23/23.
102. Beitsch, Rebecca (February 9, 2024). "Special counsel fights judge's order allowing Trump to reveal witness identities in Mar-a-Lago case". The Hill. Arch Feb 10, 2024. Retr Feb 12, 2024.
103. Garrison, Steve (2/9/24). "Feds say Mar-a-Lago witnesses face 'risks' if identified". Courthouse News. Retr 2/12/24.
104. Fins, Antonio (March 14, 2024). "Trump may appear in Fort Pierce federal court today for documents case". Palm Beach Post Archi, Retr April 10, 2024.

105. Gerstein, Josh; Cheney, Kyle April 9, 2024. "Siding with counsel, Cannon agrees to keep witness identities secret". Politico. Archi May 8, 2024. Retr April 10, 2024
106. "Federal judge denies Trump's effort to dismiss classified documents case". ny1.com. AP. 3/14/24. Archi, Retr 5/8/24.
107. Feuer, Alan (March 14, 2024). "Judge Denies One of Trump's Efforts to Derail Documents Case". The New York Times. Archi March 15, 2024. Retr May 8, 2024.
108. Barrett, Devlin; Stein, Perry March 20, 2024. "'Very troubling': Judges, lawyers flummoxed by Judge Cannon". Washington Post. Arch April 16, 2024. Retr 5/8/24
109. Legare, Robert (April 4, 2024). "Judge denies Trump's motion to dismiss documents case". CBS News. Retrieved 5/8/24.
110. Gerstein, Josh; Cheney, Kyle (April 4, 2024). "Judge denies, Trump bid to dismiss charges that he hoarded classified documents". Politico. Archi, Retr May 8, 2024
111. Cheney, Kyle (5/7/24). "Judge Cannon postpones Trump's classified docs trial". Politico Arch. on 5/8/24. Retr 5/8/24.
112. Stein, Perry; Barrett, Devlin (May 7, 2024). "Judge indefinitely delays Trump's classified documents trial in Florida". Washington Post.
113. Polantz, Katelyn; Rabinowitz, Hannah; Lybrand, Holmes; Sneed, Tierney (May 7, 2024). "Federal judge postpones Trump documents trial". CNN. Arch.& Retr 5/7/24.
114. Lowell, Hugo; Joseph, Cameron (May 8, 2024). "Judge scraps date for Trump Mar-a-Lago documents trial without rescheduling". The Guardian. Retr May 8, 2024.
115. Jansen, Bart (May 7, 2024). "Judge Cannon indefinitely postpones Donald Trump's trial for classified document retention". USA Today. Retr May 8, 2024.
116. Feuer, Alan (May 6, 2024). "Judge Pushes Back Critical Filing Deadline in Trump Documents Case". The Guardian. Archi May 7, 2024. Retr May 8, 2024.
117. Graham, David (4/9/24). "Trump's Shoot-the-Moon Legal Strategy". The Atlantic. Archived 4/10/24. Retrieved 5/9/24.
118. Samuels, Brett (July 16, 2023). "Trump praises judge overseeing his classified documents case, saying she 'loves our country'". The Hill. Archi, Retr May 9, 2024.
119. Barrett, Devlin; Stein, Perry April 4, 2024. "Trump defends Judge Cannon over classified documents trial". Washington Post Archi April 21, 2024, Retr May 9, 2024
120. Eisler, Peter; Parker, Ned; Tanfani, Joseph (May 14, 2024). "Trump blasts his trial judges. Then fans call for violence". Reuters. Archi May 16, 2024. Retr May 15, 2024.
121. Polantz, Katelyn (5/10/24). "Special counsel asks judge for gag order in Trump classified documents". CNN. Arch. 5/25/24.
122. Doyle, Katherine (May 28, 2024). "Judge denies counsel's request to impose gag order on Trump over claim about FBI raid". NBC News. Archi, Retr May 29, 2024.
123. Savage, Charlie; Feuer, Alan (June 20, 2024). "Judge in Trump Documents Case Rejected Suggestions to Step Aside". NYT. ISSN 0362-4331. Retr June 20, 2024.
124. Tait, Robert (June 20, 2024). "Judge in Trump classified documents case reportedly refused to step aside". The Guardian.
125. Johnson, Carrie (July 15, 2024). "Judge Cannon dismisses Trump documents case". NPR. Retr 7/15/24.
126. Jouvenal, Justin (July 16, 2024). "Dismissal draws scrutiny to Judge Cannon's handling of Trump case". Washington Post. ISSN 0190-8286. Retr July 16, 2024.
127. Rosenzweig, Paul (7/15/24). "Judge Cannon Has Gotten It Completely Wrong". The Atlantic. Retr 7/15/24.
128. Kochi, Sudiksha. "Monica Lewinsky wants Judge Aileen Cannon overseeing Trump classified docs case impeached". USA TODAY. Retrieved July 16, 2024.

Jack Smith, Prosecutor appointed by DOJ for the Trump Cases

John Luman Smith is an American attorney who has served in the United States Department of Justice as an assistant U.S. attorney, acting U.S. attorney, and head of the department's Public Integrity Section.
Born: 1969 (age 55 years)
Education: Harvard Law School (1994), SUNY Oneonta (1991), Liverpool High School (1987) Office: Special Counsel for US Department of Justice since 2022.

In November 2022, attorney general Merrick Garland appointed Smith an independent special counsel, responsible for overseeing two preexisting Justice Department criminal investigations into former president Donald Trump, three days after Trump announced his 2024 presidential campaign: one regarding Trump's role in the January 6 U.S. Capitol attack, and the other, alleged mishandling of government records, including classified documents. The documents case resulted in a 37-count indictment of Trump in June 2023 to which three counts were added in July.[2] In August, the January 6 case resulted in an indictment on four charges.[3]

The classified documents case was dismissed by judge Aileen Cannon in July 2024, on the grounds that Smith was unlawfully appointed as special counsel.[2] Smith's office announced that he will be appealing the decision.[4]

2. Sneed, Tierney; Cohen, Marshall; Herb, Jeremy (July 27, 2023). "Special counsel brings more charges against Trump in Mar-a-Lago documents case". CNN.
3. Sneed, Tierney; Cohen, Marshall; Cohen, Zachary; Cole, Devan; Rabinowitz, Hannah; Polantz, Katelyn; Gannon, Casey (8/1/23). "Donald Trump indicted in 2020 election interference probe". CNN. Retr 8/ 2/23.
4. Tucker, Eric (July 15, 2024). "Federal judge dismisses Trump classified documents case over concerns with prosecutor's appointment". AP. Retr 7/15/24.

Smith was born on June 5, 1969.[5] He grew up in Clay, New York, a suburb of Syracuse.[6][7] His father was a draftsman of air-conditioning systems; his mother was a homemaker for most of Smith's childhood.[8] He graduated from Liverpool High School in 1987,[9] where he played football and baseball.[10] He then studied political science at the State University of New York at Oneonta, graduating in 1991 with a Bachelor of Arts, summa cum laude.[10][11][12] Smith graduated Harvard Law School, in 1994 with the degree of Juris Doctor.[7]

5. Thrush, Glenn (June 8, 2023). "Who Is Jack Smith, Special Counsel Who Indicted Trump?". New York Times. Retr 6/11/23.
6. Yost, Pete (August 30, 2010). "DOJ's elite Public Integrity unit gets new leader". San Diego Union-Tribune. Associated Press. Retr Nov 19, 2022.
7. Savage, Charlie; Feuer, Alan (Nov 19, 2022). "In New Special Counsel, Prosecutor Schooled in Corruption Cases". NYT Retr Nov 21, 2022.
8. Roig-Franzia, Manuel (10/3/23). "What's it like to be prosecuted by Smith?". Washington Post. Retr 10/4/23.

9. Casey, Ashley M. (November 18, 2022). "Liverpool grad named special counsel to oversee Trump investigations". Eagle News Online. Retrieved Nov 19, 2022.
10. Eisenstadt, Marnie (Dec 14, 2022). "How Jack Smith went from Liverpool football bench to a starring role in Trump investigation". syracuse.com. Retr Dec 14, 2022.
11. Keller, Aaron (November 18, 2022). "Special Counsel Tapped by Merrick Garland to Investigate Trump Formerly Prosecuted Top Democrats and Republicans". Law & Crime
12. Scott, Eugene (November 18, 2022). "Who is Jack Smith, special counsel in Trump criminal investigation?". The Washington Post. Retr Nov 18, 2022.

In 2010, Smith returned to the U.S. to become chief of the U.S. Department of Justice's Public Integrity Section (PIN).[6][15] Among his first responsibilities was evaluating investigations, and he recommended closing investigations into several members of Congress.[7][a] He spent five years as chief of PIN, where he prosecuted a variety of corruption cases, including those against Virginia governor Bob McDonnell, U.S. representative Rick Renzi, Jeffrey Sterling, a Central Intelligence Agency agent who shared national secrets,[18][15] New York State Assembly speaker Sheldon Silver,[19] and North Carolina Senator John Edwards.[20]

McDonnell, Renzi, Sterling,[18] and Silver were found guilty,[19] though the Supreme Court unanimously overturned McDonnell's conviction.[21] Edwards' case ended in a mistrial.[20]

15. Feuer, Alan; Savage, Charlie (11/18/22). "Who Is Jack Smith, New Special Counsel?". NYT. Archi 12/7/22. Retr 12/8/22.
16. Tucker, Eric (11/19/22) special counsel long career on corruption". Associated Press.
17. "Jack Smith". United States Department of Justice. April 14, 2015. Arch. on November 26, 2022. Retr Dec 2, 2022. From 2008 to 2010, Jack served as Investigation Coordinator in Office of the Prosecutor at the International Criminal Court (ICC) in the Hague, Netherlands.
18. Gerstein, Josh; Cheney, Kyle (11/18/22). "Garland names Smith special counsel for Trump probes". Politico. Retr 11/18/22.
19. Hurtado, Patricia (November 20, 2022). "New Trump Special Counsel Impartial and Tough, Ex-Colleagues Say". Bloomberg. Retr April 10, 2024.
20. Lefelar, Grant (July 28, 2023). "Revisiting Trump special counsel Jack Smith's failed prosecution of John Edwards". Carolina Journal. Retrieved April 10, 2024.

On November 18, 2022, United States Attorney General Merrick Garland appointed Smith special counsel to oversee the investigations into Donald Trump's actions regarding the Jan 6 U.S. Capitol attack, and Trump's handling and storage of records, including classified documents at Mar-a-Lago estate.[14][18][30][31] He worked initially from the Netherlands while recovering from a fractured leg, injured when struck by a scooter.[7] By early January 2023, Smith returned to the U.S.[32]

On June 8, 2023, a grand jury indicted Trump on seven criminal charges on his handling of classified documents. This was the first time in American history a serving or former president has been indicted on federal criminal charge.[33]

After repeated delays and postponement,[34] Judge Aileen Cannon dismissed the case July 15, 2024, on grounds that Smith's appointment as special counsel violated the Appointments Clause of the Constitution.[35][4][36] On July 17, with permission from the Justice Department,[37][38] Smith filed a notice of appeal to the 11th U.S. Circuit Court of Appeals.[39]

On August 1, 2023, a grand jury indicted Trump on four federal charges related to his attempts to overturn the 2020 presidential election and his conduct during the January 6 Capitol attack.[3] A year later, the Supreme Court decision on immunity directed Judge Chutkan to determine what parts of the indictment may proceed,[40] whether each act was official or private; whether the official acts are part of core constitutional duties; and whether prosecuting the non-core official acts would have any "dangers of intrusion on the authority and functions of the Executive."[41][42] Chutkan set a hearing for September 5, 2024.[43]

30. Thrush, Glenn; Savage, Charlie; Haberman, Maggie; Feuer, Alan (Nov 18, 2022). "Garland Names Special Counsel for Trump Inquiries". NYT. Arch Nov18, 2022. Retr Nov 19, 2022.
31. "Appointment Special Counsel". U.S. Dept of Justice (Press release). 11/18/22. Retr 6/10/23.
32. Stein, Perry; Barrett, Devlin (January 3, 2023). "Smith returns to U.S. weeks after becoming special counsel". Washington Post. ISSN 0190-8286. Retr April 27, 2023.
33. Mangan, Dan; Bhattacharjee, Riya (June 8, 2023). "Trump indicted on seven criminal counts in classified documents case". CNBC. Retr June 8, 2023.
34. Cabral, Sam (6/22/24). "Judge Cannon, Trump trial going nowhere". BBC. Retr 8/17/24.
35. Cheney, Kyle; Gerstein, Josh; Swan, Betsy Woodruff (July 15, 2024). "Judge dismisses Trump's Mar-a-Lago classified docs case". Politico. Retr July 15, 2024.
36. Barnes, Daniel; Winter, Tom; Gregorian, Dareh (July 15, 2024). "Judge Cannon dismisses the Trump classified documents case". NBC News. Retrieved July 15, 2024.
37. Johnson, Carrie (July 15, 2024). "Judge dismisses Trump case over special counsel appointment". NPR. Retr July 17, 2024.
38. Feuer, Alan (7/15/24). "Judge Dismisses Classified Docs Case - Trump". NYT. Retr 7/16/24.
39. Mallin, Alexander (7/17/24). "Special counsel files notice of appeal in classified documents case". ABC News. Retr 7/17/24.
40. Feuer, Alan (July 1, 2024). "Ruling Further Slows Trump Election Case but Opens Door to Airing of Evidence". The New York Times. ISSN 0362-4331. Retr July 3, 2024.
41. "What is 'official' act, how will judge interpret Trump's immunity?". Washington Post. July 3, 2024. Retrieved July 4, 2024.
42. Rabinowitz, Hannah (August 2, 2024). "Judge Chutkan could jumpstart Trump election interference case now that it's back in her court". CNN. Retr August 2, 2024.
43. Lybrand, Holmes; Polantz, Katelyn; Reid, Paula; Sneed, Tierney (August 8, 2024). "First hearing in Trump DC election case after Supreme Court's immunity ruling is delayed until September". CNN. Retr August 9, 2024.

NOT THE FIRST SUCH FAILED ESCAPADE FOR JACK SMITH. SMITH'S CASES, FAILED/OVERTURNED HIGH LEVEL POLITICAL ASSASSINATIONS.

The following lists 7 cases in which Smith was overturned by high court.

1. Highly popular Virginia Governor Robert McDonnell was a strong performer in Republican Presidential Primary, only to have Smith convict McDonnell twice and then SCOTUS unanimously overturned both verdicts, the last McDonnell case was in 2016.

2. Smith and DOJ then attack NJ Senator Bob Menendez, with a Bribery conviction in 2015, ending in a 2017 mistrial.

3. Next is a DOJ/Smith case against North Carolina Senator and Presidential candidate John Edwards, only to result in a mistrial.

4. Senator John Ensign, republican of Nevada,

5. Former Majority Leader Tom Delay, Republican of Texas,

6. Late Senator Don Young, Republican of Alaska, and

7. ex-representative Alan Mollohan, democrat of West Virginia.

Here is the storyline as written by New York Times and Fox News.
(https://www.foxnews.com/media/ex-virginia-gov-who-saw-conviction-by-jack-smith-thrown-out-says-hed-rather-win-than-get-it-right)

In 2016, federal prosecutors announced they would not pursue a second case against McDonnell after the Chief Justice John Roberts-led unanimous ruling vacating the conviction. McDonnell had been accused of accepting gifts in exchange for promoting a supplement.

In vacating McDonnell's conviction, the Supreme Court ruled that setting up a meeting or organizing an event – without doing more – isn't considered an "official act," as charged by the Justice Department, where the Public Integrity Section was run by Smith. Smith, as special counsel, indicted former President Trump for mishandling classified information following a raid on his Mar-a-Lago compound.

McDonnell joined "Life, Liberty & Levin" on Sunday to sound off about his case and that of the former president.

"That stretch was exceptionally painful; three-and-a-half years from the investigation until we got unanimous vindication by the U.S. Supreme Court. I knew in my heart from the very beginning – I'm a lawyer, obviously, looking at the law and the facts – that these charges were completely wrong," he said.

McDonnell said his attorneys at the time went to the Justice Department with an "extensive brief" about why they believed Smith and his prosecutors "got the law wrong" and why he, the defendant, was innocent. "And they persisted and pulled the trigger, and the indictments started. Of course, they've got all the investigators. They got all the money; they've got access to The Washington Post through multiple leaks," he alleged.

McDonnell said even though the Roberts court vacated the conviction, it was a difficult time for him and his family.

"My walk-away from that, especially as I looked at what Smith did in the Lois Lerner case with advising people that they were okay to go after conservatives and Bob Menendez and other cases is that I think he's just overzealous," he said.

In April 2015, Justice Department indicted Menendez, a Democratic U.S. senator from New Jersey, on bribery allegations alleging he wrongfully accepted gifts from a Florida ophthalmologist. Menendez pleaded not guilty, the case ended in a mistrial in late 2017.

Outside the Newark courtroom at the time, Menendez said "the way this case started was wrong, the way it was investigated was wrong, the way it was prosecuted was wrong..."

On "Life, Liberty & Levin," McDonnell claimed Smith would "rather win than get it right," and claimed that alleged mindset is influencing some moves in the Trump case. "I think he doesn't do an honest look at the law to see if facts apply to the law," McDonnell said.

Smith also saw the campaign-finance-related prosecution of former Democratic presidential candidate then-North Carolina Sen. John Edwards declared a mistrial; Levin noted.

The New York Times at the time called it a high-profile example of several "visible efforts" by Smith's DOJ section, listing other investigations where charges were unsuccessful or not brought including against then-Sen. John Ensign, R-Nev., former House Majority Leader Tom DeLay, R-Texas, the late Rep. Don Young, R-Alaska, and ex-Rep. Alan Mollohan, D-W.Va.

Tanya Sue Chutkan

Tanya Sue Chutkan (born July 5, 1962) is an American lawyer and jurist serving as a U.S. district judge for the U.S. District Court for the District of Columbia.

She is presiding judge over the criminal trial of former U.S. president Donald Trump over his alleged attempts to overturn the result of the 2020 presidential election, including the events leading up to the attack on the United States Capitol on January 6, 2021.

Chutkan was born on July 5, 1962, in Kingston, Jamaica.[1] Chutkan has a younger brother, Norman, and a younger sister, Robynne, both of whom are physicians. Her father Winston Chutkan is an Indo-Jamaican doctor, and her mother Noelle is an Afro-Jamaican who was one of the leading dancers at National Dance Theatre Company of Jamaica.[2][3][4]

Chutkan received a Bachelor of Arts degree in 1983 from George Washington University. She later attended the University of Pennsylvania Law School, where she was an associate editor of the University of Pennsylvania Law Review. She graduated in 1987 with a Juris Doctor.[7] Noelle is daughter of Frank Hill, one of the members of the People's National Party. Through her mother, she is a cousin of former Liverpool footballer John Barnes.[5][6]

Chutkan received a Bachelor of Arts degree in 1983 from George Washington U. She later attended the U of Pennsylvania Law School, where she was an associate editor of the U of Pennsylvania Law Review. She graduated in 1987 with a Juris Doctor.[7]

1. "Attorney Tanya S Chutkan – Lawyer in". lawyercentral.com. Arch April 8, 2016. Retrieved March 28, 2016.
2. "Congressional Directory 115th Congress (2017-18)". Arch 8/5/23. Retr 8/4/23.
3. "NDTC returns to Toronto after 15-year Hiatus". Pride Magazine. 9/18/14. Arch on May 13, 2023. Retr August 4, 2023.
4. Johnson, Richard (11/28/21). "Kumina turns 50". Jamaica Observer. Archived 8/12/22. Retrieved August 4, 2023.
5. Smith, Alecia (8/3/23). "Trump can expect fair trial, says Chutkan's aunt". Jamaican Observer. Archi 8/5/23. Retr 8/4/23.
6. Shennan, Paddy (5/7/13). "Former Liverpool FC star J Barnes discovers family roots, Who Do You Think You Are". Liverpool Echo. Arch 1/17/24. Retr 8/4/23.
7. "Tanya Chutkan - Senate Judiciary Committee Questionnaire" (PDF). US Senate Committee on Judiciary. Archi Jan 19, 2023. Retr August 2, 2023.

On December 19, 2013, President Barack Obama nominated Chutkan as a United States district judge of the US District Court for the District of Columbia to a seat created pursuant to 104 Stat. 5089.[10][11]

Judge Chutkan Key Cases processed

In Garza v. Hargan (2017), Chutkan ordered the Office of Refugee Resettlement to allow a girl in its care to have an abortion.[24] That ruling was vacated by a panel of the D.C. Circuit, reinstated by the full en banc D.C. Circuit, and ultimately mooted by U.S. Supreme Court.[25] In December 2017, Chutkan granted relief to two additional pregnant minors who sued seeking access to abortion services while in ORR custody.[26] In March 2018, Chutkan certified a class action and ordered ORR to provide access to abortions to all in custody.[27]

On June 8, 2018, Chutkan blocked until June 20 the release in Syrian Democratic Forces-controlled territory of a dual-nationality Saudi American citizen alleged to have joined ISIL. The man, who is now held for nine months in Iraq, was planned to be released by the U.S. military – with a new cell phone, some food and water and $4,210 in cash, and his Professional Association of Diving Instructors (PADI) identification card, as soon as the next day.[28][29]

On March 7, 2019, Chutkan ruled that U.S. Secretary of Education Betsy DeVos illegally delayed implementation of the "Equity in IDEA" regulations. These regulations updated how states calculate racial disparities in identification of children as being eligible for special education, placement of children in restrictive classroom settings, and use exclusionary discipline. Chutkan also ruled the U.S. Department of Education violated the law concerning the spread of regulations by neglecting to provide a "reasoned explanation" for the delay, and failing to account for the costs that child, parents, and society would bear.[30]

On April 26, 2019, Chutkan sentenced Maria Butina to 18 months in prison for conspiring to be an unregistered agent of Russian government in the US.[31][32]

On November 20, 2019, Chutkan issued a preliminary injunction against the U.S. Department of Justice, finding that federal inmates sentenced to death were likely to succeed in arguing that the federal government's new lethal injection procedure – which uses a single drug, pentobarbital, rather than the three-drug combination previously in place – "exceeds statutory authority" under the Federal Death Penalty Act.[33] Chutkan's order was later reversed by a divided panel of the U.S. Court of Appeals for the D.C. Circuit,[34] and the case went to the U.S. Supreme Court.[35] The reversal of the injunction was upheld and thirteen federal inmates were executed.[36]

On November 9, 2021, Chutkan denied former President Donald Trump's motion to keep records from being released to the House Select Committee investigating the attack on the Capitol on January 6, 2021.[37][38] The D.C. Circuit affirmed, and SCOTUS declined review.[39]

Chutkan has overseen trials of more than 30 defendants in cases related to the January 6 Capitol attack. According to The Washington Post, she has been the toughest sentencing judge in those cases, ordering at least some jail or prison time in all cases, sometimes exceeding the sentence recommended by prosecutors.[40]

As of August 1, 2023, Chutkan is the judge overseeing Trump's criminal trial over his attempts to overturn results of the 2020 election, culminating in the events leading up to the January 6 Capitol attack.[41]

Ex husband of Judge Chutkan, Peter Krauthamer,1995 to 2000 assistant professor, clinical supervising attorney, Howard U. School of Law.[41, 42, 43]

24. Note, Recent Case: En Banc D.C. Circuit Upholds Order Requiring HHS to Allow an Undocumented Minor to Have an Abortion, 131 Harv. L. Rev. 1812 (2018).
25. Liptak, Adam (6/4/18). "Supreme Court Rejects Bid to Discipline A.C.L.U." New York Times. p. A14. Archived, Retr 6/18/18.
26. Astor, Maggie (Dec 18, 2017). "2 Undocumented Teenagers Must Be Allowed Abortions, Judge Rules". NYT p. A14. Arch June 18, 2018. Retr Nov 10, 2021.
27. Stevens, Matt (March 31, 2018). "Judge Temporarily Stops U.S. From Blocking Undocumented Teenagers' Abortions". NYT Arch & Retr June 18, 2018.
28. "Judge questions plan to release US detainee into Syrian war zone". Daily Star. 6/8/18. Arch. Retr 6/8/18.
29. Gresko, Jessica (6/8/18). "Government will hold off releasing American to Syria". WLNS. Arch., Retr. 6/12/18.
30. Green, Erica L. (March 8, 2019). "Judge Rules DeVos Held Up Obama-era Rule on Special Education". NYT. p. A15. Archived March 10, Retr Mar11, 2019.
31. "Russian agent jailed for targeting NRA". BBC News. April 26, 2019. Archived & Retrieved 4/26/1919.
32. Lucas, Ryan (April 26, 2019). "Russian Agent Maria Butina Sentenced To 18 Months Following Guilty Plea". NPR. Arch & Retr, 4/26/19. U.S. District Court Judge Tanya S. Chutkan ordered the 18-month sentence and said Butina would receive credit for the roughly nine months she has already served.
33. Berman, Mark (Nov 21, 2019). "Federal judge blocks Trump administration's plans to resume executions". Washington Post. Archi June 17, Retr June 16, 2020.
34. Swanson, Ian (5/20/20). "Death row inmates ask for stay while appeal to Supreme Court". The Hill. Arch & Retr 6/16/20.
35. Rubin, Jordan S. (June 9, 2020). "Trump Federal Execution Revival Back at Supreme Court (1)". news.bloomberglaw.com. Archived, Retr June 16, 2020.
36. Bart, Katie (11/20/20). "Justices clear the way for eighth federal execution this year". SCOTUSblog. Archived, Retr 2/10/22.
37. Hsu, Spencer (11/9/21). "Trump White House records can be turned over to House Jan. 6 committee, judge rules". Washington Post. Arch & Retr 11/10/21
38. "Judge refuses Trump request to block Jan. 6 records". Lethbridge News Now. Canadian Press. Nov 9, 2021. Archi May 1, 2023. Retr Nov 10, 2021.
39. Liptak, Adam (1/19/22). "Supreme Court Allows Release of Jan. 6 Files". NYT. ISSN 0362-4331. Arch 1/22/22.
40. Hsu, Spencer S.; Jackman, Tom (August 1, 2023). "Judge Chutkan is toughest Jan. 6 sentencer. Next on docket: Trump". Washington Post. Arch. Retr. 8/3/23.
41. Feuer, Alan (August 1, 2023). "Trump Indictment: Jan. 6 Riot 'Fueled by Lies' From Trump, Special Counsel Says". NYT. ISSN 0362-4331. Arch & Retr 8/1/23.
42. Draper, Robert (October 15, 2023). "Tanya Chutkan, an Unflinching Judge in the Trump Jan. 6 Trial". The New York Times. Arch & Retr Oct 16, 2023.
43. "Opening Statement of Peter A. Krauthamer" (PDF). US Senate. 11/8/11. Archived 10/9/2020. Retr 12/9/19.

Fani Taifa Willis[3]

(née Floyd; /fɑːniː/, FAH-nee;[3] born October 27, 1971)[1][2] is an American attorney. She is DA of Fulton County, Georgia, which contains most of Atlanta, serving since 2021.[4] She is the first woman to hold the office.[5] Willis investigated the 2020 presidential election in Georgia, resulted in indictments against Trump and 18 alleged co-conspirators on racketeering and other crimes.

Willis was born in Inglewood, California. Her father, John C. Floyd III, was a founder of a faction of Black Panthers but grew disillusioned by the movement's infighting.[6] When Willis was in first grade, her family moved to Washington, D.C., where her father practiced law as a criminal defense attorney. Her parents divorced and her mother moved back to California. Willis mostly stayed with her father.[1]

She graduated from Regina High School, in Maryland,[7] an all-girls Catholic High School that closed in 1989.[8] Willis studied political science at Howard University, graduating cum laude in 1993, then moved to Atlanta[1] to attend Emory University School of Law, graduating in 1996 with a Juris Doctor.[5]

1. Binelli, Mark (Feb 2, 2023). "Fani Willis Took On Atlanta's Gangs. Now She May Be Coming For Trump". New York Times. Archi April 11, 2023. Retr April 10, 2023.
2. "Happy Birthday Fani Willis!". Fani Willis for DA. Oct 27, 2020. Retr April 1, 2024.
3. Rose, Ashtin (1/20/21). "Call Her Madam DA; Fani Willis Making History As Fulton County's First Woman DA". South Atlanta Magazine. Arch., Retr July 7, 2022.
4. Murphy, Patricia; Bluestein, Greg; Mitchell, Tia (2/12/21). "The Jolt: Willis takes stage in Trump show". Atlanta Journal Constitution. Arch 2/12/21. Retr 2/13/21.
5. "Fani T. Willis, Fulton County DA". Fulton County Government. 2022. Arch 3/5/2121. Retr 5/15/22.
6. McWhirter, Cameron; Wolfe, Jan (July 16, 2023). "Fani Willis: The No-Nonsense Georgia Prosecutor on a Collision Course With Donald Trump". Wall Street Journal. Arch. Aug 15, 2023. Retr 1/1/24
7. "Your ballot explained". Archived Feb 15, 2024. Retr Feb 16, 2024.
8. "Catholic High School Celebrating 50 Years of Accomplishments". 10/4/96. Arch 2/15/24. Ret Feb 16, 2024.

District attorney of Fulton County

In 2020, Willis was elected DA for Fulton County, defeating Paul Howard Jr., a six-term incumbent, and her former boss.[14][15] In this role she is known for successfully using Georgia's RICO statute to prosecute non-mobsters,[16] and, as of 2023, is using the same statute to prosecute former president Trump and 18 alleged co-conspirators.[17]

In 2022, an employee in the Fulton County DA's Office alleged Willis fired her for uncovering plans to misuse federal grant funding.[18] In 2024, the House Judiciary Committee subpoenaed Willis regarding the former employee's whistleblower complaint after a taped conversation of the employee discussing misuse of federal funds with Willis was released.[19][20] The committee gave Willis a February 23 deadline.[21] Willis said the employee was "terminated for cause" and $488,000 in federal grant funding was utilized appropriately.[22]

Willis ran for reelection in 2024. In the Democratic Party primary election, she defeated Christian Wise Smith. Willis will face Republican Courtney Kramer in the November election.[23]

2020 election influence investigation

Main articles: 2020 Georgia election investigation and Georgia election racketeering prosecution:

On February 10, 2021, Willis launched a criminal investigation into Donald Trump's attempts to influence Georgia election officials—including the governor, attorney general, and Secretary of State Raffensperger via a telephone call—to "find" enough votes to override Biden's win in the 2020 presidential election.[24][25][26] In January 2022, she requested a special grand jury to consider charges of election interference by Trump and his allies.[27][28] In May, a 26-member special grand jury was given investigative authority and subpoena power and tasked with submitting a report to the judge and Willis on whether a crime was committed.[29]

Willis sent target letters to people being investigated related to the fake elector's plot. These include two Republican officials—State Senator Brandon Beach and David Shafer, chairman of the Georgia Republican Party[30]—and the 16 people who falsely presented themselves as electors.[31] She also sent a target letter to State Senator Burt Jones, but then a judge ruled she could not target Jones due to a conflict of interest which was created by Willis hosting a fundraiser for the Democratic candidate for lieutenant governor.[32]

After hearing 75 witnesses—including former US Senator Kelly Loeffler, former White House Counsel Pat Cipollone,[33] and possibly Sidney Powell[34]—special grand jury completed its work, dissolved January 9, 2023. On February 16, parts of the report were released.[35]

Willis's indicted Trump and 18 others on 41 charges on August 14, 2023, including 13 charges against Trump.[36] In 2024, Judge Scott McAfee quashed 6 charges, 3 against Trump, while giving prosecutors the option to refile.[37][38]

On January 8, 2024, a defendant filed a pre-trial motion to dismiss the indictment and disqualify Willis and her office from prosecuting the RICO case against them due to Willis having a conflict of interest related to her personal relationship with lead prosecutor Nathan Wade.[39][40] On February 15, 2024, Judge McAfee started an evidentiary hearing where he ruled on March 15, 2024, that either Willis – and her office - or Wade must leave the case, their relationship brought a "significant appearance of impropriety".[41]

He found no conflict of interest as there was insufficient evidence Willis benefited financially.[42][43][44][45] Based on the Judge's ruling, Nathan Wade resigned from the case a few hours later in order "...to move this case forward as quickly as possible."[46] In May 2024, Georgia Court of Appeals agreed to hear an appeal to the ruling, revisiting whether Willis may be allowed to stay on the case.[47]

13. ...
14. Boone, Christian (August 14, 2020). "After victory, Willis plans transformation of Fulton DA's office". Atlanta Journal Constitution. Arch 2/6/21. Retr 2/13/21.
15. McDonald, R. Robin (August 11, 2020). "Fani Willis Sweeps Paul Howard to be Fulton County DA". Law.com. Archi April 25, 2023. Retr Feb 13, 2021.
16. Fausset, Richard (9/29/14). "Trial Opens in Atlanta School Cheating Scandal (Pub 2014)". NYT. Archi 8/18/23, Retr 8/15/23.
17. "Here's who else was charged in Georgia (other than Trump)". Washington Post. August 15, 2023. Archived August 15, 2023. Retrieved August 15, 2023.
18. "Whistleblower lawsuit against Fulton DA claims misuse of funds". Atlanta Journal-Constitution. August 31, 2022. Archived Febr 26, 2024. Retrieved March 15, 2024.
19. "U.S. House committee subpoenas Fani Willis over federal grant funds". Atlanta Journal-Constitution. Feb 2, 2024. Archi March 8, 2024. Retr March 15, 2024.
20. "Jordan threatens Fani Willis with contempt over subpoena on federal grants". The Hill. March 14, 2024. Archived March 15, 2024. Retrieved March 15, 2024.
21. Boboltz, Sara (February 2, 2024). "House GOP Subpoenas Fani Willis, Georgia Prosecutor Who Charged Trump". HuffPost. Archi March 24, Retr Feb 2, 2024.
22. "House GOP Subpoenas Fulton County DA Fani Willis Amid Trump Criminal Case". Forbes. February 2, 2024. Archived & Retrieved March 15, 2024.
23. Brumback, Kate (May 21, 2024). "Fani Willis and judge presiding over Georgia Trump election case defeat challengers". Associated Press. Retr May 22, 2024.
24. Hakim, Danny; Fausset, Richard (Feb 13, 2021). "In Ga, a New District Attorney Starts Circling Trump and His Allies". NYT. Arch Feb 13, 2021. Retr Feb 13, 2021.
25. Morris, Jason; Cole, Devan (2/10/21). "Prosecutors in Georgia open investigation, Trump's attempt to influence election". CNN. Arch 2/10/21. Retr Feb 12, 2021.
26. Fausset, Richard; Hakim, Danny (February 10, 2021). "Georgia Prosecutors Open Criminal Inquiry Into Trump's Efforts to Subvert Election". New York Times. Archived Feb 10, 2021. Retrieved Feb 12, 2021.
27. Hakim, Danny; Fausset, Richard (Nov 6, 2021). "Georgia Grand Jury Looms in Trump Inquiry". The New York Times. Archived Jan 14, Retr Nov 7, 2021.
28. Hallerman, Tamar (January 20, 2022). "Fulton DA requests special grand jury for Trump probe". Atlanta Journal-Constitution. Archived Jan 21,Retr Jan 20, 2022.
29. Murray, Sara; Morris, Jason (May 2, 2022). "Grand jury selected in Fulton County probe of Trump election interference in Georgia". CNN. Archi May 3, May 2, 2022.
30. Fausset, Richard; Hakim, Danny (July 15, 2022). "Prosecutor Warns Georgia Officials They May Face Charges in Trump Inquiry: The investigation could prove to be one of the most perilous legal problems facing the former president and his allies". The NYT. Archived on July 15, 2022. Retrieved July 15, 2022.
31. Visser, Nick (July 20, 2022). "Fake Electors Are Now 'Targets' In Georgia Probe Of Trump's Effort To Overturn 2020 Vote". Huffington Post. Archi, Retr July 20, 2022.
32. Mangan, Dan (July 25, 2022). "Georgia prosecutor Fani Willis disqualified from investigating Trump in criminal probe". CNBC. Archi, Retr Aug 19, 2022.
33. Murray, Sara; Cohen, Zachary; Perez, Evan (Oct 20, 2022). "First on CNN: Former White House Counsel Pat Cipollone, former US Sen. Kelly Loeffler testify to grand jury in Georgia investigating 2020 election interference | CNN Politics". CNN. Archived on Oct 20, 2022. Retrieved Oct 20, 2022.
34. "Trump election probe in Georgia cites voting system breach". Associated Press. August 26, 2022. Archived August 31, 2022. Retrieved August 27, 2022.

35. Mangan, Dan; Breuninger, Kevin (Feb 16, 2023). "Ga grand jury recommends perjury indictments in Trump election meddling". CNBC. Arch, Retr. Feb 16, 2023.
36. "Trump Indicted in Georgia: Prosecutors Accuse Trump of 'Criminal Enterprise' to Overturn Election". NYT. August 14, 2023. Archi August 14, Retr August 15, 2023.
37. "Judge Quashes Six Charges in Georgia Election Case Against Trump". The New York Times. March 13, 2024. Archived March 16, 2024. Retrieved March 16, 2024.
38. "Judge in Georgia election interference case quashes some charges against Trump". NPR. March 13, 2024. Archived March 16, 2024. Retr March 16, 2024.
39. Hallerman, Tamar; Rankin, Bill (February 2, 2024). "Fulton DA Fani Willis says relationship with Trump prosecutor shouldn't disqualify her". The Atlanta Journal-Constitution. Archived & Retr 2/2/24
40. Cohen, Zachary; Morris, Jason; Rabinowitz, Hannah; Lybrand, Holmes (Feb 2, 2024). "Fulton County DA acknowledges personal relationship with lead prosecutor on Trump case, says it doesn't disqualify her". CNN. Arch, Retr 2/2/24
41. "Judge indicates he will rule within next 2 weeks on bid to remove Fani Willis from Trump case". AP. March 1, 2024. Archi on March 15, 2024. Retr March 15, 2024.
42. Quinn, Melissa; Eggleston, Jared (March 15, 2024). "Fani Willis and her office can stay on Trump Georgia 2020 election case if Nathan Wade steps aside, judge rules". CBS News. Arch 3/15, 2024. Retr 3/15, 2024.
43. Alexander, Blayne; Gregorian, Dareh; Gile, Charlie (March 15, 2024). "Fulton Co DA Fani Willis case against Trump can continue if she or special prosecutor Wade remove themselves, judge rules". NBC News. Archi, Retr March 15, 2024.
44. "Judge Says Fani Willis Can Stay on Georgia Trump Case—if Deputy Steps Asides". The Wall Street Journal. March 15, 2024. Archi, Retr March 15, 2024.
45. "Takeaways from scathing ruling that allows DA Fani Willis to remain on the Trump election subversion case". CNN. March 15, 2024. Archi, Retr March 15, 2024.
46. "Lead prosecutor in Georgia election case resigns following judge's decision DA Fani Willis to stay on". ABC News. March 15, 2024. Archi, Retr March 15, 2024.
47. "Georgia Court Will Hear Appeal of Ruling That Kept Prosecutor on Trump Case". The NYT. May 8, 2024.

2020 Georgia election investigation

In February 2021, Fulton County, Georgia, district attorney Fani Willis launched a criminal investigation into alleged efforts by then-president Donald Trump and his allies to overturn the certified 2020 election victory of Democratic candidate Joe Biden and award the state's electoral college votes to Trump. A special grand jury recommended indictments in January 2023, followed by a grand jury that indicted Trump and 18 allies in August 2023. Charges include conspiracy, racketeering and other felonies.[1]

The investigation scope includes Trump pressuring Brad Raffensperger, the Republican Georgia Secretary of State, in a recorded phone call to "find" sufficient ballots for him to win the state. Trump personal attorney Rudy Giuliani and others met with state legislators to provide specious allegations of election fraud to encourage the legislature to convene a special session to reconsider its certified electoral vote that found Biden had won. Sixteen Trump supporters convened to create slates of Trump electors. Republican senator and ardent Trump supporter Lindsey Graham asked the secretary of state if he could discard legally cast ballots.

The investigation examines one facet of many attempts to overturn the 2020 US presidential election, others are being investigated by the Dept of Justice and the Smith special counsel investigation.

Background - - Accusations of electoral fraud

Throughout his 2016 presidential campaign, Trump repeatedly sowed doubt on the election certification process. Campaigning in Colorado, Trump claimed the Democratic Party "[rigged] the election at polling booths".[2] Trump claimed widespread voter fraud occurred in the 2016 presidential election in October 2016. These statements were echoed by Rudy Giuliani, Trump's legal advisor.[3]

Attempts to overturn the 2020 presidential election

See also: Trump fake electors plot, 2020 United States presidential election in Georgia, and Post-election lawsuits, 2020 US presidential election from Georgia. Following Trump's defeat in the 2020 presidential election, an outside advisor to Trump known as Kenneth Chesebro began drafting a plot to purport Trump supporters as electors.[4][5]

Chesebro justified the plot using precedent set in the 1960 United States presidential election, by certifying a slate of electors declaring Trump the winner.[6] Attempting to overturn the results of the election, Trump called Georgia governor Brian Kemp, asking him to convene Georgia's legislators to select electors that would support him in the election, and requested an audit of absentee ballots.[7] Georgia certified the results of the election multiple times and reaffirmed Joe Biden's win in the state, including a final time on December 7, prior to the Electoral College vote a week later.[8]

Trump–Raffensperger phone call

Trump called Brad Raffensperger, Georgia Secretary of State, January 2, 2021, and pressured him to alter results of the 2020 election in Georgia.[9] Trump's call with Raffensperger was obtained by The Washington Post the following day.[10]

Investigation

Fani Willis, the DA for Fulton County, Georgia, began a criminal investigation into Trump's efforts to overturn the 2020 presidential election on February 10, 2021.[11] Willis began interviewing election officials and staff working under Raffensperger in September 2021.[12]

Willis hired three attorneys, appointed them special prosecutors; John Floyd, beginning April 1, 2021; Nathan Wade, beginning November 1, 2021, ending with his resignation March 15, 2024;[13] Anna Cross, beginning July 15, 2022.[14] 2022 special grand jury

Willis requested a special grand jury for investigation into Trump on January 20, 2022.[15] Superior Court of Fulton County granted the request four days later.[16] The special grand jury was authorized to write a report but not to indict anyone.[17]

About 75 Witnesses testified[18]

Subpoenas were issued on July 5, 2022.[19] Some to members of Trump's legal team; Kenneth Chesebro, Cleta Michell, Rudy Giuliani, Jenna Ellis, and John Eastman. Giuliani was deposed August 17, Ellis August 25,[20] and Eastman August 31.[21] Another to Capitol Hill counsel Jacki Deason, but a Texas court said she did not have to testify.[22]

U.S. Senator Lindsey Graham was subpoenaed that day, and after the subpoena was upheld by a federal judge,[23] an appeals court,[24] and U.S. Supreme Court,[25] he was deposed on November 22.[26] He testified (according to a 2024 book by journalists Michael Isikoff and Daniel Klaidman) if you told Trump, "Martians stole the election, he'd probably believe you."[27]

Later subpoenas included Georgia Governor Brian Kemp (subpoenaed August 4,[28] deposed November 15[29]) former White House Chief of Staff Mark Meadows (subpoenaed October 26,[30] deposed[31]), and former national security advisor Michael Flynn (subpoenaed November 15,[32] deposed December 8[33]).

Former Georgia Lt Governor Geoff Duncan, Georgia Secretary of State Brad Raffensperger, Georgia attorney general Chris Carr, and former Georgia Speaker of the House David Ralston testified.[34]

December 2022 report

On December 15, 2022, the grand jury completed its report. On September 8, 2023, the report was released in full to the public,[35] revealing that the grand jury had recommended charges against 39 people. (By the time this information was released, the district attorney had already charged 18 of them, plus one more the grand jury had not named.)

The 21 people not charged included Republican Senator Lindsey Graham of South Carolina, chair of the Senate Judiciary committee when the election was certified;[36] former GOP Senators David Perdue and Kelly Loeffler; and former national security adviser Michael Flynn.[37]

A previous public release revealed the grand jury's conclusion that some of the 75 witnesses may have committed perjury.[38] Partial and full releases were both by order of Fulton County Superior Court Judge Robert McBurney.[39][35]

Allegation of defense attorney's misconduct

In April 2023, Willis alleged two attorneys representing ten Georgia Republicans investigated for acting as fake electors of falsely representing they had informed their clients of immunity deals offered by investigators though they had not. Willis sought in a filing to have one of the attorneys removed from the case. One Republican under investigation who was not represented by the two attorneys had accepted immunity. One of the attorneys denied the allegation, another was not available for comment.[40]

Immunity agreements

Eight of sixteen Republicans who allegedly participated in the fake elector's scheme accepted immunity deals to cooperate with Willis.[41]

2023 grand jury

After Willis hinted an indictment might come during the first half of August 2023,[42] another grand jury was seated July 11, empowered to vote to bring charges against Trump.[18]

The grand jury indicted Trump 18 allies on August 14. This followed a day of testimony by witnesses including former Georgia state senator Jen Jordan,[43] former state representative Bee Nguyen,[44] former Georgia Lieutenant Governor Geoff Duncan and independent journalist George Chidi.[45] Gabe Sterling, a Georgia official for the Secretary of State, was seen in the courthouse that day.[46] The charges against Trump include racketeering and other felonies. Willis gave the 19 co-defendants the opportunity to voluntarily surrender no later than noon on Friday, August 25, 2023. Each defendant is charged with violating the Georgia version of federal Racketeer Influenced Corrupt Organizations (RICO) Act.[47]

Trump and Giuliani face 13 counts, other defendants face fewer.[49]

There is overlap with co-conspirators mentioned in the federal indictment of Trump issued two weeks earlier. In the federal indictment, Giuliani was co-conspirator No. 1, Eastman was #2, Powell was #3, Clark was #4, and Chesebro was #5. All five of these people, though not charged in the federal prosecution, are charged as co-defendants in the Georgia prosecution. (Co-conspirator No. 6 in the federal indictment has not yet been conclusively identified by the public.) The indictment references thirty unidentified, unindicted co-conspirators.[50]

When the indictment was unsealed, Fulton County District Attorney Fani Willis told reporters she would propose a trial date within the next six months[51] and would seek to try all 19 co-defendants together.[52]

Threats and security

At the end of July, Willis disclosed to county leaders a threatening email she had received, calling her a "corrupt nigger" and a "Jim Crow Democrat whore";[53] "I guess I am sending this as a reminder that you should stay alert over the month of August and stay safe," Willis wrote.[54] In September, the Atlanta Journal-Constitution wrote, Willis "travels with around-the-clock security detail at work and at home, and last year gave frontline staff bulletproof vests, keychains with panic buttons",[55] it noted her family has been threatened.[56]

August 1, two weeks before the indictment, sheriff Pat Labat said normal procedures, including mug shot and fingerprints, would be followed for Trump.[57]

Plea agreements

Bail bondsman Scott Hall pleaded guilty to five misdemeanor counts of conspiracy to commit intentional interference with performance of election duties, on Friday September 29, 2023. Lawyer Sidney Powell pleaded guilty to six misdemeanors accusing her of conspiring to intentionally interfere with the performance of election duties, on Thursday October 19, 2023.[58][59] Lawyer Kenneth Chesebro pled guilty to one felony, conspiracy to commit filing false documents, Friday October 20, 2023.[60] Lawyer Jenna Ellis pled guilty to one felony, aiding and abetting false statements and writings, 10/24, 2023,.[61]

Other investigations

Georgia Lieutenant Governor Burt Jones was one of thirty unidentified/ unindicted co-conspirators in the Willis indictment. Jones was a state senator in 2020, allegedly playing a prominent role seeking to replace official electors with Trump electors. After reviewing the Willis indictment, Pete Skandalakis, executive director of Prosecuting Attorneys Council of Georgia, planned to appoint a special prosecutor to examine Jones's activities.[62]

Trump's response

The President participated in two perfect phone calls regarding election integrity in Georgia, which he is entitled to do, as President, it was President Trump's Constitutional duty to ensure election safety, security, and integrity.

—Trump spokesperson Steven Cheung[63]

Upon the February 2023 release of excerpts of the special grand jury report, Trump spokesperson defended Trumps phone call made between Trump and Raffensperger.[63]

On July 14, Trump attorneys petitioned two courts to end the investigation. Georgia Supreme Court unanimously rejected this petition the next business day,[64] Fulton County Superior Court Judge Robert McBurney also rejected it on July 31.[65] Trump's team had asked to throw out evidence obtained by the special grand jury, ban prosecutors from presenting evidence to the charging grand jury and disqualify Willis from related proceedings, alleging Trump would suffer "a violation of his fundamental constitutional rights" as he sought the Republican presidential nomination.[66]

Other responses

In February 2023, Timothy J. Heaphy, the top investigator on the January 6 House select committee, said he expected "indictments both in Georgia and at the federal level."[67]

In May 2023, Georgia Republicans enacted a law that created a commission empowered to discipline or remove state prosecutors alleged to have violated their duties. As he signed the bill to create the commission, Governor Kemp said it would curb "far-left prosecutors" who are "making our communities less safe." State senator Chad Dixon announced he would file a complaint against, alleging she had weaponized justice against political opponents with an "unabashed goal to become some sort of leftist celebrity."[68][69]

On July 18, 2023, after the grand jury was seated, attorneys for David Shafer wrote to Willis arguing that Shafer's action was protected under the First, Fifth and Fourteenth Amendments. Willis had already identified Shafer as a target of the investigation.[70]

1. Hallerman, Tamar; Rankin, Bill (August 14, 2023). "Trump, 18 others indicted for trying to overthrow 2020 Georgia election". The Atlanta Journal-Constitution. ISSN 1539-7459. Archi August 15, 2023. Retr 8/14/23.
2. Bowden, M; Teague, Matt (2022). The Steal: Attempt to Overturn 2020 Election, People Who Stopped It. NYC: Grove Press. p.1. ISBN 978-0-802-15996-0
3. "US election 2016: Trump says election 'rigged at polling places'". BBC News. October 17, 2016. Archived June 18, 2021. Retr February 16, 2023.
4. Savage, Charlie (Oct 12, 2022). "Lawyers Ask Court to Sanction Chesebro Over Trump Fake Electors". NYT. Archived Feb 17, 2023. Retrieved Feb 16, 2023.
5. Haberman, Maggie; Savage, Charlie; Broadwater, Luke (August 8, 2023). "Previously Secret Memo Laid Out Strategy for Trump to Overturn Biden's Win - The House Jan. 6 committee's investigation did not uncover the memo, whose existence first came to light in last week's indictment". The New York Times. Archived August 9, 2023. Retrieved August 10, 2023.
6. Feuer, Alan; Benner, Katie (July 27, 2022). "The Fake Electors Scheme Explained". The New York Times. Archived August 1, 2023. Retr Feb 16, 2023.

7. Holmes, Kristen; Stracqualursi, Veronica (Dec 5, 2020). "Trump pressured Ga gov. in call to help overturn Biden's win". CNN. Arch Feb 17, 2023. Retr 2/16/23.
8. Duster, Chandelis (Dec 7, 2020). "Georgia reaffirms Biden victory after recount, blow to Trump attempt overturn". CNN. Arch Jan 10, 2021. Retr Feb 16, 2023.
9. Shear, Michael; Saul, Stephanie (Jan 3, 2021). "Trump, in Taped Call, Pressured Ga Official, 'Find' Votes to Overturn Election". NYT. Arch 1/4/21. Retr 2/16/23.
10. Scanlan, Quinn (Jan 3, 2021). "Trump demands Georgia secretary of state 'find' enough votes to hand him win". ABC News. Archi Jan 4, 2021. Retr Feb 16, 2023.
11. Hakim, Danny; Fausset, Richard (Feb 13, 2021). "In Georgia, New District Att. Starts Circling Trump and His Allies. NYT. Archi Feb 13, Retr Feb 16, 2023.
12. Murray, Sara; Morris, Jason (September 17, 2021). "Georgia criminal probe into Trump's attempts to overturn 2020 election quietly moves forward". CNN. Archived on February 23, 2023. Retr Feb 22, 2023.
13. Boboltz, Sara; Blumenthal, Paul; O'Connor, Lydia (March 15, 2024). "Prosecutor Steps Down, Trump's Ga Case After Judge's Ultimatum". HuffPost. Retr 3/15/24.
14. "Fulton County DA Fani Willis explosive accusations: New documents in special prosecutor controversy". FOX 5 Atlanta. January 19, 2024. Retr January 31, 2024.
15. Gringlas, Sam (January 20, 2022). "District attorney in Georgia asks for a special grand jury for Trump election probe". NPR. Archi Feb 23, Retr February 22, 2023.
16. "A special grand jury has been granted in Fulton County's Trump investigation". NPR. 1/24/22. Archi 2/23/23. Retr 2/22/23.
17. Brumback, Kate (Feb 23, 2023). "What's a special grand jury and how does it work?". AP. Arch., Retr July 16, 2023.
18. Brumback, Kate (July 11, 2023). "Grand Jury Seated Tuesday May Decide If Trump Is Charged Over Georgia Election". HuffPost. Archi July 11, Retr 7/11/23
19. Brown, Matthew (July 5, 2022). "Georgia grand jury subpoenas Sen. Graham, Giuliani and Trump legal team". Washington Post. Archi Feb 19, Retr 7/11/23
20. "Trump legal adviser Jenna Ellis appears before special grand jury in 2020 election probe". CBS News. August 25, 2022. Archived, Retr Feb 17, 2023.
21. Cohen, Zachary; Murray, Sara; Morris, Jason (August 31, 2022). "Former Trump attorney John Eastman appears before Fulton County grand jury". CNN. Archived August 15, 2023. Retrieved February 17, 2023.
22. Murray, Sara; Morris, Jason (Sept 7, 2022). "Texas lawyer wins subpoena fight against Ga prosecutors investigating Trump's efforts to overturn 2020 election". CNN. Arch Aug 15, 2023. Retr 2/17/23.
23. Hamburger, Tom; Scott, Eugene (Aug 15, 2022). "Giuliani target in Ga. criminal probe 2020 election". Washington Post. Archi Feb 19, 20 Retr Feb 17, 2023.
24. Sneed, Tierney (10/20/22). "Atlanta investigators can subpoena Lindsey Graham in 2020 election investigation, fed court rules". CNN. Arch. 2/1/23. Retr 2/17/23.
25. de Vogue, Ariane; Murray, Sara; Sneed, Tierney (Nov 1, 2022). "Supreme Court rejects Graham's request to block Ga subpoena". CNN. Arch, Retr Feb 17, 2023.
26. Murray, Sara; Youd, Chris (Nov 22, 2022). "Lindsey Graham testifies before Ga grand jury investigating 2020 election". CNN. Archi Jan 26, Retr Feb 17, 2023.
27. Lizza, Ryan; Daniels, Eugene; Bade, Rachael (Jan 24, 2024). "Playbook: 'That's the guy we will beat'". POLITICO. Retrieved January 25, 2024.
28. Cheney, Kyle; Wu, Nicholas (Aug17, 2022). "Kemp fights subpoena from Atlanta-area Trump probe after talks break down". Politico. Archi, Retr Feb 17, 2023.
29. Johnson, Kevin (November 15, 2022). "Georgia Gov. Brian Kemp appears before Atlanta grand jury in election probe". USA Today. Archi Dec 3, Retr Febr 17, 2023.
30. Sneed, Tierney (October 26, 2022). "Mark Meadows ordered by court to testify in Georgia 2020 election meddling probe". CNN. Archi on Jan 10, Retr Feb 17, 2023.

31. Cohen, Marshall; Carver, Katie; Cole, Devan (Feb 21, 2023). "Foreperson on Georgia grand jury investigating Trump and 2020 election: 'I don't think you will be shocked' by indictments". CNN Politics. Arch July 15, 2023. Retr July 16, 2023.
32. Morris, Jason; Sneed, Tierney (Nov 15, 2022). "Flynn ordered to testify in Atlanta grand jury probe, Trump's election subversion". CNN. Arch 1/30/23. Retr 2/17/23.
33. Morris, Jason; Fiegel, Eric (Dec 8, 2022). "Flynn appears before Atlanta grand jury probe into Trump's election subversion". CNN. Archi Jan 28, Retr Feb 17, 2023.
34. "Photos: Who's testified before Fulton Trump grand jury?". AJC. Retr Oct 2, 2023.
35. Sangal, Aditi (9/8/23). "Read the Georgia special grand jury report on 2020 election interference". CNN. Retr 9/8/23.
36. Aftergut, Dennis (Sept 11, 2023). "Opinion: Why Lindsey Graham wasn't indicted". CNN. Retr 3/26/24.
37. Sangal, Aditi (9/8/23). "Georgia special grand jury recommended charges against 39 people". CNN. Retrieved 9/8/23.
38. Bailey, Holly (Feb 16, 2023). "Georgia grand jury: 'Perjury may have been committed' in Trump election probe". Washington Post. Arch & Retr Feb 22, 2023.
39. Bailey, Holly (Feb 13, 2023). "Part of Georgia grand jury report on Trump election interference to be released". Washington Post. Archi Febr 13, Retr Feb 22, 2023.
40. Danny Hakim; Richard Fausset (April 18, 2023). "Atlanta Prosecutor Seeks Removal of Lawyer in Trump Case". New York Times. Archi Retr April 19, 2023.
41. Amy Gardner; Holly Bailey (5/5/23). "At least eight Trump electors have accepted immunity in Georgia investigation". Washington Post. Arch & Retr May 6, 2023.
42. Brown, Matthew; Bailey, Holly (May 19, 2023). "Georgia D.A. investigating Trump hints time frame for charges". Washington Post. ISSN 0190-8286. Arch. on May 19, 2023. Retr July 13, 2023.
43. Hellerman, Tamar (August 14, 2023). "Former state Sen. Jordan: 'It's about time'". The Atlanta Journal-Constitution. Archived August 14, 2023. Retr August 14, 2023.
44. Bluestein, Greg (August 14, 2023). "Nguyen testifies to grand jury: 'No individual above the law.'" Atlanta Journal-Constitution. Archi Aug 15, Retr Aug 14, 2023.
45. Bluestein, Greg; Hellerman, Tamar (Aug 14, 2023). "Chidi, Duncan to testify ahead of schedule Monday". Atlanta Journal-Constitution. Arch., Retr 8/14/23
46. Hellerman, Tamar (Aug 14, 2023) "Gabriel Sterling, top Secretary of State official, spotted in courthouse". Atlanta Journal-Constitution. Arch & Retr Aug 14, 2023
47. "READ: Trump indictment in Fulton County, Georgia, probe". CNN Politics. August 15, 2023. Retr 8/15/23.
48. Cole, Devan; Murray, Sara; Morris, Jason; Cohen, Marshall (August 14, 2023). "Live updates: Trump indicted in Georgia election probe by Fulton County grand jury". CNN. Arch August 15, 2023. Retr 8/15/23.
49. Herb, Jeremy (8/15/23). "Giuliani faces 13 charges, more than any other defendant except Trump". CNN. Retr 8/15/23.
50. Wickert, David (August 15, 2023). "Following Trump indictment, agency moves on investigation of Lt. Gov. Jones". Atlanta Journal-Constitution.
51. "Fulton County district attorney says her office will propose Trump election trial to happen within the next 6 months". CNN. August 15, 2023. Retr August 15, 2023.
52. Murray, Sara (8/15/23). "Fulton County DA said she intends to try all 19 defendants together". CNN. Retrieved 8/15/23.
53. Alexander, Blayne (August 1, 2023). "Fulton County DA Fani Willis shares racist threat as Trump probe nears a conclusion". NBC News. Archi, Retr 8/1/23
54. Murphy, Patricia; Bluestein, Greg; Michell, Tia July 31, 2023 "The Jolt: Fani Willis warns Fulton leaders 'stay alert'". Atlanta Journal-Constitution. Archi, Aug 1, 2023.
55. Joyner, Chris (Sept 25, 2023). "Judge in Trump RICO case orders protections for jurors". The Atlanta Journal-Constitution. ISSN 1539-7459. Retr Sept 26, 2023.

56. Papp, Jozsef; Jordan, Mike (September 26, 2023). "Fulton DA prosecuting Trump, Young Thug says her family has been threatened". The Atlanta Journal-Constitution. ISSN 1539-7459. Retrieved 9/27/23.
57. Elliot, Richard (August 1, 2023). "Fulton Co sheriff says, 'mugshot' if Trump is indicted locally". WSB-TV Channel 2 - Atlanta. Arch 8/2/23. Retr 8/3/23.
58. Richard Fausset; Danny Hakim (10/19/23). "Sidney Powell Pleads Guilty in Georgia Trump Case". NYT.
59. Becket, Stefan; Hymes, Clare; Legare, Robert (Oct 19, 2023). "Sidney Powell pleads guilty to conspiracy in Ga 2020 election case". CBS News. Retr 10/19/23.
60. "Lawyer Kenneth Chesebro pleads guilty over efforts to overturn Trump's 2020 loss in Georgia". AP News. Oct 20, 2023. Retrieved October 20, 2023.
61. Fausset, Richard; Hakim, Danny (10/24/23). "Jenna Ellis, Former Trump Lawyer, Pleads Guilty in Ga Election Case". NYT. Arch., Oct 24, 2023. Retr Nov 23, 2023.
62. Wickert, David (August 15, 2023). "Following Trump indictment, agency moves on investigation of Lt. Gov. Jones". Atlanta Journal-Constitution.
63. Holmes, Kristen; Morris, Jason (Feb 16, 2023). "Trump touts "perfect" phone calls to Georgia election officials, says did nothing wrong". CNN. Arch, Retr 2/16/2023
64. Breuninger, Kevin (July 17, 2023). "Georgia Supreme Court rejects Trump bid to block grand jury report in election probe". CNBC. Archi, Retr July 17, 2023.
65. Sara Murray; Jason Morris (July 31, 2023). "Georgia judge rejects Trump's efforts to toss evidence in Fulton probe, disqualify DA". CNN. Arch., Retr July 31, 2023.
66. Cohen, Marshall (July 14, 2023). "Trump asks courts to throw out evidence and disqualify DA in Georgia probe of 2020 election". CNN. Archi , Retr July 14, 2023.
67. LeBlanc, Paul (Feb 23, 2023). "House Jan 6 investigator says 'likely' 2020 election subversion probes to produce indictments". CNN Politics. Archi, Retr 2/25/23
68. Amy, Jeff (May 5, 2023). "Ga enacts law lets panel punish, oust prosecutors". AP
69. Bluestein, Greg (August 21, 2023). "State senator eyes new panel as way to punish Fani Willis over Trump indictments". Atlanta Journal-Constitution.
70. Rankin, Bill. "Former Georgia GOP chair argues against indictment in Trump probe". Atlanta Journal-Constitution. ISSN 1539-7459. Archi &Retr July 20, 2023.

Special Prosecutor Nathan Wade, Fulton Co v. Trump

Prosecutorial impropriety Background

On January 8, 2024, Mike Roman's attorney filed with the court alleging that Fani Willis and Nathan Wade had a romantic relationship.[156][157][158] Willis had hired Wade as special prosecutor in the Trump case in November 2021.[159] The filing asserted Willis went on vacations with Wade and so Willis profited from hiring him, which would be a conflict of interest. The filing requested charges against Roman be dropped. It also requested Willis be disqualified from the case; Willis's office said it would motion to have this request dismissed.[156][157][158] On January 25, Trump joined Roman's effort by filing a similar complaint.[160]

Wade was concurrently involved with divorce proceedings from his wife, Joycelyn, which had also begun in November 2021. On January 8, 2024, Joycelyn's attorneys subpoenaed Willis to testify in the divorce case.[159] On January 19, Joycelyn filed in her divorce case that Nathan had purchased a 2022 trip for himself and Willis to Miami with a Royal Caribbean cruise and a 2023 trip to San Francisco and a Napa Valley hotel. Clara Bowman (reportedly Nathan's mother) came too.[161]

On January 22, a judge in Cobb Co Superior Court unsealed records of the Wades' ongoing divorce.[162] The unsealed records had no reference to an alleged affair between Nathan and Willis.[163] On Jan 30, Nathan and Joycelyn Wade reached a temporary agreement on some of their issues.[164] Willis and Nathan scheduled to testify in Wades' divorce.[159]

On January 14, Willis made public comments about the allegation, saying Wade is qualified for his role and is paid the same as the other two special prosecutors on the case.[165] According to The New York Times, Wade had little prior experience beyond being employed about a year in late 1990s by the Cobb Co Solicitor's Office, which prosecutes misdemeanors and traffic citations.[166]

Hearing

On January 18, with Willis's unwillingness to recuse herself,[167] Judge McAfee scheduled a hearing on Roman's request to dismiss her from the case. On February 2, the court deadline for Willis to respond to the allegation,[168] she acknowledged she had been in a personal relationship with Wade since 2022 but said she had no financial or personal conflict of interest and there were no grounds for dismissal.[169] Willis and Wade were subpoenaed to testify at the February 15 hearing.[170]

Seventeen ethics experts, former prosecutors and defense attorneys filed a "friend of the court" brief with Judge McAfee on February 5. They found that, even if all of Roman's allegations were true, they would "not even come close" to requiring Willis be removed, or that the charges be dropped.[171]

On February 12, McAfee said he would consider removing Willis from the case if he finds a financial conflict of interest. McAfee clarified that not all of Roman's complaints are relevant and that, at a February 15 hearing, he would consider details of the Willis–Wade relationship only in the context of whether the relationship led to financial benefit.[172]

At the first day of the hearing, Roman's lawyers questioned whether prosecutors had lied in their affidavit about when they began their romantic relationship.[173] On February 27, Wade's former law partner Terrence Bradley testified that he did not know when Wade and Willis's relationship began.

Although Bradley had previously informed the defense team[174] that the relationship began in "late 2019," he testified that "I speculated on some things."[175] On March 4, Shafer's attorneys asked to subpoena Cindi Lee Yeager, a co-chief deputy district attorney for Cobb County, should McAfee reopen hearings.[176]

Ruling and aftermath

On March 15, Judge Scott McAfee ruled that either Willis (along with her office) or Wade must leave the case, because their relationship brought about a "significant appearance of impropriety".[177][178] Willis committed a "tremendous lapse in judgment" and her "testimony during the evidentiary hearing" was "unprofessional", but "simply making bad choices – even repeatedly" does not establish an actual conflict of interest under Georgia law, stated McAfee.[177][179] As there was not enough evidence that Willis "acquired a personal stake in the prosecution, or that her financial arrangements had any impact on the case", an actual conflict of interest was not proven, ruled McAfee.[180] Later that day, Wade resigned from the case.[181][155]

On May 6, ABC's Good Morning America aired an interview with Wade regarding the matter.[182][183]

Appeal to dismiss Fani Willis from the case

After Wade resigned, satisfying McAfee's March 15 ruling, Trump continued to seek Willis's removal from the case. On March 20, McAfee allowed Trump to turn to the Georgia Court of Appeals,[184] though McAfee clarified Trump's appeal would not delay "the many other unrelated pending pretrial motions" McAfee was addressing.[185] On March 29, Trump submitted the appeal.[186] On April 8, Willis asked the court to reject it.[187]

On May 8, the Georgia Court of Appeals said it would hear the appeal to dismiss Willis,[188] and on June 5, it paused the election racketeering case until it decides about Willis.[6] Oral arguments were tentatively set for October 4 before judges E. Trenton Brown III, Benjamin A. Land, and Todd Markle,[189] then delayed to December 5.[7] While such cases usually rely on legal briefs, Trump's team asked the court to hear oral arguments.[190]

156.Hakim, Danny; Fausset, Richard (January 11, 2024). "Atlanta Prosecutor Faces Upheaval in Trump Inquiry". New York Times. Retr January 11, 2024.

157. Blumenthal, Paul (Jan 13, 2024). "Could Allegations Against DA Fani Willis Derail The Case Against Trump In Georgia?". HuffPost. Retr March 7, 2024.

158. Gardner, Amy; Bailey, Holly (1/18/24). "Judge in Trump Georgia case orders hearing on Fani Willis misconduct claims". Washington Post. ISSN 0190-8286. Retrieved 1/18/24 a scheduled Jan. 31 hearing in Cobb County Superior Court over motion to unseal records in Wade's divorce case. Merchant said she believes records in that case will substantiate her allegations of wrongdoing by Willis and Wade.

159. Rankin, Bill; Minshew, Charles (1/30/24). "Wade settles divorce case, canceling court hearing". Atlanta Journal-Constitution. ISSN 1539-7459. Retr Jan 31, 2024.
160. Karanth, Sanjana (January 25, 2024). "Trump Joins Legal Effort To Disqualify DA Fani Willis From Georgia Election Case". HuffPost. Retrieved January 25, 2024.
161. Fankin, Bill (January 19, 2024). "Bank records: DA Willis and special prosecutor traveled together during Trump probe". Atlanta Journal-Constitution. ISSN 1539-7459. Archived Jan 25, 2024. Retrieved Jan 19, 2024.
162. "Timeline of allegations against Fulton DA Fani Willis". The Atlanta Journal-Constitution. Jan 22, 2024. ISSN 1539-7459. Archived Janu 25, Retr Jan 24, 2024.
163. Brumback, Kate; Richer, Alanna Durkin (1/22/24). "Judge orders unsealing divorce case, Trump special prosecutor in Ga accused of affair". AP. Retr 1/24/24
164. "Wade divorce case: Couple reaches agreement ahead of scheduled hearing". FOX 5 Atlanta. 1/30/24. Retr 3/17/24
165. Abusaid, Shaddi (Jan 14, 2024). "Fulton DA defends special prosecutor during church speech". The Atlanta Journal-Constitution. Archived Jan 25, Retr Jan 14, 2024.
166. Bogel-Burroughs, Nicholas; Fausset, Richard (Jan 10, 2024). "Lawyer Tapped to Prosecute Trump in Georgia Is Now Under Scrutiny Himself". NYT. Retr Mar 7, 2024.
167. Cohen, Zachary (Feb 1, 2024). "Exclusive: Embattled Georgia prosecutor will not recuse amid affair allegations in Trump election case". CNN. Retr Feb 1, 2024.
168. Grenoble, Ryan (1/18/24). "Georgia Judge Calls Hearing On Fani Willis Improper Relationship". HuffPost. Retr 1/18/24.
169. Rubin, Olivia (February 2, 2024). "Filing from DA in Trump case admits 'personal relationship' with prosecutor but denies wrongdoing". ABC News. Retr Feb 2, 2024.
170. Boboltz, Sara (January 31, 2024). "Fulton County DA Fani Willis Subpoenaed For Alleged Misconduct: Reports". HuffPost. Retr Feb 1, 2024.
171. Hallerman, Tamar (Feb 6, 2024). "Ethics pro back up Fulton DA in Trump conflict-of-interest dispute". Atlanta Journal-Constitution. Archi Feb 14, Retr March 7, 2024.
172. Lybrand, Holmes; Cohen, Zachary; Valencia, Nick; Morris, Jason (Feb12, 2024). "Fulton County DA could be disqualified from Trump case if financially benefitted from relationship with prosecutor". CNN. Retr 2/13/24.
173. Polantz, Katelyn (2/15/24). "Here's what defense lawyers trying to do in the Fani Willis hearing". CNN. Ret Feb 15, 2024.
174. Valencia, Nick; Cohen, Zachary; Morris, Jason (Feb 28, 2024). "Exclusive: Texts reveal role witness played in DA push to disqualify Willis". CNN. Retr March 1, 2024.
175. Bailey, Holly; Gardner, Amy (Feb 28, 2024). "'Star witness' testifies claims about Fani Willis were 'speculation'". Washington Post. ISSN 0190-8286. Retr Feb 28, 2024.
176. Vlachou, Marita (March 5, 2024). "Trump Co-Defendant Offers New Witness To Testify In Effort To Remove Willis". HuffPost. Retr March 5, 2024.
177. Quinn, Melissa; Eggleston, Jared (March 15, 2024). "Fani Willis and her office can stay on Trump Georgia 2020 election case if Nathan Wade steps aside, judge rules". CBS News. Retrieved March 15, 2024.
178. Meyer, Josh (March 15, 2024). "DA Fani Willis can stay on Georgia Trump case - if she fires special prosecutor, judge says". USA Today. March 15, 2024.
179. Alexander, Blayne; Gregorian, Dareh; Gile, Charlie (Mar 15, 2024). "Fulton County DA Willis case against Trump can continue if she or prosecutor remove themselves, judge rules". NBC News. Retr Mar 15, 2024.
180. Butler, Megan (3/15/24). "Special prosecutor out in Georgia election subversion case". Courthouse News. Retr 3/1624.
181. Boboltz, Sara; Blumenthal, Paul; O'Connor, Lydia (March 15, 2024). "Prosecutor Steps Down From Georgia Case After Judge's Ultimatum". HuffPost. Retr 3/15/24
182. Davis, Linsey (5/6/24). "Former special prosecutor Nathan Wade speaks out". Good Morning America. Retrieved 5/6/24.
183. Rubin, Olivia; Schlosberg, Jon (May 6, 2024). "Ex-Fulton County prosecutor Wade says, 'day of reckoning' coming in Trump case". ABC News. Retr May 6, 2024.

184. "Judge Clears Way For Trump To Appeal Ruling Keeping Willis On Ga. Election Case". HuffPost. 3/20/24. Retr 3/20/24.
185. Rubin, Olivia (3/20/24). "Judge allows Trump to appeal Fani Willis disqualification ruling". ABC News. Retrieved 3/20/24.
186. Brumback, Kate (March 29, 2024). "Trump Appeals Ruling Allowing Fani Willis To Remain On Georgia Election Case". HuffPost. Retr March 29, 2024.
187. Visser, Nick (4/9/24). "Willis Asks Court To Reject Trump's Effort To See Her Thrown Off Case". HuffPost. Retr 4/9/24.
188. Cole, Devan; Lybrand, Holmes (May 8, 2024). "Georgia appeals court will consider Trump's effort to disqualify DA Willis from election case". Retr May 8, 2024.
189. Rankin, Bill; Hallerman, Tamar (June 3, 2024). "Georgia court sets Oct. 4 as tentative hearing date in Fani Willis appeal". The Atlanta Journal-Constitution.
190. Rankin, Bill; Hallerman, Tamar (June 10, 2024). "Trump's lawyer seeks oral arguments on Fani Willis appeal in Georgia case". The Atlanta Journal-Constitution. ISSN 1539-7459. Retrieved June 10, 2024.

Scott F. McAfee

Scott F. McAfee (born 1988 or 1989) is an American judge serving on the Fulton County Superior Court in Georgia since 2023. Judge McAfee was the Georgia inspector general from 2021 to 2023. Prior to his current appointment, he served as a senior assistant DA in Fulton County and an assistant US Attorney for Northern District of Georgia.

In August 2023, McAfee garnered national attention when he was assigned to preside over the Fulton County district attorney's criminal racketeering case against Donald Trump.

McAfee was born in 1989.[1] He was raised in Kennesaw, Georgia.[2] He is an Eagle Scout.[3][4] McAfee received a cello scholarship to Emory University symphony orchestra.[5][4] In 2010, he completed a bachelor's degree in political science and music.[6]

In 2012, McAfee was a judicial intern for Georgia Supreme Court justice Keith R. Blackwell.[7] He also interned for justice David Nahmias.[5][4] In 2013, he graduated from Univ of Georgia School of Law, cum laude. While in law school, he was the VP of the school's Federalist Society chapter, treasurer of Law Republicans and inducted into The Order of Barristers.[1][5][4][6]

McAfee was an assistant district attorney in the Barrow County, Piedmont Judicial Circuit.[8] He joined the office of the district attorney in Fulton Co in April 2015, initially working on the early stages of criminal cases.[9] He later was promoted to prosecutor in the complex trial division, which was then headed by prosecutor Fani Willis, who was later elected as Fulton County district attorney.[1][10] McAfee was eventually promoted to senior assistant DA in the major case division, where he prosecuted felony cases including armed robbery and murder.[5][1]

In 2019, McAfee was appointed as an assistant US Attorney for the US District Court for the Northern District of Georgia.[1] He worked in the criminal division where he investigated and prosecuted drug trafficking organizations, fraud, and illegal firearms possession.[5][1][4] On April 1, 2021, Georgia governor Kemp appointed McAfee as the state inspector general.[5][1][11]

In December 2022, Kemp appointed McAfee to the Fulton County Superior Court following Christopher S. Brasher's retirement.[12] He was sworn in on February 1, 2023.[1]

In August 2023, he was assigned to preside over the racketeering case, State of Georgia v. Donald J. Trump, et al, in which former president Donald Trump and 18 co-defendants are accused of conspiring to overturn the Georgia presidential election results.[7][13] Fani Willis is overseeing the prosecution.[1]

As Inspector General appointed by Governor Kemp, now presiding Judge, appointed by Governor Kemp, McAfee has all the evidence of 2020 Georgia voter fraud and has failed to disclose his knowledge or participation to the Parties.[14]

1. Bogel-Burroughs, Nicholas (8/15/23). "Judge on Trump Case Once Worked Under Fani Willis". NYT. Retrieved 8/15/23.
2. Mizelle, Shawna (8/15/23). "Who is Scott McAfee, the judge assigned to Trump case in Georgia?". CNN. Retr 8/15/23.
3. Redmon, Jeremy; Rankin, Bill (8/17/23). "34-year-old judge to oversee Trump prosecution in Ga". The Atlanta Journal-Constitution. Arch 8/20/23. Retr 9/28/23.
4. "U.S. Attorney Pak announces the appointment of thirteen new Assistant U.S. Attorneys". Northern District of Georgia (Press release). US Dept of Justice. Feb 8, 2019. Retrieved August 15, 2023
5. "Kemp appoints Scott McAfee Inspector General". Albany Herald. 3/31/21. Archi 9/3/23. Retr 8/15/23.
6. McWhirter, Cameron (August 16, 2023). "McAfee Has Been a Judge Six Months. Assigned Trump's Ga Case". Wall Street Journal. ISSN 0099-9660. Retr 8/16/23

Judge Beryl A. Howell, Appellate Judge in Giuliani Defamation Case

Beryl Alaine Howell (born December 3, 1956) is an American lawyer and jurist who serves as a senior United States district judge of the United States District Court for the District of Columbia. She was district's chief judge from 2016 to 2023. As chief judge, she supervised federal grand juries in the District, including for Mueller special counsel investigation into Russian interference in the 2016 United States elections and investigations into attempts to overturn the 2020 United States presidential election.[1][2]

Howell was born in 1956 in Fort Benning, Georgia.[3] She is the daughter of an Army officer and is Jewish.[4] She attended elementary secondary school in six states and Germany.[5] Howell graduated Bryn Mawr College in 1978 with a Bachelor of Arts in philosophy with honors. From 1978 to 1980, Howell was legal assistant at law firm Shanley & Fisher (now Faegre Drinker). She attended Columbia Law School, graduating in 1983 with a Juris Doctor as a Harlan Fiske Stone Scholar.[6]

After law school, Howell was a law clerk for Judge Dickinson Richards Debevoise of the United States District Court for the District of New Jersey from 1983 to 1984. From 1985 to 1987, she was in private practice at the New York City law firm of Schulte Roth & Zabel.[5][6]

From 1987 to 1993, Howell was an assistant US attorney for the United States District Court for the Eastern District of New York, where she became deputy chief of the Narcotics section.[7] From 1993 to 2003, Howell served on the staff of the US Senate Committee on the Judiciary as a senior advisor to Chairman Patrick Leahy, including as the committee's general counsel starting in 1997.[6]

While working for Senator Leahy, Howell helped craft the E-FOIA amendments, which expanded electronic access to government records.[8] She also helped Sen. Leahy fend off proposals to impose new limits on the FOIA.[8] In 2001, she was honored by the Coalition to Support and Expand the Freedom of Information Act,[8] and in 2004, her FOIA work was honored by the Society of Professional Journalists.[7]

Howell was involved crafting legislation for investigation and prosecution of computer crime and copyright infringement, including the Anti-Cybersquatting Consumer Protection Act,[9] the National Information Infrastructure Protection Act,[9] the Computer Fraud and Abuse Act,[9] the Communications Assistance for Law Enforcement Act (CALEA),[10] the No Electronic Theft Act (NET Act),[7][10] the Digital Millennium Copyright Act (DMCA),[7][9][10] and the Digital Theft Deterrence and Copyright Damages Improvement Act of 1999.[7][10]

Howell was involved in national security issues,[11] including creation of the USA PATRIOT Act,[7][10] which she defended in a 2005 article for the Pa Bar Assoc Quarterly.[12] Center for Democracy and Technology lists Howell as "board alum".[13] From 2004 to 2010, she was a member of the US Sentencing Commission, appointed by President G. W. Bush.[5][7]

In November 2023, Howell received the Champion Award for people who advance opportunities for women in "the white collar field".[14] In her acceptance speech, she said: "My D.C. judicial colleagues and I regularly see the impact of big lies at the sentencing of hundreds, hundreds of individuals who have been convicted for offense conduct on Jan. 6, 2021, when they disrupted the certification of the 2020 presidential election at the U.S. Capitol." She also cited historian Heather Cox Richardson's book Democracy Awakening.[15]

Representative Elise Stefanik, a Republican from NY, filed a complaint of judicial misconduct alleging Howell's remarks were "conduct unbecoming of a federal judge".[16]

From 2004 to 2009,[7][17][18] Howell was executive VP,[8] executive managing director,[11] and general counsel[11] at Stroz Friedberg, a global digital risk management and investigations firm. Howell's work at Stroz Friedberg included lobbying on behalf of Recording Industry Association of America,[7][18][19][20] and Universal Music Group.[7][21]

In 2008, Howell was a member of the Commission on Cybersecurity for the 44th Presidency, sponsored by Center for Strategic and International Studies.[11][22] Howell teaches legal ethics as an adjunct professor at the American University's Washington College of Law.[9][23]

Federal judicial service

On July 14, 2010, Howell was nominated by President Barack Obama to the seat vacated by Judge Paul L. Friedman, who assumed senior status on December 31, 2009.[5][24] She was confirmed by the U.S. Senate on December 22, 2010. She received her judicial commission on December 27, 2010. She served as chief judge from March 17, 2016, to March 17, 2023. She assumed senior status on February 1, 2024.[6] A 2015 analysis by Ravel Law found Howell to be the second most-cited district court judge appointed in previous five years.[25]

Notable decisions

In 2011, Harold Hodge Jr. stood outside the U.S. Supreme Court wearing a sign that protested the American government's treatment of Black and Hispanic people.[26] He did so in violation of a 1949 federal law that makes such protests a crime. Hodge sued the Marshal of the United States Supreme Court and the U.S. Attorney for the District of Columbia under the First Amendment. In a June 2013 decision, Howell struck down the law as violating the First Amendment's guarantee of free speech.[27] The judge wrote, "The absolute prohibition on expressive activity in the statute is unreasonable, substantially overbroad and irreconcilable with the First Amendment." Defendants appealed the decision to the U.S. Court of Appeals for the District of Columbia, which reversed Howell's decision and reinstated the law as it applies to the Supreme Court Plaza and steps. Hodge v. Talkin, 799 F. 3d 1145 (D.C. Cir. 2015).

In 2018, Howell struck down a regulation of the Federal Election Commission allowing dark money groups, certain nonprofit organizations engaged in political activities, to conceal their donors. She wrote that the regulation "blatantly undercuts the congressional goal of fully disclosing the sources of money flowing into federal political campaigns, and thereby suppresses the benefits intended to accrue from disclosure."[28] SCOTUS later declined to review the decision.[29]

In that same year, Howell became the supervising judge for the grand jury working for special counsel Robert Mueller's investigation into Russian interference in the 2016 United States elections.[1] On October 25, 2019, she ruled in favor of the House Judiciary Committee, which had sought grand jury materials from the Mueller investigation, finding their impeachment inquiry into President Donald Trump to be a judicial proceeding.[30] Justice Department attorneys had previously asserted congressional investigators had "not yet exhausted their available discovery tools," arguments Howell said "smack of farce," as administration openly stated it would stonewall the investigation.[31]

1. Neuborne, Burt (11/29/18). "Trump may fire Mueller, but can't fire Mueller's grand jury". Los Angeles Times. Retr 11/30/18.
2. Savage, Charlie (March 13, 2023). "Gavel to Pass to New Chief Judge Overseeing Grand Jury in Trump Inquiry". NYT.
3. "Senate Judiciary Committee Questionnaire – Beryl Howell". Retr Aug 16, 2023.
4. Hsu, Spencer (9/26/16). "judge released 200 secret government surveillance requests". Washington Post.
5. "President Obama Names Five to US District Court" (Press release). Washington, D.C.: The White House. July 14, 2010. Archi Jan 18, 2017. Retr 3/1/23. article incorporates text from this source, public domain.
6. Beryl Howell Bio Directory of Federal Judges, publication of Fed Judicial Center.
7. Anderson, Nate (3/28/11). "RIAA lobbyist becomes federal judge, rules on file-sharing cases". Ars Technica. Retr 3/4/13.
8. "Practicing at Intersection of Law, Policy and Technology". Science and Tech newsletter. Bryn Mawr College. Oct 2003. Arch., Jan 5, Retr March 4, 2013.
9. "Statement Of Senator Patrick Leahy (D-Vt.), Chairman, Senate Judiciary Committee, Nomination Of Beryl Howell To Be US District Court Judge, District Of Columbia". 7/28/10. Arch., Dec 16, 2012. Retr 3/4/13.
10. "Stroz Friedberg LLC – Professionals – Howell, Beryl A." Stroz Friedberg, LLC. Arch 10/12/07. Retr 3/6/13.
11. "Beryl Howell". Center for Democracy and Technology. Arch 4/12/10. Retr 3/4/13
12. Howell, Beryl. "Perspectives on the USA PATRIOT Act" Archi, Retr March 4, 2016.
13. "Staff". Center for Democracy and Technology. Retr March 4, 2013.
14. "Awards Program - Women's White Collar Defense Association". www.wwcda.org. Retrieved Dec16, 2023.
15. 2023 WWCDA Awards Gala Full Video, YouTube, Retr Dec 16, 2023
16. Rajkumar, Shruti (December 16, 2023). "Rep. Elise Stefanik Lodges Complaint Against Judge Who Oversaw Jan. 6, Trump Cases". HuffPost. Retr Dec 16, 2023.
17. "Revolving Door: Beryl A Howell Employment Summary – OpenSecrets". www.opensecrets.org.
18. U.S. Copyright Surveillance Machine About To Be Switched On, Promises of Transparency Already Broken, Electronic Frontier Foundation, Nov 15, 2012.
19. RIAA lobbying data (public record) published by OpenSecrets.org for 2004, 2005, 2006, 2007, 2008, 2009.
20. Stroz Frieberg lobbying data (public record) published by OpenSecrets.org 2004, 2005, 2006, 2007, 2008.
21. Stroz Frieberg lobbying data (public record) published by OpenSecrets.org 2005
22. "Commission Members" (PDF). Center for Strategic and International Studies. Archived (PDF) on June 4, 2011. Retrieved March 4, 2013.
23. "The Honorable Beryl Howell : Adjunct Professor of Law". Faculty. American Uni Washington College of Law. Archi March 17, 2014. Retr April 4, 2013.
24. "Presidential Nominations and Withdrawal Sent to Senate, 7/14/10" (Press release). Washington, D.C.: White House. Arch 7/16/10, Retr July 14, 2010.
25. Kassam, Kerry (April 23, 2015). "Judging The Judges: Who Are the Most-Cited New Jurists On The Federal Bench?". Above the Law.
26. "Supreme Court Issues New Rule Barring Protests on Plaza". NYT. June 13, 2013. Retr Sept25, 2014.
27. "Protest challenge SCOTUS speech-free zone". Watchdog.org. Ret 10/25/14.

28. Griffiths, Brent D. (Aug 4, 2018). "Judge's ruling invalidates regulation allowing anonymous donations to 'dark money' groups". Politico. Retr May 22, 2021
29. Lee, Michelle Ye Hee; Barnes, Robert (Sept 18, 2018). "Political nonprofits must name their donors under federal court ruling after Supreme Court declines to intervene". Washington Post. Retr 5/22/21.
30. Savage, Charlie; Cochrane, Emily (October 25, 2019). "Impeachment Inquiry Is Legal, Judge Rules, Giving Democrats a Victory". The New York Times.
31. "Federal Judge Calls Trump Admin's Legal Arguments a 'Farce' in Order Filled with Jabs at DOJ Attorneys". lawandcrime.com. October 25, 2019.

11th Circuit US Court of appeals Judge William Pryor

William Holcombe Pryor Jr. (born 1962) is an American lawyer who has served as the chief judge of the US Court of Appeals for the Eleventh Circuit since 2020. He was appointed as a US circuit judge of the court by President Geoge W. Bush in 2004. He is a former commissioner of the US Sentencing Commission.[1] Previously, he was the AG of Alabama, from 1997 to 2004.

Pryor was born in 1962 in Mobile, Alabama, the son of William Holcombe Pryor and Laura Louise Bowles. Pryor was raised in a devoutly Roman Catholic family.[2] He and his siblings attended McGill–Toolen Catholic School in Mobile.

Pryor attended Northeast Louisiana University on a band scholarship, graduating in 1984 with Bachelor of Arts, magna cum laude. He attended Tulane Univ Law School. He was editor-in-chief of Tulane Law Review, graduated in 1987 as Juris Doctor, magna cum laude.[3]

After law school, Pryor served as a law clerk to judge John Minor Wisdom of the U.S. Court of Appeals for the Fifth Circuit from 1987 to 1988.[4] He then entered private practice with the Birmingham, Alabama, law firm Cabaniss, Johnston, Gardner, Dumas & O'Neal. He served as an adjunct professor of maritime law at the Cumberland School of Law at Samford University from 1989 to 1995. Pryor is a visiting professor at the University of Alabama School of Law[5] and an adjunct professor at Cumberland School of Law at Samford University.[6]

In 1994, Pryor was introduced to Jeff Sessions, who was then campaigning to become the attorney general of Alabama.[7] Sessions won, and from 1995 to 1997 Pryor served as Alabama's deputy attorney general.[7] When Sessions became a U.S. Senator in 1997, Alabama Governor Fob James made Pryor the state's AG.[7] He was, at that time, the youngest state attorney general in the US. Pryor was elected in 1998 and reelected in 2002. At reelection, Pryor received nearly 59% of the vote, the highest percentage of any statewide candidate.[8]

Pryor received national attention in 2003 when he called for the removal of Alabama chief justice Roy Moore, who disobeyed a federal court order to remove a Ten Commandments monument from the Alabama judicial building. Pryor said that although he agreed with the propriety of displaying the Ten Commandments in a courthouse, he was bound to follow the court order and uphold rule of law. Pryor personally prosecuted Moore for violations of canons of judicial ethics, Alabama Court of the Judiciary unanimously removed Moore from office.[9]

1. U.S. Sentencing Commission. "Bio Commissioners". Arch 4/8/16. Retr 11/8/13.
2. "Pryor: Perhaps the most polarizing Supreme Court justice possibility". Washington Post. Retr Oct 5, 2018.
3. "Pryor, William Holcombe, Jr. Fed Judicial Center". www.fjc.gov. Retr Oct 5, 2018.
4. Russell, Kevin; Davis, Charles (1/10/17). "Potential nominee profile: William Pryor (Expanded)". SCOTUS blog. Retr 7/2/18.
5. University of Alabama. "Faculty Page". Retrieved November 8, 2013.
6. Cumberland School of Law. "Adjunct Faculty Page". Arch Nov 9, Retr 11/8/13
7. Stolberg, Sheryl Gay June 10, 2005. "A Different Timpanist" NYT Retr 7/2/18
8. Alabama Dept of Archives & History (Aug 25, 2009). Alabama Attorneys General.
9. Ten Commandments Judge Removed From Office, CNN Nov 14, 2003

Eleventh Circuit nomination and confirmation

Pryor was nominated to the United States Court of Appeals for the Eleventh Circuit by president George W. Bush on April 9, 2003, to fill a seat vacated by judge Emmett Ripley Cox, who had assumed senior status.[15] Originally, William H. Steele had been nominated to the seat in 2001, but his nomination had become stalled in the Democratic-controlled Senate Judiciary Committee during the 107th United States Congress because African-American groups protested his decisions in two civil rights cases as a magistrate judge.

15. "Presidential Nomination 512, 108th United States Congress". US Congress. 4/99, 2003. Retr 7/2/18

Due to a filibuster of his nomination, George W. Bush installed Pryor as a circuit court judge on February 20, 2004, using a recess appointment to bypass the regular Senate confirmation process.[22] Pryor resigned as Alabama's attorney general that same day and took his judicial oath for a term lasting until the end of the first session of the 109th Congress (Dec 22, 2005), when his appointment would have ended had he not been eventually confirmed.[23]

On May 23, 2005, senator John McCain announced an agreement between seven Republican and seven Democratic U.S. senators, the Gang of 14, to ensure an up-or-down vote on Pryor and two other stalled Bush nominees, Priscilla Owen, and Janice Rogers Brown. On June 9, 2005, Pryor was confirmed to the Eleventh Circuit by a 53–45 vote.[24][25]

22. Lewis, Neil A. (2/21, 2004). "Bypassing Senate Second Time, Bush Seats Judge". NYT. Retr July 2, 2018.
23. "Recess Appointments". CNN. Aug 2, 2005. Retr Dec 18, 2016.
24. "Presidential Nomination 200, 109th US Congress". United States Congress. 2/14/05. Retr 7/2, 2018.
25. "On the Nomination (Confirmation William H. Pryor, Jr., of Alabama, to be U.S. Circuit Judge)". senate.gov. Retr 7/8/18.

Notable opinions

Georgia v. Meadows (11th Cir. 2023). Pryor was part of a panel that denied the appeal of Mark Meadows, to remove his case from state to federal court.[36]

Trump v. United States (11th Cir. 2022). Pryor was part of a panel that issued a per curiam opinion vacating U.S. District Judge Aileen M. Cannon's September 5 Order in the Mar-a-Lago documents case. The opinion held that the district court's exercise of equitable jurisdiction constituted an abuse of discretion and accordingly remanded the matter with instructions for the district court to dismiss the case. In doing so, the opinion rejected the notion that the execution of a search warrant at the home of a former president is sufficient to warrant an exercise of equitable jurisdiction.[37]

36. https://media.ca11.uscourts.gov/opinions/pub/files/202312958.pdf
37. "Trump v. United States".

Justice of Supreme Court consideration

On May 16, 2016, then-presidential candidate Donald Trump released a list of eleven individuals from which he would pick to fill the vacancy left on the Supreme Court by the death of Antonin Scalia, including Pryor.[61]

At a Republican primary debate in, Trump said "we could have a Diane Sykes or you could have Bill Pryor, we have some fantastic people."[62]

It was reported in mid-December, Trump had narrowed his choices to "three or four individuals", with the top two leading candidates being Sykes and Pryor.[63]

Trump announced Neil Gorsuch for his pick on Jan 31, 2017.[64]

61. "SHOW YOUR SUPPORT FOR DONALD TRUMP". www.donaldjtrump.com. Archived 1/11/17. Retr 1/3/17.
62. CBSN (Feb 15, 2016), Full CBS News South Carolina Republican Debate, archived 12/13/21, Retr 1/3/17
63. "Bill Pryor, former Alabama AG, among Trump's top 2 Supreme Court prospects: Reports". AL.com. Retr 1/3/17.
64. Trump to announce Supreme Court pick on Tuesday, usatoday.com, January 30, 2017; accessed 2/1417.

Merrick Garland, US Attorney General appoints Jack Smith

This chapter is heavy reading, albeit essential to understand the background and career progression of Merrick Garland. While Garland legal cases sometimes appear balanced, he has been a maverick working heavily against any and all Republican/Conservative interests, while a strong supporter of Democrat causes, thus what the reader should see as a destructive force in 2024 attempts to reduce and eliminate treason level election cheating.

Merrick Brian Garland (born November 13, 1952) is an American lawyer and jurist who serves as 86th United States attorney general. He previously served as circuit judge of the United States Court of Appeals for the District of Columbia Circuit from 1997 to 2021. In 2016, President Obama nominated Garland to the U.S. Supreme Court, but Republican-led U.S. Senate blocked Garland's appointment.

A native of the Chicago area, Garland attended Harvard University and Harvard Law, where he was an editor of the Harvard Law Review. He served as a law clerk to Judge Henry Friendly of the US Court of Appeals for the Second Circuit and to U.S. Supreme Court Justice William J. Brennan Jr., and then practiced corporate litigation at Arnold & Porter, after which he worked as a federal prosecutor in the US DOJ, where he supervised the investigation and prosecution of the Oklahoma City bombers. President Clinton appointed Garland to the D.C. Court of Appeals in 1997, and served as chief judge, 2013 to 2020.

President Barack Obama, a Democrat, nominated Garland to serve as an associate justice of the Supreme Court in March 2016. However, the Republican Senate majority refused to hold a hearing or vote on his nomination. The unprecedented refusal of a Senate majority to consider a Supreme Court nomination was highly controversial. Garland's nomination lasted 293 days (the longest to date), and it expired on January 3, 2017, at the end of the 114th Congress. Eventually, President Donald Trump, a Republican, nominated Neil Gorsuch to the vacant seat, and the Republican Senate majority confirmed him.

President Biden nominated Garland as U.S. attorney general. He was confirmed by the Senate in a 70–30 vote, and took office in March 2021.

Young life and education

Garland was born on November 13, 1952, in Chicago.[1] His mother Shirley (née Horwitz; 1925–2016)[2] was a director of volunteer services at Chicago's Council for Jewish Elderly (now called CJE Senior LIFE).

His father, Cyril Garland (1915–2000),[3] headed Garland Advertising, a small business run out of the family home.[4][5][6] Garland was raised in Conservative Judaism; the family name changed from Garfinkel generations earlier.

His grandparents left the "Pale of Settlement" in Russia in the early 20th century, fleeing antisemitism in what is now Ukraine and Poland, seeking a better life for their children in USA.[6][7] Two of his grandmother's siblings were murdered in the Holocaust.[8] He is a cousin of Republican Iowa Governor, Ambassador to China Terry Branstad.[9]

Garland grew up in the north Chicago border suburb of Lincolnwood.[10][4] He attended Niles West High School in Skokie, Illinois, where he was president of the student council, acted in theatrical productions, and was a member of the debate team.[11] He graduated in 1970 as the class valedictorian.[4][10] Garland was also a Presidential Scholar and National Merit Scholar.[12][13] He then studied social studies at Harvard University.[4][14][15] He initially wanted to become a physician, but soon decided to become a lawyer instead.[11]

He allied himself with his future boss, Jamie Gorelick, when he was elected the only freshman member of a campus-wide committee on which Gorelick also served.[16] During his college summers Garland volunteered as a speechwriter to Congressman Abner J. Mikva.[16] After President Jimmy Carter appointed Mikva to the D.C. Circuit, Mikva would rely on Garland when hiring law clerks.[17] At Harvard, Garland wrote news articles and theater reviews for the Harvard Crimson, and was a resident of Quincy House.[18][19] Garland wrote his 235-page honors thesis on industrial mergers in Britain in the 1960s.[16][20] Garland graduated Harvard in 1974 with an Bachelor of Arts, summa cum laude, and was elected to Phi Beta Kappa.

Garland then attended Harvard Law School,[14] where he was a member of the Harvard Law Review. Garland ran for the presidency of the Law Review but lost to Susan Estrich, so he served as an articles editor instead.[16][15] As an articles editor, Garland assigned himself to edit a submission by U.S. Supreme Court Justice William Brennan on the topic of the role of state constitutions in safeguarding individual rights.[16][17][21] This correspondence with Brennan later contributed to his winning a clerkship with the justice.[21] Garland graduated from Harvard Law School in 1977 with a Juris Doctor, magna cum laude.

Garland briefly returned to Arnold & Porter, from 1992 to 1993.[16] In 1993, Garland joined the new Clinton administration as deputy assistant attorney general in the Criminal Division of the US Department of Justice.[4] The following year, Deputy AG Jamie Gorelick – a key mentor of Garland's[25] – asked Garland to be principal associate deputy AG.[4][26]

In that role, Garland's responsibilities included supervision of high-profile domestic-terrorism cases, including the Oklahoma City bombing, Ted Kaczynski (also known as the "Unabomber"), and the Atlanta Olympics bombings.[4][27]

Garland insisted on being sent to Oklahoma City after the attack, to examine the crime scene and oversee the investigation in preparation for the prosecution.[28]

He represented the government at preliminary hearings of the two main defendants, Timothy McVeigh and Terry Nichols.[28] Garland offered to lead the trial team, but could not because he was needed at Justice Department headquarters.

In 2003, Garland was elected to the Harvard Board of Overseers, completing the unexpired term of Deval Patrick, who stepped down.[30]

After winning the November 1996 presidential election, Clinton renominated Garland on January 7, 1997.[36] He was confirmed on March 19, 1997, by a 76–23 vote.[37] The majority of Republican senators voted to confirm Garland, including John McCain, Orrin Hatch, Susan Collins, and Jim Inhofe.[38] Senators Mitch McConnell, Chuck Grassley, and Jeff Sessions were among those who voted against Garland.[38] All of the 23 "no" votes came from Republicans, and all were based "on whether there was even a need for an eleventh seat" on the D.C. Circuit.[39] He received his judicial commission March 20, 1997.[40]

Garland has been described as "a moderate liberal, with a definite pro-prosecution bent in criminal cases".[4]

1. Bio Directory of the Federal Judiciary. Bernan Press. 2001. p. 511. ISBN 978-0890592588. Arch 11/2/16.
2. "Garland (obituary)". Chicago Tribune. 11/27/00. Archi 2/2216. Retr 9/11/21.
3. "Garland". Chicago Tribune. November 27, 2000.
4. Totenberg, Nina; Johnson, Carrie (3/16, 2016). "Garland Has A Reputation of Collegiality, Record of Republican Support". NPR. Archest March 20, 2016.
5. "Lynn Rosenman Married". NYT. 9/20/87. Archi 4/14/10. Retr April 10,2010
6. Nathan-Kazis, Josh (March 16, 2016). "Garland Offers Poignant Story About Anti-Semitism Supreme Court Battle Looms". The Forward. Arch & Retr 3/20/16.
7. Margolick, David (3/18/16). "What's in Merrick Garland's Name?". Tablet. Arch 3/24/16. Retr 8/18/16.
8. Garland, Merrick (Sept 17, 2022). "Attorney General Merrick B. Garland Administers the Oath of Allegiance and Delivers Congratulatory Remarks at Island Ceremony in Celebration of Constitution Week and Citizenship Day". Justice.gov. Retrieved Sept 19, 2022. My grandmother was one of five children born in Belarus. Three made it to the US, including my grandmother who came through Port of Baltimore. Two killed in the Holocaust.
9. McKinney, Kait (March 16, 2016). "Branstad Has Connection to SCOTUS Nominee Garland". WHO-HD Channel 13. Arch March 21,2016. Retr 3/16/16
10. Sweet, Lynn (3/16/16). "Obama Supreme Court pick: Chicago native Merrick Garland". Chicago Sun-Times. Arch&Retr March 20, 2016.
11. Stolberg, Sheryl Gay; Liptak, Adam (3/16/16). "Garland's Path to Nomination Marked by Deference, With Limits". NYT. p. A1. ISSN 0362-4331. Retr 3/20/16.
12. "145 in Chicago, Suburbs Earn Merit Scholarships". Chicago Trib. 4/30/70. Arch May 25, 2011.
13. "Nixon Urges Scholars to Take Active Role in Communities". Chicago Tribune. 6/5/70. Arch 7/29/17.
14. Elving, Ron, Apr 9,2010."Who Succeed Justice Stevens?". NPR. Sept 11,2021
15. Official Directory: 116th Congress (2019–2020) (PDF). U. S. Gov Printing Office. 2020. p. 870. ISBN 978-0160953866. Archi Sept 13, 2021. Retr March 16, 2016.
16. Goldstein, Amy; Hamburger, Tom (March 27, 2016). "For Merrick Garland, a methodical life of ambition". The Washington Post. p. A1. Retr March 29, 2016.
17. Stolberg, Sheryl Gay; Apuzzo, Matt; Seelye, Katharine Q. (3/27/16). "Garland Is a Deft Navigator of Washington's Legal Circles". NYT. p. A1. Retr March 29, 2016.
18. Parker, Claire E. (3/17/16). "Supreme Court Nominee Maintains Close Harvard Ties". Harvard Crimson. Retr 3/20/16.

19. Rosen, Andy; Ellement, John R. (March 16, 2016). "Obama Supreme Court nominee Garland strong ties to Harvard U". Boston Globe. Retr March 20, 2016.
20. Garland, Merrick Brian (1974). Industrial reorg in Britain; interpret government/ industry relations 1960's (Thesis). Harvard U. OCLC 76985796. Retr 2/22/21
21. Mauro, Tony (March 26, 2018). "How Merrick Garland Landed a Supreme Court Clerkship With Brennan". National Law Journal. Retrieved September 11, 2021.
22. Garland, Merrick B. (1985). "Deregulation Judicial Review". Harvard Law Review. **98** (3): 505–591. doi:10.2307/1340869. ISSN 0017-811X. JSTOR 1340869.
23. Goldstein, Tom (4/26/10). "Potential Nomination of Garland". SCOTUSBlog. Retrieved April 30, 2010.
24. Perry, Stein (8/17/16). "Garland and D.C. politics: His role in voting rights and Marion Barry's imprisonment". Washington Post. Washington DC. Retr 3/18/16.
25. "Washington Insight "LA Times. 7/6/5. Archi 3/23/16.Retr March 16,2016
26. "Merrick B. Garland: Selected Primary Material" (PDF). U.S. Congressional Research Service. 3/17/16. Retrieved 8/27/18.
27. Lee, Carol E.; Peterson, Kristina; Bravin, Jess (March 16, 2016). "Obama Picks Garland to Fill Supreme Court Seat". Wall Street Journal. Retr March 20, 2016.
28. Savage, Charles (4/27/10). "How Bombing Case Helped Shape Career of a Potential Justice". The NYT. Retrieved 4/30/10.
29. "Hon. Merrick B. Garland". Federalist Society. Nov 19, 2012. Retr March 16, 2016
30. "Harvard Board of Overseers election". Harvard Gazette. 6/12/03. Retr 7/1/10.
31. "Board elects officers". Harvard Gazette. April 23, 2009. Retr Sept 11, 2021.
32. "Ratings of Article III Judicial Nominees (105th Congress) (1997–1998)" . ABA Standing Committee, Judiciary Fed. American Bar Association. 1997. Retr 3/1,12.
33. "104th Congress (1995-96):1/4/95-1/3/96: Senate Committee Meetings by Date".1/4/95. Arch Nov 10, 2005.
34. Palazzolo, Joe (3/16/16). "Judge Merrick Garland, In His Own Words". Wall Street Journal. Retr 3/16/16.
35. Lewis, Neil A. (November 30, 1995). "Partisan Gridlock Blocks Senate Confirmations of Federal Judges". NYT ISSN 0362-4331. Retr March 16, 2016.
36. "President Nominates Twenty Two to Federal Bench" (Press release). White House. 1/7/97. Arch 9/23/20.
37. "U.S. Senate: Roll Call Vote: PN6". U.S. Senate. January 27, 2015.
38. Wheaton, Sarah; Gerstein, Josh; Seung Min, Kim (March 16, 2016). "Obama picks Merrick Garland for Supreme Court". Politico. Retrieved March 16, 2016.
39. Steigerwalt, Amy (2010). Battle over Bench: Senators, Interest Groups, and Lower Court Confirmations. University of Virginia Press. p. 224. ISBN 9780813929989.
40. Merrick Garland at the Biographical Directory of Federal Judges, a publication of the Federal Judicial Center. Retr 9/11/21.

Notable cases

Administrative and environmental law

Garland has tended to favor deference to regulatory agencies.[50] For example, in In re Aiken County (2013), Garland dissented when the court issued mandamus ordering the Nuclear Regulatory Commission to process the Yucca Mountain nuclear waste repository license.[51] In Americans for Safe Access v. Drug Enforcement Administration (2013), Garland joined a divided court upholding the DEA's classification of marijuana as a Schedule I drug.[11] According to Goldstein, in a number of split decisions on environmental law Garland "favored contested EPA regulations and actions when challenged by industry, and in other cases he has accepted challenges brought by environmental groups."[23]

Criminal law and whistleblower protection

While on the bench, Garland has shown a tendency to be deferential to the government in criminal cases, siding with prosecutors in ten of the fourteen criminal cases in which he disagreed with a colleague.[54] Garland has taken a broad view of whistleblower protections, such as the False Claims Act (FCA),[56] which creates a private cause of action against those defrauding the federal government.[55]

National security

During Garland's tenure, the D.C. Circuit reviewed cases arising from the Guantanamo Bay detention camp. In al Odah v. United States (2003), a panel that included Garland unanimously held that federal courts could not hear challenges from Guantanamo detainees.[23] In July 2011, Garland wrote for the unanimous panel when it rejected Guantanamo detainee Moath Hamza Ahmed al Alawi's petition for habeas corpus.[59][60] In Parhat v. Gates (2008), Garland wrote for a panel that unanimously overturned the Combatant Status Review Tribunal's determination that a captured Uyghur was enemy combatant.[61]

First Amendment

According to Goldstein, Garland has "tended to take a broader view" of First Amendment rights.[23] In cases involving the Freedom of Information Act and similar provisions related to government transparency, "Garland's rulings reflect a preference for open government."[23]

In ACLU v. CIA (2013), Garland wrote for a panel unanimously rejecting the agency's Glomar response and ordering it to process the ACLU's FOIA request regarding targeted killings by CIA drones.[65] In Cause of Action v. FTC (2015), Garland wrote for a panel unanimously overturning the agency's limitation on FOIA fee waivers to large news outlets.[65]

In Initiative & Referendum Institute v. U.S. Postal Service (2005), Garland wrote for the court, holding that a U.S. Postal Service regulation banning signature-gathering for petitions at post offices violated the First Amendment.[23][66]

54. Savage, Charlie (March 23, 2016). "In Criminal Rulings, Garland Has Usually Sided With Law Enforcement". The New York Times. p. A13. Retr March 24, 2016.
55. Barnes, Robert (3/18/15). "respectful disagreements Judge Merrick Garland". Washington Post. Retr 3/23/16.
56. Loughran, Matthew; Swann, James (March 18, 2016). "Judge Garland Would Be Good for HHS, CMS, Attorneys Say". Bloomberg BNA. Retrieved March 20, 2016.
57. US ex rel. Totten v. Bombardier Corp., 380 F.3d 488 (D.C. Cir. 2004). (citing Henry J. Friendly, Benchmarks (1967)).

58. Palazzolo, Joe (March 17, 2016). "Judge Garland's Career in Dissent". Wall Street Journal. Retr 3/23/16.
59. Recent Case: D.C. Circuit Holds Government's Authority Has Not Unraveled, 132 Harv. L. Rev. 1542 (2019).
60. Al-Alwi v. Obama, 653 F3d 11 (D.C. Cir. 2011).
61. Glaberson, William (June 24, 2008). "Court Voids Finding on Guantánamo Detainee". The NYT. Retrieved June 24, 2008.
62. Richey, Warren (June 27, 2011). "Supreme Court declines to take up Abu Ghraib detainee lawsuit". Christian Science Monitor. Retrieved July 1, 2011.
63. Gibney, Mark (2015). "Litigating Transnational Human Rights Obligations". In Vandenhole, Wouter (ed.). Challenging Territoriality in Human Rights Law: Building Blocks for Plural Diverse Duty-Bearer. Routledge.
p. 103. ISBN 9781317628965.
64. Liptak, Adam (March 18, 2016). "Where Merrick Garland Stands: A Close Look at His Judicial Record". The New York Times. p. A1. Retrieved March 24, 2016.
65. "Judge Merrick Garland's media law cases". Reporters Committee-Freedom of Press. 3/18/16. Retr 6/8/16.
66. Almanac Fed Judiciary. Vol.1. Aspen Publishers. 2011. p.7. ISBN 978-0735568891.

Supreme Court nomination

Garland was considered twice to fill seats on the United States Supreme Court in 2009 and 2010, before finally being nominated in 2016 by President Barack Obama for the seat left vacant by the death of Associate Justice Antonin Scalia.[74]

2009 and 2010 SCOTUS considerations

In 2009, following the announcement by Justice David Souter that he would retire, Garland was considered one of nine finalists, which ultimately went to Sonia Sotomayor, a judge of the Second Circuit.[75]

After the April 2010 announcement by Justice John Paul Stevens that he would retire, Garland was again widely seen as a leading contender for a nomination to the Supreme Court of the United States.[76][77][78] President Obama interviewed Garland, among others, for the vacancy.[48] In May 2010, Senator Orrin Hatch, Republican of Utah, said he would help Obama if Garland was nominated, calling Garland "a consensus nominee" and predicting that Garland would win Senate confirmation with bipartisan support.[79][80] Obama nominated Solicitor General of the U.S. Elena Kagan, who was confirmed in August 2010.[48]

Scalia vacancy and 2016 nomination

On February 13, 2016, Supreme Court Justice Antonin Scalia died.[81] Later that day, Senate Republicans Majority Leader Mitch McConnell issued a statement that they would not consider any nominee put forth by Obama, and a Supreme Court nomination should be left to the next president.[82][83][84]

President Obama responded he intended to "fulfill my constitutional duty to appoint a judge to our highest court,"[85][86] and there was no "well established tradition" that a president could not fill a Supreme Court vacancy during their last year in office.[87]

In early March 2016, The New York Times reported that Garland was being vetted by the Obama administration as a potential nominee. A week later, Garland was named as one of three judges on the President's "short list" (along with Judge Sri Srinivasan, also of the D.C. Circuit, and Judge Paul J. Watford of the Ninth Circuit). Obama interviewed all three leading contenders, as well as two others who were being considered: Judge Jane L. Kelly of the U.S. Court of Appeals for the Eighth Circuit and Judge Ketanji Brown Jackson of the U.S. District Court for the District of Columbia.[88] Soon afterward, Senator Orrin Hatch, President pro tempore of the US Senate and the most senior Republican Senator, predicted that President Obama would "name someone the liberal Democratic base wants" even though he "could easily name Merrick Garland, who is a fine man."[89] Five days later, March 16, Obama nominated Garland to the post of Associate Justice of SCOTUS.[90][91]

Garland had more federal judicial experience than any other Supreme Court nominee in history,[38] and was the oldest Supreme Court nominee since Lewis F. Powell Jr. in 1971.[92] The American Bar Association (ABA) Standing Committee on the Federal Judiciary unanimously rated Garland "well-qualified" (its highest rating) to sit on the Supreme Court.

Senate Republican majority refused to consider Garland nomination.[94][95][96] McConnell's categorical refusal to hold hearings on Garland's was described by political scientists and legal scholars as unprecedented,[95][97][98] McConnell's choice to lead a Republican blockade of the nomination was described as a "culmination of [his] confrontational style,"[99] an example of constitutional hardball.[100]

After a period of 293 days, Garland's nomination expired on January 3, 2017, at the end of the 114th Congress, the 15th nomination to the Supreme Court to lapse at the end of a session of Congress.[102][103] It was the longest pending period of a Supreme Court nominee in history, far exceeding the 125-day delay faced by the ultimately confirmed Justice Louis Brandeis in 1916.[104] On January 31, 2017, President Donald Trump nominated Neil Gorsuch to fill the vacancy.[105] On April 7, 2017, the Senate confirmed Gorsuch's to the Supreme Court.

McConnell went on to boast about stopping Garland's nomination, saying in August 2016, "one of my proudest moments was when I looked Barack Obama in the eye and I said, 'Mr. President, you will not fill the Supreme Court vacancy.'"[106][107] In April 2018, McConnell said the decision not to act upon the Garland nomination was "the most consequential decision I've made in my entire public career".[108]

Attorney General (2021–present)

President-elect Joe Biden selected Garland for the position of United States attorney general, on January 6, 2021.[109][110] He was formally nominated by Biden on January 20, after Biden took office.[111] In Senate Judiciary Committee confirmation hearings, Garland vowed to oversee vigorous prosecution of those who stormed the United States Capitol, and other domestic extremists, drawing on his prosecuting perpetrators of the Oklahoma City bombing.[112][113][114] Garland said it was likely the Biden administration would place a moratorium on use of the federal death penalty and expressed reservations about the death penalty in light of the "almost randomness or arbitrariness of its application."[114] He pledged to protect equal justice under law and reinvigorate the DOJ Civil Rights Division, which, according to some media figures, languished under the Trump administration.[113][115] Garland affirmed that the Justice Department would remain independent under his leadership.[114] The Senate Judiciary Committee voted 15–7 to advance Garland's nomination to the Senate floor,[116][117] and on March 10, the Senate confirmed Garland's nomination by a vote of 70–30.[118][112][119] He was sworn in on March 11, 2021, by Assistant AG for Administration Lee Lofthus.[120]

In April 2021, Russia imposed sanctions against Garland, including prohibiting him from entering Russia. Retaliation was for U.S. expulsion of 10 Russian diplomats, a sanction imposed by the U.S. against Russia for its SolarWinds hack, aggression against Ukraine, and interference in the 2020 U.S. election.[121]

In May 2021, the DOJ appealed in part a ruling by Judge Amy Berman Jackson of the District Court for the District of Columbia to make public most of a DOJ memo detailing former AG Bill Barr's rationale for clearing Trump of obstruction of justice in the Special Counsel investigation.[122][123][124][125]

On June 7, 2021, the Justice Department continued its defense of a defamation lawsuit by E. Jean Carroll, arguing that President Trump could not be sued because he had denied her rape allegation in offending statements in his capacity as president. Garland had been deeply involved in the decision. The White House quickly distanced itself from the decision.[122][123][126] Garland in a House Judiciary Committee hearing on October 21 stated that the DOJ's briefing was solely on the question of the application of the Federal Tort Claims Act.[127][128]

On July 1, 2021, Garland imposed a moratorium on all federal executions pending a review of relevant policies and procedures.[129] The review will examine "the risk of pain and suffering associated with the use of pentobarbital," and "December 2020 and January 2021 changes to expedite execution of capital sentences."[129][130][131]

This was consistent with Biden's pledge to push for legislation to end the federal death penalty. Garland has continued to pursue the death penalty in cases wherein a previous administration had sought the death penalty against terrorists.[132] Trump administration resumed federal executions in 2019, and executed 13 inmates, first in 17 years, including the first woman in 70 years.[130][131]

Voting rights

In June 2021, Garland pledged to double the department's enforcement staff for protecting the right to vote, in response to Republican Party efforts to restrict voting following the 2020 presidential election,[133][134] The same month, Garland announced a DOJ lawsuit against the state of Georgia over its newly passed restrictions on voting; the DOJ complaint said that the state targeted Black Americans in violation of the Voting Rights Act of 1965.[135]

In July 2021, the Justice Department released two guidance documents re: election law and post-election audits, reminding states that DOJ was closely observing states' compliance with federal election and civil rights laws.[122][136][137]

In November 2021, DOJ sued Texas over Senate Bill 1 which required rejection of mail ballots "for immaterial errors and omissions," alleging it would restrict voting for those with limited English proficiency, soldiers deployed, voters overseas.[138][139]

In a separate suit by DOJ against Texas the following month, the federal government alleged Texas' redistricting plans discriminated against Latino and Black voters in violation of the Section 2 of the Voting Rights Act.[140][141][142][143]

Civil rights

During Garland's tenure as AG, Justice Department emphasized protection of civil rights.[144] Garland rescinded a Trump administration policy (imposed by Jeff Sessions) that curtailed DOJ investigations into police department misconduct ("pattern-and-practice" investigations) and restricted consent decrees to reform police departments.[144][145][146]

On April 21, 2021, Garland announced DOJ was opening a pattern-and-practice investigation of Minneapolis Police Dept after the murder of George Floyd, examining use of force, its treatment of people with behavioral health issues, and the department's current accountability systems.[147] On April 26, Garland announced another investigation into the Louisville Metro Police Department in the aftermath of the killing of Breonna Taylor, examining the execution of search warrants.[148][149] On August 5, Garland opened another investigation into the Phoenix Police Dept over its policies on dealing with the homeless.[150][151]

On December 3, DOJ opened another investigation into Mount Vernon Police Dept to assess if it engaged in discriminatory policing, involving use of force, strip, and body cavity searches, how it handles evidence, and accountability.[152][153]

In June 2021, DOJ, Deputy AG Lisa Monaco, reversed a Trump-era policy that banned federal officers/agents from body-worn cameras; the memo mandated use of body-worn cameras for federal law enforcement in certain circumstances (including carrying out planned arrests or search warrants).[154][155][156]

On September 14, 2021, DOJ announced a civil investigation into prisons in Georgia, focusing on prison violence and sexual abuse of LGBTQ prisoners by prisoners and staff, continuing an initial investigation launched in 2016.[157][158][159]

In September 2021, the DOJ in a memo limited the use of chokeholds and carotid restraints by federal officers during arrests, (i.e., unless the officer reasonably believes "that the subject of such force poses an imminent danger of death or serious physical injury to the officer or to another person").

The memo also limited the use of unannounced ("no-knock") entries when executing warrants, directing officers to knock-and-announce except "where an agent has reasonable grounds to believe that knocking and announcing the agent's presence would create an imminent threat of physical violence to the agent and/or another person."[160][161][162]

On October 13, 2021, the DOJ launched another investigation into five juvenile detention facilities in Texas for systemic physical or sexual abuse of children.[158][163]

January 6 U.S. Capitol attack

On July 26, 2021, DOJ sent letters to former DOJ officials of the Trump administration, including Acting Attorney General Jeffrey A. Rosen, Acting Deputy Attorney General Richard Donoghue, Associate Deputy Attorney General Patrick Hovakimian, U.S. Attorney for the Northern District of Georgia Byung J. "BJay" Pak, Acting U.S. Attorney for the Northern District of Georgia Bobby L. Christine, and United States Assistant Attorney General for the Environment and Natural Resources Division and Civil Division Jeffrey Clark.[164] The letters relayed that DOJ would not exert executive privilege over their testimony as witnesses to Trump's attempts to overturn the 2020 US presidential election or the 2021 US Capitol attack, and that they were free to provide "unrestricted testimony" "irrespective of potential privilege" to House Oversight Committee and Senate Judiciary Committee.[164][165][166][167]

On July 28, 2021, the DOJ further rejected Rep. Mo Brooks's request to protect him in Eric Swalwell's civil lawsuit against him and President Trump concerning his comments and actions in the attack. The DOJ in a court filing determined Brooks' relevant comments and actions were outside his official responsibilities as a member of Congress.[168]

On October 21, 2021, the U.S. House of Representatives voted to refer Steve Bannon, to the DOJ for criminal contempt of Congress due to defying a subpoena from the House's January 6 select committee over claims of executive privilege. After Speaker Nancy Pelosi certified the contempt referral, it was sent to the U.S. Attorney for DC, who will then decide whether to send the referral to a grand jury for indictment, with Garland having the final say.[169] He stated that "the Department of Justice will do what it always does, we'll apply facts and law and make a decision, consistent with principles of prosecution."[127][128][169][170]

Days after Trump announced his 2024 presidential campaign, Garland appointed Jack Smith, special counsel for investigations of Trump.[171][172]

Robert Hur report

On February 8, 2024, the Department of Justice released a report authored by special counsel Robert Hur into President Biden's handling of classified documents, concluding charges were not necessary in the incident. As reasoning not to charge Biden, the report mentioned perceived problems with memory and mental acuity.[173]

Garland has been criticized by supporters of Biden and some former prosecutors for his decision to release Hur's report referring to Biden as an "elderly man with a poor memory." They alleged that Hur's report included gratuitous language about Biden that could be used to reinforce perceptions that Biden is fading mentally and physically.[174]

Associate deputy AG Bradley Weinsheimer, rejected criticisms, stating the report's comments "fall within the department's standards for public release".[175] Garland said Hur never proposed an investigative step he found inappropriate.[176]

Pace of Trump prosecution - - Smith special counsel investigation

Garland has been criticized for the pace of the prosecution of former president Donald Trump. Some observers, reportedly including President Joe Biden, assign him some responsibility for the fact that none of the indictments obtained by special counsel Jack Smith are likely to go to trial before the November 2024 election.[177]

California Representative Adam Schiff is quoted as saying "The department bears some of that responsibility."[178] Others have defended Garland, such as Marcy Wheeler, who cited "unavoidable" delays caused by the COVID-19 pandemic, use of encrypted messaging apps by defendants, and invocations of attorney–client and executive privilege claims that needed to be litigated before any case could go to trial, while highlighting avoidable delays caused by the January 6 committee, which pushed back the Proud Boys trial by several months.[179]

School board memo

In October 2021, Garland issued a memo addressing an "increase in harassment, intimidation, and threats of violence against school administrators, board members, teachers, and staff"; the memo directed FBI and US attorneys' to set up meetings with federal, state and local law enforcement to establish tiplines for threat reporting and discussing strategies to address threats.[180][181][127][182] He issued the memo after National School Boards Association wrote Biden to request whether they constitute domestic terrorism and hate crimes.[183][184][185][186]

The memo prompted criticism from Republicans in House and Senate, who accused Garland of treating parents like domestic terrorists.[182] McConnell wrote Garland that parents "absolutely should be telling" local schools what to teach regarding contentious public issues.[181][187] In House and Senate Judiciary Committee hearings, Garland pushed back on claims that DOJ were treating parents like "domestic terrorists" and investigating political speech, testifying the DOJ "[were] not investigating peaceful protest or parent involvement at school board meetings."[127][128][188][189] Senate Republicans called on Garland to resign over the memo.[190] Seventeen Republican state attorneys general, numerous House Republicans, wrote Biden and Garland requesting withdrawal.[182][186][188]

Contempt of congress charges

The House Judiciary Committee and the House Oversight Committee issued subpoenas for Garland to turn over materials on Hur's investigation, particularly audio of Hur's interview with Biden.[191][192] Biden subsequently invoked executive privilege to block the release of materials, preventing Garland from turning them over.[193] On June 12, 2024, Garland was held in contempt by the House of Representatives for defying the subpoenas and refusing to disclose audio of Hur's interview with Biden.[194] The DOJ stated Garland cannot be prosecuted for contempt due to Biden's invocation of executive privilege.[195]

Speaker Johnson said he will move in federal court to enforce a subpoena against Garland to obtain audio recordings of Biden, after DOJ declined to act.[196]

Three lawsuits have been filed by organizations seeking access to audio recordings of the Biden interview. Judicial Watch, Heritage Foundation and CNN are plaintiffs in the lawsuits, based on failure of DOJ to provide audio in response to Freedom of Information Act requests. CNN's lawsuit is joined by eleven news organizations. Three lawsuits are consolidated and pending before Judge Kelly.[197]

74. Harris, Gardiner (3/16/16). "Garland, Third Time Was Charm". NYT. Retr 3/20/16.
75. Baker, Peter; Nagourney, Adam (May 27, 2009). "Sotomayor Pick a Product of Lessons From Past Battles". The NYT. Arch March 16, 2015. Retr June 1, 2009.
76. "Profiles of three possible successors to Justice John Paul Stevens". Los Angeles Times. April 10, 2010. Archived on January 9, 2021. Retrieved May 12, 2010.
77. de Vogue, Ariane (February 4, 2010). "White House Prepares for Possibility of 2 Supreme Court Vacancies". ABC News. Retrieved March 1, 2010.
78. Bravin, Jess (February 8, 2010). "Democrats Divide on Voice of Possible Top-Court Pick". The Wall Street Journal. Retrieved March 1, 2010.
79. Ferraro, Tho (5/6/10). "Republicans back Garland, SCOTUS" Reuters. 3/16/16.
80. Burr, Thomas (March 16, 2016). "White House notes Hatch called Supreme Court nominee a 'consensus' pick in 2010". Salt Lake Tribune. Retrieved March 16, 2016.
81. Hirschfeld Davis, Julie (March 4, 2016). "Three More Judges Said to be Vetted for Supreme Court". The New York Times. Arch August 24, 2018. Retrieved Feb 11, 2017.
82. Everett, Burgess (February 13, 2016). "McConnell throws down the gauntlet: No Scalia replacement under Obama". Politico. Arch Sept 19, 2020. Retr March 16, 2016.
83. Chait, Jonathan (February 23, 2016). "No, the Senate's Supreme Court Blockade Has Never Happened in American History". New York. Retrieved March 1, 2016.
84. McAuliff, Michael; Bendery, Jennifer (March 10, 2016). "Republican Admits Supreme Court Blockade Unprecedented". The Huffington Post. Retr March 30, 2016.
85. Obama, Barack (Feb 24, 2016). "Responsibility I Take Seriously". SCOTUSBlog.
86. Liptak, Adam (February 24, 2016). "Obama's Scotusblog Post: Reading Between the Lines". The New York Times. Retrieved March 1, 2016.
87. Ramsey, David (Feb 24, 2016). "President Obama responds to Mitch McConnell on Supreme Court vacancy". Arkansas Times. Retr March 1, 2016. The one thing I think is important to dispel is any notion . . . well established tradition, or constitutional principle, that a president in his last year in office cannot fill a Supreme Court vacancy.
88. Totenberg, Nina (3/8/20/16). "Obama Meets SCOTUS Candidates". Retr 3/30/16.
89. Shepherd, Alex (March 16, 2016). "Orrin Hatch once said there was "no question" Garland could be confirmed to Supreme Court". New Republic. Retr Sept 11, 2021.
90. Shear, Michael D.; Harris, Gardiner (March 16, 2016). "Obama Chooses Garland for Supreme Court". The NYT. Archived on March 16, 2016. Retrieved Feb 11, 2017.
91. Eilperin, Juliet; DeBonis, Mike; Markon, Jerry (3/16/16). "President Obama nominates Garland to the Supreme Court". The Washington Post. Retr Sept 11, 2021.
92. Roeder, Oliver (March 16, 2016). "Merrick Garland Is The Oldest Supreme Court Nominee Since Nixon Was President". FiveThirtyEight. Retrieved September 11, 2021.
93. "Ratings Article III and IV Judicial Nominees (114th Congress)" (PDF). American Bar Association Standing Committee on Federal Judiciary. 2016. Retr 9/11/21.
94. Totenberg, Nina (September 6, 2016). "170-Plus Days And Counting: GOP Unlikely To End Supreme Court Blockade Soon". NPR. Arch 9/30/18. Retr 9/11/21

95. Liptak, Adam (June 14, 2016). "Study Calls Snub of Obama's Supreme Court Pick Unprecedented" The NYT. Retr Sept 11, 2021. After a comprehensive look at every past Supreme Court vacancy, two law professors concluded it is an unprecedented development ... That categorical stance is new in nation's history, professors, Robin Bradley Kar, Jason Mazzone, a study published online by New York U Law Review.
96. McConnell, Mitch (March 16, 2016). "McConnell On Supreme Court Nomination". republicanleader.senate.gov. Retrieved September 21, 2020.
97. Schier, Steven E.; Eberly, Todd E. (2017). Trump Presidency: Outsider in Oval Office. Rowman & Littlefield. p. 71. ISBN 9781538105757. Arch 9/11/21. Retr 10/11/18.
98. Handelsman Shugerman, Jed (2019). "Constitutional Hardball vs. Beanball: Identifying Antidemocratic Tactics". Columbia Law Review. Archi, Retr May 30, 2019.
99. Ashbee, Edward; Dumbrell, John, eds. (2017). The Obama Presidency and the Politics of Change. Palgrave Macmillan. pp. 55, 62. doi:10.1007/978-3-319-41033-3. ISBN 978-3-319-41032-
6. Archived Nov 30, 2018. Retrieved October 6, 2018.
100. Fishkin, Joseph; Pozen, David E. (2018). "Asymmetric Constitutional Hardball". Columbia Law Review. Vol. 118, no. 3. Arch Jan 19, 2019. Retr September 11, 2021.
101. Mounk, Yascha (2018). The People vs. Democracy. Harvard University Press. ISBN 9780674976825. Archived Nov 27, 2018. Retrieved March 14, 2019.
102. Bravin, Jess (Jan 3, 2017). "President Obama's Supreme Court Nomination of Merrick Garland Expires". Wall Street Journal. Arch 3-10, 2017 Retr 9-11, 2021.
103. McMillion, Barry. "Supreme Court Nominations, 1789 to 2020: Actions by Senate, Judiciary Committee, President". Congressional Research Service. Retr June 5, 2024.
104. Martin, Phillip (July 18, 2016). "Obama's SCOTUS Nominee Suffers Longest Confirmation Delay in History". Progress Texas. Retrieved January 22, 2021.
105. Barnes, Robert (Jan 31, 2017). "Trump picks Colo. appeals court judge Neil Gorsuch for Supreme Court". Washington Post. Arch Feb 1, 2017. Retr Feb 1, 2017.
106. Scarce, Ed (Aug 9, 2016). "Mitch McConnell: Proud Moment When Told Obama 'You Will Not Fill Vacancy'". Crooks and Liars. Archi July 12,2018. Retr Aug 2, 2018.
107. Roarty, Alex (August 8, 2016). "Tea Party-Aligned Kentucky Gov May End 95-Year Democratic Reign". rollcall.com. Arch August 22, 2016. Retr August 21, 2016.
108. Alford, Roger (April 3, 2018). "McConnell on midterm elections: 'The wind is going to be in our face'". Kentucky Today. Archived April 4, 2018. Retr April 5, 2018.
109. "Judge Garland, Attorney General". Buildbackbetter.gov. Arch, Retr Jan 7, 2021.
110. Bravin, Jess; Gurman, Sadie; Viswanatha, Aruna (January 6, 2021). "Biden to Name Merrick Garland as Attorney General". The Wall Street Journal.
111. "PN78-7 – Merrick Brian Garland – Department of Justice". 117th Congress. March 10, 2021. Retrieved September 11, 2021 – via Congress.gov.
112. Benner, Katie (March 10, 2021). "Merrick Garland Is Confirmed as Attorney General". The New York Times. Archived from the original on December 28, 2021.
113. Pengelly, Martin (February 21, 2021). "Merrick Garland vows to target white supremacists as attorney general". The Guardian. Retrieved September 11, 2021.
114. Tucker, Eric; Jalonick, Mary Clare; Balsamo, Michael (Feb 23, 2021). "Garland vows sharp focus on Capitol riot as attorney general". AP. Retr Sept 12, 2021.
115. Wolfe, Jan; Lynch, Sarah N. (February 20, 2021). "Biden's attorney general nominee Garland vows to prioritize civil rights". Reuters. Retrieved March 11, 2021.
116. Shabad, Rebecca (March 1, 2021). "Senate committee advances Merrick Garland's nomination for attorney general". NBC News. Retrieved March 1, 2021.
117. Higgins, Tucker (March 1, 2021). "Merrick Garland's nomination to be attorney general advances to full Senate". CNBC. Retrieved March 10, 2021.
118. "On the Nomination (Confirmation: Merrick Brian Garland, of Maryland, to be Attorney General)". U.S. Senate. March 10, 2021. Retrieved March 11, 2021.
119. Rogers, Alex (3/10/21). "Senate confirms Garland AG". CNN. Retr 3/11 /21.
120. @TheJusticeDept (March 11, 2021). "Judge Merrick Garland takes his oath of office as

the 86th Attorney General of the United States as he is sworn in by Assistant AG for Administration Lee Lofthus" (Tweet). Retr March 11, 2021 – via Twitter.
121. "Russia retaliates US expulsions". BBC. April 16, 2021. Retr Sept 11, 2021.
122. Perez, Evan (July 28, 2021). "Liberals may end up liking much of Garland's Justice Department after all". CNN. Retrieved July 29, 2021.
123. Benner, Katie (July 9, 2021). "Garland Settles In but Trump Era Still Shadows the Justice Dept". The New York Times. ISSN 0362-4331. Retrieved July 29, 2021.
124. Savage, Charlie (May 25,2021). "Justice Dept. Fight to keep secret a Barr memo whether Trump obstructed Russia inquiry". NYT. ISSN 0362-4331. Retr July 29, 2021.
125. Schmidt, Michael (May 4, 2021). "Judge Says Barr Misled on How His Dept. View Trump's Actions". NYT . ISSN 0362-4331. Arch May 4, 2021. Retr July 29, 2021
126. Feuer, Alan; Weiser, Benjamin (June 8, 2021). "Biden Justice Dept Seeks to Defend Trump in Suit Over Rape Denial". NYT. ISSN 0362-4331. Retr July 29, 2021.
127. Sneed, Tierney (October 31, 2021). "Takeaways from Merrick Garland's hearing with the House Judiciary Committee". CNN. Retrieved October 21, 2021.
128. Sneed, Tierney (October 21, 2021). "Garland: DOJ 'will apply the facts and the law' when considering Bannon referral". CNN. Retrieved October 21, 2021.
129. "AG Merrick B. Garland Imposes a Moratorium on Federal Executions; Orders Review of Policies and Procedures". justice.gov (Press release). 71/21. Retr 7/29/21.
130. Swanson, Ian (7/1/21). "Garland moratorium on federal executions". The Hill.
131. Lynch, Sarah N.; Beech, Eric (July 1, 2021). "U.S. attorney general imposes moratorium on federal executions". Reuters. Retrieved July 29, 2021.
132. Weiser, Benjamin (January 7, 2023). "Suspect in Bike Path Killing Faces First Death Penalty Trial Under Biden". NYT. ISSN 0362-4331. Retrieved January 8, 2023.
133. "Attorney General Merrick B. Garland Delivered a Policy Address Regarding Voting Rights". justice.gov. June 11, 2021. Retrieved June 12, 2021.
134. Phillips, Kristine (June 11, 2021). "AG Merrick Garland vows to protect voting rights, beef up DOJ civil rights division". USA TODAY. Retrieved June 12, 2021.
135. Cole, Devan; Carrega, Christina; Schouten, Fredreka; Perez, Evan; de Vogue, Ariane; Gallagher, Dianne "Justice Dept sue Ga., vote restrictions". CNN. (6/25/21).
136. "Justice Dept Issues Guidance on Federal Statutes Re Voting Methods and Post-Election "Audits"". justice.gov (Press release). July 28, 2021. Retrieved July 29, 2021.
137. Sneed, Tierney (July 28, 2021). "Justice Department puts states on notice about post-election audits and election law changes". CNN. Retrieved July 29, 2021.
138. "Justice Department Files Lawsuit Against the State of Texas to Protect Voting Rights". justice.gov (Press release). November 4, 2021. Retrieved November 5, 2021.
139. Perez, Evan (11/4/21). "Justice Dept sues Tx, vote restrictions". CNN. Retr 5/5/21
140. "Justice Department Files Lawsuit Against State of Texas to Challenge Statewide Redistricting Plans". justice.gov (Press release). Dec 6, 2021.Retr Dec 9, 2021
141 "AG Garland Delivers Remarks Announcing Lawsuit Against State of Texas to Challenge Statewide Redistricting Plan". justice.gov. Dec 6, 2021. Retr Dec 9, 2021.
142. Timm, Jane C. (December 6, 2021). "In lawsuit, DOJ says Texas voting maps discriminate against Black and Latino voters". NBC News. Retrieved Dec 9, 2021.
143. Sneed, Tierney; Carrega, Christina (December 6, 2021). "DOJ sues Texas over Republican-approved redistricting maps". CNN. Retrieved December 29, 2021.
144. Balsamo, Michael (April 17, 2021). "Garland rescinds Trump-era memo curtailing consent decrees". Associated Press. Retrieved September 11, 2021.
145. Benner, Katie (April 16, 2021). "Justice Dept. Restores Use of Consent Decrees for Police Abuses". The New York Times. Retrieved September 11, 2021.

146. Carrega, Christina; Cole, Devan (August 5, 2021). "DOJ opens investigation how Phoenix Police Dept treats city's homeless residents". CNN. Retrieved August 6, 2021.
147. Balsamo, Michael; Forliti, Amy (April 21, 2021). "Garland announces sweeping police probe after Floyd verdict". Associated Press. Retrieved October 15, 2021.
148. Farivar, Masood (April 26, 2021). "2nd Police Department Under Investigation Following Chauvin Conviction". Voice of America. Retrieved October 15, 2021.

149. Levine, Mike; Mallin, Alexander (April 26, 2021). "AG Garland announces investigation of Louisville PD's policing practices". ABC News. Retrieved Oct 15, 2021.
150. Nakamura, David (August 5, 2021). "Justice Dept. opens civil rights investigation into Phoenix police dept". Washington Post. ISSN 0190-8286. Retr Oct 15, 2021.
151. "Justice Department Announces Investigation of City of Phoenix and Phoenix Police Department". justice.gov (Press release). August 5, 2021. Retr Oct 15, 2021.
152. "Justice Department Launches Investigation of the Mount Vernon Police Department". justice.gov (Press release). December 3, 2021. Retr Dec 10, 2021.
153. Reimann, Nicholas (Dec 3, 2021). "Feds Launch Sweeping Probe Of Suburban N.Y. Police Department Over Discrimination Claims". Forbes. Retrieved Dec 10, 2021.
154. Carrega, Christina; Campbell, Josh (June 7, 2021). "DOJ ends policy that prohibited federal officers from using body-worn cameras". CNN. Retr Sept 16, 2021.
155. Zapotosky, Matt (June 7, 2021). "Justice Dept. will require law enforcement to use body cameras in certain circumstances". The Washington Post. Archived 10/10/22
156. "Justice Department Announces First Federal Agents to Use Body-Worn Cameras". justice.gov (Press release). Sept 1, 2021. Retrieved Sept 16, 2021.
157. Carrega, Christina (September 14, 2021). "Justice Department announces investigation into Georgia prisons". CNN. Retrieved October 21, 2021.
158. Sneed, Tierney (October 20, 2021). "'Big, big shifts': How Biden's civil rights pros have reoriented the Justice Department". CNN. Retrieved October 21, 2021.
159. "Justice Department Announces Investigation into Conditions in Georgia Prisons". justice.gov (Press release). Sept 14, 2021. Retrieved Oct 21, 2021.
160. "Department of Justice Announces Department-Wide Policy on Chokeholds and 'No-Knock' Entries". justice.gov (Press release). Sept 14, 2021. Retr Sept 16, 2021.
161. Carrega, Christina; Nickeas, Peter (September 14, 2021). "Justice Department limits use of chokeholds and 'no-knock' warrants". CNN. Retrieved Sept 16, 2021.
162. Tucker, Emma (Sept 15, 2021). "Bans on chokeholds for federal officers latest in nationwide push to hold police to a 'higher standard'". CNN. Retr Sept 16, 2021.
163. "Justice Department Announces Investigation into Conditions at Five Juvenile Facilities in Texas". justice.gov (Press release). Oct 13, 2021. Retrieved Oct 21, 2021.
164. Weinsheimer, Bradley (7/26/21). "Testimony to Congress" (PDF). Letter to Jeffrey A. Rosen. Arch (PDF) July 27, 2021. Retr August 27, 2021 – via justsecurity.org.
165. Perez, Evan (July 27, 2021). "Trump officials can testify on former President's actions leading to insurrection, Justice Department decides". CNN. Retr July 30, 2021
166. Benner, Katie (July 27, 2021). "Trump officials can testify into efforts to subvert election outcome/Jan 6, Justice Dept. says". NYT. ISSN 0362-4331. Retr 7/30/21
167. Swan, Betsy Woodruff; Desiderio, Andrew (July 27, 2021). "DOJ: Former Trump officials can testify about Jan 6 Capitol attack". Politico. Retrieved July 30, 2021.
168. Cohen, Marshall; Sneed, Tierney (July 28, 2021). "DOJ won't protect GOP Rep. Mo Brooks in insurrection lawsuit". CNN. Retrieved July 29, 2021.
169. Foran, Clare; Cohen, Zachary; Nobles, Ryan (October 21, 2021). "House votes to hold Steve Bannon in contempt for defying subpoena". CNN. Retr Oct 21, 2021.
170. Sneed, Tierney; Schneider, Jessica (Oct 20, 2021). "Bannon contempt vote puts AG Garland in center of legal and political storm". CNN. Retr Oct 21, 2021.
171. Gerstein, Josh; Cheney, Kyle (November 18, 2022). "Garland names Jack Smith special counsel for Trump criminal probes". Politico. Retrieved November 18, 2022.
172 Thrush, Glenn; Savage, Charlie; Haberman, Maggie; Feuer, Alan (Nov 18, 2022). "Garland Names Special Counsel for Trump Inquiries". NYT. Retrieved Nov 19, 2022.
173. Swan, Betsy Woodruff (February 8, 2024). "Special counsel passes on charging Biden but paints damning portrait of him". Politico. Retrieved August 20, 2024.
174. Gerstein, Josh. "Garland: 'Absurd' to think he should've censored special counsel report on Biden". Politico. Retrieved June 7, 2024.
175. Savage, Charlie (February 15, 2024). "White House Clashed With Justice Dept. Over Special Counsel Report". NYT. Arch Feb 15, 2024. Retr Feb 15, 2024.
176. Gurman, Sadie; Barber, C. Ryan (Feb 10, 2024). "Special Counsel Expected Heat for

Biden Inquiry. Report Sparked Inferno". WSJ. Arch&Retr Feb 10, 2024
177. Lemire, Jonathan (2/9/24). "White House frustration Garland grows". Politico.
178. Thrush, Glenn (3/22/24). "Inside Garland's Effort to Prosecute Trump". NYT
179. Wheeler, Marcy (March 6, 2024). "Opinion | Merrick Garland isn't to blame for delays in Trump's election interference case". MSNBC. Retrieved August 20, 2024.
180. "Justice Department Addresses Violent Threats Against School Officials and Teachers". justice.gov (Press release). October 4, 2021. Retrieved October 21, 2021.
181. LeBlanc, Paul (Oct 9, 2021). "McConnell challenges Garland, effort to address threats re: public school board members and teachers". CNN. Retr Oct 21, 2021
182. Feuer, Alan (November 5, 2021). "'I Don't Want to Die for It': School Board Members Face Rising Threats". New York Times. Retrieved June 21, 2022.
183. "NSBA, AASA Joint Statement for End to Threats and Violence, Safe School Opening Decisions". National School Boards Assoc. Sept 22, 2021. Retr Oct 28, 2021.
184. "National School Boards Assoc Asks Federal Assistance to Stop Threats and Acts of Violence Against Education Leaders". . Sept 30, 2021. Retr Oct 28, 2021.
185. "National School Boards Assoc Statement in Response to Justice Department Action to Address Threats Against School Personnel". Oct 4, 2021. Retr Oct 28, 2021.
186. Quilantan, Bianca (October 25, 2021). "School board group backtracks on letter for security help from DOJ". Politico. Retrieved October 28, 2021.
187. Kennedy, Brigid (Oct 21, 2021). "9 House Republicans vote with Democrats to hold Bannon in contempt for defying Jan. 6 subpoena". The Week. Retr Oct 21, 2021.
188. Perez, Evan; Sneed, Tierney (Oct 26, 2021). "Garland faces relentless GOP pressure after issuing memo on school board threats". CNN. Retr Oct 28, 2021.
189. Sneed, Tierney (Oct 27, 2021). "AG Garland defends memo responding to threats of violence against school board members". CNN. Retr Oct 28, 2021.
190. "GOP senators erupt at Garland in heated hearing. Cooper says they misrepresent the facts". CNN. October 28, 2021. Retrieved October 28, 2021.
191. " DOJ rejects GOP bid audio of Biden interview". CBS. April 8, 2024.
192. "GOP advances Garland contempt charges after White House exerts executive privilege over Biden audio". Associated Press. May 17, 2024.
193. "As Congress threatens contempt for Garland, White House says Hur tapes are privileged". Washington Post. May 16, 2024.
194. "House GOP holds Garland in contempt, DOJ feud". Politico. June 12, 2024.
195. "DOJ says Garland not be prosecuted Biden-Hur audio". The Hill. June 12, 2024.
196. Sneed, Tierney (June 14, 2024). "Johnson says House will go to court for Biden recordings after DOJ says it won't prosecute Garland`". CNN. CNN. Retr 6/17/24
197. Gerstein, Josh (May 17, 2024). "Conservative group tries to accelerate court fight over Biden-Hur audio". Politico. Retrieved June 17, 2024.

By any means of evaluation, Garland is in violation of "conflict of interest" on many counts and should resign as a result of the ongoing Trump cases.

Nearly every paragraph of Garland career indicates opposition to Republicans. Then Garland finds Jack Smith and his innate ability to push failed cases by lower courts, only to be reversed by SCOTUS.

Could it be Garland that has emerged as the force that has coordinated countless cases against Trump. Are these cases bad Judicature, or 198 instances of Conflict of Interest by democrats, or an outright instance of Treason?

Are we witnessing an instance in which one of the three branches of government specified by America's Founding Fathers has fully and completely lost the way forward?

It seems abundantly clear from the many cases against Donald Trump, along with the clear conflict of interest on the part of all investigators, Prosecutors, and Judges deployed against Donald Trump, we must find the correct fix so that these issues never occur again.

CHAPTER 14. CONFLICT OF INTEREST AGAINST TRUMP

This chapter will detail the extent of Conflict of Interest this Judiciary has applied to Donald Trump. In previous chapters, we provided many pages of text dealing with those specific Judicial traits that fly in the face of conservative standards. In this chapter, we will indicate specifics applying to each of the judges. The end result will indicate some 200 points of conflict of interest contrary to Donald Trump.

Ursula Ungaro, Steele Dossier allowed to print

Judge Ungaro is a Cuban-American, born in Miami. We have no information on her parents' immigration status, nor that of her husband. Ungaro is not a Cuban name. She was appointed by President George Bush. Her notable cases are leftist:

- ruled that an Establishment Clause challenge to Congress's 1954 addition of the words "under God" in the Pledge of Allegiance was "so patently lacking in merit as to be frivolous." A California Court overturned her leftist ruling.
- an order issued by Florida Governor Rick Scott to randomly drug test 80,000 Florida state workers was unconstitutional.
- Allowed publication of the STEELE DOSSIER while intelligence agencies of USA and Great Britian declared nothing of merit was contained.

It is clear the actions of Judge Ungaro in the Steele matter would become the launch point for all unfounded cases against Trump.

Judge Lewis Kaplan, case of E. Jean Carrol against Trump

- Long serving Judge in New York.
- Appointed by Bill Clinton.
- Democrat
- Minority Ethnicity
- Judge in the E. Jean Carrol case of sexual abuse and defamation. This was a case of "he said, she said" having zero witnesses, yet Trump was convicted. As for the "defamation" charge, clearly, we are allowed to defend ourselves, therefore, Trump was within rights under US Constitution to state his case.
- In a case called "Sullivan," politicians have long been granted broadened "free speech," yet this judge decided against Trump.
- The American Prospect, by Walker Bragman, David Sirota--July 14, 2020 -- "The Government Gave Big Oil the Power to Prosecute Its Biggest Critic". July 14, 2020. (Case against CHEVRON partners)
- He married former NYT reporter and former vice president of Random House Lesley Oelsner on February 29, 2004.[5] NYT is known to support Democrats.

Linda V. Parker (Case to overturn Michigan general election Dec. 2020)

- Appointed by President Obama
- Worked little but Civil Rights cases prior to Judgeship
- Minority Ethnicity
- Democrat
- Dismissed Case to overturn Michigan election, saying it was full of "theories, conjecture and speculation" adding "the people of Michigan have spoken."[7]
- On August 25, 2021, Parker ruled "Plaintiffs' counsel filed this lawsuit in bad faith and for improper purpose", sanctioned those attorneys

Ballotpedia list of AWARDS AND ACHIEVEMENTS:

- 2009: Oakland County NAACP Freedom Fighter Award
- 2008: National Association of Human Rights Workers
- 2008: Salute to Diversity Award - Diversity Business Leader, CORP! Magazine
- 2008: Women of Courage Women of Change Award,
- 2007: Professional Woman of the Year, Detroit Club National Association of Negro Business and Professional Women's Clubs
- 2006: Women of Achievement Award, Anti-Defamation League

Associations

- 2013: Board Member, Cesar Chavez Academy
- 2004-Present: Board Member, Michigan Roundtable for Diversity & Inclusion
- 2003-2006, 2008-Present: Active Board Member and Advisory Board Member, American Civil Liberties Union of Michigan

Judge Emmett Sullivan   A case against General Flynn

Early in career, Sullivan appeared even-handed, which went away during the Flynn trial, which was charged upon Steele Dossier, now proven the dossier was garbage.

- Minority Ethnicity
- Democrat
- Allowed Flynn to plead guilty
- Did not wish to hear a redaction of the guilty plea
- Found Flynn guilty and sentenced him
- Appeals Court ordered Sullivan to dismiss the case against Flynn
- Sullivan appeals to the entire DC Court
- In 8-2 decision, DC Appeals Court orders to proceed. 8 democrats- 2 republican
- In 2020, DOJ ordered case dismissed (Steele Dossier discredited)

Judge Amit Mehta   Jan 06 cases

- Minority Ethnicity
- Democrat
- Born in India.
- Judge on the US Foreign Intelligence Surveillance Court.
- Many FISA actions launched against Trump and Trump Appointees
- FISA is slated for Congressional removal.
- Ordered Trump to disclose Financial Records.
- India born; he rejected Trump immunity claims entrenched in Constitution.

Alvin Bragg and the Trump Cases

- Ethnic Minority
- Democrat
- Took Trump to Court on White House policies
- Took Trump to Court on Trump Charitable Foundation
- As candidate for District Attorney, he cited work against Trump
- As DA, ordered prosecutors NOT TO SEEK JAIL time for low level offenses
- Police and Democrats say Bragg soft against crime.
- GOP Gov. Candidate Zeldin promised to remove Bragg if elected
- Refused to prosecute those who brawled with Police
- Prosecuted Trump CFO on tax charge, whereas no jurisdiction
- Prosecuted Trump on financial charges, whereas Accounting firms audited and found no problems.
- Repeated case decided in 2016, violation of "statute of limitations."

It seems clear, Bragg and these judges are criminals in all the cases listed above.

Judge Juan Merchan NY cases against Trump

- Ethnic Minority
- Democrat
- Born in Bogota Columbia, live there until age of six.
- ACTING JUDGE, not fully confirmed by Judicial process
- Judged the cases brought by Alvin Bragg
- Judged Tax case against Trump Org, IRS had full jurisdiction
- Judged Tax case against Trump CFO. Not his jurisdiction.

- Judged cases for which he had no jurisdiction.
- Set as Judge in the Steve Bannon cases.
- His daughter raised over $93 million for democrat elections
- Adam Schiff raised over $20 million by advertising this Trump Case
- Democrat Super PAC raised $15 million, advertising Trump Case
- Daughter Loren was "Chief of Digital Persuasion" for Harris Campaign.

Alan Dershowitz comments:

The Author awards the final word on Merchan to "Constitutional and criminal law attorney Alan Dershowitz, who said if the judge's daughter is involved in anti-Trump politics, "there seems to be a basis for recusal of the father."

"Under the law, close relationships can sometimes constitute a basis for recusal," he told The Post.

Judge Arthur F. Engoron NY Civil cases on Trump

- Democrat
- Judge of all Civil cases brought against Trump by Alvin Bragg

Judge Aileen Cannon Mar a Lago cases

- Born in Cali, Colombia - - Father from Indiana
- Ordered special Master to review Trump Records at Mar a Lago
- Eleventh Circuit overturned the special master
- Cannon resumed the Jack Smith prosecuted case.
- Cannon ordered that Jack Smith was illegally appointed by DOJ
- Finding above has "handcuffed" many other cases
- Trump filed his Immunity case,
- Immunity Case upheld by US Supreme Court.
- Immunity principle, limits on immunity, written into US Constitution, other cases.

No Conflict of Interest with Judge Cannon

Merrick Garland Appoints Jack Smith

- Chicago native
- Bill Clinton appointed to DC Court of Appeals
- Conservative Judaism, (Russia, Ukraine, Poland)
- Obama nominated him to SCOTUS, Twice nominated
- All republicans led by Mitch McConnell voted against Garland
- Trump nominated Gorsuch to fill Vacancy, not Garland
- First Notable case Oklahoma City Bombing Investigation
- Elected to Harvard Board of Overseers
- Garland case decision tend to favor Regulatory Agencies
- Tends to favor Environmental Groups in Court
- Appointed Attorney General of the United States by Joe Biden
- DOJ top officer as Attorney General
- Appealed a ruling in favor of Trump AG Bill Barr
- Continued to defend a case although beyond "statute of limitations"
- Continues to attack GOP attempts to implement Election Integrity
- Sues Texas for rejecting mail-in ballots for errors and omissions
- Sues Texas over redistricting plans
- Increased investigations, Police Misconduct. AG Sessions cut back the practice
- Blocks constitutional Executive Privilege in Jan06 cases.
- Acted against Alabama US Congressman Mo Brooks
- Acted against Trump Advisor Steve Bannon
- Appointed Jack Smith to Prosecute Trump Cases.
- Launched investigations of Parents who complain to school boards
- Possibly treats school Parents like "Domestic Terrorists."
- Garland declared "In Contempt of Congress"

Jack Smith, Prosecutor appointed by DOJ for the Trump Cases

- Presumed Democrat
- First Law Job as Assistant DA in Manhattan
- Promoted to Lead DOJ Public Integrity Section (PIN)
- Prosecuted former Republican Governor of Virginia Bob McDonnell
- Prosecuted McDonnell during McDonnell Presidential Campaign
- Prosecuted former Presidential Candidate John Edwards
- Prosecuted Edwards during Presidential Campaign
- NJ Menendez Bribery conviction overturned

- Prosecutes GOP Senator John Ensign, of Nevada, loses case
- Prosecutes former GOP House Majority Leader Tom Delay, loses
- Prosecutes late GOP Senator Don Young, Alaska, and loses
- Prosecutes ex-rep Alan Mollohan, democrat, West Virginia, loses
- SCOTUS Overturned McDonnell case
- Edwards Case declared a mistrial
- Garland appoints Smith to lead Trump Cases
- Mar a Lago case dismissed; Smith was illegally appointed.
- Trump files SCOTUS case seeking Presidential Immunity
- SCOTUS concurs, Trump immunity case and moots many cases
- Some cases continue pending, as this book goes to press
- Smith's wife is successful documentary produced and won awards for a video production on life of Michelle Obama.

Judge Tanya Chutkan, DC Jan 06 against Trump

- Ethnic Minority
- Born Kingston, Jamaica
- Democrat
- Obama nominated her U.S. District Court for District of Columbia
- Ordered an abortion for a minor
- Order was vacated by DC Court
- Reinstated by the full en banc D.C. Circuit
- Mooted by SCOTUS
- Granted abortions for 2 minors, Office of Resettlement custody
- Ordered ORR to provide access to abortions, minors in custody
- Ruled U.S. Secretary of Education DeVos delayed "Equity in IDEA"
- Ruled U.S. Dept. of Education violated law concerning regulations
- Denied Trump to seal records from House Select Committee
- Washington Post declared Chutkan toughest sentencing judge in Jan06 cases
- Many of those cases are being reduced and overturned.
- Judge of Trump's trial, attempts to overturn the 2020 election
- Chutkan trial of Trump, reduced by SCOTUS immunity decision.
- Her husband was assistant professor/ attorney at Howard U. School of Law

Fani Willis, Fulton County DA prosecuting Trump

- Ethnic Minority
- Democrat
- Father is noted Black Panther Lawyer
- Grew up in Washington, DC
- Willis investigated the 2020 presidential election in Georgia,
- Willis indicted Donald Trump and 18 alleged co-conspirators
- Novel racketeering case to refer to Presidential Election actions.
- Elected Fulton, Co DA in 2020
- Novice DA attacking incumbent President of the United States.
- Accused by subordinates of misusing Federal Funds
- Willis accused of conflict of interest re: love affair with Prosecutor
- Judge ordered that either Willis or the prosecutor must recuse
- Prosecutor recused; Willis remained on the case
- Willis continues to prosecute through countless steps
- Georgia appeals court to hear dismissal of Willis in late 2024
- Fulton County Elections Commission resigns
- New Commission begins removing barriers to honest election in Fulton, Co.

Nathan Wade Special Prosecutor in Fulton Co cases against Trump

- Ethnic Minority
- Democrat
- Colleague reports Wade and Willis involved in extra-marital affair
- Evidence shows Wade and Willis take expensive trips together
- Was DA office budget charged for those expenses
- Trial of Trump continues
- Wade less than 1 year experience to prosecute POTUS
- Appeal ultimately gets Wade dismissed from case involvement.

Judge Scott McAfee Fulton County Cases

- Elected Democrat, Fulton County in 2023. (very young Judge)
- 10 years beyond law school he is Judge against POTUS.
- Judge McAfee reported to Fani Willis early in career.
- In earlier law job, McAfee was privy to Election evidence.

Judge Beryl A. Howell, Appellate Judge in Giuliani Defamation Case

- Ethnic Minority
- Child of Army Officer, born at Ft. Benning
- Columbia Law School
- Democrat
- Worked for NJ Senator Patrick Leahy
- BIO makes clear she has been in and out of the Judiciary
- Supervising Judge for Mueller investigation (Steele)
- Ordered Mueller to give Grand Jury Info to House Judiciary
-

Judge William Pryor 11th Circuit US Court of Appeals

- Republican
- Alabama Attorney General upon election of US Senator Sessions
- Ordered Chief Justice Roy Moore to remove 10 Commandments
- Allowed Minority group to auction new auto to Minority Voters
- Appointed to 11th Circuit by George W. Bush
- John McCain engineered Pryor vote to 11th Circuit
- Rumored to be Candidate for SCOTUS
- Trump twice nominated and secured SCOTUS for 2 other Judges
- Denied Trump Chief of Staff Meadows, not to remove case
- Vacated Judge Cannon first opinion in Mar a Lago case
- SCOTUS Trump Immunity decision mooted issue above.

TOTAL CONFLICT OF INTEREST POINTS ABOVE - -198

The Author counts 198 points of conflict of interest (total count of bullet points) between these judges and Trump, solidly proven by the information contained herein alone, and therefore, all should have recused immediately. Now all but a couple should face American Bar Association Disciplinary action at minimum.

CHAPTER 15. DOMINION AND SMARTMATIC FILE CASES

SMARTMATIC NEWSMAX IN ELECTION CASE
CONTINUANCE OF CONFLICT OF INTEREST AGAINST FREEDOM

https://thehill.com/regulation/court-battles/4877817-judge-rules-smartmatic-lawsuit-newsmax-trial/

Judge rules defamation suit V. Newsmax can go to trial.
by Lauren Irwin - 09/12/24 11:05 PM ET

A voting machine company's defamation lawsuit against Newsmax appears headed to trial following a Delaware judge's ruling on Thursday.

Florida based Smartmatic accused Newsmax of airing defamatory statements that implied DOMINION rigged results of the 2020 election. Newsmax argued it was reporting newsworthy allegations made by former President Trump and his allies, the company previously issued a clarification saying, "not reported as true certain claims made about these companies."

Newsmax and Smartmatic asked Superior Court Judge Eric Davis to rule in their favor without trial. Davis granted partial summary judgment but said a jury will decide key issues. The trial is scheduled to start Sept. 30, The AP reported.

Smartmatic has maintained it provided election machinery and software for 2020 election only in Los Angeles, not where Trump contested the results.

Smartmatic's lawsuit against Newsmax is similar to one filed against One America News Network (OANN). Smartmatic and OANN had "resolved its litigation" in April through a "confidential settlement." Smartmatic's defamation litigation against Fox News is still pending.

The judge said Thursday, not all allegedly defamatory statements by Newsmax against the voting company was materially false, so he allowed the media organization to "contest falsity" of Smartmatic's connections with Venezuela, which Newsmax made statements about.

A federal grand jury in Florida indicted three current and former Smartmatic executives for a $1 million scheme to put voting machines in the Philippines. Newsmax detailed Smartmatic's "checkered history" in court papers, AP reported.

David ruled Smartmatic is a "limited public figure," meaning for defamation, the company must show Newsmax acted with "actual malice" by purposefully disregarding the truth. He also determined that Newsmax could assert a "neutral reporting privilege," which the company says it did since the statements of election fraud were made by third parties on non-Newsmax platforms.

Still, the judge determined there was no evidence that Newsmax acted with "evil intent." A jury must decide whether the company acted with actual malice and whether Smartmatic is entitled to damages, Davis ruled, according to the AP.

Smartmatic said it "very much" looks forward to explaining the company's losses to a jury to receive damages, though it's unlikely Newsmax would want the case to go before a jury and might settle.

In a statement to The Hill, Smartmatic said it will review the ruling but argues Newsmax knew it was reporting false allegations.

"Smartmatic is pleased to have the opportunity to prove this to a jury in court," Erik Connolly, Smartmatic's lead trial attorney, said in a statement. "The court's decision is the latest victory for Smartmatic in lawsuits it filed against individuals and media organizations that defamed the company after the 2020 US election."

Newsmax told The Hill the company itself never made "a claim of impropriety about Smartmatic, its ownership or software."

The Hill reached out to Newsmax for comment about Thursday's ruling, the company accused Davis of hampering the free press in a statement to CNN.

"While Newsmax is disappointed that any part of Smartmatic's lawsuit is going to trial, as we believe it is a threat to a free press, we are pleased the Court found no evidence that Newsmax acted with evil intent and that neutral and fair reporting privileges are available to Newsmax at trial," spokesperson Bill Daddi said in a statement to CNN.

The Associated Press contributed.

The writer of this book identifies scurrilous statements from Smartmatic, allowed by the judge -Smartmatic claims only to have equipment in Los Angeles in 2020, whereas their equipment has been in use in many more election cycles.

This is yet another in the continuing string of Democrats Court activity that poses strong resemblance to Racketeering, as we have yet another Democrat Judge joining the election cheating fray.

Meet the judge deciding $1.6 billion defamation case against Fox

The Honorable Eric M. Davis became a Judge of the Superior Court of the State of Delaware on December 21, 2012. Judge Davis was appointed by Delaware Democrat Jack Markell. Judge Davis has also been assigned another case filed against Donald Trump.

February 15, 20235:00 AM ET
By Karl Baker, David Folkenflik

https://www.npr.org/2023/02/15/1156610403/dominion-voting-vs-fox-news-judge-smartmatic-newsmax
https://trellis.law/judge/eric.m.davis

Davis is also overseeing a separate defamation case filed by Smartmatic, against Fox's smaller rival, Newsmax, over similar claims.

Davis earlier this month denied Newsmax's request to toss out Smartmatic's defamation claim. Davis ruled that the facts pleaded by Smartmatic lead him to "reasonably infer" that Newsmax's airing of stolen-election claims was reckless enough to meet the high legal bar required for defamation.

Finally, Davis ruled that Smartmatic could reasonably allege that Newsmax defamed the company even in statements that did not name it. He said Newsmax "seemingly wants the court to make a hyper-literal reading of every statement."

"It seems pretty clear to me that the judge was not having any of the Newsmax arguments – nor should he have, by the way," says John Culhane, a professor at Delaware Law School. But the judge said he did not find that Smartmatic had fully proven its claims.

In its defense against Dominion, Fox News' legal team argues the network simply relayed stark claims about national elections, either as "questions to a newsmaker on newsworthy subjects" or by "accurately reporting on pending allegations." As sitting U.S. president, Trump was among the most newsworthy people, Fox and Newsmax attorneys argue.

Smartmatic also sued Fox for $2.7 billion, but that suit is not as far along as Dominion's. On Tuesday, a New York state appellate court rejected Fox News' motion to have the Smartmatic case against the network and several of its stars dismissed. The ruling dismissed claims against Fox Corp, saying no cause stated.

Smartmatic attorney Erik Connolly said it would file an amended complaint that "details the involvement of Fox Corp. leaders Rupert and Lachlan Murdoch."

Fox News issued a statement yesterday echoing earlier remarks: "There is nothing more newsworthy than covering the president of the United States and his lawyers making allegations of voter fraud. We are confident we will prevail as freedom of the press is foundational to our democracy and must be protected."

Much like Fox's lawyers in New York and Delaware, Newsmax's attorneys similarly cite a legal privilege, known as neutral reportage, allowing it to present "unprecedented allegations without adopting them as true, so that the public could draw its own conclusions" about "a news story of extraordinary public interest."

That approach failed to win favor with Davis.

The following information deals with NY Appeals Judges on Dominion.

- https://en.wikipedia.org/wiki/New_York_State_Supreme_Court,_Appellate_Division,_First_Department
- https://www.nycourts.gov/courts/ad1/justicesofthecourt/Justice_Higgitt.shtml
- https://www.nycourts.gov/courts/ad1/calendar/List_Word/2023/02_Feb/14/PDF/Smartmatic%20 v%20Fox%20Corp%20(2022-01291).pdf
- https://www.npr.org/2023/02/15/1156610403/dominion-voting-vs-fox-news-judge-smartmatic-newsmax

As this book goes to press, even more democrat led cases against Trump and his Presidential staff continue to move forward. As has been the pattern of practice in this entire scandalous affair, Democrat Judges lead all activity.

CHAPTER 16. EXECUTIVE BRANCH CONSTITUTION ANNOTATED
(Oath of Office, Take Care Clause, Presidential Immunity)

Given the litany of cases against Trump, many people ask, "just what executive powers are vested into a President of the United States. Those powers are more numerous than we can detail within this book. We will concentrate on constitutional powers granted the Executive Branch, and the President of the U.S. Herein, we present a great amount of information pulled fully from the United States Constitution and found in the following internet link. https://constitution.congress.gov/browse/article-2/section-1/

Article II Executive Branch

Art II.S1.C1.1 Overview of Executive Vesting Clause (Powers of the President)

Article II, Section 1, Clause 1:

The executive Power shall be vested in a President of the United States of America. He shall hold his Office during the Term of four Years, and, together with the Vice President, chosen for the same Term, be elected, as follows

Under Article II, Section 1, Clause 1, the executive power is vested in a single person—the President of the United States. The nature and extent of the executive power is less clear.[1] Article II identifies exclusive powers of the President, including the President's authority as Commander in Chief and the power to pardon;[2] powers the President shares with the Senate, including appointments and treaty-making powers;[3] and the President's duties, most important of which is the duty to take Care that the Laws be faithfully executed.[4] Moreover, the Supreme Court has recognized that [b]because no single person could fulfill that responsibility, the *Take Care Clause implicitly provides the President with authority to supervise subordinate officers assisting with this responsibility*.[5] Likewise, Article I provides the President a role in the legislative process, including authority to veto legislation, subject to potential override by a two-thirds vote of both Houses of Congress.[6]

It is less clear from the text of the Constitution whether the executive powers expressly identified in the Constitution are exclusive or illustrative. Whereas the Article I Legislative Vesting Clause provides that All legislative Powers *herein granted* shall be vested in a Congress,[7] thereby distinguishing the powers granted by states from those they retained, the Article II Executive Vesting Clause does not limit the executive Power in any way.[8] Since the earliest days of the Republic, parameters of the executive power and, in particular, what implicit or residual powers such executive power encompasses have been the subject of debate.

1. U.S. Const. art. II, § 1, cl. 1.
2. *Id.* art. II, § 2, cl. 1. *See* ArtII.S2.C1.1.1 Historical Background on Commander in Chief Clause.
3. *Id.* art. II, § 2, cl. 2. *See* ArtII.S2.C1.3.1 Overview of Pardon Power.
4. *Id.* art. II, § 3. *See* ArtII.S3.3.1 Overview of Take Care Clause.
5. Seila Law LLC v. Consumer Fin. Protection Bureau, No. 19-7, slip op. at 2 (U.S. June 29, 2020). *See also* Free Enter. Fund v. Pub. Co. Acct. Oversight Bd., 561 U.S. 477, 492–93 (2010).
6. U.S. Const. art. I, § 7, cl. 2. *See* ArtI.S7.C2.1 Overview of Presidential Approval or Veto of Bills.
7. *Id.* art. I, § 1, cl. 1 (emphasis added). *See* ArtI.S1.1 Overview of Legislative Vesting Clause.
8. *Id.* art. II, § 1, cl. 1.

Art II.S1.C8.1 Oath of Office for the Presidency

Article II, Section 1, Clause 8:
Before he enter on the Execution of his Office, he shall take the following Oath or Affirmation:–I do solemnly swear (or affirm) that I will faithfully execute the Office of President of the United States, and will to the best of my Ability, preserve, protect and defend the Constitution of the United States.

That the oath the President is required to take might be considered to add anything to the powers of the President, because of his obligation to preserve, protect and defend the Constitution, might appear to be rather a fanciful idea. But in **President Andrew Jackson's** message announcing his veto of the act renewing the Bank of the United States there is language which suggests that the President has the right to refuse to enforce both statutes and judicial decisions based on his own independent decision that they were unwarranted by the Constitution.[2] The idea next turned up in a message by **President Abraham Lincoln** justifying his suspension of the writ of habeas corpus without obtaining congressional authorization.[3] And counsel to **President Andrew Johnson** during his impeachment trial adverted to the theory, but only in passing.[4] Beyond these isolated instances, it does not appear to be seriously contended that the oath adds anything to the President's powers.

[2] 2 J. Richardson, *supra*, at 576. Chief Justice Taney, who as a member of Jackson's Cabinet had drafted the message, later repudiated this possible reading of the message. 2 C. Warren, The Supreme Court In United States History 223–224 (1926).
[3] 6 J. Richardson, *supra*, at 25.
[4] 2 Trial Of Andrew Johnson 200, 293, 296 (1868).

Art II.S3.3.1 Overview of Take Care Clause

He shall from time to time give to the Congress Information of the State of the Union, and recommend to their Consideration such Measures as he shall judge necessary and expedient; he may, on extraordinary Occasions, convene both Houses, or either of them, and in Case of Disagreement between them, with Respect to the Time of Adjournment, he may adjourn them to such Time as he shall think proper; he shall receive Ambassadors and other public Ministers; he shall take Care that the Laws be faithfully executed, and Commission all Officers of the US.

The Constitution provides that the President shall take Care that the Laws be faithfully executed   This duty potentially implicates at least five categories of executive power, including: (1) powers the Constitution confers directly upon the President by the opening and succeeding clauses of Article II; (2) powers that congressional acts directly confer upon the President; (3) powers that congressional acts confer upon heads of departments and other executive agencies of the federal government; (4) power that stems implicitly from the duty to enforce the criminal statutes of the United States; and (5) power to carry out the so-called ministerial duties, regarding which an executive officer can exercise limited discretion as to the occasion or manner of their discharge. The following essays explore some of the questions raised by these executive powers, including how the President may exercise the powers which the Constitution or the statutes confer upon him, the relationship between the Take Care Clause and the President's power to remove—and thus supervise—those who wield executive power on his behalf, and the extent to which Congress can direct actions of executive officials.

Art II.S3.3.2 Who Can Fulfill the Take Care Duty
https://constitution.congress.gov/browse/essay/artII-S3-3-2/ALDE_00000217/

Article II, Section 3:

He shall from time to time give to the Congress Information of the State of the Union, and recommend to their Consideration such Measures as he shall judge necessary and expedient; he may, on extraordinary Occasions, convene both Houses, or either of them, and in Case of Disagreement between them, with Respect to the Time of Adjournment, he may adjourn them to such Time as he shall think proper; he shall receive Ambassadors and other public Ministers; he shall take Care that the Laws be faithfully executed, and Commission all Officers of the US.

Whereas the British monarch is constitutionally required to always act through agents if his acts are to receive legal recognition, the President is presumed to exercise certain of his constitutional powers personally. In an 1855 opinion, Attorney General Caleb Cushing identified several such examples, including the President's granting of reprieves and pardons for offenses against the United States and his role as the supreme commander in chief of the Army and Navy of the US, and of the militia of the States when called into the actual service.[1]

According to Cushing, the President's power as Commander in Chief is constitutionally inherent in the person of the President such that [n]o act of Congress, no act even of the President himself, can, by constitutional possibility, authorize or create any military officer not subordinate to the President.[2]

Moreover, according to Cushing, the President's obligation to act personally may be sometimes enlarged by statute. The act organizing the President with other designated officials into an Establishment by name of the Smithsonian Institute, in Cushing's view, is one such example. Cushing also believed that expenditures from the secret service fund, in order to be valid, must be vouched for by the President personally.[3] On like grounds the Supreme Court once held void a court martial decree because it was not specifically approved by the President as required by the 65th Article of War.[4] The Court has effectively overruled this case, and such cases are exceptional.[5]

Over time, the general rule that developed is that when any duty is cast by law upon the President, it may be exercised by him through the head of the appropriate department, whose acts, if performed within the law, become the President's acts.[6] In Williams v. United States,[7] for instance, the Supreme Court considered a statute that prohibited the advance of public money in any case whatsoever to disbursing officers of the United States, except under special direction by the President.[8] The Supreme Court held that the act did not require the personal performance by the President of this duty.[9] Such a practice, said the Court, would absorb the duties of the various departments of the government in the personal acts of one chief executive officer and be not just impracticable but impossible.[10] While [t]he President's duty in general requires his superintendence of the administration, the Court reasoned that he cannot be required to become the administrative officer of every department and bureau, or to perform in person the numerous details incident to services which he is technically required by the Constitution and applicable laws to perform.[11] As a matter of practice, most orders and instructions are attributed to the heads of departments, even though such orders and instructions are based on powers conferred by statute on the President.[12]

1. 7 Ops. Atty. Gen. 453, 464–65 (1855).
2. Id.
3. Cf. Act of May 10, 1800, 2 Stat. 78. The provision has long since dropped out of the statute book.
4. Runkle v. United States, 122 U.S. 543 (1887).
5. Cf. In In re Chapman, 166 U.S. 661, 670–671 (1897), Supreme Court held that presumptions in favor of official action preclude collateral attack on sentences of courts-martial. See also US v. Fletcher, 148 U.S. 84, 88–89 (1893); Bishop v. US, 97 U.S. 334, 341–42 (1905), both of which in effect repudiate Runkle.

6. In exercising his or her executive power under the Constitution, the President speaks and acts through heads of several departments in relation to subjects which appertain to their respective duties. The heads of the departments are the President's authorized assistants . . ., their official acts, promulgated in regular course of business, are presumptively the President's acts. Wilcox v. McConnel, 38 U.S. (13 Pet.) 498, 513 (1839). See also US v. Eliason, 41 U.S. (16 Pet.) 291 (1842); Williams v. US, 42 U.S. (1 How.) 290, 297 (1843); US v. Jones, 59 U.S. (18 How.) 92, 95 (1856); The Confiscation Cases, 87 U.S. (20 Wall.) 92 (1874); US v. Farden, 99 U.S. 10 (1879); Wolsey v. Chapman, 101 U.S. 755 (1880).
7. 42 U.S. (1 How.) 290 (1843).
8. 3 Stat. 723 (1823) (codified at 31 U.S.C. § 3324).
9. See Williams, 42 U.S. at 297.
10. Id.
11. Id. at 297–98.
12. See 38 Ops. Atty. Gen. 457, 458 (1936). If the President exercises his or her duty through subordinates, the President must appoint them or appoint the officers who appoint them, Buckley v. Valeo, 424 U.S. 1, 109–143 (1976), and he or she must have the power to discharge those officers in the Executive Branch, Myers v. United States, 272 U.S. 52 (1926).

Art II.S3.3.3 Relationship of Take Care Clause and President's Removal Power
https://constitution.congress.gov/browse/essay/artII-S3-3-3/ALDE_00000097/

Article II, Section 3:

He shall from time to time give to the Congress Information of the State of the Union, and recommend to their Consideration such Measures as he shall judge necessary and expedient; he may, on extraordinary Occasions, convene both Houses, or either of them, and in Case of Disagreement between them, with Respect to the Time of Adjournment, he may adjourn them to such Time as he shall think proper; he shall receive Ambassadors and other public Ministers; he shall take Care that the Laws be faithfully executed, and shall Commission all the Officers of the United States.

As the Supreme Court has observed, the Constitution vests all executive power in the President, who must take Care that laws be faithfully executed.[1] Because no single person could fulfill that responsibility alone, the Court notes, the Framers expected that the President would rely on subordinate officers for assistance.[2] As a result, the Court reasoned that [t]he President's power to remove-and thus supervise-those who wield executive power follows from Article II.[3]

Some early views of the President's removal power grounds this authority in large part in the Take Care Clause. In a 1789 debate in the First Congress concerning whether the Constitution authorizes the President to remove Executive Branch officers unilaterally, for instance, Representative James Madison expressed the view that the heads of certain executive departments should be removable by the President alone.

According to him, it was the intention of the Constitution, expressed especially in the faithful execution clause, that the first magistrate should be responsible for the executive department, and this responsibility carried with it the power to inspect and control the conduct of subordinate Executive Officers.[4] Vesting removal power in Senate jointly with the President would, in Madison's view, abolish at once the great principle of unity and responsibility in the executive department, intended for the security of liberty and the public good.[5]

Over time, however, as the Supreme Court refined its jurisprudence on the President's removal power, it came to characterize the basis of this power as stemming more generally from separation of power principles embedded in the Constitution's scheme, as evidenced by provisions including the Vesting Clause, Take Care Clause, and the Appointment Clause.[6]

1. Seila Law LLC v. CFPB, No. 19-7, slip op. 2 (U.S. 2020).
2. Id.
3. Id.
4. 1 Annals of Cong. 495, 499 (1789). For more information about the 1789 debate, also known as the decision of 1789, see ArtII.S2.C2.3.15.2 Decision of 1789 and Removals in Early Republic.
5. Id. Shortly thereafter, however, when the question arose as to the power of Congress to regulate the tenure of the Comptroller of the Treasury, Madison assumed a very different position. He conceded in effect that this office was to be an arm of certain of Congress's own powers and should therefore be protected against the President's removal power. Id. at 611–612. In Marbury v. Madison, 5 U.S. (1 Cr.) 137 (1803), Justice Marshall drew a parallel distinction between the duties of the Secretary of State under the original act which had created a Dept of Foreign Affairs and those which had been added by a later act. Id. at 166. The former duties were, according to Chief Justice Marshall, entirely political and thus must conform precisely to the will of the President. Id. The latter duties, on the other hand, were exclusively of statutory origin and sprang from the powers of Congress. Id. Chief Justice Marshall reasoned that with respect to these duties, the Secretary was an officer of the law and amenable to the law for his conduct, suggesting Congress may exercise certain removal power over Executive Officers.
6. For detailed discussion of President's removal power and evolution in its interpretation, see ArtII.S3.3.1 Overview of Take Care Clause through ArtII.S2.C2.3.15.7 Twenty-First Century Cases on Removal.

CHAPTER 17. CONSTITUTION ANNOTATED, PRESIDENTIAL IMMUNITY

US Constitution Annotated sections addressing The Executive Branch represent quite a huge book of information. Understand that Footnotes and Documentation of Sources is as important to the documentation of US Constitution along with Court Case and Legislative updates that all those points are essential to the establishment of a Constitutional Law.

Our Book will provide only those Constitutional Articles and Sections that fully apply to issues of Presidential actions that could conceivably and legally be used in response to a flawed Presidential election.

https://constitution.congress.gov/browse/article-2/
The URL above takes the reader to the section of the website that features all clauses of the US Constitution along with any and all SCOTUS decisions that impact each of the clauses.

SECTION 2 PRESIDENTIAL POWERS and PRESIDENTIAL IMMUNITY

Clause 1 Military, Administrative, and Clemency

The President shall be Commander in Chief of the Army and Navy of the United States, and of the Militia of the several States, when called into the actual Service of the United States; he may require the Opinion, in writing, of the principal Officer in each of the executive Departments, upon any Subject relating to the Duties of their respective Offices, and he shall have Power to grant Reprieves and Pardons for Offences against the United States, except in Cases of Impeachment.

- Art II.S2.C1.1 Commander in Chief
  - Art II.S2.C1.1.1Historical Background on Commander in Chief Clause
  - Art II.S2.C1.1.2Prize Cases and Commander in Chief Clause
  - Art II.S2.C1.1.11Presidential Power and Commander in Chief Clause
  - Art II.S2.C1.1.12Congressional Control Over President's Discretion
  - Art II.S2.C1.1.13President as Commander of Armed Forces

- Art II.S2.C2.3 Appointments
  - Art II.S2.C2.3.1Overview of Appointments Clause
  - Art II.S2.C2.3.2Historical Background on Appointments Clause
  - Art II.S2.C2.3.3Process of Appointment for Principal Officers

Clause 3 Senate Recess

- The President shall have Power to fill all Vacancies that may happen during Recess of the Senate, by granting Commissions which expire at the End of their next Session.
- ArtII.S2.C3.1Overview of Recess Appointments Clause
- ArtII.S2.C3.2Recess Appointments of Article III Judges

Section 3 Duties

He shall from time to time give to the Congress Information of the State of the Union, and recommend to their Consideration such Measures as he shall judge necessary and expedient; he may, on extraordinary Occasions, convene both Houses, or either of them, and in Case of Disagreement between them, with Respect to the Time of Adjournment, he may adjourn them to such Time as he shall think proper; he shall receive Ambassadors and other public Ministers; he shall take Care that the Laws be faithfully executed, and shall Commission all the Officers of the U.S.

Art II.S3.1The President's Legislative Role

□ Art II.S3.3 Enforcer of Laws
- Art II.S3.3.1Overview of Take Care Clause
- Art II.S3.3.2Who Can Fulfill the Take Care Duty
- Art II.S3.3.3Relationship Between Take Care Clause and President's Removal Power
- Art II.S3.3.5Interpretations of Law, Part of President's Take Care Duties

- Art II.S3.3.6President's Take Care Duties and International Law

□ Art II.S3.4 Executive Privilege
- Art II.S3.4.1Overview of Executive Privilege
- Art II.S3.4.2Defining Executive Privileges
- Art II.S3.4.8Separation of Powers and Communications Privilege
- Art II.S3.4.9Former Presidents and Communications Privilege

□ Art II.S3.5 Presidential Immunity
- Art II.S3.5.1Presidential Immunity to Suits and Official Conduct
- Art II.S3.5.2Presidential Immunity to Suits and Unofficial Conduct
- Art II.S3.5.3Qualified Immunity Doctrine
- Art II.S3.5.4Criminal Prosecution, Presidential Immunity, Former Presidents

Article VI Supreme Law

- Art VI.1Overview of Article VI, Supreme Law
- Clause 2 Supremacy Clause
- This Constitution, and the Laws of the United States which shall be made in Pursuance thereof; and all Treaties made, or which shall be made, under the Authority of the United States, shall be the supreme Law of the Land; and the Judges in every State shall be bound thereby, any Thing in the Constitution or Laws of any State to the Contrary notwithstanding.
- Art VI.C2.1Overview of Supremacy Clause
- Art VI.C2.2 Historical Background
    - Art VI.C2.2.1Articles of Confederation, Supremacy of Federal Law
    - Art VI.C2.2.2Supremacy Clause and the Constitutional Convention
    - Art VI.C2.2.3Debate and Ratification of Supremacy Clause
- Art VI.C2.3 Doctrine
    - Art VI.C2.3.1Early Doctrine on Supremacy Clause
    - Art VI.C2.3.2Dual Federalism in Late Nineteenth and Early Twentieth Centuries
    - Art VI.C2.3.3New Deal and Presumption Against Preemption
    - Art VI.C2.3.4Modern Doctrine on Supremacy

Clause 3 Oaths of Office

The Senators and Representatives before mentioned, and the Members of the several State Legislatures, and all executive and judicial Officers, both of the United States and of the several States, shall be bound by Oath or Affirmation, to support this Constitution; but no religious Test shall ever be required as a Qualification to any Office or public Trust under the United States.

Clause 1 Military, Administrative, and Clemency

The President shall be Commander in Chief of the Army and Navy of the United States, and of the Militia of the several States, when called into the actual Service of the United States; he may require the Opinion, in writing, of the principal Officer in each of the executive Departments, upon any Subject relating to the Duties of their respective Offices, and he shall have Power to grant Reprieves and Pardons for Offences against the United States, except in Cases of Impeachment.

Art II.S2.C1.1 Commander in Chief

- Art II.S2.C1.1.1Historical Background on Commander in Chief Clause
- Art II.S2.C1.1.2Prize Cases and Commander in Chief Clause
- Art II.S2.C1.1.11Presidential Power and Commander in Chief Clause
- Art II.S2.C1.1.12Congressional Control Over President's Discretion
- Art II.S2.C1.1.13President as Commander of Armed Forces

Art II.S2.C1.1.1 Historical Background on Commander in Chief Clause

The President shall be Commander in Chief of the Army and Navy of the United States, and of the Militia of the several States, when called into the actual Service of the United States; he may require the Opinion, in writing, of the principal Officer in each of the executive Departments, upon any Subject relating to the Duties of their respective Offices, and he shall have Power to grant Reprieves and Pardons for Offences against the United States, except in Cases of Impeachment.

Surprisingly, little discussion of the Commander in Chief Clause occurred in the Constitutional Convention or in ratifying debates. From evidence available, it appears the Framers vested the duty in the President because experience in the Continental Congress had disclosed the expediency of vesting command in a single official[1] and because the lesson of English history was that danger lurked in vesting command in a person separate from the responsible political leaders.[2]

Early cases and commentary emphasized the purely military aspects of the Commander in Chiefship. Alexander Hamilton said the office would amount to nothing more than the supreme command and direction of the Military and naval forces, as first general and admiral of the confederacy.[3] In his Commentaries on the Constitution of the United States, Justice Joseph Story wrote of the debates accompanying the ratification of the Constitution, stating: The propriety of admitting the president to be commander in chief, so far as to give orders, and have a general superintendency, was admitted.[4] Justice Story took note of the debate regarding the propriety of the President taking command of the armed forces in person, explaining the apparent consensus. He stated: Though the president might, there was no necessity that he should, take the command in person; and there was no probability that he would do so, except in extraordinary emergencies, and when he possessed superior military talents.[5]

Supreme Court did not think it apparent that the Commander in Chief Power necessarily entailed all of the attributes available to a sovereign under the laws and usages of war, even in cases of war declared by Congress.[6]

The Court held that a declaration of war, by itself, did not empower the President to confiscate enemy property.[7]

Chief Justice John Marshall, while suggesting that the President might, during the limited war authorized against France, have the authority as Commander in Chief to issue orders pertaining to the capture of certain vessels in the absence of legislation, denied the validity of such an order where Congress had enacted a contradictory staute.[8] A U.S. commander had captured, pursuant to presidential instructions, what he believed was a U.S. merchant ship bound from a French port, allegedly carrying contraband material.[9] Congress had, enacted the Non-Intercourse Act, which only provided for the seizure of such vessels bound to French ports.[10] The Court held that the President's instructions exceeded authority granted by Congress and were not to be given force of law, the captain could be held liable for damages.[11]

In 1850, Chief Justice Roger Taney, writing for the Supreme Court, explained the President's power during wartime:

His duty and his power are purely military. As Commander in Chief, he is authorized to direct the movements of the naval and military forces placed by law at his command, and to employ them in the manner he may deem most effectual to harass and conquer and subdue the enemy. He may invade the hostile country, and subject it to the sovereignty and authority of the United States. But his conquests do not enlarge the boundaries of this Union, nor extend operation of our institutions and laws beyond limits before assigned to them by legislative power.[12]

Justice Taney continued and distinguished the role of the Commander in Chief and that of the British King:

But in the distribution of political power between the great departments of government, there is such a wide difference between the power conferred on the President of the United States, and authority and sovereignty which belong to the English crown, that it would be altogether unsafe to reason from any supposed resemblance between them, as regards conquest in war, or any other subject where rights and powers of the executive arm of government are brought into question.[13] Even after the Civil War, a powerful minority of the Court, led by Chief Justice Salmon Chase, described the role of President as Commander in Chief, as the command of forces and conduct of campaigns.[14]

1. Earnest R. May, The President Shall Be Commander in Chief, in The Ultimate Decision: The President as Commander In Chief 3, 6–7 (E. May ed., 1960). During North Carolina Ratify Convention, James Iredell said: From the nature of the thing, command of armies ought to be delegated to only one person. The secrecy, dispatch, and decision, which are necessary in military operations can only be expected from one person. 4 Jonathan Elliot, Debates in the Several State Conventions on the Adoption of the Federal Constitution 107 (2d ed.1836).
2. May, supra note 1, at 18. Virginia ratifying convention, Madison, replying to Patrick Henry's objection that danger lurked in giving the President control of the military, said: Would the member say that the sword ought to be put in the hands of representatives of the people, or in other hands independent of the government altogether? 3 Elliot, supra note 1, at 393.
3. The Federalist No. 69 (Alexander Hamilton).

4. 3 Joseph Story, Commentaries on Constitution Of The US § 1492 (1833).
5. Id.
6. See, e.g., The Thomas Gibbons, 12 U.S. (8 Cranch) 421, 427–28 (1814) (As to authority of the president, we do not think it necessary to consider how far he would be entitled, in his character of commander in chief of the army and navy of the US, independent of any statute provision, to issue instructions for government and direction of privateers. That question deserves grave consideration; and we should not be disposed to entertain the discussion unless it become unavoidable.).
7. Brown v. United States, 12 U.S. (8 Cranch) 110, 128–29 (1814) (appears to the Court, power of confiscating enemy property is in legislature, the legislature has not declared its will to confiscate property in our territory at declaration of war.)
8. Little v. Barreme, 6 U.S. (2 Cranch) 170, 177–78 (1804).
9. Id. at 177 (with reference to the Law of February 9, 1799, 1 Stat. 613).
10. Id.
11. Id. at 179. See also Talbot v. Seeman, 5 U.S. (1 Cranch) 1, (1801) (The whole powers of war being by the constitution of the US, vested in congress, the acts of that body can alone be restored to as our guides in this enquiry.).
12. Fleming v. Page, 50 U.S. (9 How.) 603, 615 (1850). Court explained, acquisition of foreign territory could be accomplished only by treaty-making power or legislative authority, is not a part of the power conferred upon the President by declaration of war. Id. Congress had declared war against Mexico in 1846. Act of May 13, 1846, ch. 16, 9 Stat. 9.
13. Fleming, 50 U.S. (9 How.) at 618.
14. Ex parte Milligan, 71 U.S. (4 Wall.) 2, 139 (1866).

Art II.S2.C1.1.2 Prize Cases and Commander in Chief Clause

The President shall be Commander in Chief of the Army and Navy of the United States, and of the Militia of the several States, when called into the actual Service of the United States; he may require the Opinion, in writing, of the principal Officer in each of the executive Departments, upon any Subject relating to the Duties of their respective Offices, and he shall have Power to grant Reprieves and Pardons for Offences against the United States, except in Cases of Impeachment.

The basis for a broader conception of the role of Commander in Chief was laid in certain early acts of Congress authorizing the President to employ military force in the execution of the laws.[1] In his famous message to Congress on July 4, 1861,[2] Abraham Lincoln advanced the claim that the war power was his for the purpose of suppressing rebellion, and in the Prize Cases[3] of 1863 a divided Court sustained this theory. The immediate issue was validity of the blockade of Southern ports that the President had established following the attack on Fort Sumter.[4]

The argument was advanced that, in order for a blockade to be valid, it must be established during an incident of a public war validly declared, and that only Congress could, by virtue of its power to declare war, constitutionally impart to a military situation this character and scope.[5]

Speaking for the majority of the Court, Justice Robert Grier answered:

> If a war be made by invasion of a foreign nation, the President is not only authorized but bound to resist force by force. He does not initiate the war, but is bound to accept the challenge without waiting for any special legislative authority. And whether the hostile party be a foreign invader, or States organized in rebellion, it is none the less a war, although the declaration of it be 'unilateral.'[6]

To support this principle with historical precedent, Justice Grier explained that the battles of Palo Alto and Resaca de la Palma had been fought before the enactment of the Act of Congress of May 13, 1846, which recognized 'a state of war as existing by the act of the Republic of Mexico.'[7] Justice Grier stated, This act not only provided for the future prosecution of the war, but was itself a vindication and ratification of the Act of the President in accepting the challenge without a previous formal declaration of war by Congress.[8]

The Court might have rested its opinion wholly on the President's authorities under statute to suppress insurrections and repel invasions,[9] coupled with Congress's ratification of the President's actions,[10] but it instead emphasized Executive power and duty:

> The President was bound to meet it in the shape it presented itself, without waiting for Congress to baptize it with a name; and no name given to it by him or them could change the fact . . . .
>
> Whether the President in fulfilling his duties, as Commander in-chief, in suppressing an insurrection, has met with such armed hostile resistance, and a civil war of such alarming proportions as will compel him to accord to them the character of belligerents, is a question to be decided by him, and this Court must be governed by the decisions and acts of the political department of the government to which this power was entrusted. 'He must determine what degree of force the crisis demands.' The proclamation of blockade is itself official and conclusive evidence to the Court that a state of war existed which demanded and authorized a recourse to such a measure, under circumstances peculiar to the case.[11]

In brief, the powers that may be claimed for the President under the Commander in Chief Clause at a time of widespread insurrection were equated with his powers under the clause at a time when the United States is engaged in a formally declared foreign war.[12]

No attention was given the fact that Lincoln had asked Congress to ratify and confirm his acts, which Congress promptly had,[13] with the exception of his suspension of habeas corpus, a power that many attributed to the President in the situation then existing, by virtue of his duty to take care that the laws be faithfully executed.[14] On the other hand, where Lincoln's proclamation suspending habeas corpus varied from legislation enacted to ratify it, the Court looked to the statute[15] rather than the proclamation[16] to determine breadth of its application in case of Ex parte Milligan.[17]

In a partial concurrence to the majority's decision in Milligan, Chief Justice Chase described the allocation of war powers as follows:

> The power to make the necessary laws is in Congress; the power to execute is the President. Both powers imply many subordinate and auxiliary powers. Each includes all authorities essential to its due exercise. But neither can the President, in war more than in peace, intrude upon the proper authority of Congress, nor Congress upon the proper authority of the President [18]
>
> The Chief Justice described the Commander in Chief Power as entailing the command of forces and conduct of campaigns,[19] but nevertheless agreed that military trials of civilians accused of violating the law of war in Union states were invalid without congressional approval, despite the government's assertion that the [Commander in Chief's] power to make an effectual use of his forces [must include the] power to arrest and punish one who arms men to join the enemy in the field against him.[20]

1. 1 Stat. 424 (1795) (Militia Act of 1795); 2 Stat. 443 (1807) (Insurrection Act of 1807) (codified at 10 U.S.C. §§ 251–254). See also Martin v. Mott, 25 U.S. (12 Wheat.) 19, 32–33 (1827) (asserting finality of President's judgment of existence of facts requiring his exercise of powers conferred by act of 1795).
2. 7 Messages and Papers of the Presidents 3221, 3224 (J. Richardson ed. 1897) (So viewing the issue, no choice was left but to call out the war power of the Government and so to resist force employed for its destruction by force for its preservation.). Later in the address, President Lincoln submitted: Recurring to the action of the Government, it may be stated that at first a call was made for 75,000 militia, and rapidly following this a proclamation was issued for closing the ports of the insurrectionary districts by proceedings in the nature of blockade. So far all was believed to be strictly legal. At this point, the insurrectionists announced their purpose to enter upon the practice of privateering.

   Other calls were made for volunteers to serve three years unless sooner discharged, and also for large additions to the Regular Army and Navy. These measures, whether strictly legal or not, were ventured upon under what appeared to be a popular demand and a public necessity, trusting then, as now, that Congress would readily ratify them. It is believed that nothing has been done beyond the constitutional competency of Congress. Id. at 3225.
3. 367 U.S. (2 Black) 635 (1863).
4. Id. at 665.
5. Id. at 644–45 (argument).

6. Id. at 668–70.
7. Id. at 668.
8. Id.
9. Id. at 668.
10. 67 U.S. (2 Black) at 670–71 (taking note of statutes and stating, Without admitting that act was necessary under circumstances, it is plain that if President had in any manner assumed powers necessary, should have authority or sanction of Congress, . .this ratification has operated to perfectly cure the defect.).
11. Id. at 669–70.
12. See generally, Edward Corwin, Total War, and the Constitution (1946).
13. 12 Stat. 326 (1861).
14. J. G. Randall, Constitutional Problems Under Lincoln 118–139 (rev. ed. 1951).
15. Act of Mar. 3, 1863, 12 Stat. 755 (authorizing suspension of habeas corpus, with limitations in Union states to those prisoners of war; all others indicted or freed.)
16. Proclamation of Sept. 15, 1863, 13 Stat. 734 (suspending habeas corpus with respect to those in federal custody as military offenders or as prisoners of war, spies, or aiders and abettors of the enemy).
17. Ex parte Milligan, 71 U.S. (4 Wall.) 2, 115–16 (1866).
18. Id. at 139 (Chase, C.J., concurring and dissenting in part).
19. Id. at 139–40 (Congress cannot direct conduct of campaigns, nor can the President, or any commander under him, without the sanction of Congress, institute tribunals for trial and punishment of offences, either of soldiers or civilians, unless in cases of controlling necessity
20. Id. at 17 (government argument).

Art II.S2.C1.1.11 Presidential Power and Commander in Chief Clause

The President shall be Commander in Chief of the Army and Navy of the US, and of the Militia of the several States, when called into the actual Service of the US; he may require the Opinion, in writing, of the principal Officer in each of the executive Departments, upon any Subject relating to the Duties of their respective Offices, and he shall have Power to grant Reprieves and Pardons for Offences against the US, except in Cases of Impeachment.

The President's power with regard to armed forces has long been debated. In defense of executive action in Indochina, the Legal Adviser of the State Department, in a widely circulated document, contended:

Under the Constitution, the President, in addition to being Chief Executive, is Commander in Chief of the Army and Navy. He holds the prime responsibility for the conduct of United States foreign relations. These duties carry broad powers, including the power to deploy American forces abroad and commit them to military operations when the President deems such action necessary to maintain the security and defense of the United States.

In 1787 the world was a far larger place, and the framers probably had in mind attacks upon the United States. In the 20th century, the world has grown much smaller. An attack on a country far from our shores can impinge directly on the Nation's security. In the SEATO treaty, for example, it is formally declared that an armed attack against Viet Nam would endanger peace and security of the U.S.

Under our Constitution it is the President who must decide when an armed attack has occurred. He has also the constitutional responsibility for determining what measures of defense are required when the peace and safety of the United States are endangered. If he considers that deployment of U.S. forces to South Viet Nam is required, and that military measures against the source of Communist aggression in North Viet Nam are necessary, he is constitutionally empowered to take those measures.[1]

Opponents of such expanded presidential powers have contended, however, that the authority to initiate war was not divided between the Executive and Congress but was vested exclusively in Congress. The President had the duty and the power to repel sudden attacks and act in other emergencies, and in his role as Commander in Chief he was empowered to direct the armed forces for any purpose specified by Congress.[2] Though Congress asserted itself in some respects, it never really managed to confront the President's power with any sort of effective limitation, until the 1970s.

1. Leonard C. Meeker, Legality of US Participation in Defense of Viet Nam, 54 Dep't State Bull. 474, 484–485 (1966). See John N. Moore, The National Executive and Use of Armed Forces Abroad, 21 Naval War College Rev. 28 (1969); Quincy Wright, Power of the Executive to Use Military Forces Abroad, 10 Va. J. Int. L. 43 (1969); Documents Relating to War Powers of Congress, President's Authority as Commander in Chief and War in Indochina, S. Comm. on Foreign Rels., 91st Cong. 1 (1970) (Under Secretary of State Katzenbach), 90 (J. Stevenson, Legal Adviser, Dept of State), 120 (Professor Moore), 175 (Asst Att'y Gen. Rehnquist).
2. E.g., F. Wormuth & E. Firmage, To Chain the Dog of War (1989), F.J. Ely, War and Responsibility: Constitutional Lessons of the Vietnam War and its Aftermath (1993); U.S. Commitments to Foreign Powers: Hearings Before the S. Comm. on Foreign Rels., 90th Cong. 9 (1967) (Bartlett); War Powers Legislation: Hearings Before the S. Comm. on Foreign Rels., 92d Cong. 7 (1971).

Art II.S2.C1.1.12 Congressional Control Over President's Discretion

The President shall be Commander in Chief of the Army and Navy of the United States, and of the Militia of the several States, when called into the actual Service of the United States; he may require the Opinion, in writing, of the principal Officer in each of the executive Departments, upon any Subject relating to the Duties of their respective Offices, and he shall have Power to grant Reprieves and Pardons for Offences against the United States, except in Cases of Impeachment. Over the President's veto, Congress enacted in 1973 the War Powers Resolution,[1] designed to redistribute war powers between President and Congress. Although ambiguous in some respects, the Resolution appears to define restrictively the President's powers, to require him to report fully to Congress upon the introduction of troops into foreign areas, to specify a maximum time limitation on engagement of hostilities absent affirmative congressional action, to provide a means for Congress to require cessation of hostilities in advance of time set.

The Resolution states that the President's power to commit United States troops into hostilities, or into situations of imminent involvement in hostilities, is limited to instances of (1) a declaration of war, (2) a specific statutory authorization, or (3) a national emergency created by an attack on the United States, its territories or possessions, or its armed forces.[2] In the absence of a declaration of war, a President must within 48 hours report to Congress whenever he introduces troops
(1) into hostilities or situations of imminent hostilities, (2) into a foreign nation while equipped for combat, except in certain nonhostile situations, or (3) in numbers which substantially enlarge United States troops equipped for combat already located in a foreign nation.[3] If the President introduces troops in the first of these three situations, then he must terminate the use of troops within 60 days after his report was submitted or was required to be submitted to Congress, unless Congress (1) has declared war, (2) has extended the period, or (3) is unable to meet as a result of an attack on the United States, but the period can be extended another 30 days by the President's certification to Congress of unavoidable military necessity respecting the safety of the troops.[4] Congress may through the passage of a concurrent resolution require the President to remove the troops sooner.[5] The Resolution further states that no legislation, whether enacted prior to or subsequent to passage of the Resolution will be taken to empower the President to use troops abroad unless the legislation specifically does so and that no treaty may so empower the President unless it is supplemented by legislation specifically addressed to the issue.[6]

Aside from its use as a rhetorical device, War Powers Resolution has been of little worth in reordering presidential-congressional relations in the years since its enactment. In general, Presidents operating under it have expressly or implicitly considered it to be at least in part an unconstitutional infringement on presidential powers,[7] and on each occasion of use abroad of United States troops the President in reporting to Congress has done so consistently with the reporting section but not pursuant to the provision.[8] Upon the invasion of Kuwait by Iraqi troops in 1990, President George H.W. Bush sought not congressional authorization but a United Nations Security Council resolution authorizing the use of force by member Nations. Only at the last moment did the President seek authorization from Congress, he and his officials contending he had the power to act unilaterally.[9] After intensive debate, Congress voted, 250 to 183 in the House of Representatives and 53 to 46 in the Senate, to authorize the President to use US troops pursuant to U.N. resolution and purporting to bring the act within context of War Powers Resolution.[10]

Presidents have continued to claim independent authority to commit U.S. Armed Forces to involvements abroad absent any congressional participation other than consultation and after-the-fact financing.

In 1994, for example, President Bill Clinton based his authority to order the participation of U.S. forces in NATO actions in Bosnia-Herzegovina on his constitutional authority to conduct U.S. foreign relations and as his role as Commander in Chief,[11] and protested efforts to restrict the use of military forces there and elsewhere as an improper and possibly unconstitutional limitation on his command and control of U.S. forces.[12] In March 2011, President Barack Obama ordered U.S. military forces to take action as part of an international coalition to enforce U.N. Security Council Resolution 1973, which authorized U.N. Member States to take all necessary measures (other than through military occupation) to protect civilians from attacks by the Libyan government and to establish a no-fly zone over the country. Although these operations had not been authorized by legislation, the Executive Branch submitted a report to Congress which claimed that the President has the constitutional authority, as Commander in Chief and Chief Executive and pursuant to his foreign affairs powers, to direct such limited military operations abroad.[13]

By contrast, President George W. Bush sought a resolution from Congress in 2002 to approve the eventual invasion of Iraq before seeking a U.N. Security Council resolution, all the while denying that express authorization from Congress, or, the U.N. Security Council, was necessary to renew hostilities in Iraq. Prior to adjourning for its midterm elections, Congress passed the Authorization for Use of Military Force against Iraq Resolution of 2002,[14] which it styled as specific statutory authorization within the meaning of section 5(b) of the War Powers Resolution. On signing the measure, the President noted he had sought an additional resolution of support from Congress, and expressed appreciation for receiving that support, but stated, my request did not, and my signing this resolution does not, constitute any change in the long-standing positions of the executive branch on either the President's constitutional authority to use force to deter, prevent, or respond to aggression or other threats to U.S. interests or on constitutionality of the War Powers Resolution.[15] In the Bush administration's view, the primary benefit of receiving authorization from Congress seems to be the message of political unity it conveyed to the world rather than fulfillment of constitutional requirements.

There is talk within Congress to amend.

1. Pub. L. No. 93-148, 87 Stat. 555 (1973) (codified at 50 U.S.C. §§ 1541–1548). For congressional intent and explanation, see H. Rep. No. 93-287, S. Rep. No. 9-220, & H. Rep. No. 93-547 , 93d Cong. (1973)(Conf. Rep.). President's veto message is H. Doc. No. 93-171, 93d Cong. (1973); The War Powers Resolution: Relevant Documents, Reports, Correspondence, H. Comm. on Foreign Affs., 103d Cong. 1–46 (1994) (Comm. Print). For account of passage, assessment of disputed compliance - congressional point of view, see War Powers Resolution, Special Study, H. Comm. on Foreign Affs., 102d Cong. (1982)(Comm. Print).
2. Pub. L. No. 93-147, 87 Stat. 554, § 2(c) (1973) (codified at 50 U.S.C. § 1541).
3. 350 U.S.C. § 1543(a).
4. 450 U.S.C. § 1544(b).
5. Id. at § 1544(c). Following INS v. Chadha, 462 U.S. 919 (1983), Congress subsequently enacted expedited procedures for considering joint resolutions or bills to require removing U.S. Armed Forces from situations of hostilities. Department of State Authorization Act, Fiscal Years 1984 and 1985, Pub. L. No. 98–164 § 1013, 97 Stat. 1062 (1983) (codified at 50 U.S.C. § 1546(a)).
6. 650 U.S.C. § 1547(a).
7. See generally Dep't of Just., Authority of the President under Domestic and International Law to Use Military Force against Iraq, 26 Op. O.L.C. 1, 39–45 (2002) (discussing presidential views and Dep't of Justice opinions concerning constitutionality of War Powers Resolution).
8. See The War Powers Resolution: Relevant Documents, Reports, Correspondence, H. Comm. on Foreign Affs., 103d Cong. 47 (1994) (Comm. Print) (Pres. Ford on refugees from Danang), 55 (Pres. Carter on attempted rescue of Iranian hostages), 73 (Pres. Reagan on use of troops in Lebanon), 113 (Pres. Reagan on Grenada), 144 (Pres G. H.W. Bush on Panama), 147, 149 (Pres. G. H.W. Bush on Persian Gulf), 189 (Pres. G. H.W. Bush on Somalia), 262 (Pres. Clinton on Haiti).
9. See Crisis in the Persian Gulf: U.S. Policy Options and Implications: Hearings Before the S. Comm. on Armed Servs., 101st Cong. 701 (1990) (Secretary Cheney) (President did not require additional authorization from Congress before attacking Iraq). The day following his request for supporting legislation from Congress, President George H.W. Bush answered a question about the requested action, stating: I don't think I need it. I feel that I have the authority to fully implement UN resolutions. 27 Weekly Comp. Pres. Doc. 25 (1/8/91).
10. Pub. L. No. 102-1, 105 Stat. 3 (1991).
11. 30 Weekly Comp. Pres. Doc. 406 (March 2, 1994).
12. See Interview with Radio Reporters, 1993 Pub. Papers 1763–64.
13. Report to the House of Representatives on US Activities in Libya (2011). The Dept of Justice's Office of Legal Counsel issued a legal opinion which claimed that the President possessed independent constitutional authority to commence U.S. military operations in Libya without prior congressional authorization because these operations would be limited in scope, the President could reasonably determine that such use of force was in the national interest. Dep't of Just., Authority to Use Military Force in Libya, 35 Op. O.L.C. 20 (2011). Opinion stated prolonged and substantial military engagements, typically involving exposure of U.S. military personnel to significant risk over a substantial period may require congressional authorization, but claimed that historical practice of presidential military action without congressional approval precludes any suggestion that Congress's authority to declare war covers every military, however limited, President initiates. Id. at 8.
14. Pub. L. No. 107-243, 116 Stat. 1498 (2002). House approved resolution by vote of 296-133. Senate passed House version of H.J. Res. 114 by a vote of 77-23. 148 Cong. Rec. S10342 (daily ed. Oct. 11, 2002).
15. Presidential Statement, Signing H.J.Res.114,38 Weekly Comp. Pres. Doc.1777 (2002).
16. Proposals to amend and on congressional responsibility, see John Hart Ely, War And Responsibility: Constitutional Lessons Vietnam ,Aftermath 115–138 (1993).

Art II.S2.C1.1.13 President as Commander of Armed Forces

The President shall be Commander in Chief of the Army and Navy of the United States, and of the Militia of the several States, when called into the actual Service of the US; he may require the Opinion, in writing, of the principal Officer in each of the executive Departments, upon any Subject relating to the Duties of their respective Offices, and he shall have Power to grant Reprieves and Pardons for Offences against the U.S. except Impeachment.

While the President customarily delegates supreme command of the forces in active service, there is no constitutional reason he should do so, and he has been known to resolve personally important questions of military policy. President Abraham Lincoln early in 1862 issued orders for a general advance in the hopes of stimulating General George McClellan to action; President Woodrow Wilson in 1918 settled the question of an independent American command on the Western Front; President Harry Truman in 1945 ordered that the bomb be dropped on Hiroshima and Nagasaki.[1] As against an enemy in the field, the President possesses all the powers accorded by international law to any supreme commander. He may invade the hostile country, and subject it to the sovereignty and authority of the United States.[2] In the absence of attempts by Congress to limit his or her power, President may establish and prescribe the jurisdiction and procedure of military commissions, and of tribunals in the nature of such commissions, in territory occupied by Armed Forces of the United States, and his or her authority to do this sometimes survives cessation of hostilities.[3] The President may employ secret agents to enter the enemy's lines and obtain information as to its strength, resources, and movements.[4] He or she may, at least with the assent of Congress, authorize commercial intercourse with the enemy.[5] The President may also requisition property and compel services from American citizens and friendly aliens who are situated within the theater of military operations when necessity requires, thereby incurring for the United States the obligation to render just compensation.[6] By the same warrant, a President may bring hostilities to a conclusion by arranging an armistice, stipulating conditions that may determine to a great extent the ensuing peace.[7] The President may not, effect a permanent acquisition of territory,[8] though he or she may govern recently acquired territory until Congress sets up a more permanent regime.[9]

The President is the ultimate tribunal for the enforcement of the rules and regulations that Congress adopts for the government of the forces, and that are enforced through courts-martial.[10] Indeed, until 1830, courts-martial were convened solely on the President's authority as Commander in Chief.[11]

Such rules and regulations are, moreover, it seems, subject in wartime to his or her amendment at discretion.[12] Similarly, the power of Congress to make rules for the government and regulation of the land and naval forces did not prevent President Lincoln from promulgating, in April 1863, a code of rules to govern the conduct in the field of the armies of the US, which was prepared at his instance by a commission headed by Francis Lieber and which later became the basis of all similar codifications both here and abroad.[13] One important power that the President lacks is that of choosing his or her subordinates, whose grades and qualifications are determined by Congress and whose appointment is ordinarily made by and with the advice and consent of the Senate, though undoubtedly Congress could if it wished vest their appointment in the President alone.[14] Also, the President's power to dismiss an officer from the service, once unlimited, is today confined by statute in time of peace to dismissal pursuant to a sentence of a general court-martial or in commutation of a sentence of a court-martial.[15] The provision is not regarded by the Court as preventing the President from displacing an officer of Army or Navy by appointing with advice and consent of the Senate another person in his or her place.[16] Congress did not limit the President's power of dismissal in time of war.

1. For a review of how several wartime Presidents operated in this sphere, see The Ultimate Decision: President As Commander In Chief (Ernest R. May ed. 1960).
2. Fleming v. Page, 50 U.S. (9 How.) 603, 615 (1850).
3. Madsen v. Kinsella, 343 U.S. 341, 348 (1952). See also Johnson v. Eisentrager, 339 U.S. 763, 789 (1950).
4. Totten v. United States, 92 U.S. 105 (1876).
5. Hamilton v. Dillin, 88 U.S. (21 Wall.) 73 (1875); Haver v. Yaker, 76 U.S. (9 Wall.) 32 (1869).
6. Mitchell v. Harmony, 54 U.S. (13 How.) 115 (1852); US v. Russell, 80 U.S. (13 Wall.) 623 (1871); Totten v. US, 92 U.S. 105 (1876); 40 Ops. Atty. Gen. 250, 253 (1942).
7. Cf. the Protocol of 8/12/1898, foreshadowed the Peace of Paris, 30 Stat. 1742 and Pres Wilson's Fourteen Points, incorporated in the Armistice of Nov 11, 1918.
8. Fleming v. Page, 50 U.S. (9 How.) 603, 615 (1850).
9. Santiago v. Nogueras, 214 U.S. 260 (1909). As to temporarily occupied territory, see Dooley v. United States, 182 U.S. 222, 230–31 (1901).
10. Approval of Court-Martial Sentence, 15 Ops. Atty. Gen. 290, 297 n. (1877). Cf. New Trials before Courts-Martial, 1 Ops. Atty. Gen. 233, 234 (1818) (Attorney General Wirt stating the contrary view).
11. Swaim v. U.S., 165 U.S. 553 (1897); cases there reviewed. See also Givens v. Zerbst, 255 U.S. 11 (1921).
12. Ex parte Quirin, 317 U.S. 1, 28–29 (1942).
13. U.S. Const. art. I, § 8, cl. 14; General Orders, No. 100 (Apr. 24, 1863), reprinted in 3 The War of the Rebellion: Official Records of the Union and Confederate Armies (Ser. III) (Robert N. Scott ed. 1880-1901).
14. See, e.g., Mimmack v. US, 97 U.S. 426, 437 (1878); United States v. Corson, 114 U.S. 619 (1885).
15. 10 U.S.C. § 1161. 10 U.S.C. § 804 (permits officer dismissed by presidential order to demand court-martial
16. Mullan v. United States, 140 U.S. 240 (1891); Wallace v. US, 257 U.S. 541 (1922).

Art II.S2.C2.3 Appointments

- Art II.S2.C2.3.1Overview of Appointments Clause
- Art II.S2.C2.3.2Historical Background on Appointments Clause
- Art II.S2.C2.3.3Process of Appointment for Principal

Officers Art II.S2.C3.2 Recess Appointments of Article III Judges

The President shall have Power to fill Vacancies that happen during Recess of the Senate, by granting Commissions which expire at the End of next Session.

Federal judges clearly fall within the terms of the Recess Appointments Clause, in the sense that the Clause broadly authorizes temporary appointments for all Vacancies. Nonetheless, other constitutional provisions could suggest hesitation before applying the Clause to Article III judges—although historically, Presidents have in fact made recess appointments to Article III courts.[1] The constitutional concern stems from the fact that Article III judges are appointed during good behavior, subject only to removal through impeachment.[2] A judge, however, who is given a recess appointment may be removed by the Senate's failure to advise and consent to his appointment; moreover, on the bench, prior to Senate confirmation, he or she may be subject to influence not felt by other judges. Although Supreme Court has not considered this issue, some appeals courts have rejected constitutional attacks upon federal judges given recess appointments.[3]

1. See generally, e.g., Edward A. Hartnett, Recess Appointments of Article III Judges: Three Constitutional Questions, 26 Cardozo L. Rev. 377 (2005).
2. See ArtIII.S1.10.2.1 Overview of Good Behavior Clause.
3. United States v. Woodley, 751 F.2d 1008, 1012 (9th Cir. 1985) (en banc), cert. denied, 475 U.S. 1048 (1986). Other cases holding that the President's power under the Recess Appointments Clause extends to filling judicial vacancies in Article III courts include United States v. Allocco, 305 F.2d 704 (2d Cir. 1962), cert. denied, 371 U.S. 964 (1963), and Evans v. Stephens, 387 F.3d 1220 (11th Cir. 2004), cert. denied, 544
U.S. 942 (2005). The opinions in the courts of appeals provide a wealth of data on the historical practice of giving recess appointments to judges, including the developments in the Eisenhower Administration, when three Justices, Earl Warren, William Brennan, and Potter Stewart, were so appointed and later confirmed after participation on the Court. The Senate in 1960 adopted a sense of the Senate resolution suggesting that the practice was not a promising idea. 106 Cong. Rec. 18130–18145 (1960).

Section 3 Duties

He shall from time to time give to the Congress Information of the State of the Union, and recommend to their Consideration such Measures as he shall judge necessary and expedient; he may, on extraordinary Occasions, convene both Houses, or either of them, and in Case of Disagreement between them, with Respect to the Time of Adjournment, he may adjourn them to such Time as he shall think proper; he shall receive Ambassadors and other public Ministers; he shall take Care that the Laws be faithfully executed, and shall Commission all the Officers of the US.

Art II.S3.1The President's Legislative Role

He shall from time to time give to Congress Information of State of the Union, and recommend to their Consideration such Measures as he shall judge necessary and expedient; he may, on extraordinary Occasions, convene both Houses, or either, and in Case of Disagreement between them, with Respect to the Time of Adjournment, he may adjourn them to such Time as he shall think proper; he shall receive Ambassadors and other public Ministers; he shall take Care that the Laws be faithfully executed, and Commission Officers of the US.

The first two clauses of Article II, Section 3, relate to the President's legislative role. The first clause, directing the President to report to the Congress on the state of the union, imposes a duty rather than confers a power and serves as the formal basis of the President's legislative leadership. The President's legislative role has grown substantially since 1900. This development reflects changes in political and social forces rather than any pronounced change in constitutional interpretation. The rise of parties and the accompanying recognition of the President as party leader, the appearance of the National Nominating Convention and the Party Platform, and the introduction of the Spoils System all contributed to the growth of the President's legislative role.[1] While certain pre-Civil War Presidents, mostly of Whigs, professed hesitation regarding usurping legislative powers,[2] still earlier Presidents including George Washington, Thomas Jefferson, and Andrew Jackson, took a very different line, albeit less boldly and persistently than later successors.[2] Today, there is no subject on which the President may not appropriately communicate to Congress, in as precise terms as he chooses, his conception of its duty. The President is not obliged by this Clause to impart information which, in his judgment, in the public interest be withheld.

Second clause of Article II, Section 3 authorizes the President to convene or adjourn the Congress in certain circumstances. The President has frequently summoned both Houses into extra or special sessions for legislative purposes, and the Senate alone for the consideration of nominations and treaties. His power to adjourn the Houses has never been exercised.

1. N. Small, Some Presidential Interpretations of the Presidency (1932); W. Binkley, President and Congress (2d ed. 1962); Edward Corwin, Total War, and the Constitution chapters 1, 7 (1946).
2. Presidents Harrison, Polk, Taylor, Fillmore had sentiments to this effect. See 4 Messages and Papers of Presidents 1860, 1864 (J. Richardson ed. 1896); 6 id. at 2513–19, 2561–62, 2608, 2615.

Art II.S3.3 Enforcer of Laws

- Art II.S3.3.1Overview of Take Care Clause
- Art II.S3.3.2Who Can Fulfill the Take Care Duty
- Art II.S3.3.3Relationship - Take Care Clause and President's Removal Power
- Art II.S3.3.5Interpretations of Law as Part of the President's Take Care Duties
- Art II.S3.3.6The President's Take Care Duties and International Law

Art II.S3.3.1 Overview of Take Care Clause

He shall from time to time give to the Congress Information of the State of the Union, and recommend to their Consideration such Measures as he shall judge necessary and expedient; he may, on extraordinary Occasions, convene both Houses, or either of them, and in Case of Disagreement between them, with Respect to the Time of Adjournment, he may adjourn them to such Time as he shall think proper; he shall receive Ambassadors and other public Ministers; he shall take Care that Laws be faithfully executed, Commission Officers of US.

The Constitution provides that the President shall take Care that the Laws be faithfully executed This duty potentially implicates at least five categories of executive power, including: (1) powers the Constitution confers directly upon the President by the opening and succeeding clauses of Article II; (2) powers that congressional acts directly confer upon the President; (3) powers that congressional acts confer upon heads of departments and other executive agencies of the federal government; (4) power that stems implicitly from the duty to enforce the criminal statutes of the United States; and (5) power to carry out the so-called ministerial duties, regarding which an executive officer can exercise limited discretion as to the occasion or manner of their discharge. The following essays explore some of the questions raised by these executive powers, including how the President may exercise the powers which the Constitution or the statutes confer upon him, the relationship between the Take Care Clause and the President's power to remove—and thus supervise—those who wield executive power on his behalf, and extent to which Congress can direct the actions of executive officials.

Art II.S3.3.2 Who Can Fulfill the Take Care Duty

He shall from time to time give to the Congress Information of the State of the Union, and recommend to their Consideration such Measures as he shall judge necessary and expedient; he may, on extraordinary Occasions, convene both Houses, or either of them, and in Case of Disagreement between them, with respect to the Time of Adjournment, he may adjourn them to such Time as he shall think proper; he shall receive Ambassadors and other public Ministers; he shall take Care that the Laws be faithfully executed, and Commission all Officers of the US.

Whereas the British monarch is constitutionally required to always act through agents if his acts are to receive legal recognition, the President is presumed to exercise certain of his constitutional powers personally. In an 1855 opinion, Attorney General Caleb Cushing identified several such examples, including the President's granting of reprieves and pardons for offenses against the United States and his role as the supreme commander in chief of the Army and Navy of the United States, and of the militia of the several States when called into the actual service of the United States.[1] According to Cushing, the President's power as Commander in Chief is constitutionally inherent in the person of the President such that [n]o act of Congress, no act even of the President himself, can, by constitutional possibility, authorize or create any military officer not subordinate to the President.[2] Moreover, according to Cushing, the President's obligation to act personally may be sometimes enlarged by statute. The act organizing the President with other designated officials into an Establishment by name of the Smithsonian Institute, in Cushing's view, is one such example. Cushing also believed that expenditures from the secret service fund, in order to be valid, must be vouched for by the President personally.[3] On like grounds the Supreme Court once held void a court martial decree because it was not specifically approved by the President as required by the 65th Article of War.[4] The Court has effectively overruled this case, and at any rate such cases are exceptional.[5]

Over time, the general rule that developed is that when any duty is cast by law upon the President, it may be exercised by him through the head of the appropriate department, whose acts, if performed within the law, become the President's acts.[6] In Williams v. United States,[7] for instance, the Supreme Court considered a statute that prohibited the advance of public money in any case whatsoever to disbursing officers of the United States, except under special direction by the President.[8] The Supreme Court held that the act did not require the personal performance by the President of this duty.[9] Such a practice, said the Court, would absorb the duties of the various departments of the government in the personal acts of one chief executive officer and be not just impracticable but impossible.[10] While [t]he President's duty in general requires his superintendence of the administration, the Court reasoned that he cannot be required to become the administrative officer of every department and bureau, or to perform in person the numerous details incident to services which he is technically required by the Constitution and applicable laws to perform.[11] As a matter of administrative practice, most orders and instructions are attributed to heads of departments, even though orders and instructions are based on powers conferred to the President.[12]

1. 7 Ops. Atty. Gen. 453, 464–65 (1855).
2. Id.
3. Cf. Act of May 10, 1800, 2 Stat. 78. provision has long since dropped out of the statute book.
4. Runkle v. United States, 122 U.S. 543 (1887).
5. Cf. In In re Chapman, 166 U.S. 661, 670–671 (1897), the Supreme Court held that presumptions in favor of official action preclude collateral attack on the sentences of courts-martial. See also US v. Fletcher, 148
U.S. 84, 88–89 (1893); Bishop v. US, 97 U.S. 334, 341–42 (1905), both of which repudiate Runkle.
6. In exercising his or her executive power under the Constitution, the President speaks and acts through the heads of the several departments in relation to subjects which appertain to their respective duties. The heads of the departments are the President's authorized assistants . . . , and their official acts, promulgated in the regular course of business, are presumptively the President's acts. Wilcox v. McConnel, 38 U.S. (13

7. Pet.) 498, 513 (1839). See also US v. Eliason, 41 U.S. (16 Pet.) 291 (1842); Williams v. US, 42 U.S. (1 How.) 290, 297 (1843); US v. Jones, 59 U.S. (18 How.) 92, 95 (1856); Confiscation Cases, 87 U.S. (20 Wall.) 92(1874); US v. Farden, 99 U.S. 10 (1879); Wolsey v. Chapman, 101 U.S. 755 (1880).
8. 742 U.S. (1 How.) 290 (1843).
9. 3 Stat. 723 (1823) (codified at 31 U.S.C. § 3324).
10. See Williams, 42 U.S. at 297.
11. Id.
12. Id. at 297–98.
13. See 38 Ops. Atty. Gen. 457, 458 (1936). If President exercises his or her duty through subordinates, President must appoint them or the officers who appoint, Buckley v. Valeo, 424 U.S. 1, 109–143 (1976), and he or she must have power to discharge those officers in Executive Branch, Myers v. US, 272 U.S. 52 (1926).

Art II.S3.3.3 Relationship- Take Care Clause and President's Removal Power

He shall from time to time give to the Congress Information of the State of the Union, and recommend to their Consideration such Measures as he shall judge necessary and expedient; he may, on extraordinary Occasions, convene both Houses, or either of them, and in Case of Disagreement between them, with Respect to the Time of Adjournment, he may adjourn them to such Time as he shall think proper; he shall receive Ambassadors and other public Ministers; he shall take Care that Laws be faithfully executed, and shall Commission all Officers of the US.

As the Supreme Court has observed, the Constitution vests all executive power in the President, who must take Care that laws be faithfully executed.[1] Because no single person could fulfill that responsibility alone, the Court notes, the Framers expected that the President would rely on subordinate officers for assistance.[2] As a result, the Court reasoned that [t]he President's power to remove—and thus supervise—those who wield executive power on his behalf follows from the text of Article II.[3]

Some early views of the President's removal power grounds this authority in large part in the Take Care Clause. In a 1789 debate in the First Congress concerning whether the Constitution authorizes the President to remove Executive Branch officers unilaterally, for instance, Representative James Madison expressed the view that the heads of certain executive departments should be removable by the President alone. According to him, it was the intention of the Constitution, expressed especially in the faithful execution clause, that the first magistrate should be responsible for the executive department, and this responsibility carried with it the power to inspect and control the conduct of subordinate Executive Officers.[4] Vesting removal power in the Senate jointly with the President would, in Madison's view, abolish the great principle of unity and responsibility in executive department, which was intended for the security of liberty and public good.[5]

As Supreme Court refined jurisprudence on President's removal power, it came to characterize the basis of this power as stemming generally from separation of power principles in the Constitution, as evidenced by provisions including the Vesting Clause, Take Care Clause, and Appointment Clause.[6]

1. Seila Law LLC v. CFPB, No. 19-7, slip op. 2 (U.S. 2020).
2. Id.
3. Id.
4. 1 Annals of Cong. 495, 499 (1789). For more info about 1789 debate, Decision of 1789, see ArtII.S2.C2.3.15.2 Decision of 1789, Removals in Early Republic.
5. Id. Shortly thereafter, when the question arose as to the power of Congress to regulate the tenure of the Comptroller of the Treasury, Madison assumed a very different position. He conceded in effect that this office was to be an arm of certain of Congress's own powers and should therefore be protected against President's removal power. Id. at 611–612. In Marbury v. Madison, 5 U.S. (1 Cr.) 137 (1803), Justice Marshall drew a parallel distinction between the duties of the Secretary of State under the original act which had created a Dept of Foreign Affairs and those which had been added by a later act. Id. at 166. The former duties were, according to CJ Marshall, entirely political and thus must conform precisely to the will of the President. Id. The latter duties, on the other hand, were exclusively of statutory origin and sprang from the powers of Congress. Id. Chief Justice Marshall reasoned that with respect to these duties, the Secretary was an officer of the law and amenable to the law for his conduct, suggesting that Congress may exercise certain removal power over Executive Officers.
6. For discussion of President's removal power and evolution in its interpretation, see ArtII.S3.3.1 Overview of Take Care Clause through ArtII.S2.C2.3.15.7 21st Century Cases on Removal.

Art II.S3.3.5 Interpretations of Law as Part of the President's Take Care Duties

He shall from time to time give to the Congress Information of the State of the Union, and recommend to their Consideration such Measures as he shall judge necessary and expedient; he may, on extraordinary Occasions, convene both Houses, or either of them, and in Case of Disagreement between them, with Respect to the Time of Adjournment, he may adjourn them to such Time as he shall think proper; he shall receive Ambassadors and other public Ministers; he shall take Care that the Laws be faithfully executed, and shall Commission all Officers of US.

Because the interpretation of law and its scope is a necessary prerequisite to any enforcement action, the precise scope of the President's authority to take Care that the laws be faithfully executed is informed and shaped by this interpretive task. The power accruing to the President from such interpretations is daily illustrated in relation to the Anti-Trust Acts, the Taft-Hartley Act, other statutes.

Nor is this interpretive task the whole story. Not only do all presidential regulations and orders based on statutes that vest power in him or on his own constitutional powers have the force of law, provided they do not transgress the Supreme Court's reading of such statutes or of the Constitution,[1] but in several early cases, the Supreme Court has suggested that the President can sometimes make law in a more special sense.

In the famous Neagle case,[2] an order of the Attorney General to a United States marshal to protect a Justice of the Supreme Court whose life has been threatened by a suitor was attributed to the President and held to be a law of the United States in the sense of section 753 of the Revised Statutes, and as such to afford basis for a writ of habeas corpus transferring the marshal, who had killed the attacker, from state to national custody. Speaking for the Court, Justice Samuel Miller inquired: Is this duty [the duty of the President to take care that the laws be faithfully executed] limited to the enforcement of acts of Congress or of treaties of the US according to their express terms, or does it include the rights, duties and obligations growing out of the Constitution itself, our international relations, and all the protection implied by the nature of the government under the Constitution?[3] The Court assumed an affirmative answer to the second branch of this inquiry, after noting several historical precedents.[4] And, in United States v. Midwest Oil Co.,[5] the Court ruled that the President had, by dint of repeated assertion of it from an early date, acquired the right to withdraw, via the Land Department, public lands, both mineral and non-mineral, from private acquisition, particularly given that Congress had never repudiated the practice.[6]

1. US v. Eliason, 41 U.S. (16 Pet.) 291, 301–02 (1842); Kurtz v. Moffitt, 115 U.S. 487, 503 (1885); Smith v. Whitney, 116 U.S. 167, 180–81 (1886). For analysis of approach determining validity of presidential, or other executive, regulations and orders under congressional delegations or implied executive power, see Chrysler Corp. v. Brown, 441 U.S. 281, 301–16 (1979).
2. In re Neagle, 135 U.S. 1 (1890).
3. 135 U.S. at 64. The phrase, a law of the United States, came from the Act of March 2, 1833, 4 Stat. 632. However, in the Act of June 25, 1948, 62 Stat. 965 (codified at 28 U.S.C. § 2241(c)(2)), the phrase is replaced by the term, an act of Congress, eliminating the basis of the holding in Neagle.
4. Neagle, 135 U.S. at 64–65.
5. 236 U.S. 459 (1915). See also Mason v. United States, 260 U.S. 545 (1923).
6. See Midwest Oil, 236 U.S. at 471–72.

Art II.S3.3.6 The President's Take Care Duties and International Law

He shall from time to time give to the Congress Information of the State of the Union, and recommend to their Consideration such Measures as he shall judge necessary and expedient; he may, on extraordinary Occasions, convene both Houses, or either of them, and in Case of Disagreement between them, with Respect to the Time of Adjournment, he may adjourn them to such Time as he shall think proper; he shall receive Ambassadors and other public Ministers; he shall take Care that the Laws be faithfully executed, and shall Commission all the Officers of the United States.

The President's duty to discharge the responsibilities of the United States in international law raises unique foreign relations considerations.

One example of a significant exercise of the President's powers in this context was the closure of the Marconi Wireless Station at Siasconset, Massachusetts, by President Woodrow Wilson—in effort to avoid difficulties with other foreign governments—on the outbreak of the European War in 1914, after the company refused to assure that it would comply with naval censorship regulations. Justifying this drastic invasion of private rights, Attorney General Thomas Gregory said:

> The President of the United States is at the head of one of the three great coordinate departments of the Government. He is Commander in Chief of the Army and the Navy. . . . If the President is of the opinion that the relations of this country with foreign nations are, or are likely to be endangered, by action deemed by him inconsistent with a due neutrality, it is his right and duty to protect such relations; and in doing so, in the absence of any statutory restrictions, he may act through such executive office or department as appears best adapted to effectuate the desired end. I do not hesitate, in view of the extraordinary conditions existing, to advise that the President, through the Secretary of the Navy or any appropriate department, close down, or take charge of and operate, the plant . . . should he deem it necessary in securing obedience to his proclamation of neutrality.[1]

1. 30 Ops. Atty. Gen. 291 (1914).

Art II.S3.4 Executive Privilege

- Art II.S3.4.1Overview of Executive Privilege
- Art II.S3.4.2Defining Executive Privileges
- Art II.S3.4.8Separation of Powers and Communications Privilege
- Art II.S3.4.9Former Presidents and Communications

Privilege Art II.S3.4.1 Overview of Executive Privilege

He shall from time to time give to the Congress Information of the State of the Union, and recommend to their Consideration such Measures as he shall judge necessary and expedient; he may, on extraordinary Occasions, convene both Houses, or either of them, and in Case of Disagreement between them, with Respect to the Time of Adjournment, he may adjourn them to such Time as he shall think proper; he shall receive Ambassadors and other public Ministers; he shall take Care that the Laws be faithfully executed, and shall Commission all the Officers of the United States.

The doctrine of executive privilege defines the authority of the President to withhold documents or information in his possession or in the possession of the Executive Branch from the Legislative or Judicial Branch of the government.

While the Constitution does not expressly confer upon Executive Branch any such privilege, the Supreme Court has held that executive privilege derives from constitutional separation of powers and from a necessary and proper concept respecting the carrying out of duties of the presidency imposed by the Constitution.[1] Although there are various and distinct components to executive privilege,[2] the privilege's foundation lies in the proposition that in making judgments and reaching decisions, the President and advisors must be free to discuss issues, express opinions, explore options without fear those deliberations will later be made public.[3]

Conceptually, the doctrine of executive privilege may well reflect different considerations in different factual situations. Congress may seek information within the possession of the President in the course of exercising its investigatory powers;[4] government prosecutors may seek information in the course of investigating and prosecuting crimes;[5] and private parties may seek information in the possession of the President for use as evidence in either a criminal or civil proceeding.[6] In all of these contexts, the courts have generally assessed any asserted privilege by weighing the President's need for confidentiality against the interests of the party seeking the information.[7]

Today, it is apparent that executive privilege is qualified rather than absolute. For the vast majority of U.S. history, however, the existence and appropriate scope of the privilege was uncertain and nearly untouched by the courts.[8] Chief Justice John Marshall referred to the confidentiality of presidential communications in Marbury v. Madison and during the treason trial of former Vice President Aaron Burr,[9] but in neither instance [ ] was Marshall forced to definitively decide whether such a presidential privilege existed and if so, in what form.[10] In fact, the judiciary's involvement in addressing the privilege's use in resisting disclosure in the face of either judicial or legislative subpoenas did not begin in earnest until the 1970s Administration of Richard Nixon.[11] Prior to the Nixon era, executive privilege's contours were defined, if at all, by historical practice and the actions and interpretations of Congress and the President. And with little further explication coming from the Supreme Court since, the Nixon era remains the defining era of judicial consideration of the privilege.

This lack of judicial involvement is most pronounced in the context of executive privilege disputes between Congress and the President. The Supreme Court has never directly considered the application of executive privilege in the context of a congressional investigation.[12] Lower federal court decisions are similarly scarce. The only appellate-level decision to reach the merits of an executive privilege dispute between Congress and a sitting President occurred nearly 50 years ago.[13] In light of this near judicial vacuum, the historical actions and interpretations of the branches necessarily play a significant role in establishing the meaning of executive privilege.

1. See US v. Nixon, 418 U.S. 683, 711 (1974) (Nowhere in the Constitution . . . is there explicit reference to a privilege of confidentiality, to the extent this interest relates to effective discharge of a President's powers, it is constitutionally based).
2. See Todd Garvey, Cong. Rsch. Serv., R47102, Executive Privilege and Presidential Communications: Judicial Principles (2022).
3. Id. at 708.
4. See, e.g., S. Select Comm. On Presidential Campaign Activities v. Nixon, 498 F.2d 725 (D.C. Cir. 1974).
5. See, e.g., Nixon, 418 U.S. at 686.
6. See, e.g., Dellums v. Powell, 561 F.2d 242 (D.C. Cir. 1977).
7. Nixon, 418 U.S. at 707.
8. See Nixon v. Adm'r of Gen. Servs., 433 U.S. 425 (1977).
9. Marbury v. Madison, 5 U.S. (1 Cranch) 137, 169–70 (1803) (suggesting the intimate political relation, subsisting between president of the US and heads of depts, necessarily renders any legal investigation of the acts of one of those high officers peculiarly irksome, as well as delicate; and excites some hesitation with respect to the propriety of entering such investigation); US v. Burr, 25 F. Cas. 30, 37 (noting if a letter to Pres Jefferson contains a matter which would be imprudent to disclose, which it is not the wish of the executive to disclose, such matter, if it be not immediately and essentially applicable, will, be suppressed).
10. In re Sealed Case, 121 F.3d 729, 738 (D.C. Cir. 1997).
11. Id. at 739–40 ([I]t was not until the 1970s and Watergate-related lawsuits seeking access to President Nixon's tapes as well as other materials that the existence of the presidential privilege was definitively established as a necessary derivation from the President's constitutional status in a separation of powers regime.); see also Id. at 742 (These lawsuits, referred to generically as the Nixon cases, remain a quarter century later the leading—if not the only—decisions on scope of the presidential communications privilege.).
12. The Supreme Court recently issued an opinion addressing congressional subpoenas for presidential records, but that case did not involve an assertion of executive privilege. See Trump v. Mazars USA, LLP, No. 19-760, slip op. at 5 (U.S. July 9, 2020) (The President did not resist the subpoenas by arguing that any of the requested records were protected by executive privilege.); Id. at 2 (We have never addressed a congressional subpoena for the President's information.).
13. See S. Select Comm. on Presidential Campaign Activities v. Nixon, 498 F.2d 725 (D.C. Cir. 1974). The D.C. Circuit recently reached the merits of a dispute between the House and a former President. Trump v. Thompson, 20 F.4th 10 (D.C. Cir. 2021), cert. denied, No. 21A272, slip op. (U.S. Jan. 20, 2022) (2022).

Art II.S3.4.2 Defining Executive Privileges

He shall from time to time give to the Congress Information of the State of the Union, and recommend to their Consideration such Measures as he shall judge necessary and expedient; he may, on extraordinary Occasions, convene both Houses, or either of them, and in Case of Disagreement between them, with Respect to the Time of Adjournment, he may adjourn them to such Time as he shall think proper; he shall receive Ambassadors and other public Ministers; he shall take Care that Laws be faithfully executed, and shall Commission all Officers of the US. There is not a single executive privilege. Instead, a suite of distinct privileges exists, each of different—though sometimes overlapping—scope.[1] The political branches, in support of their often-competing interests and priorities, have adopted somewhat divergent views on these different component privileges.

Whereas Congress has generally interpreted executive privilege narrowly, limiting its application to the types of presidential, national security, and diplomatic communications referenced by judicial decisions,[2] the Executive Branch has historically viewed executive privilege more broadly, providing protections to different categories of documents and communications that implicate Executive Branch confidentiality interests.[3] Under the Executive Branch's interpretation, these privileges include:

- the State Secrets Privilege, which protects certain military, diplomatic, and national security information;[4]
- the Presidential Communications Privilege, which generally protects confidential communications between the President and his advisers that relate to presidential decision making, as well as a certain subset of communications not involving the President but that are still made for purposes of advising the President;[5]
- the Deliberative Process Privilege, which protects pre-decisional and deliberative communications within Executive Branch agencies;[6] and
- the Law Enforcement Privilege, which protects the contents of open (and sometimes closed) law enforcement files, including communications related to investigative and prosecutorial decisionmaking.[7]

Executive Branch has tended to consolidate these various privileges into one executive privilege, particularly when responding to congressional investigative requests.[8] Congressional committees, on the other hand, typically distinguished among the different individual privileges.[9]

The executive privileges may appropriately be treated as distinct, not only because of the different communications they protect, but also because the privileges appear to arise from different sources of law, with some more firmly established in judicial precedent than others. In short, the different privileges apply with different strengths and, in the congressional context, are balanced against Congress's Article I powers differently. For example, courts have traditionally shown the utmost deference to presidential claims of a need to protect military or diplomatic secrets.[10] The President's more generalized interest in the confidentiality of his other communications, though arising implicitly from the Constitution, has not been extended this high degree of deference.[11] Because the other privileges have been given less weight, they are assessed differently in the face of an exercise of Congress's investigative powers. For example, when compared to the Presidential Communications Privilege, the Deliberative Process Privilege is more easily overcome by Congress and disappears altogether when there is any reason to believe government misconduct occurred.[12]

Its legal source also appears to be different from the Presidential Communications Privilege, as it arises primarily from the common law,[13] but may have a constitutional dimension.[14] Least potent are those executive privileges that arise purely from the common law, which have generally been viewed, at least by Congress, as legally insufficient to justify noncompliance with a congressional subpoena.[15]

1. In re Sealed Case, 121 F.3d at 736 (noting that executive officials have claimed a variety of privileges to resist disclosure of information). See also John E. Bies, Primer on Executive Privilege and the Executive Branch Approach to Congressional Oversight, Lawfare (June 16, 2017), https://www.lawfareblog.com/primer-executive-privilege-and-executive-branch-approach-congressional-oversight ([A] review of Executive Branch practice identifies a number of categories of information that the Executive Branch, at least, believes may be protected by an invocation of the privilege.).
2. See Rep. on President Bush's Assertion of Executive Privilege in Response to the Committee Subpoena to Attorney General Michael B. Mukasey, H. Comm. on Oversight and Gov't Reform, 110th Cong. 8 (Comm. Print 2008) (rejecting an executive privilege claim on the grounds that [t]he Attorney General did not cite a single judicial decision recognizing this alleged privilege); H.R. Rep. No. 105–728, at 16 n. 43 (1998) (As the D.C. Circuit has recently held, the doctrine of executive privilege which arises from the constitutional separation of powers applies only to decision-making of the President. Since the subject of the Committee's subpoena is not one that does (or legally could) involve Presidential decision-making, no constitutional privilege could be invoked here.) (citations omitted)).
3. See Assertion of Executive Privilege Over Documents Generated in Response to Congressional Investigation into Operation Fast and Furious, 8 Op. O.L.C. 101, 116 (2012) (The scope of executive privilege includes several related areas in which confidentiality within the Executive Branch is necessary for the effective execution of the laws.).
4. Id. at 116–17.
5. Id. at 116.
6. See Assertion of Exec Privilege Over Documents Generated re: Congressional Investigation into Operation Fast and Furious, 36 Op. O.L.C. 1 (2012).
7. See Protective Assertion of Executive Privilege Over Unredacted Mueller Report and Related Investigative Files, 43 Op. O.L.C. 374 (2019).
8. See 8 Op. O.L.C. 101, 116 (1984) (reasoning that [t]the scope of executive privilege includes several related areas); 13 Op. O.L.C. 153, 154 (1989) (reasoning that the Executive Branch's interest in keeping the information confidential is usually discussed in terms of 'executive privilege').
9. See , Rep. on President Bush's Assertion of Executive Privilege in Response to the Committee Subpoena to Attorney General Michael B. Mukasey H. Comm. on Oversight and Gov't Reform, 110th Cong. 8 (Comm. Print 2008) (The Attorney General's argument that the subpoena implicates the 'law enforcement component' of executive privilege is equally flawed. There is no basis to support the proposition that a Law Enforcement Privilege, particularly one applied to closed investigations, can shield from congressional scrutiny information that is important for addressing congressional oversight concerns. The Attorney General did not cite a single judicial decision recognizing this alleged privilege.); H.R. Rep. No. 105–728, at 16 n. 43 (1998) (As the D.C. Circuit has recently held, the doctrine of executive privilege which arises from the constitutional separation of powers applies only to decision making of the President. Since the subject of the Committee's subpoena is not one that does (or could) involve Presidential decision making, no constitutional privilege could be here.)
10. United States v. Nixon, 418 U.S. 683, 710 (1974).
11. Id. at 711.
12. In re Sealed Case, 121 F.3d 729, 746 (D.C. Cir. 1997). Given its broad scope, the Deliberative Process Privilege is the most frequent form of executive privilege raised. Id. at 737.

13. In In re Sealed Case, D.C. Circuit determined the deliberative process privilege is primarily a common law privilege, but that some aspects of the privilege, for example the protection accorded mental processes of agency officials, have roots in constitutional separation of powers. 121 F.3d at 745, 737 n.4.
14. Comm. on Oversight & Gov't Reform v. Lynch, 156 F. Supp. 3d 101, 104 (D.D.C. 2016). The scope and source of the Law Enforcement Privilege is unclear, particularly when asserted in the context of congressional investigations where committees have voiced consistent objections to its use. Congress has previously viewed the Executive Branch's position on the confidentiality of law enforcement information as a nondisclosure policy rather than a constitutionally based privilege. See Rep. on President Bush's Assertion of Executive Privilege in Response to the Committee Subpoena to Attorney General Michael B. Mukasey,
H. Comm. on Oversight and Gov't Reform, 110th Cong. 8 (Comm. Print 2008).
15. The Supreme Court recently stated in dicta that the recipients of a congressional subpoena have long been understood to retain common law . . . privileges with respect to certain materials Trump v. Mazars USA,
LLP, No. 19-760, slip op. at 12 (U.S. July 9, 2020). This statement is in tension with the congressional practice of treating common law privileges as discretionary and has been subject to some criticism. See Christopher M. Davis, Todd Garvey, Ben Wilhelm, et al. Cong. Rsch. Serv., RL30240, Congressional Oversight Manual, at 62–63 (2022).

ArtII.S3.4.8 Separation of Powers and Communications Privilege

He shall from time to time give to the Congress Information of the State of the Union, and recommend to their Consideration such Measures as he shall judge necessary and expedient; he may, on extraordinary Occasions, convene both Houses, or either of them, and in Case of Disagreement between them, with Respect to the Time of Adjournment, he may adjourn them to such Time as he shall think proper; he shall receive Ambassadors and other public Ministers; he shall take Care that the Laws be faithfully executed, and Commission all Officers of the US.

In 2004, the Supreme Court issued Cheney v. United States District Court[1] in which it reaffirmed distinctions first articulated in the Nixon-era cases between civil and criminal proceedings and expounded on the relationship between the Communications Privilege and the separation of powers.

The Cheney decision interacted with the Communications Privilege in a complicated procedural posture, and for this reason the implications of the decision to more traditional scenarios, especially to the congressional context, are difficult to discern. In Cheney, a federal district court had entered orders in a Federal Advisory Committee Act (FACA) lawsuit allowing discovery of documents relating to the structure and operation of the National Energy Policy Development Group (NEPDG), a task force chaired by the Vice President and established to give policy recommendations on energy issues to the President.[2] The George W. Bush Administration, though not asserting executive privilege, challenged that discovery order on the ground that it represented a substantial intrusion[ ] on the process by which those in closest operational proximity to the President advise the President in violation of the separation of powers.[3]

The district court and the D.C. Circuit rejected the Administration's arguments, mainly because the Administration had another means to protect its interests; it could assert executive privilege in response to the civil discovery subpoena.[4]

The Supreme Court reversed, holding that when a lower court has allowed unnecessarily broad discovery, reviewing courts have authority to explore other avenues, short of forcing the Executive to invoke privilege.[5] The Court reasoned that to require the Executive Branch to assert the Communications Privilege in such a scenario would ignore the weighty separation of powers objections raised in the case, because [o]once executive privilege is asserted, coequal branches of the Government are set on a collision course.[6] The Court determined that the lower courts had labored under the mistaken assumption that the assertion of executive privilege is a necessary precondition to the Government's separation of powers objections.[7] Cheney, therefore, appears to suggest that there are separation of powers concerns associated with executive confidentiality issues that attach even before executive privilege is asserted.[8]

Cheney also reaffirmed the principle that the confidentiality interests associated with the Communications Privilege are weighed differently in different types of proceedings. In fact, the nature of proceeding, whether civil or criminal, appears to affect both sides of the judicially developed balancing test. As for the requesting party, the Court held that [t]he need for information for use in civil cases, while far from negligible, does not share the urgency or significance of [a] criminal subpoena, where the need for the information is much weightier.[9]

As for the President's interest, the court viewed the potential for a civil subpoena to disrupt the functioning of the Executive Branch as far greater than a criminal subpoena. In the criminal context, there are various constraints . . . to filter out insubstantial legal claims, but there are no analogous checks in the civil discovery process.[10] Like past cases, however, Cheney did not address how a congressional proceeding relates to either civil or criminal proceedings.[11]

1. Cheney v. U.S. Dist. Ct., 542 U.S. 367, 383–91 (2004)
2. Id. at 376.
3. Id. at 381. That action was in the form of mandamus, which . . . requires a party to show that there is no other adequate means to attain the relief desired. Id. at 403.
4. Id. at 376–77.
5. Id. at 390.
6. Id. at 391, 389.
7. Cheney, 542 U.S. at 391.
8. Id. at 385 (special considerations control when Executive Branch's interests in maintaining autonomy of office and safeguarding confidentiality of communications are implicated.). See, Karnoski v. Trump, 926 F.3d 1180, 1205–06 (9th Cir. 2019).
9. Cheney, 542 U.S. at 384.

10. Id. at 386 (noting that in the criminal system decisions are made by a publicly accountable prosecutor subject to budgetary considerations and subject to the responsible exercise of prosecutorial discretion).
11. The Supreme Court did appear to draw a distinction between the criminal process and the legislative process in Trump v. Mazars USA, LLP, No. 19-715 (U.S. May 12, 2020) (Unlike in criminal proceedings, where '[t]he very integrity of the judicial system' would be undermined without 'full disclosure of all the facts,' efforts to craft legislation involve predictive policy judgments that are 'not hamper[ed] . . . in quite the same way' when every scrap of potentially relevant evidence is not available. While we certainly recognize Congress's important interests in obtaining information through appropriate inquiries, those interests are not sufficiently powerful to justify access to the President's personal papers when other sources could provide Congress the information it needs.) (citations omitted).

Art II.S3.4.9 Former Presidents and Communications Privilege

He shall from time to time give to the Congress Information of the State of the Union, and recommend to their Consideration such Measures as he shall judge necessary and expedient; he may, on extraordinary Occasions, convene both Houses, or either of them, and in Case of Disagreement between them, with Respect to the Time of Adjournment, he may adjourn them to such Time as he shall think proper; he shall receive Ambassadors and other public Ministers; he shall take Care that the Laws be faithfully executed, and Commission all Officers of the US.

In Nixon II, Supreme Court determined the Communications Privilege continues to protect presidential communications after the conclusion of the Administration within which the communication occurred and may be asserted by the former President.[1] As described above, the Court found that a former President may legitimately assert the Communications Privilege to prevent disclosure of his official records after he has left office.[2]

The Court reasoned that the confidentiality necessary to ensure the free exchange of ideas between the President and his advisers while the President is in office cannot be measured by the few months or years between the submission of the information and the end of the President's tenure; the privilege is not for the benefit of the President as an individual, but for the benefit of the Republic. Therefore, the privilege survives the individual President's tenure.[3]

The Court's determination appears to have rested on the reasoning that the general purpose of the Communications Privilege—ensuring the provision of frank advice to the President—could be threatened or undermined no matter when the disclosure of the covered communications occurs. Nixon II distinguished former Presidents from incumbents in three important ways. First, the Court explicitly stated that to the extent that the privilege serves as a shield for executive officials against burdensome requests for information which might interfere with proper performance of their duties, a former President is in less need of it than an incumbent.[4]

Second, the Court concluded that the expectation of the confidentiality of executive communications is subject to erosion over time after an administration leaves office.[5] Thus, the strength of a former President's Communications Privilege claim appears to dwindle as time passes.

Third and most importantly, the Court determined that because only the sitting President is charged with performance of executive duty under the Constitution, he is in the best position to assess present and future needs of the Executive Branch, and support invocation of the privilege accordingly.[6] In Nixon II, the fact that President Carte—the sitting President at the time—did not support former President Nixon's privilege claim detract[ed] from the weight of Nixon's assertion.[7] In the Court's view, it is the incumbent President who is better situated to make determinations about executive confidentiality, because it is the incumbent President who may suffer the harm that the Communications Privilege purports to protect against if privileged documents were disclosed (namely that current advisers would be dissuaded from giving the incumbent President candid advice).[8] As a result, when the incumbent President does not support a former President's privilege claim, the strength of the claim declines.

The importance of the incumbent's concurrence to a privilege claim by a former President was recently reaffirmed in Trump v. Thompson.[9] Thompson arose from the inquiry conducted by the House Select Committee to Investigate the January 6th Attack on the U.S. Capitol (Select Committee). As part of its investigation, the Select Committee requested National Archives and Records Administration (NARA) produce relevant presidential records from the former Trump Administration pursuant to the Presidential Records Act (PRA).[10] The request sought various categories of White House communications and documents created on or around January 6, 2021. Under the PRA, if any congressional committee requests a presidential record on a matter within its jurisdiction that is needed for the conduct of its business and that is not otherwise available, the National Archives shall make the record available.[11] However, consistent with principles established in Nixon and Nixon II, the PRA also preserves the right of both current and former Presidents to assert privilege claims by providing that disclosure by NARA is subject to any rights, defenses, or privileges which the US or any agency or person may invoke.[12]

Shortly thereafter, President Joseph Biden determined that under the unique extraordinary circumstances because of Congress's compelling need to understand the events of January 6, asserting executive privilege over the requested documents would not be in the best interests of the United States.[13] Former President Trump disagreed and notified the Archivist that he was asserting the Communications Privilege.

After President Biden clarified that he would not uphold the former President's assertion of Privilege, former President Trump filed suit in federal district court to block NARA from disclosing privileged documents to the Select Committee.[14]

The D.C. District Court in Thompson viewed the case as a dispute between a former and incumbent President.[15] Citing to Nixon II, the court stated that because the incumbent President is best suited to identify and determine the best interests of the Executive Branch, former President Trump's Privilege claim was outweighed by President Biden's decision not to uphold the Privilege.[16] Moreover, the court reasoned that to side with the former President would not only second guess the sitting President's judgment, but also the Legislative Branch's judgment—for both President Biden and the House agree, requested documents should be disclosed.[17] The D.C. Circuit affirmed the district court decision on appeal. The court acknowledged, with reference to Nixon II, that there was no question that former President Trump could assert the Communications Privilege and that the Communications Privilege was of constitutional stature.[18] The court held that a rare and formidable alignment of [three] factors supported disclosure of the documents to the Committee and outweighed the former President's interest in confidentiality.[19]

First, the court stated that President Biden's determination that it was neither in the Executive Branch's nor the public's interest to assert Privilege over the requested documents carries immense weight in overcoming the former President's claim.[20] Consistent with previous case law, the court viewed President Biden as principal holder and keeper of executive privilege and the judiciary as ill equipped to . .second guess expert judgment of the sitting President.[21]

Second, the House had a uniquely weighty interest in investigating the causes and circumstances of the January 6 attack on the U.S. Capitol.[22] Indeed, the court noted that having presented a sound factual predicate for the requested documents, there would seem to be few, if any, more imperative interests squarely within Congress's wheelhouse than ensuring the safe and uninterrupted conduct of its constitutionally assigned business.[23]

Third, and weighing still more heavily against former President Trump, was the fact that the judgment of the Political Branches is unified as to these particular documents.[24] The court was unwilling to needlessly disturb 'the compromises and working arrangements that the Congress and the President had already reached.[25]

In light of these three factors, the D.C. Circuit held that the profound interests in disclosure advanced by President Biden and the January 6th Committee far exceed [former President Trump's] generalized concerns for Executive Branch confidentiality.[26]

That holding was given added significance by the court's determination that it would have been compelled to reach that conclusion under any of the tests advocated by former President Trump, including the demonstrated, specific need standard from Nixon or the demonstrably critical standard from Senate Select.[27] As such, it appears the Select Committee would have been able to overcome the Communications Privilege in this circumstance even if President Biden had supported former President Trump's Privilege claim.

The Supreme Court picked up on this point in denying former President Trump's petition to stay the D.C. Circuit decision.[28] In interpreting the opinion below, the Supreme Court—in an unsigned order—reasoned that Mr. Trump's status as a former President made no difference to the court's decision since the D.C. Circuit had concluded that President Trump's claims would have failed even if he were an incumbent.[29] Because the former President's assertion of privilege would have been unsuccessful either way, the Court declared the D.C. Circuit's discussion . . . to be nonbinding dictum.[29]

1. Nixon v. Adm'r of Gen. Servs. (Nixon II), 433 U.S. 425, 446-49 (1977).
2. Id. at 449.
3. Id. (citations omitted).
4. Id. at 448.
5. Id. at 451.
6. Id. at 449.
7. Id., at 449.
8. Id.
9. Trump v. Thompson, 20 F.4th 10 (D.C. Cir. 2021), cert. denied, No. 21A272 (U.S. Jan. 20, 2022).
10. Id. at 16.
11. 44 U.S.C. § 2205(2)(C).
12. Id. at § 2205(2).
13. Thompson, 20 F.4th at 20–21.
14. Id. at 21–22.
15. Trump v. Thompson, 573 F. Supp. 3d 1, 26 (D.D.C. 2021).
16. Id. at 29.
17. Id. at 27–29.
18. Thompson, 20 F. 4th at 32.
19. Id. at 33.
20. Id.
21. Id. at 35.
22. Id.
23. Id. at 35–36.
24. Id., at 37.
25. Id. at 38 (quoting Trump v. Mazars USA, LLP, No. 19-715 (U.S. May 12, 2020)).
26. Id. at 33.
27. Id. at 41 (legislative interest at stake passes muster under any tests pressed by former President Trump.).
28. Trump v. Thompson, No. 21A272 (U.S. Jan. 20, 2022). The Supreme Court later denied certiorari. No. 21A272 (U.S. Jan. 20, 2022).
29. Id. Justice Clarence Thomas would have granted the former President's application. Justice Brett Kavanaugh authored a concurrence to clarify his position that [a] former President must be able to successfully invoke the Presidential communications privilege for communications that occurred during his Presidency. Id. (Kavanaugh, J., concurring). Once invoked, it appears to be Justice Kavanaugh's view that tests from Nixon and Senate Select may apply to a former President's privilege claim as they do to a current President's privilege claim. Id.

Art II.S3.5 Presidential Immunity

- Art II.S3.5.1Presidential Immunity to Suits and Official Conduct
- Art II.S3.5.2Presidential Immunity, Suits, and Unofficial Conduct
- Art II.S3.5.3Qualified Immunity Doctrine
- Art II.S3.5.4Criminal Prosecution, Presidential Immunity, Former Presidents

Art II.S3.5.1 Presidential Immunity to Suits and Official Conduct

He shall from time to time give to the Congress Information of the State of the Union, and recommend to their Consideration such Measures as he shall judge necessary and expedient; he may, on extraordinary Occasions, convene both Houses, or either of them, and in Case of Disagreement between them, with Respect to the Time of Adjournment, he may adjourn them to such Time as he shall think proper; he shall receive Ambassadors and other public Ministers; he shall take Care that the Laws be faithfully executed, and Commission all Officers of the US.

In its 1867 decision Mississippi v. Johnson, the Supreme Court established that the President is largely beyond the reach of the judiciary by holding that it could not direct President Andrew Johnson in how he exercised his purely executive and political powers.[1] The Court stated, it had no jurisdiction . . . to enjoin the President in the performance of his official duties.[2]

In subsequent decisions, however, the Court made clear that Johnson does not stand for the proposition that the President is immune from judicial process. For example, in United States v. Nixon,[3] the Court held that President Richard Nixon was amenable to a subpoena to produce evidence for use in a federal criminal case. There, the President had argued that he was immune to judicial process, claiming that the independence of the Executive Branch within its own sphere insulates a President from a judicial subpoena in an ongoing criminal prosecution.[4] The Supreme Court unanimously disagreed, holding that neither the doctrine of separation of powers, nor the need for confidentiality of high-level communications, without more, can sustain an absolute, unqualified Presidential privilege of immunity from judicial process under all circumstances.[5] The Court noted that the constitutional duty of courts to do justice in criminal prosecutions was counterbalanced by the claim of presidential immunity. To accept the President's argument, the Court further reasoned, would undermine the separation of powers that was at the core of a workable government as well as gravely impair the role of the courts under Art. III.[6]

Throughout the Watergate investigation, it was unclear whether the President could be subject to criminal prosecution prior to being convicted upon impeachment.[7] The Court, however, resolved that courts may require the President to testify or produce documents in criminal proceedings.[8] This principle dates to the earliest days of the Republic, when Chief Justice John Marshall presided as the Circuit Justice for Virginia over the treason trial of Aaron Burr. In that case, Chief Justice Marshall concluded that President Thomas Jefferson could be subject to a subpoena to provide a document relevant to the trial.[9] Specifically, Chief Justice Marshall declared that, in contrast to common law privileges afforded the King of England, the President was not exempt from general provisions of the constitution, like the Sixth Amendment, which provides the defense compulsory process.[10]

Chief Justice Marshall recognized that while the President could be subject to a criminal subpoena, the President could still withhold information from disclosure based on executive privilege.[11] In the two centuries since the Burr trial, the Executive Branch's practices[12] and Supreme Court rulings unequivocally and emphatically endorsed Chief Justice Marshall's position that the President was subject to federal criminal process.[13] In its 2020 opinion in Trump v. Vance, the Court extended this precedent to state criminal proceedings, concluding that President was not absolutely immune from state criminal subpoenas.[14]

Finally, with respect to civil liability, the Court held in Nixon v. Fitzgerald that the President is absolutely immune in actions for civil damages for all acts within the outer perimeter of his official duties.[15] The Court's close decision was premised on the President's unique position in the constitutional scheme, that is, the Court conducted a kind of 'public policy' analysis of the policies and principles that may be considered implicit in the nature of the President's office in a system structured to achieve effective government under a constitutionally mandated separation of powers.[16] Although the Constitution expressly afforded Members of Congress immunity in matters arising from speech or debate and was silent on presidential immunity, the Court nonetheless considered immunity to be a functionally mandated incident of the President's unique office, rooted in the constitutional tradition of the separation of powers and supported by our history.[17]

While the Court relied, in part, upon its practice of finding immunity for officers, such as judges, for whom the Constitution is silent, but for which a long common-law history exists, and in part upon historical evidence, which it admitted was fragmentary and ambiguous,[18] the Court focused on the fact that the President is different from all other executive officials.

The President is charged with a long list of supervisory and policy responsibilities of utmost discretion and sensitivity,[19,] and diversion of his energies by concerns with private lawsuits would raise unique risks to the effective functioning of government.[20] Moreover, the presidential privilege is rooted in the separation of powers doctrine, counseling courts to tread carefully before intruding. While some interests are important enough to require judicial action, the Court reasoned that merely private suit[s] for damages based on a President's official acts do not serve this broad public interest necessitating the courts to act.[21] Finally, qualified immunity would not adequately protect the President, because judicial inquiry into analysis of his actions would bring the evil immunity it was to prevent; absolute immunity was required.[22]

1. 71 U.S. (4 Wall.) 475 (1867). The Court declined to express an opinion on whether, in any case, the President of the United States may be required, by the process of this court, to perform a purely ministerial act under a positive law, or may be held amenable, otherwise than by impeachment for crime. Id., at 498. See Franklin v. Massachusetts, 505 U.S. 788, 825–28 (1992) (Scalia, J., concurring). In NTEU v. Nixon, 492 F.2d 587 (D.C. Cir. 1974), the court held it could issue a writ of mandamus to compel President to perform a ministerial act, although it said that if another officer were available, it should be applied to him.
2. Johnson, 71 U.S. at 501.
3. United States v. Nixon, 418 U.S. 683 (1974)
4. Id. at 706.
5. Id.
6. Id. at 706–07. The lower courts considered the issue more fully. In re Grand Jury Subpoena to Richard M. Nixon, 360 F. Supp. 1, 6–10 (D.D.C. 1973) (Judge Sirica), aff'd sub nom., Nixon v. Sirica, 487 F.2d 700, 708–712 (D.C. Cir. 1973) (en banc) (refusing to find President immune from process). Assessments of the subpoena of President Jefferson in the Burr trial have conflicted. US v. Burr, 25 F. Cas. 187 (No. 14694) (C.C.D.Va. 1807). For history, see Paul Freund, Foreword: On Presidential Privilege, The Supreme Court, 1973 Term, 88 Harv. L. Rev. 13, 23–30 (1974).
7. Impeachment Clause provides that a party convicted upon impeachment shall nonetheless be liable for criminal proceedings. U.S. Const. art. I, § 3, cl. 7. Gouverneur Morris in Convention, Alexander Hamilton in Federalist Papers asserted a criminal trial would follow a successful impeachment. See 2 Records of the Federal Convention of 1787, at 500 (Max Farrand ed., 1937); The Federalist Nos. 65 & 69.
8. See Trump v. Vance, No. 19-635 (July 9, 2020) (recognizing the public has a right to every man's evidence).
9. See United States v. Burr, 25 F. Cas. 30, 34 (C.C.D. Va. 1807) (No. 14,692D).
10. See id. (observing that while the King is born to power and can do no wrong, the President, by contrast, is of the people and subject to the law).
11. See United States v. Burr, 25 F. Cas. 187, 192 (C.C.D. Va. 1807) (No. 14,694).
12. See Vance, No. 19-635, slip op. at 7–9 (discussing historical practices of Presidents Monroe, U S. Grant, Ford, Carter, and Clinton).
13. Clinton v. Jones, 520 U.S. 681, 704 (1997) (citing US v. Nixon, 418 U.S. 683, 706 (1974)). In rejecting separation of powers challenges to claims that the President is immune from federal criminal process, the Court rejected the argument that criminal subpoenas rise to the level of constitutionally forbidden impairment of the Executive's ability to perform its constitutionally mandated functions. Id. at 702–03.
14. See Vance, No. 19-635, slip op. at 12–15 (rejecting the categorical argument that state criminal subpoenas would unduly distract the President, impose a stigma on the presidency, or result in harassment by state prosecutors). The Vance Court also rejected the argument that a state prosecutor should satisfy a heightened standard of need when seeking a sitting President's records. Id. at 15–16. More important, in Vance, the state prosecutor sought private presidential records, and executive privilege was not at issue. Id. (Kavanaugh, J., concurring). The Court refused to extend the heightened-need standard in Nixon to private records, reasoning that: (1) Burr and its progeny foreclosed that argument; (2) the heightened-need standard was unnecessary to allow the President to fulfill his Article II functions; (3) the public interest in fair and effective law enforcement favors access to evidence. Id. (majority opinion).

15. Nixon v. Fitzgerald, 457 U.S. 731 (1982)
16. Id. at 748.
17. Id. at 749.
18. Id. at 750–52 n.31.
19. Id. at 750.
20. Id. at 751.
21. Id. at 754.
22. Id. at 755–57. Justices Byron White, William Brennan, Thurgood Marshall, and Henry Blackmun dissented. The Court reserved decision on whether Congress could expressly create a damages action against the President and abrogate immunity, id. at 748–49 n.27, thus appearing to disclaim that the Constitution mandated the decision; Chief Justice Warren Burger disagreed with the implication of this footnote, id. at 763–64 n.7 (concurring opinion), and the dissenters noted they agreed with the Chief Justice on this point. Id. at 770 & n.4.

Art II.S3.5.2 Presidential Immunity to Suits and Unofficial Conduct

He shall from time to time give to the Congress Information of the State of the Union, and recommend to their Consideration such Measures as he shall judge necessary and expedient; he may, on extraordinary Occasions, convene both Houses, or either of them, and in Case of Disagreement between them, with Respect to the Time of Adjournment, he may adjourn them to such Time as he shall think proper; he shall receive Ambassadors and other public Ministers; he shall take Care that the Laws be faithfully executed, and Commission all Officers of the US.

.In Clinton v. Jones,[1] the Court, in a case of first impression, held that President William Clinton did not have qualified immunity from civil suit for conduct alleged to have taken place prior to his election, and therefore denied President Clinton's request to delay both the trial and discovery. The Court held that its precedents affording the President immunity from suit for his official conduct—primarily so that the President could perform his duties effectively absent fear that a particular decision might lead to personal liability—did not apply when the alleged conduct at issue had occurred before his election. Moreover, the Supreme Court observed, the separation of powers doctrine did not require a stay of all private actions against the President, as the trial court had sufficient powers to accommodate the President's schedule and his workload so as not to impede the President from performing his duties. Finally, the Court stated that allowing such suits to proceed would not generate a large volume of politically motivated harassing frivolous litigation. Congress has power, the Court advised, if it think necessary, to protect the President.[2].

While courts may be unable to compel the President to act or prevent him from acting, his acts, when performed, are generally subject to judicial review and disallowance. Typically, the President's subordinates, through whom he acts, may be sued pursuant to a legal fiction to enjoin committing acts that might lead to irreparable damage[3] or to compel by writ of mandamus performing a duty required by law.[4]

Such suits are usually brought in the United States District Court for the District of Columbia.[5] In common law, courts may hold a subordinate executive officer personally liable for damages that resulted from any act the officer committed that was beyond his authority,[6] although he has immunity for anything, even malicious wrongdoing, that he does in performing his duties.[7]

Different rules prevail when a plaintiff sues an officer for a constitutional tort.[8] The Court has suggested that, in some sensitive areas, officers acting in the outer perimeter of their duties may be accorded absolute immunity from liability.[9] To reach such officers for acts for which they can be held responsible, courts must use the general federal question jurisdictional statute.[10]. On deleting the jurisdictional amount, see Pub. L. No. 94-574, 90 Stat. 2721 (1976); Pub. L. No. 96-486, 94 Stat. 2369 (1980). If suits are brought in state courts, they can be removed to federal district courts. 28 U.S.C. § 1442(a). 28 U.S.C. § 1331.

1. 520 U.S. 681 (1997)
2. 457 U.S. at 749.
3. E.g., Youngstown Sheet & Tube Co. v. Sawyer, 343 U.S. 579 (1952) (suit to enjoin Secretary of Commerce to return steel mills seized on President's order); Dames & Moore v. Regan, 453 U.S. 654 (1981) (suit against Secretary of Treasury to nullify presidential orders on Iranian assets). See also Noble v. Union River Logging Railroad, 147 U.S. 165 (1893); Philadelphia Co. v. Stimson, 223 U.S. 605 (1912).
4. E.g., Marbury v. Madison, 5 U.S. (1 Cr.) 137 (1803) (suit against Secretary of State to compel delivery of commissions of office); Kendall v. United States ex rel. Stokes, 37 U.S. (12 Pet.) 524 (1838) (suit against Postmaster General to compel payment of money owed under act of Congress); Decatur v. Paulding, 39 U.S. (14 Pet.) 497 (1840) (suit to compel Secretary of Navy to pay a pension).
5. This was based on the theory that Supreme Court of the District of Columbia had inherited, via common law of Maryland, jurisdiction of the King's Bench over inferior jurisdictions and officers. Kendall v. United States ex rel. Stokes, 37 U.S. (12 Pet.) 524, 614, 620–(1838). Congress has since authorized federal district courts outside District of Columbia to entertain such suits. Act of Oct 5, 1962, Pub. L. No. 87-748, 76 Stat. 744 (codified at 28 U.S.C. § 1361).
6. E.g., Little v. Barreme, 6 U.S. (2 Cr.) 170 (1804); Bates v. Clark, 95 U.S. 204 (1877); US v. Lee, 106 U.S. 196 (1882); Virginia Coupon Cases (Poindexter v. Greenhow), 114 U.S. 270 (1885); Belknap v. Schild, 161 U.S. 10 (1896).
7. Spalding v. Vilas, 161 U.S. 483 (1896); Barr v. Matteo, 360 U.S. 564 (1959). See Westfall v. Erwin, 484 U.S. 292 (1988) (an action must be discretionary in nature as well as within the scope of employment, before a federal official is entitled to absolute immunity). Following the Westfall decision, Congress enacted the Federal Employees Liability Reform and Tort Compensation Act of 1988 (the Westfall Act), which authorized the Attorney General to certify that an employee was acting within the scope of his office or employment at the time an incident occurred that led to a lawsuit; upon certification, the employee is dismissed from the action, and the United States is substituted. As a result, sometimes the action will be dismissed against the government because the government has not waived sovereign immunity under the Federal Tort Claims Act. United States v. Smith, 499 U.S. 160 (1991) (the Westfall Act bars suit against federal employee even if sovereign immunity forecloses suit against the government). Cognizant of temptation of the government to immunize itself and its employee, the Court in Gutierrez de Martinez v. Lamagno, 515 U.S. 417 (1995), held, an Attorney General's certification is subject to judicial review.

8. The Supreme Court recognized an implied cause of action against officers accused of constitutional violations in Bivens v. Six Unknown Named Agents of the Federal Bureau of Narcotics, 403 U.S. 388 (1971). In Butz v. Economou, 438 U.S. 478 (1978), which concerned a Bivens action, the Court distinguished between common-law torts and constitutional torts and denied high federal officials, including cabinet secretaries, absolute immunity, in favor of the qualified immunity Congress had previously accorded high state officials under 42 U.S.C. § 1983. In Harlow v. Fitzgerald, 457 U.S. 800 (1982), the Court denied presidential aides derivative absolute presidential immunity, but it modified the rules of qualified immunity, making it more difficult to hold such aides, other federal officials, and state and local officials, liable for constitutional torts. In Mitchell v. Forsyth, 472 U.S. 511 (1985), the Court extended qualified immunity to the AG for authorizing a warrantless wiretap in a case involving domestic national security. Although Court later held warrantless wiretaps violated Fourth Amendment, at time of Attorney General's authorization, this interpretation was not clearly established, and Harlow immunity protected officials exercising discretion on open questions. See Anderson v. Creighton, 483 U.S. 635 (1987) (in an exceedingly opaque opinion, Court extended immunity to FBI agents conducting warrantless search).
9. Jump to essay-Harlow v. Fitzgerald, 457 U.S. 800, 812 (1982)
10. See 28 U.S.C. § 1331. On deleting the jurisdictional amount, see Pub. L. No. 94-574, 90 Stat. 2721 (1976); Pub. L. No. 96-486, 94 Stat. 2369 (1980). If such suits are brought in state courts, they can be removed to federal district courts. 28 U.S.C. § 1442(a). See 28 U.S.C. § 1331.

Art II.S3.5.3 Qualified Immunity Doctrine

He shall have Power, by and with the Advice and Consent of the Senate, to make Treaties, provided two thirds of the Senators present concur; and he shall nominate, and by and with the Advice and Consent of the Senate, shall appoint Ambassadors, other public Ministers and Consuls, Judges of the supreme Court, and all other Officers of the United States, whose Appointments are not herein otherwise provided for, and which shall be established by Law: but the Congress may by Law vest the Appointment of such inferior Officers, as they think proper, in the President alone, in Courts of Law, or in Heads of Departments.

While the courts may be unable to compel the President to act or to prevent him from acting, his acts, when performed, are in proper cases subject to judicial review and disallowance. Typically, the subordinates through whom he acts may be sued, in a form of legal fiction, to enjoin the commission of acts which might lead to irreparable damage[1] or to compel by writ of mandamus the performance of a duty required by law.[2] Such suits are usually brought in the US District Court for the District of Columbia.[3] In suits under the common law, a subordinate executive officer may be held personally liable in damages for any act done in excess of authority,[4] although immunity exists for anything, even malicious wrongdoing, done in course of his duties.[5]

Different rules prevail when an official is sued for a constitutional tort for wrongs allegedly in violation of our basic charter,[6] although the Court has hinted that in sensitive areas officials acting in the outer perimeter of their duties may be accorded an absolute immunity from liability.[7] Jurisdiction to reach such officers for acts for which they can be held responsible must be under general federal question jurisdictional statute, as amended, requires no jurisdictional amount.[8]

1. E.g., Youngstown Sheet & Tube Co. v. Sawyer, 343 U.S. 579 (1952) (suit to enjoin Secretary of Commerce to return steel mills seized on President's order); Dames & Moore v. Regan, 453 U.S. 654 (1981) (suit against Secretary of Treasury to nullify presidential orders on Iranian assets). See also Noble v. Union River Logging R.R., 147 U.S. 165 (1893); Phila. Co. v. Stimson, 223 U.S. 605 (1912).
2. E.g., Marbury v. Madison, 5 U.S. (1 Cr.) 137 (1803) (suit against Secretary of State to compel delivery of commissions of office); Kendall v. United States ex rel. Stokes, 37 U.S. (12 Pet.) 524 (1838) (suit against Postmaster General to compel payment of money owed under act of Congress); Decatur v. Paulding, 39 U.S. (14 Pet.) 497 (1840) (suit to compel Secretary of Navy to pay a pension).
3. This was originally on the theory that the Supreme Court of the District of Columbia had inherited, via the common law of Maryland, the jurisdiction of the King's Bench over inferior jurisdictions and officers. Kendall
v. United States ex rel. Stokes, 37 U.S. (12 Pet.) 524, 614, 620–21 (1838). Congress has authorized federal district courts outside District of Columbia also to entertain such suits. Act of Oct 5, 1962, Pub. L. No. 87-748, 76 Stat. 744 (codified at 28 U.S.C. § 1361).
4. E.g., Little v. Barreme, 6 U.S. (2 Cr.) 170 (1804); Bates v. Clark, 95 U.S. 204 (1877); U.S. v. Lee, 106 U.S. 196 (1882); Virginia Coupon Cases (Poindexter v. Greenhow), 114 U.S. 270 (1885); Belknap v. Schild, 161 U.S. 10 (1896).
5. Spalding v. Vilas, 161 U.S. 483 (1896); Barr v. Matteo, 360 U.S. 564 (1959). See Westfall v. Erwin, 484 U.S. 292 (1988) (action must be discretionary in nature as well as being within the scope of employment, before federal official is entitled to absolute immunity). Following the Westfall decision, Congress enacted the Federal Employees Liability Reform and Tort Compensation Act of 1988 (the Westfall Act), which authorized the AG to certify that an employee was acting within the scope of his office or employment at the time of the incident out of which a suit arose; upon certification, the employee is dismissed from the action, and the US is substituted, the Federal Tort Claims Act (FTCA) then governing the action, which means that sometimes the action must be dismissed against government because FTCA has not waived sovereign immunity. US v. Smith, 499 U.S. 160 (1991) (Westfall Act bars suit against federal employee even when an exception in the FTCA bars suit against the government). Cognizant of temptation of government to immunize both itself and its employee, the Court in Gutierrez de Martinez v. Lamagno, 515 U.S. 417 (1995), held the AG's certification is subject to judicial review.
6. An implied cause of action against officers accused of constitutional violations was recognized in Bivens v. Six Unknown Named Agents of the Federal Bureau of Narcotics, 403 U.S. 388 (1971). In Butz v. Economou, 438 U.S. 478 (1978), a Bivens action, the Court distinguished between common-law torts and constitutional torts and denied high federal officials, including cabinet secretaries, absolute immunity, in favor of the qualified immunity previously accorded high state officials under 42 U.S.C. § 1983. In Harlow v. Fitzgerald, 457 U.S. 800 (1982), the Court denied presidential aides derivative absolute presidential immunity, but it modified the rules of qualified immunity, making it more difficult to hold such aides, other federal officials, and indeed state and local officials, liable for constitutional torts. In Mitchell v. Forsyth, 472 U.S. 511 (1985), the Court extended qualified immunity to the AG for authorizing a warrantless wiretap in a case involving domestic national security. Although the Court later held such warrantless wiretaps violated the Fourth Amendment, at the time of the AG's authorization this interpretation was not clearly established, and Harlow immunity protected officials exercising discretion on such open questions. See also Anderson v. Creighton, 483 U.S. 635 (1987) (in an exceedingly opaque opinion, the Court extended similar qualified immunity to FBI agents who conducted a warrantless search).
7. Harlow v. Fitzgerald, 457 U.S. 800, 812 (1982).
8. See 28 U.S.C. § 1331. On deleting the jurisdictional amount, see Pub. L. No. 94-574, 90 Stat. 2721 (1976), and Pub. L. No. 96-486, 94 Stat. 2369 (1980). If such suits are brought in state courts, they can be removed to federal district courts. 28 U.S.C. § 1442(a).

Art II.S3.5.4 Criminal Prosecution, Presidential Immunity and Former Presidents

In *Trump v. United States*, Supreme Court addressed how principles of presidential immunity apply to a criminal prosecution of a former president[1] for actions taken while in office.[2] The case concerned an indictment against former President Trump for allegedly attempting to overturn the results of the 2020 election.[3] In evaluating President Trump's claim that he was immune from prosecution, the Supreme Court announced a three-part framework for evaluating a former president's immunity from criminal prosecution.

The Court held that former presidents are entitled to absolute immunity from criminal prosecution for actions in the exclusive sphere of their constitutional authority while in office.[4] Certain core presidential powers, such as granting pardons,[5] removing executive officers whom the president has appointed,[6] and discussing potential investigations and prosecutions with the Justice Department, including those concerning allegations of election crime,[7] are exclusive and preclusive—meaning other branches of government have no constitutional power to restrict them, the Court explained.[8] For example, President Trump acted in this exclusive sphere of authority, the Court held, when he allegedly attempted to leverage Justice Department's power and authority to convince States to replace their legitimate electors with Trump's fraudulent slates of electors.[9]

Because the President cannot be prosecuted for conduct within his exclusive constitutional authority,[10] the Court explained, the former President is absolutely immune from prosecution for the alleged conduct involving his discussions with Justice Department officials.[11]

The second facet of the framework addresses conduct that falls outside the exclusive sphere of presidential power but still constitutes an official act by the President.[12] Although not protected in the same manner as core executive powers, official acts may still be protected by immunity, the Court reasoned, in order to safeguard the independence and effectiveness of the presidency and to enable presidents to perform their constitutional responsibilities without being overly cautious or concerned with future prosecutions.[13] Official acts are at least presumptively immune from criminal prosecution,[14] the Supreme Court held, unless the government can show that prosecuting a former President in that instance would pose no 'dangers of intrusion on the authority and functions of the Executive Branch.'[15] The Court held that President Trump's official acts included his alleged attempt to pressure the former Vice President to take certain acts in connection with certifying the electoral vote count, and the Court remanded for lower courts to determine whether the United States could rebut the presumption that immunity applied to those acts.[16]

Finally, the Supreme Court held former presidents do not have immunity for their unofficial acts.[17] The Court observed that the process of distinguishing the President's official acts from his unofficial can be difficult[,][18] especially in the context of the former President's public communications on social media and in a public speech.[19] Because official acts analysis requires a fact-specific evaluation that lower courts did not conduct, the Supreme Court remanded the case for further consideration on whether certain activity qualifies as official or unofficial.[20]

Although the Supreme Court left questions of immunity unresolved in *Trump v. United States*, it did definitively address Trump's argument that a former President can only be prosecuted after being impeached in the House and convicted in the Senate.[21] Supreme Court rejected the view that impeachment is a perquisite to a criminal conviction, reasoning that transforming the political process of impeachment into an essential first step in a criminal prosecution did not have support in the Constitution's text or structure of the US government.[22]

1. Because criminal charges have never been filed against a sitting President, the Supreme Court has never considered a case addressing whether a sitting President could be prosecuted. The executive branch has expressed the view sitting Presidents enjoy absolute immunity from criminal prosecution. *See* Memorandum from Randolph D. Moss, Assistant Atty. Gen., Office of Legal Counsel, to the Atty. Gen.: A Sitting President's Amenability to Indictment and Criminal Prosecution, 24 Op. OLC 222, 222 (Oct. 16, 2000) ([T]he indictment or criminal prosecution of a sitting President would impermissibly undermine the capacity of the executive branch to perform its constitutionally assigned functions.).
2. Trump v. United States, No. 23-939, slip op. at 1 (U.S. July 1, 2024).
3. A federal grand jury indicted President Trump on four criminal counts: (1) conspiracy to defraud the United States by overturning the election results under (18 United States Code, section 371), (2) conspiracy to obstruct an official proceeding— in this case, Congress's certification of the electoral vote (18 United States Code, section 1512(k)); (3) obstruction of, and attempt to obstruct, the certification of the electoral vote (18 United States Code, section 1512(c)(2)); and (4) conspiracy against the rights of persons to vote and to have their votes counted (18 United States Code, section 241). In *Fischer v. United States*—a different case arising out of the January 6, 2021, unrest at the U.S. Capitol issued during the same term as the Trump decision—the Supreme Court interpreted the statute on which the third count is based, 18 United States Code, section 1512(c)(2). No. 23-5572., slip op. at 1 (U.S. June 28, 2024). In *Fischer*, the Court held that charges under section 1512(c)(2) must be based on alleged impairment (or attempted impairment) of records, documents, objects, or other things used an official proceeding. *Id.* at 16. For a more detailed discussion of the charges in the Trump indictment, see Peter G. Berris, Cong. Rsch. Serv. LSB1116, Overview of the Indictment of Former President Trump Related to the 2020 Election,
4. https://crsreports.congress.gov/product/pdf/LSB/LSB11016.
5. Trump v. United States, No. 23-939, slip op. at 9.
6. *Id.* at 7-8.
7. *Id.* at 8.
8. *Id.* at 20.
9. *Id.* at 8 (quoting Youngstown Sheet & Tube Co. v. Sawyer, 343 U.S. 579, 638 (1952) (Jackson, J., concurring)). *See also id* at 19 (The Government does not dispute that the indictment's allegations regarding the Justice Department involve Trump's 'use of official power.' The allegations in fact plainly implicate Trump's 'conclusive and preclusive' authority. 'Investigation and prosecution of crimes is a quintessentially executive function.')(citations omitted).
10. *Id.* at 19.
11. *Id.* at 21.

12. *See id.* The Court explained: The indictment's allegations that the requested investigations were 'sham[s]' or proposed for an improper purpose do not divest the President of exclusive authority over the investigative and prosecutorial functions of the Justice Department and its officials. And the President cannot be prosecuted for conduct within his exclusive constitutional authority. *Id.* (citations omitted).
13. *See id.* at 9.
14. *Id.* at 12-15.
15. *Id.* at 23, 36.
16. *Id.* at 14 (quoting Nixon v. Fitzgerald, 457 U.S. 731, 754 (1982)).
17. *Id.* at 23-24.
18. *Id.* at 15.
19. *Id.* at 17.
20. *Id.* at 28-30.
21. *Id.* at 28.
22. *Id.* at 32-34.
23. *Id.* at 34.
24.

Art VI.C2.3.2 Dual Federalism in Late Nineteenth and Early Twentieth Centuries

This Constitution, and the Laws of the United States which shall be made in Pursuance thereof; and all Treaties made, or which shall be made, under the Authority of the US, shall be the supreme Law of the Land; and Judges in every State shall be bound thereby, any Thing in the Constitution or Laws of any State to the Contrary notwithstanding.

The Supreme Court continued to apply the basic principle of federal supremacy throughout the late nineteenth and early twentieth centuries. But the Supremacy Clause's role during that era was limited by other aspects of the Court's federalism jurisprudence. Through this period, the Court embraced what academics call the doctrine of dual federalism, under which the federal government and states occupied largely distinct, non-overlapping zones of constitutional authority.[1] Applying this framework, the Court adopted a narrow interpretation of Congress's Commerce Clause authorities[2] and construed the Tenth Amendment as imposing strict additional limitations on federal power.[3] The Court also relied on the Dormant Commerce Clause to conclude states lacked the power to regulate subjects of exclusive federal concern.[4] While federal supremacy persisted as a background principle during late nineteenth and early twentieth centuries, the Court's bifurcation of federal and state authority minimized instances in which the two could conflict.[5] To the extent that the Supremacy Clause played an explicit role in the federalism disputes of this era, the Court applied it in ways that reinforced the sharp division of federal and state power. In a series of early-twentieth-century decisions, the Court developed a precursor to the doctrine of field preemption—the principle that some federal legislation implicitly prevents states from adopting any laws regulating the same general subject. For example, in Southern Railway v. Reid, the Court held that the Interstate Commerce Act (ICA)—which regulated railroad rates—superseded a state law requiring railroads to transport tendered freight.[6]

The Court reasoned that Congress had taken possession of the field of railroad rate regulation with the ICA, thereby precluding even supplementary state regulations.[7] In another decision, the Court held that a different federal law requiring railroads to secure the safe transportation of property upon reasonable terms displaced a state law compelling railroads to settle certain claims within forty days.[8] In his opinion, Justice Oliver Wendell Holmes rejected the argument that state law did not conflict with federal law, explaining that absence of such a conflict was immaterial, because coincidence is as ineffective as opposition when Congress has taken [a] particular subject-matter in hand.[9] In yet another field-preemption case, the Court held that a federal law involving railroads' liability for employee injuries superseded state common law claims based on such injuries.[10]

While the Supreme Court's reasoning in these cases varied, one commentator has noted the readiness with which the Court concluded that federal law preempted the relevant fields.[11] For example, in one decision, the Court appeared to suggest that any federal legislation in certain fields precluded states from adopting even supplementary regulations of the same subject.[12] Under this theory of automatic preemption, Congress's authority over certain subjects was one of latent exclusivity, meaning the power of the states ended as soon as Congress chose to exercise its regulatory power in those fields.[13] However, this view of federal power—which was related to notions of dual federalism—would soon give way to broader legal and political trends.

Footnotes

1. See Edward S. Corwin, The Passing of Dual Federalism, 36 Va. L. Rev. 1, 4 (1950) (defining Dual Federalism as involving the following postulates: 1. The national government is one of enumerated powers only; 2. Also the purposes which it may constitutionally promote are few; 3. Within their respective spheres the two centers of government are 'sovereign' and hence 'equal'; 4. The relation of the two centers with each other is one of tension rather than collaboration.).
2. See, e.g., Carter v. Carter Coal Co., 298 U.S. 238, 303–04 (1936) (holding that the Bituminous Coal Conservation Act of 1935 exceeded the scope of Congress's Commerce Clause authority); ALA Schechter Poultry Corp. v. US, 295 U.S. 495, 546 (1935) (holding that a code of fair competition adopted under the National Industrial Recovery Act exceeded the scope of the Commerce Power); US v. E.C. Knight, 156 U.S. 1, 12 (1895) (holding that the Sherman Antitrust Act's application to acquisitions in sugar refining industry exceeded scope of Commerce Power).
3. See, e.g., Hammer v. Dagenhart, 247 U.S. 251, 273–74 (1918) (holding that a federal law prohibiting the interstate shipment of goods produced using child labor violated the Tenth Amendment).
4. See, e.g., Wabash, St. Louis & Pac. Ry. Co. v. Illinois, 118 U.S. 557, 575 (1886) (holding that a state law regulating railroad rates violated the Dormant Commerce Clause); Welton v. Missouri, 91 U.S. 275, 281 (1876) (holding that a state law requiring peddlers of out-of-state merchandise to pay a tax and obtain a license violated the Dormant Commerce Clause because it regulated a subject of national importance); see also Cooley v. Bd. of Wardens, 53 U.S. 299, 319–20 (1851) (distinguishing between subjects of the Commerce Power that were in their nature national, and therefore subject to exclusive federal regulation, and those that were subject to concurrent federal and state regulation).

5. Davis v. Elmira Sav. Bank, 161 U.S. 275, 284 (1896) (holding National Bank Act superseded state law regarding distribution of insolvent national bank's assets).
6. 222 U.S. 424, 438 (1912).
7. Id. at 442.
8. Charleston & W. Carolina Ry. v. Varnville Furniture Co., 237U.S.597, 603–04 (1915
9. Id. at 604.
10. N.Y. Cent. & Hudson River R.R. v. Tonsellito, 244 U.S. 360, 362 (1917).
11. Stephen A. Gardbaum, Nature of Preemption, 49 Cornell L. Rev. 767, 783 (1994).
12. See Chi., Rock Island & Pac. Ry. v. Hardwick Farmers Elevator Co., 226 U.S. 426, 435 (1913) ([I]t must follow in consequence of action of Congress . . . that power of State over subject matter ceased to exist from the moment Congress exerted its paramount and all-embracing authority over the subject. We say this because the elementary and long settled doctrine is there can be no divided authority over interstate commerce and regulations of Congress on that subject are supreme.).
13. Gardbaum, supra note 11, at 783.

CHAPTER 18. NATIONAL EMERGENCIES AND PRESIDENTIAL POWER

https://www.newsmax.com/judgeandrewpnapolitano/constitution-presidential-powers/2024/05/31/id/1166951/

It is essential that the reader understand and comprehend the weighty issues that have occurred in America in the past 3 centuries. Many times, bloody points of defiance of the law have occurred. In many instances, sitting Presidents found it necessary to commit military and militia forces in order to bring these issues to a solution. We commence this chapter with comments from noted Constitutional Scholars regarding the dire need for Presidential Powers.

QUESTION: What are the extreme issues that may arise that give a sitting President authority to react with superior power?

By Judge Andrew P. Napolitano

The Economist magazine column asking if America is dictator-proof got me thinking if our constitutional guarantees are secure.
Stated differently: Can the custodians of our constitutional norms be trusted to restrain a deliberate attempt to ignore, diminish or evade the Constitution? The short answer is NO.

The history of what I will charitably call constitutional indifference is long and tortuous. It goes back to the earliest days of the republic when, in a period of eight years, Congress enacted, and Presidents Washington and John Adams signed into law legislation that directly defied restraints upon federal government.

And this constitutional indifference gave birth to the steady radical growth of government — usually in wartime and based on fears of foreign persons — at expense of personal liberty.

In 1791, over a fierce and eloquent objection by then-Congressman James Madison — largely the author of the Constitution — Congress enacted a series of statutes that created the first National Bank of the United States. The bank's purpose was to enable elites to enrich themselves by controlling the flow of cash.

Madison, in his famous Bank Speech, the best articulation of limited constitutional government by any Founding Father, argued that because the Constitution intentionally did not authorize Congress to establish a bank — it reserved bank regulation to the states — Congress was without lawful authority to establish one. Congress enacted the legislation, nevertheless.

In 1792, Congress enacted the Insurrection Act, over Madison's objections. That law enabled the president to declare an emergency and call the military to address the emergency.

The definition of emergency has been and remains the subjective choice of the president. This statute enabled the president to use federal troops to enforce federal and state laws, and to seize state militias from state governors and use them in presidentially declared emergencies for presidentially directed purposes.

And in 1798, again over Madison's objections, and in defiance of the First Amendment's command that "Congress shall make no law ... abridging the freedom of speech," Congress enacted the Alien and Sedition Acts, which criminalized public criticism of the government's foreign policy and of the president personally.

These are the initial monstrous examples of constitutional indifference that set the government's path on regular, consistent, and systematic growth, ignoring restraints Madison built into the Constitution. These early constitutional aberrations established the precedent and pattern in Congress for giving power to any president that will enable him to become an American Caesar.

Today there are around 135 of these largely unknown-to-the-public statutes that permit the president to close federal highways, confiscate bank accounts in federally insured banks and shut down the internet — all to address a self-willed emergency, all without due process, all in defiance of basic constitutional norms.

What is an emergency? The courts have defined it as a state of affairs whereby courts cannot sit to address due process. By that definition, we have never had an emergency in our history, including the War Between the States and immediately after 9/11 New York City.

Yet, with the congressionally indifferent attitude that emergency somehow creates lawful power where none existed before the so-called emergency, presidents have from time to time become Caesar.

When President Abraham Lincoln declared speech critical of his war machine to be an emergency, he claimed he was thereby able to use federal troops to arrest more than 3,000 journalists and editors in the North and confine them without charges. By the time one cases reached the Supreme Court, after the war's end and Lincoln's death, the court ruled that the Constitution tolerates no emergency powers, and its meaning applies in good or bad time.

Nevertheless, constitutionally indifferent presidents have defined emergency to suit their political needs and violated constitutional norms.

President Woodrow Wilson declared the prevalence of anti-war speech during World War I to be an emergency, and thereby he claimed the emergency enabled him to arrest Princeton University students who recited the Declaration of Independence aloud outside draft offices in Trenton, New Jersey.

President Franklin D. Roosevelt declared the presence of Americans of Japanese ancestry in the western parts of the United States to be an emergency, and thereby he claimed the emergency enabled him to arrest without charge and incarcerate more than 120,000 Americans without trial until end of World War II.

President George W. Bush claimed that 9/11 was an emergency that somehow authorized him to authorize the NSA to spy on all Americans without suspicion, probable cause, or search warrants.

President Obama claimed the presence of Moammar Gadhafi as the leader of Libya was an American emergency such that he needed to be removed from office without a congressional declaration of war, so he had CIA bomb Libya.

President Donald Trump declared the entry of undocumented immigrants into the United States at the Texas/Mexico border to be an emergency, and thereby he claimed this so-called emergency enabled him to begin construction of a border fence, in defiance of Congress, which had refused to fund it.

President Joe Biden declared the unfulfilled obligation of former students to repay their college loans to be an emergency; thereby permitting him to forgive loans in defiance of the Supreme Court, which ruled only Congress can do this.

And last month, U.S. Secretary of State Antony Blinken filed documents with Congress claiming the Israeli war in Gaza was an American emergency of such magnitude that weapons and supplies needed to be sent to the Israeli government before Congress could authorize them, and so they were sent.

The national bank is still with us as the Federal Reserve. The Insurrection Act remains available today for all presidents to employ on a whim. The Alien and Seditions Acts have been reborn under the guise of the Espionage Act of 1917 and Antisemitism Awareness Act of 2024.

Why do we repose the Constitution for safe-keeping into the hands of those deliberately indifferent to it? Can anyone seriously argue that America is dictator-proof? Who or what will save us from those who'd crush our freedoms to enhance their own powers?

Judge Andrew P. Napolitano, a graduate of Princeton University and the University of Notre Dame Law School, was the youngest life-tenured Superior Court judge in the history of New Jersey. He is the author of five books on the U.S. Constitution.

LIST OF EXTREME GOVERNMENT ACTIONS- PRESIDENTIAL IMMUNITY
https://en.wikipedia.org/wiki/List_of_incidents_of_civil_unrest_in_the_United_States

The following are actual times in American history in which our US Constitution provides means by which a sitting President may deploy Military, National Guard, or Militia, to protect public safety, clearly that President must be immune from such.

TAX REBELLIONS in earliest days following ratification of the US Constitution.

1. Shays' Rebellion (central and western Massachusetts, 1786–87)
2. Whiskey Rebellion (western Pennsylvania, 1794).
3. Fries's Rebellion, also called House Tax Rebellion, Home Tax Rebellion, in Pennsylvania German, the Hesses-Wasser Uffschtand, was an armed tax revolt among Pennsylvania Dutch farmers,1799 and 1800. In each of these cases, Federal government sent US Marshalls and Armed Troops often with state ordered Militia assistance to help local officials put down these acts.

1811 German Coast uprising, slave revolt in the Territory of Orleans
1812 Baltimore riots took place shortly before the War of 1812
1824 Hard Scrabble- Snow Town Riots, 1824&1831, Providence, RI (race riots)
1831 Nat Turner's Rebellion, August 21–23, Southampton County, Va
1834 – Anti-abolitionist riot, New York City
1834 – Philadelphia race riot, August 14
1835 – Baltimore bank riot, August 6–9
1835 – Snow Riot, Washington D.C.; race riot caused by labor
1837 – Flour Riots (Wheat), New York City
1839 – Anti-Rent War, Hudson Valley, New York
1842 – Lombard Street Riot (a.k.a. Abolition Riots), Aug 1, Philadelphia
1844 – Philadelphia Nativist Riots, May 6–8, July 6–7, (anti-Catholic)
1849 – Astor Place riot, May 10, New York City, (anti-British)
1855 – Portland Rum Riot, June 2, Portland, Maine
1856 - Bleeding Kansas, Sacking of Lawrence, Kansas, May 21, 1856,
1856 – Battle of Seattle (1856)
1856 – Pottawatomie massacre, May 24, Franklin County, Kansas
1856 – Baltimore Know-Nothing riots of 1856, (anti-immigration)
1856 – San Francisco Vigilance Movement, San Francisco
1857 – Know-Nothing Riot, June 1, Washington D.C. (anti-immigration)
1857 – New York City Police Riot, June 16, New York City
1857 – Dead Rabbits Riot, July 4–5, NYC, Gangs vs. Police
1859 – John Brown's raid, October 16, Harpers Ferry, Virginia

War and riots brought about by Civil War and Reconstruction 1860–1877

1861–1865: American Civil War, April 12 – 9, United States
1861 – Baltimore Riot of 1861, April 19, (the Pratt Street Riot)
1861 – Camp Jackson Affair, May 10, Union forces clash with Confederate sympathizers on streets of St. Louis, 28 dead, 100 injured St. Louis, Mo.
1862 – Brooklyn Riot of 1862 occurred August 4 between New York Police against a white mob attacking African Am strike-breakers at a Factory[4]
1862 – Buffalo riot of 1862, August 12, Buffalo, NY (labor riot)
1863 – Detroit race riot of 1863, March 6
1863 - Tally's War/Skunk River War, Keokuk County, Iowa
1863 – Southern bread riots, April 2, Riots broke out in the South during the Civil War due to food shortages throughout the Confederate States
1863 – Battle of Fort Fizzle, June, known as Holmes County Draft Riots, active resistance to draft during Civil War, Holmes County, Ohio
1863 – New York City draft riots, July 13–16, (anti-draft)
1864 – Charleston Riot, March 28, Charleston, Illinois
1865 – April 1–3, 1865 Burning of Richmond, end of Civil War
1866 – Memphis Riots 1866, May 1–3, Race riot,
1866 – New Orleans riot, July 30, New Orleans, 1867
1867 - Franklin riot, July 10, Franklin, Tennessee[5]
1867 – Rogersville riot, July 26, Rogersville, Tennessee[6]
1868 – Pulaski Riot, Pulaski, Tennessee (race riot)
1870 – First New York City Orange riot, Catholics vs Protestant
1870 – Kirk-Holden war, July–Nov, Caswell and Alamance NC, labor riot between Italian and Irish laborers
1870 – Eutaw Riot, Alabama, KKK attacked a Republican rally[7]
1871 – Second New York City Orange riot
1871 – Meridian race riot of 1871, March, Meridian, Mississippi
1871 – Los Angeles anti-Chinese riot, Los Angeles, California
1873 – Colfax massacre, April 13, Colfax, Louisiana (race)
1874 – Coushatta La massacre, August, Attack, White League
on Republican officeholders and freedmen
1874 – Election Riot of 1874, Barbour County, Alabama
1874 – Tompkins Square Riot, New York City (poverty)
1874 – Battle of Liberty Place, New Orleans,(anti-reconstruction)
1874–1875 – Vicksburg massacre, Miss. (anti-Reconstruction)
1876 – South Carolina civil disturbances 1876 (race riots)
1877 – San Francisco Riot of 1877 (anti-Chinese immigration)

Widespread rioting across the US was part of the Great Railroad Strike 1877:

Baltimore railroad strike in Baltimore, Maryland
Chicago railroad strike of 1877, Chicago, Illinois
Philadelphia Railroad Strike, Philadelphia,
Pennsylvania Pittsburgh Railway Riots, in Pittsburgh,
Pennsylvania Reading Railroad massacre, Reading,
Pennsylvania Saint Louis general strike, July, East St.
Louis, Illinois Scranton General Strike, in Scranton,
Pennsylvania Shamokin uprising, Shamokin,

1884 – Cincinnati riots of 1884, March 28–30, Cincinnati, Ohio
1885 – Rock Springs, WY massacre, white's vs Chinese; 28
killed 1886 – Seattle riot of 1886, February 6–9 (anti-Chinese)
1886 – Bay View Massacre, May 4; 1400 workers march for 8 hour workday
7 killed, several more wounded after confrontation with National Guard
Milwaukee, Wisconsin
1887 – Thibodaux La. Massacre, November 22–25; a labor/racial
attack mounted by white paramilitary groups
1888 – Jaybird-Woodpecker War, 1888–90, two factions of
Democratic Party fight for control, Fort Bend County, Tx
1889 – Forrest City riot, May 18, Arkansas (race riot)
1891 - Morewood massacre, United Mine Workers strike
1892 – Homestead strike, July 6, 1892, Homestead, Pennsylvania
1894 – American Railway Union striking Pullman factory workers near Chicago
1894 – Pullman strike American Railway Union strike versus
federal troops, many cities west of Detroit
1894 – Bituminous Coal Miners' Strike, coal mining regions
1897 Lattimer massacre, near Hazleton, Pa (labor)
1898 – Tampa riot, Florida; between white and black soldiers
1898 – Battle of Virden, Ill Coal strike; 11 killed, 35 wounded
1898 – Phoenix election riot, Nov 8,SC (race/electoral)
1899 – Coeur d'Alene, Idaho labor confrontation of 1899

1900's Actions

1900 – Akron Riot of 1900, Akron, Ohio Gov sent troops
1900 --New Orleans(race riots) Gov sent State Police
1900 – 1900 Liberty County riot, August 18, Georgia Cavalry
1901 – Denver Riots, Colorado Jobs, Gov troops and militia
1903 – Colorado Labor Wars, 1903–1904 National Guard Sent
1903 – Anthracite Coal Strike, Eastern Pa Gov sent NG,
1903 – Evansville Race Riot, Evansville, Indiana Militia sent
1903 – Motormen's Riot, Richmond, Va 16 companies militia
1906 – Rioting/looting 1906 San Fran earthquake Military
1906 – Atlanta Race Riot, Jobs, Race, Ga. National Guard
1908 – Springfield Race Riot, Illinois (anti-Black riots) militia
1910–1919 – Bandit War Southern Texas Tx Rangers, Army
1910 – Philadelphia strike (1910), Philadelphia National Guard
1912 – Lawrence, Mass textile strike, State Militia, and police
1912 – Grabow riot; (labor riot) working conditions, militia
1913 – Copper Country Strike, Michigan national guard
1913 – Colorado Coalfield War, 1914, Southern Co (labor) NG
1913 – Indianapolis streetcar strike NG, Martial Law
1914 – Ludlow massacre, April 20, Colorado (labor) NG
1916 – Everett massacre, Washington (labor massacre) militia
1917 – St. Louis Race Riots, July 2, St. Louis, Missouri & East
St. Louis, Illinois (labor competition) NG
1917 – Chester, Pa race riot, July 25–29, NG State Police
1917 – Houston Race riot, August 23, Houston, military
1919 – Seattle General Strike, Feb 6–11, police, military
1919 – May Day Riots, May 1, Cleveland, Ohio, Boston, Mass., New York
City, NY (state) (labor riots triggered by Eugene V. Debs' conviction,
and American intervention in Russian Civil War) Army and Police
1919 – Red Summer, white riots against blacks 36 cities, Army,
1919 – Boston Police Strike, Sept 9–11, Mass Militia,
1919 – Steel Strike Pennsylvania jobs, police, army
1920 – Lexington, KY serial killer riots, NG, Police, Army
1920 – Battle of Matewan, West Virginia (labor) police
1921 – Tulsa, Ok Race Massacre, black man white woman, NG
1921 – Battle of Blair Mountain, Logan County, W Va; labor
up to 100 people were killed Army, NG
1922 – Herrin, Ill Massacre, (labor massacre) union, NG

The following indicates our Constitution provided means by which a sitting President may deploy Military, National Guard, or Militia.
https://crsreports.congress.gov/product/pdf/LSB/LSB10121

The President's Authority to Use the National Guard or the Armed Forces to Secure the Border -- - Updated June 15, 2023

On May 2, 2023, the Biden Administration announced that Secretary of Defense Lloyd Austin approved a request from Secretary of Homeland Security Alejandro Mayorkas to send an additional 1,500 active-duty members of the Armed Forces to assist U.S. Customs and Border Protection (CBP) agents with a potential influx of migrants after pandemic-era health restrictions ended in May 2023. (Does not include the thousands of Texas National Guard troops deployed to the border as part of Texas's Operation Lone Star.) The federal deployment is to last up to 90 days and add to the 2,500 National Guard members already deployed to the border with Mexico. The Department of Defense (DOD) said the troops will provide "ground-based detection and monitoring, data entry, and warehouse support" and will not "directly participate in law enforcement activities." This Sidebar addresses precedent for deploying troops to the border and President's legal authorities to use the National Guard or the Armed Forces to assist securing the southwestern border.

There is precedent for deploying National Guard units to the southwestern border to assist with immigration control. President Trump deployed units there in April 2018 to "stop the flow of deadly drugs and other contraband, gang members and other criminals, and illegal aliens" pursuant to Title 32 authority. (In "Title 32 status," National Guard members remain under control of governors of their states and are not considered to be performing active-duty service as part of regular Armed Forces. Mobilization of National Guard members under Title 10 differs from mobilization under Title 32 in a number of ways.) President Trump also ordered the Pentagon to deploy active-duty troops to the southwest border in October 2018.

The Pentagon reportedly sent 5,800 soldiers to the border mission.

From 2006 to 2008, President George W. Bush called on the National Guard to participate in Operation Jump Start, in which National Guard troops were called to duty to assist CBP to secure the border. National Guard members participating in this operation did not serve in a direct law enforcement role but rather reinforced the U.S. Border Patrol, including by performing missions involving engineering; aviation; entry identification; and a wide range of technical, logistical, and administrative support. President Barack Obama used National Guard troops in a 2010 during Operation Phalanx, a successor operation to Operation Jump Start.

Authority to Deploy the National Guard

Section 502 of Title 32, U.S. Code, provides the authority for the Secretary of the Army and the Secretary of the Air Force to call National Guard units to active duty under Title 32 status for training purposes. It also permits individual members to be called to active duty to perform training "or other duty in addition to" the mandatory training described earlier in Section 502. This is the provision of law that was used to provide federal pay and benefits to the National Guard personnel who provided security at many of the nation's airports after September 11, 2001, and who participated in disaster relief operations in response to hurricanes Katrina and Rita in 2005. Title 32 authority under Section 502(f) was also used for Operation Jump Start and Operation Phalanx, discussed above. Although National Guard members did not engage in direct law enforcement activities during these two border security operations, it is possible that states might consider giving them that authority in future operations.

As a matter of statute, other duty under Section 502(f) may also include "homeland defense activities."

Such activities are statutorily defined to mean activities undertaken for the military protection of the territory or domestic population of the United States, or of infrastructure or other assets of the US determined by Secretary of Defense as being critical to national security, from a threat or aggression against the US.

Federal funding for some aspects of Title 32 missions may be available upon a determination by the Secretary of Defense that the participation of National Guard units or members for a qualifying operation is necessary and appropriate. The governor of a state wishing to use its National Guard resources for homeland defense activities may also request funding assistance.

There is also a provision for ordering National Guard troops to duty for drug interdiction operations at the state level. Federal funding may be provided to a state for the implementation of a drug interdiction program in accordance with 32 U.S.C.

§ 112. Under this provision, the Secretary of Defense may grant funding to the governor of a state who submits a "drug interdiction and counterdrug activities plan" that satisfies certain statutory requirements. The Secretary of Defense is responsible for examining the sufficiency of the drug interdiction plan and determining whether the distribution of funds for its implementation would be proper. It appears that a state plan might include border security and immigration-related functions that overlap with drug interdiction activities.

Authority to Deploy the Armed Forces

In the event Armed Forces are used to assist securing the border, a number of legal considerations arise. For example, use of military to enforce immigration or criminal laws at the border could run afoul of the Posse Comitatus Act, unless exception applies. Posse Comitatus Act provides:

> Whoever, except in cases and under circumstances expressly authorized by the Constitution or Act of Congress, willfully uses any part of the Army, the Navy, the Marine Corps, the Air Force, or the Space Force as a posse comitatus or otherwise to execute the laws shall be fined under this title or imprisoned not more than two years, or both.

Consequently, there must be constitutional or statutory authority to use federal troops in law enforcement capacity to stop aliens from entering the country unlawfully, apprehend gang members, or seize contraband. (The Posse Comitatus Act does not apply to National Guard unless activated for federal service.)

The Constitution empowers Congress to authorize the militia to be called forth to execute federal law. Congress has used this power to authorize the President to use the regular Armed Forces and the National Guard in cases of insurrection against state governments, obstruction of federal laws, or protecting civil rights. These authorities permit use of federal Armed Forces to execute a law enforcement role notwithstanding the Posse Comitatus Act. It also seems settled the President has constitutional authority as to employ Armed Forces to defend against an armed attack against the US, its territories, or Armed Forces.

The Armed Forces do not appear to have a direct legislative mandate to protect or patrol the border or to engage in immigration enforcement. Chapter 15 of Title 10, U.S. Code—Military Support for Civilian Law Enforcement Agencies, however, provides general legislative authority for the Armed Forces to provide certain types of support to federal, state, and local law enforcement agencies and, in particular, to assist in counterdrug and counterterrorism efforts. Such authorities might permit the military to provide indirect border security and immigration control assistance. These authorities permit DOD to share information collected during the normal course of military operations, loan equipment and facilities, provide expert advice and training, and maintain such equipment. For federal law enforcement agencies, military personnel may be made available to maintain and operate equipment in conjunction with counterterrorism operations or the enforcement of counterdrug laws, immigration laws, and customs requirements. Military personnel are permitted under this authority to maintain and operate equipment only for specific purposes, including aerial reconnaissance and the detection, monitoring, and communication of the movement of air and sea traffic and of surface traffic outside the US or within 25 miles of U.S. borders if detected outside the border.

Congress placed several stipulations on Chapter 15 assistance. For example, the recipient law enforcement agency must reimburse DOD for the support it provides unless the support "is provided in the normal course of military training or operations" or if it "results in a benefit ... substantially equivalent to that which would otherwise be obtained from military operations or training." DOD can also provide such assistance only where it does not adversely affect "military preparedness of the US." Congress incorporated posse comitatus restrictions into Chapter 15 support activities, providing that the authorized assistance "does not include or permit direct participation by a member of the Army, Navy, Air Force, or Marine Corps in a search, seizure, arrest, or other similar activity unless participation in such activity by member otherwise authorized by law."

With respect to counterdrug operations and activities to counter other transnational crimes along the border, beginning in 1989, Congress expanded the military's support role in a number of other ways. For example, Congress directed DOD, to the maximum extent practicable, to conduct military training exercises in drug interdiction areas and made DOD the lead federal agency for the detection and monitoring of aerial and maritime transit of illegal drugs into the US. Congress later provided additional authorities for military support to law enforcement agencies specifically for counterdrug purposes in the National Defense Authorization Act for FY1991. Section 1004 of the law authorized DOD to extend support in several areas to any federal, state, and local (and sometimes foreign) law enforcement agency requesting counterdrug assistance, subject to restrictions against military direct participation in law enforcement. This section was extended a number of times but was repealed at the end of 2016, when it was superseded by similar authority now codified at 10 U.S.C. § 284 to provide assistance in drug interdiction and activities to control transnational organized crime. Authorized assistance is limited to maintenance or upgrade of equipment, transportation of personnel, establishment and operation of operations or training bases, training of law enforcement personnel, detecting and monitoring traffic within 25 miles of the border, constructing roads and fences, installing lights along smuggling corridors, establishing command and control centers and computer networks, providing linguist and intelligence analysis services, and conducting aerial and ground reconnaissance.

As noted, these Chapter 15 authorities restrict military personnel from participating directly in law enforcement activities, but military reconnaissance patrols along the border may be armed and permitted to fire in self-defense under applicable rules governing the use of force. Controversy arose in 1997 after a group of U.S. Marines conducting drug interdiction surveillance fired upon and killed an American teenage goatherd they believed posed a threat.

Author Information Jennifer K. Elsea Legislative Attorney
Disclaimer: This document was prepared by the Congressional Research Service.

Now the reader should see the developing degree to which Presidential Immunity has been essential across the history of The United States. Oath of Office plus Take Care provides much immunity, and helps to provide a means by which a sitting president may act on most extreme emergencies.

We must include another case of repetition of this mass of Constitutionally authorized Presidential powers.

Clause 1 Military, Administrative, and Clemency

The President shall be Commander in Chief of the Army and Navy of the United States, and of the Militia of the several States, when called into the actual Service of the United States; he may require the Opinion, in writing, of the principal Officer in each of the executive Departments, upon any Subject relating to the Duties of their respective Offices, and he shall have Power to grant Reprieves and Pardons for Offences against the United States, except in Cases of Impeachment.

Art II.S2.C1.1 Commander in Chief

- Art II.S2.C1.1.1Historical Background on Commander in Chief Clause
- Art II.S2.C1.1.2Prize Cases and Commander in Chief Clause
- Art II.S2.C1.1.11Presidential Power and Commander in Chief Clause
- Art II.S2.C1.1.12Congressional Control Over President's Discretion
- Art II.S2.C1.1.13President as Commander of Armed Forces

Art II.S2.C1.1.1 Historical Background on Commander in Chief Clause

The President shall be Commander in Chief of the Army and Navy of the United States, and of the Militia of the several States, when called into the actual Service of the United States; he may require the Opinion, in writing, of the principal Officer in each of the executive Departments, upon any Subject relating to the Duties of their respective Offices, and he shall have Power to grant Reprieves and Pardons for Offences against the United States, except in Cases of Impeachment.

Surprisingly, little discussion of the Commander in Chief Clause occurred in the Constitutional Convention or in the ratifying debates. From the evidence available, it appears the Framers vested the duty in the President because experience in the Continental Congress had disclosed the expediency of vesting command in a single official[1] and because the lesson of English history was that danger lurked in vesting command in a person separate from the responsible political leaders.[2]

Early cases and commentary emphasized the purely military aspects of the Commander in Chiefship. Alexander Hamilton said the office would amount to nothing more than the supreme command and direction of the Military and naval forces, as first general and admiral of the confederacy.[3] In his Commentaries on the Constitution of the United States, Justice Joseph Story wrote of the debates accompanying the ratification of the Constitution, stating: The propriety of admitting the president to be commander in chief, so far as to give orders, and have a general superintendency, was admitted.[4] Justice Story took note of the debate regarding the propriety of the President taking command of the armed forces in person, explaining the apparent consensus. He stated: Though the president might, there was no necessity that he should, take the command in person; and there was no probability that he would do so, except in extraordinary emergencies, and when he possessed superior military talents.[5]

Supreme Court did not think it apparent that the Commander in Chief Power necessarily entailed all the attributes available to a sovereign under the laws and usages of war, even in cases of war declared by Congress.[6] The Court held that a declaration of war, by itself, did not empower the President to confiscate enemy property.[7]

Chief Justice John Marshall, while suggesting that the President might, during the limited war authorized against France, have the authority as Commander in Chief to issue orders pertaining to the capture of certain vessels in the absence of legislation, denied the validity of such an order where Congress had enacted a contradictory staute.[8] A U.S. commander had captured, pursuant to presidential instructions, what he believed was a U.S. merchant ship bound from a French port, allegedly carrying contraband material.[9] Congress had, enacted the Non-Intercourse Act, which only provided for the seizure of such vessels bound to French ports.[10] The Court held that the President's instructions exceeded authority granted by Congress and were not to be given force of law, the captain could be held liable for damages.[11]

In 1850, Chief Justice Roger Taney, writing for the Supreme Court, explained the President's power during wartime:

His duty and his power are purely military. As Commander in Chief, he is authorized to direct movements of the naval and military forces placed by law at his command, and to employ them in the manner he may deem most effectual to harass and conquer and subdue the enemy. He may invade the hostile country, and subject it to the sovereignty and authority of the US. But his conquests do not enlarge the boundaries of this Union, nor extend the operation of our institutions and laws beyond limits before assigned to them by legislative power.[12]

Justice Taney continued and distinguished the role of the Commander in Chief and that of the British King:

But in the distribution of political power between the great departments of government, there is such a wide difference between the power conferred on the President of the United States, and the authority and sovereignty which belong to the English crown, that it would be altogether unsafe to reason from any supposed resemblance between them, either as regards conquest in war, or any other subject where the rights and powers of the executive arm of the government are brought into question.[13]

Even after the Civil War, a powerful minority of the Court, led by Chief Justice Salmon Chase, described the role of President as Commander in Chief simply as the command of the forces and the conduct of campaigns.[14]

15. Earnest R. May, The President Shall Be Commander in Chief, in The Ultimate Decision: The President as Commander In Chief 3, 6–7 (E. May ed., 1960). During North Carolina Ratify Convention, James Iredell said: From the nature of the thing, command of armies ought to be delegated to only one person. The secrecy, dispatch, and decision, which are necessary in military operations can only be expected from one person. 4 Jonathan Elliot, Debates in the Several State Conventions on the Adoption of the Federal Constitution 107 (2d ed.1836).
16. May, supra note 1, at 18. Virginia ratifying convention, Madison, replying to Patrick Henry's objection that danger lurked in giving the President control of the military, said: Would the member say that the sword ought to be put in the hands of representatives of the people, or in other hands independent of the government altogether? 3 Elliot, supra note 1, at 393.
17. The Federalist No. 69 (Alexander Hamilton).
18. 3 Joseph Story, Commentaries on Constitution Of The US § 1492 (1833).
19. Id.
20. See, e.g., The Thomas Gibbons, 12 U.S. (8 Cranch) 421, 427–28 (1814) (As to authority of the president, we do not think it necessary to consider how far he would be entitled, in his character of commander in chief of the army and navy of the US, independent of any statute provision, to issue instructions for government and direction of privateers. That question deserves grave consideration; and we should not be disposed to entertain the discussion unless it become unavoidable.).
21. Brown v. United States, 12 U.S. (8 Cranch) 110, 128–29 (1814) (appears to the Court, power of confiscating enemy property is in legislature, the legislature has not declared its will to confiscate property in our territory at declaration of war.)
22. Little v. Barreme, 6 U.S. (2 Cranch) 170, 177–78 (1804).
23. Id. at 177 (with reference to the Law of February 9, 1799, 1 Stat. 613).
24. Id.
25. Id. at 179. See also Talbot v. Seeman, 5 U.S. (1 Cranch) 1, (1801) (The whole powers of war being by the constitution of the US, vested in congress, the acts of that body can alone be restored to as our guides in this enquiry.).
26. Fleming v. Page, 50 U.S. (9 How.) 603, 615 (1850). Court explained, acquisition of foreign territory could be accomplished only by treaty-making power or legislative authority, is not a part of the power conferred upon the President by declaration of war. Id. Congress had declared war against Mexico in 1846. Act of May 13, 1846, ch. 16, 9 Stat. 9.
27. Fleming, 50 U.S. (9 How.) at 618.
28. Ex parte Milligan, 71 U.S. (4 Wall.) 2, 139 (1866).

Art II.S2.C1.1.2 Prize Cases and Commander in Chief Clause

The President shall be Commander in Chief of the Army and Navy of the United States, and of the Militia of the several States, when called into the actual Service of the United States; he may require the Opinion, in writing, of the principal Officer in each of the executive Departments, upon any Subject relating to the Duties of their respective Offices, and he shall have Power to grant Reprieves and Pardons for Offences against the United States, except in Cases of Impeachment.

The basis for a broader conception of the role of Commander in Chief was laid in certain early acts of Congress authorizing the President to employ military force in the execution of the laws.[1] In his famous message to Congress on July 4, 1861,[2] Abraham Lincoln advanced the claim that the war power was his for the purpose of suppressing rebellion, and in the Prize Cases[3] of 1863 a divided Court sustained this theory. The immediate issue was the validity of the blockade of the Southern ports that the President had established following the attack on Fort Sumter.[4] The argument was advanced that, in order for a blockade to be valid, it must be established during an incident of a public war validly declared, and that only Congress could, by virtue of its power to declare war, constitutionally impart to a military situation this character and scope.[5] Speaking for the majority of the Court, Justice Robert Grier answered:

> If a war be made by invasion of a foreign nation, the President is not only authorized but bound to resist force by force. He does not initiate the war, but is bound to accept the challenge without waiting for any special legislative authority. And whether the hostile party be a foreign invader, or States organized in rebellion, it is none the less a war, although the declaration of it be 'unilateral.'[6]

To support this principle with historical precedent, Justice Grier explained that the battles of Palo Alto and Resaca de la Palma had been fought before the enactment of the Act of Congress of May 13, 1846, which recognized 'a state of war as existing by the act of the Republic of Mexico.'[7] Justice Grier stated, This act not only provided for the future prosecution of the war, but was itself a vindication and ratification of the Act of the President in accepting the challenge without a previous formal declaration of war by Congress.[8]

The Court might have rested its opinion wholly on the President's authorities under statute to suppress insurrections and repel invasions,[9] coupled with Congress's ratification of the President's actions,[10] but it instead emphasized Executive power and duty:

> The President was bound to meet it in the shape it presented itself, without waiting for Congress to baptize it with a name; and no name given to it by him or them could change the fact . . . Whether the President in fulfilling his duties, as Commander in-chief, in suppressing an insurrection, has met with such armed hostile resistance, and a civil war of such alarming proportions as will compel him to accord to them the character of belligerents, is a question to be decided by him, and this Court must be governed by the decisions and acts of the political department of the government to which this power was entrusted. 'He must determine what degree of force the crisis demands.' The proclamation of blockade is itself official and conclusive evidence to the Court that a state of war existed which demanded and authorized a recourse to such measure, under circumstances peculiar to the case.[11]

In brief, the powers that may be claimed for the President under the Commander in Chief Clause at a time of widespread insurrection were equated with his powers under the clause at a time when the United States is engaged in a formally declared foreign war.[12] No attention was given the fact that Lincoln had asked Congress to ratify and confirm his acts, which Congress promptly had,[13] with the exception of his suspension of habeas corpus, a power that many attributed to the President in the situation then existing, by virtue of his duty to take care that the laws be faithfully executed.[14] On the other hand, where Lincoln's proclamation suspending habeas corpus varied from legislation enacted to ratify it, the Court looked to the statute[15] rather than the proclamation[16] to determine breadth of its application in case of Ex parte Milligan.[17] In a partial concurrence to the majority's decision in Milligan, Chief Justice Chase described the allocation of war powers as follows:

> The power to make the necessary laws is in Congress; the power to execute is the President. Both powers imply many subordinate and auxiliary powers. Each includes all authorities essential to its due exercise. But neither can the President, in war more than in peace, intrude upon the proper authority of Congress, nor Congress upon the proper authority of the President.[18]

> The Chief Justice described the Commander in Chief Power as entailing the command of forces and conduct of campaigns,[19] but nevertheless agreed that military trials of civilians accused of violating the law of war in Union states were invalid without congressional approval, despite the government's assertion that the [Commander in Chief's] power to make an effectual use of his forces [must include the] power to arrest and punish one who arms men to join the enemy in the field against him.[20]

Footnotes

21. 1 Stat. 424 (1795) (Militia Act of 1795); 2 Stat. 443 (1807) (Insurrection Act of 1807) (codified at 10 U.S.C. §§ 251–254). See also Martin v. Mott, 25 U.S. (12 Wheat.) 19, 32–33 (1827) (asserting finality of President's judgment of existence of a state of facts requiring his exercise of powers conferred by act of 1795).
22. 7 Messages and Papers of the Presidents 3221, 3224 (J. Richardson ed. 1897) (So viewing the issue, no choice was left but to call out the war power of the Government and so to resist force employed for its destruction by force for its preservation.). Later in the address, President Lincoln submitted: Recurring to the action of the Government, it may be stated that at first a call was made for 75,000 militia, and rapidly following this a proclamation was issued for closing the ports of the insurrectionary districts by proceedings in the nature of blockade. So far all was believed to be strictly legal. At this point, the insurrectionists announced their purpose to enter upon the practice of privateering.

    Other calls were made for volunteers to serve three years unless sooner discharged, and also for large additions to the Regular Army and Navy. These measures, whether strictly legal or not, were ventured upon under what appeared to be a popular demand and a public necessity, trusting then, as now, that Congress would readily ratify them. It is believed that nothing has been done beyond the constitutional competency of Congress. Id. at 3225.
23. 367 U.S. (2 Black) 635 (1863).
24. Id. at 665.
25. Id. at 644–45 (argument).
26. Id. at 668–70.
27. Id. at 668.
28. Id.
29. Id. at 668.
30. 67 U.S. (2 Black) at 670–71 (taking note of statutes and stating, Without admitting that act was necessary under circumstances, it is plain that if President had in any manner assumed powers which it was necessary should have authority or sanction of Congress, . .this ratification has operated to perfectly cure the defect.).
31. Id. at 669–70.
32. See generally, Edward Corwin, Total War, and the Constitution (1946).
33. 12 Stat. 326 (1861).
34. J. G. Randall, Constitutional Problems Under Lincoln 118–139 (rev. ed. 1951).
35. Act of Mar. 3, 1863, 12 Stat. 755 (authorizing suspension of habeas corpus, with limitations in Union states to those prisoners of war; all others indicted or freed.)
36. Proclamation of Sept. 15, 1863, 13 Stat. 734 (suspending habeas corpus with respect to those in federal custody as military offenders or as prisoners of war, spies, or aiders and abettors of the enemy).
37. Ex parte Milligan, 71 U.S. (4 Wall.) 2, 115–16 (1866).
38. Id. at 139 (Chase, C.J., concurring and dissenting in part).
39. Id. at 139–40 (Congress cannot direct conduct of campaigns, nor can the President, or any commander under him, without the sanction of Congress, institute tribunals for trial and punishment of offences, either of soldiers or civilians, unless in cases of controlling necessity
40. Id. at 17 (government argument).

Art II.S2.C1.1.11 Presidential Power and Commander in Chief Clause

The President shall be Commander in Chief of the Army and Navy of the US, and of the Militia of the several States, when called into the actual Service of the US; he may require the Opinion, in writing, of the principal Officer in each of the executive Departments, upon any Subject relating to the Duties of their respective Offices, and he shall have Power to grant Reprieves and Pardons for Offences against the US, except in Cases of Impeachment.

The President's power with regard to armed forces has long been debated. In defense of executive action in Indochina, the Legal Adviser of the State Department, in a widely circulated document, contended:

Under the Constitution, the President, in addition to being Chief Executive, is Commander in Chief of the Army and Navy. He holds the prime responsibility for the conduct of United States foreign relations. These duties carry broad powers, including the power to deploy American forces abroad and commit them to military operations when the President deems such action necessary to maintain the security and defense of the United States.

In 1787 the world was a far larger place, and the framers probably had in mind attacks upon the United States. In the 20th century, the world has grown much smaller. An attack on a country far from our shores can impinge directly on the Nation's security. In the SEATO treaty, for example, it is formally declared that an armed attack against Viet Nam would endanger peace and security of the U.S.

Under our Constitution it is the President who must decide when an armed attack has occurred. He has also the constitutional responsibility for determining what measures of defense are required when the peace and safety of the United States are endangered. If he considers that deployment of U.S. forces to South Viet Nam is required, and that military measures against the source of Communist aggression in North Viet Nam are necessary, he is constitutionally empowered to take those measures.[1]

Opponents of such expanded presidential powers have contended, however, that the authority to initiate war was not divided between the Executive and Congress but was vested exclusively in Congress. The President had the duty and the power to repel sudden attacks and act in other emergencies, and in his role as Commander in Chief he was empowered to direct the armed forces for any purpose specified by Congress.[2] Though Congress asserted itself in some respects, it never really managed to confront the President's power with any sort of effective limitation, until the 1970s.

Footnotes

3. Leonard C. Meeker, Legality of US Participation in Defense of Viet Nam, 54 Dep't State Bull. 474, 484–485 (1966). See John N. Moore, The National Executive and the Use of Armed Forces Abroad, 21 Naval War College Rev. 28 (1969); Quincy Wright, Power of the Executive to Use Military Forces Abroad, 10 Va. J. Int.

   L. 43 (1969); Documents Relating to the War Powers of Congress, The President's Authority as Commander in Chief and War in Indochina, S. Comm. on Foreign Rels., 91st Cong. 1 (1970) (Under Secretary of State Katzenbach), 90 (J. Stevenson, Legal Adviser, Dept of State), 120 (Professor Moore), 175 (Asst Att'y Gen. Rehnquist).
4. E.g., F. Wormuth & E. Firmage, To Chain the Dog of War (1989), F.J. Ely, War and Responsibility: Constitutional Lessons of the Vietnam War and its Aftermath (1993); U.S. Commitments to Foreign Powers: Hearings Before the S. Comm. on Foreign Rels., 90th Cong. 9 (1967) (Bartlett); War Powers Legislation: Hearings Before the S. Comm. on Foreign Rels., 92d Cong. 7 (1971).

It is intended that the reader learn from these many US Constitution passages and Courts discussion - - sitting Presidents have held many powers over and above those granted to US Congress and our Court system. Those powers are quite similar to those of Chief Executive Officers (CEO) of corporations large and small. It is a sheer impossibility to detail all those vitally important powers in writing. The very purpose of those powers is to ensure that America can always be properly represented and that necessary actions must and shall be taken in cases of civil situations as well as the serious emergency issues.

CHAPTER 19. GRECO-ROMAN ELECTIONS AND VOTING SOLUTIONS

The many forces arrayed against Donald Trump have become legend, as they are all seriously conflicted Democrats, with two exceptions. At minimum, all those people are in violation of any possible definition of CONFLICT OF INTEREST, (possibly CRIMINAL conflict of interest.)

Historical points that preceded these bad actors:

Cicero:

We included a discussion of the ultimate execution of Roman Leader Cicero in an earlier chapter. Julius Ceasar and his cohorts convicted and chased Cicero to his ultimate execution. Ceasar did not live to see the execution as he was assassinated at Ides of March a few years earlier.

The many cases against Trump were all launched due to Donald Trump performing his oath of office fully and working to attempt to prevent a most serious breach of law, due to the many breaches of voting and elections law we have documented in earlier chapters.

Even the ancient Greek/Athenian and Roman governments experienced problems with voting. Sometimes experimenting with voting and political methods, they always reverted to the most secure methods of limiting those allowed to vote.

Source:
Greek voting elections, Chapter 27, Demokratia to Democracy, The Requiem by George McCarley
Rome voting, elections Chapter 28, Demokratia to Democracy, The Requiem by George McCarley

No examination of our voting and elections problems today can be complete unless we reflect upon the many issues in the Roman and Athenian/Greek early democracies and republics. We see many of the same objectionable issues in ancient days as we see today. As you read, you will learn that in each case of abuse or experimentation with voting and elections changes, those early governments would return to the basics and often cease their experimentation - - typically returning to a more conservative and tightly controlled process. Quite clearly, that is where we must and shall return today.

ANCIENT GREEK DEMOCRACY DEVELOPS[1]
(EXCERPTED FROM DEMOKRATIA TO DEMOCRACY, THE REQUIEM by G. McCarley Chapter 27 and 28)

In the late 6th century B.C., the Greek city-state of Athens began to lay the foundations for a new kind of political system. This *demokratia* as it became known, was a direct democracy that gave political power to free male Athenian citizens rather than a ruling aristocratic class or dictator, which had largely been the norm in Athens for several hundred years before.

Athens' demokratia, which lasted until 322 B.C., is one of the earliest known examples of democracy; and although recent scholarship has complicated the Eurocentric view that it was the first democracy, this ancient political system was extremely influential in the Mediterranean region. It inspired similar political systems in other Greek city-states and influenced the ancient Roman Republic.

Athenian Men Join the Assembly

The last *tyrannos*, or tyrant, to rule Athens was Hippias, who fled the city when Sparta invaded in 510 B.C. Two or three years later, an Athenian aristocrat named Cleisthenes helped introduce democratic reforms. Over the next several decades, subsequent reforms expanded this political system while also narrowing the definition of who counted as an Athenian citizen.

What was Cleisthenes' motivation for initiating these changes? Unfortunately, "we don't have any good contemporary historical Athenian sources that tell us what's going on," says Paul Cartledge, a classics professor at the University of Cambridge. After the 514 B.C. assassination of Hippias' brother, Cleisthenes may have sensed there was growing public support for a system in which the city-state was not governed by an elite ruling class.

"Cleisthenes, I think probably partly for his own personal self-promotion, put himself forward as champion of the majority view, which was that we must have some form of popular, 'people' regime," Cartledge says.

To participate in the demokratia, a person had to be free, male, and Athenian. In the beginning of the democratic period, Athenian men had to have an Athenian father and a free mother. By the mid-5th century B.C., Athens changed the law so that only men with Athenian fathers *and* mothers could claim citizenship.

Because there were no birth certificates (or DNA tests) to prove parentage, a young Athenian man's political life began when his father introduced him at their local *demos*, or political unit, by swearing that he was his father and bringing witnesses to attest to this, Cartledge says.

The Athenian democracy was direct, rather than representative, meaning that Athenian men themselves made up the Assembly. Because there were no population censuses, we don't know exactly how many Athenian men there were in the 5th century B.C., but historians have commonly estimated the number to be around 30,000. Of those, around 5,000 might regularly attend Assembly meetings. In addition, Athenian men served on juries and were annually selected by lot to serve on the Council of 500.

There were other government positions that were in theory open to all Athenian men, although wealth and location played a large role in whether a man could take on a full-time government job or even make it to the Assembly to vote in the first place. Still, there were some positions that were only open to elites: the treasurers were always wealthy (ostensibly because wealthy men knew how to handle finances), and the 10 generals who occupied the top government office were always elite, well-known men.

Political Citizenship Remained Narrow

And then, of course, there were all the other people in Athens who were completely cut off from political participation.

Assuming that there were about 30,000 Athenian men when the city-state developed its democracy, historians estimate there were probably about 90,000 other people living in Athens. A sizable portion of these people would have been non-Athenians who were enslaved (by law, Athenians could not enslave other Athenians). Others were "resident aliens" who were free and lived in Athens but did not meet the requirements for Athenian citizenship. The rest were Athenian women and children, both of whom could not join the Assembly.

Although these groups never gained the same political rights as Athenian men, there was some debate about whether they should be able to, says Josiah Ober, classics professor at Stanford. "We know the question of 'could women be political beings?' was debated," he says. In 391 B.C., the Greek playwright Aristophanes wrote a comedy, *Assemblywomen,* in which women take over Athens' government. "It's meant to be funny in some ways, but there's a serious thought behind it," he says. Although Aristotle thought women were not psychologically fit for politics, Ober notes that Aristotle's teacher, Plato, wrote in *The Republic* (circa 375 B.C.) that an ideal political system would include women and men.

In addition, "there were moves several times in Athenian crisis history to…free large numbers of slaves to make them citizens, or make them resident aliens, on the argument that [Athens] needed more people who were full participants in the war effort," Ober says. However, "these tended to get defeated."

Athens' democratic period also coincided with the city-state's tightening of its control over what was originally a voluntary alliance of Greek city-states but had now become an Athenian empire. The city-states had their own governments, some of which were influenced by Athens' democratic system, but did not have any political power in Athens' demokratia.

Athens' democracy officially ended in 322 B.C., as Macedonia imposed an oligarchic government on Athens after defeating the city-state in battle. One of the Athenian democracy's major legacies was its influence on the Roman Republic, which lasted until 27 B.C. The Roman Republic took the idea of direct democracy and amended it to create a representative democracy—a form of government that European colonists liked, centuries later.

ATHENIAN DEMOKRATIA ORIGINAL FORMAT

Your reading of this chapter will make it clear just how avant-garde the Greek Philosophers and leaders were in this period that began as early as 800 BC. The demokratia system charted and described herein is strikingly similar to that practiced by Western Nations in 21st Century. It was a simpler system and in fact, it was all the system they needed in a day in which the entire population of Amphictyonic League Greece was in the range of 2 or 3 million people. They made errors that will be clear as you read, and yet Greece became known as the longest-lived democracy, of some 800 years. Read on to learn how and why they failed.

Athenian democracy developed around the 6th century BC in the Greek city-state (known as a polis) of Athens, comprising the city of Athens and the surrounding territory of Attica. Although Athens is the most famous ancient Greek democratic city-state, it was not the only one, nor was it the first; multiple other city-states adopted similar democratic constitutions before Athens.[1][2] Ober (2015) argues that by the late 4th century BC as many as half of the one thousand Greek city-states might have been democracies.[3]

Athens practiced a political system of legislation and executive bills. Participation was open to adult, male citizens (i.e., not a foreign resident, regardless of how many generations of the family had lived in the city, nor a slave, nor a woman), "probably no more than 30 percent of the total adult population".[4]

Solon (in 594 BC), Cleisthenes (in 508–07 BC), and Ephialtes (in 462 BC) contributed to the development of Athenian democracy. Cleisthenes broke up the unlimited power of the nobility by organizing citizens into ten groups based on where they lived, rather than on their wealth.[5] The longest-lasting democratic leader was Pericles. After his death, Athenian democracy was interrupted by oligarchic revolutions towards the end of the Peloponnesian War. It was modified somewhat after it was restored under Eucleides; the most detailed accounts of the system are of this fourth-century modification, rather than the Periclean system. Democracy was suppressed by the Macedonians in 322 BC. The Athenian institutions were later revived, but how close they were to a real democracy is debatable.

Etymology

The word "democracy" (Greek: *dēmokratia*, combines the *dêmos* which means "people") and *krátos* which means "force" or "power"), and thus means literally "people power". In the words "monarchy" and "oligarchy", the second element comes from arche (ἀρχή), meaning "beginning (that which comes first)", and hence also "first place or power", "sovereignty". One might expect, by analogy, that the term "demarchy" would have been adopted for the new form of government introduced by Athenian democrats. However, the word "demarchy" had been applied meaning "mayoralty", office, or high municipal magistrate. (In present-day use, "demarchy" has acquired new meaning.)

It is unknown whether the word "democracy" was in existence when systems that came to be called democratic were first instituted. The first conceptual articulation of the term is generally accepted to be c. 470 BC with Aeschylus' *The Suppliants* (l. 604) with the line sung by the Chorus: *dēmou kratousa cheir* (δήμου κρατούσα χειρ). This approximately translates as the "people's hand of power", and in the context of the play it acts as a counterpoint to inclination of the votes cast by the people, i.e., that authority as implemented by the people in the Assembly has power.

The word is then completely attested in the works of Herodotus (*Histories* 6.43.3) with the terms *dēmokrateomai* and *dēmokratia*. Herodotus wrote some of the earliest surviving Greek prose, but this might not have been before 440 or 430 BC. Around 460 BC an individual known with the name of Democrates,[6] a name possibly coined as a gesture of democratic loyalty; the name can also be found in Aeolian Temnus.[7]

History / Development / *Athenian Revolution*

Athens was not the only polis in Greece to institute demokratia. Aristotle points to other cities that adopted governments in the democratic style. Accounts of the rise of democratic institutions are in reference to Athens, since only this city-state had sufficient historical records to speculate on the rise and nature of Greek democracy.[8]

Before the first attempt at democratic government, Athens was ruled by a series of archons or chief magistrates, and the Areopagus, made up of ex-archons. Members of these institutions were generally aristocrats. In 621 BC, Draco replaced the prevailing system of oral law by a written code to be enforced only by a court of law.[9][10] While the laws, later come to be known as the Draconian Constitution, were harsh and restrictive, with nearly all of them later being repealed, the written legal code was one of the first of its kind and considered to be one of the earliest developments of Athenian democracy.[11] In 594 BC, Solon was appointed premier archon and began issuing economic and constitutional reforms in an attempt to alleviate the conflict that was beginning to arise from the inequities that permeated throughout Athenian society. His reforms redefined citizenship in a way that gave each free resident of Attica a political function: Athenian citizens had the right to participate in assembly meetings.

Solon sought to break away from the strong influence noble families had on the government by broadening the government's structure to include a wider range of property classes rather than just aristocracy. His reforms included establishing four property classes: the *pentakosiomedimnoi*, the *hippeis*, the *zeugitai*, and the *thetes*.[12] Classifications were based on *medimnoi*, income of a man's estate per year with the *pentakosiomedimnoi* making at least 500 medimnoi, the *hippeis* making 300-500 medimnoi, the *zeugitai* making 200-300 medimnoi, and the *thetes* making under 200 medimnoi.[12] By granting the formerly aristocratic role to every free citizen of Athens who owned property, Solon reshaped the social framework of the city-state. Under these reforms, the *boule* (a council of 400 members, with 100 citizens from each of Athens's four tribes) ran daily affairs and set the political agenda.[9] The Areopagus, which formerly took on this role, remained but thereafter carried on the role of "guardianship of the laws".[13] Another major contribution to democracy was Solon's setting up of an *Ecclesia* or Assembly, which was open to all male citizens. Solon also made significant economic reforms including cancelling debts, freeing debtors, no longer allowing borrowing on the security of one's own person as a means of restructuring enslavement and debt.[14]

Cleisthenes

In 561 BC, the nascent democracy was overthrown by Peisistratos but was reinstated after expulsion of his son, Hippias, in 510. Cleisthenes issued reforms in 508 and 507 BC that undermined the domination of the aristocratic families and connected every Athenian to the city's rule. Cleisthenes formally identified free inhabitants of Attica as citizens of Athens, which gave them power and a role in a sense of civic solidarity.[15] He did this by making the traditional tribes politically irrelevant, instituting ten new tribes, made up of three trittyes (geographical divisions), each consisting of several demes (further subdivisions). Every male citizen over 18 had to be registered in his deme.[16]

The third set of reforms was instigated by Ephialtes in 462 BC. While Ephialtes's opponents assisted the Spartans, he persuaded the Assembly to reduce powers of the Areopagus to criminal court for homicide and sacrilege. Membership of the Areopagus was extended to lower level propertied citizenship.[17]

In the wake of Athens's disastrous defeat by Sicily in 413 BC, a group of citizens took steps to limit the radical democracy they thought was leading the city to ruin. Their efforts, initially conducted through constitutional channels, culminated in establishment of an oligarchy, the Council of 400, in the Athenian coup of 411 BC. The oligarchy endured four months before it was replaced by more democratic government. Democratic regimes governed until Athens surrendered to Sparta in 404 BC, into the hands of the so-called Thirty Tyrants, pro-Spartan oligarchs.[18] After a year, pro-democracy elements regained control, and democratic forms persisted until the Macedonian army of Phillip II conquered Athens in 338 BC.[19]

Aftermath

Philip II had led a coalition of the Greek states to war with Persia in 336 BC, but his Greek soldiers were hostages for the behavior of their states as much as allies. Alexander The Great's relations with Athens later strained when he returned to Babylon in 324 BC; after his death, Athens and Sparta led several states to war with Macedonia and lost.[20]This led to the Hellenistic control of Athens, with the Macedonian king appointing a local agent as political governor in Athens. However, the governors, like Demetrius of Phalerum, appointed by Cassander, kept some of the traditional institutions in formal existence, although the Athenian public would consider them nothing more than Macedonian puppet dictators. Once Demetrius Poliorcetes ended Cassander's rule over Athens, Demetrius of Phalerum went into exile and the democracy was restored in 307 BC. However, by now Athens had become "politically impotent".[21]

An example of this, in 307, in order to curry favour with Macedonia and Egypt, three new tribes were created, two in honour of the Macedonian king and his son, the other to honour the Egyptian king.

When Rome fought Macedonia in 200, Athens abolished the first two new tribes and created a twelfth tribe to honour the Pergamene king. Athenians declared for Rome, in 146 BC Athens became an autonomous *civitas foederata*, able to manage internal affairs. This allowed Athens to practice democracy, though Rome ensured the constitution strengthened the city's aristocracy.[22]

Under Roman rule, the archons ranked as the highest officials. They were elected, and even foreigners Domitian and Hadrian held the office as a mark of honour. Four presided over judicial administration. The council (numbers varied from 300 to 750) was appointed by lot. It was superseded in importance by the Areopagus, which recruited from the elected archons, had aristocratic character and was entrusted with wide powers. At the time of Hadrian, an imperial curator superintended finance. The shadow of the old constitution lingered, and Archons and Areopagus survived the fall of the Roman Empire.[22] In 88 BC, there was a revolution under Athenion, as tyrant, he forced the Assembly to elect whomever he wished. Athenion allied with Mithridates and went to war with Rome; he was killed in the war and replaced by Aristion. The victorious Roman general, Publius Cornelius Sulla, gave the Athenians their lives and did not sell them into slavery; restored previous government, in 86 BC.[23] After Rome became an Empire under Augustus, independence of Athens dissolved and its government converged to a Roman type municipality, with a Senate of *decuriones*.[24]

Size and make-up of the Athenian population
Slavery in ancient Greece

Estimates of the population of ancient Athens vary. During the 4th century BC, there might well have been some 250,000–300,000 people in Attica.[4] Citizen families could have amounted to 100,000 people and out of these some 30,000 would have been the adult male citizens entitled to vote in the assembly. In the mid-5th century, the number of adult male citizens was perhaps as high as 60,000, but this number fell precipitously during the Peloponnesian War.[25] This slump was permanent, due to the introduction of a stricter definition of citizen described below. From a modern perspective these figures may seem small, but among Greek city-states Athens was huge: most of the thousand or so Greek cities could only muster 1,000–1,500 adult male citizens each; and Corinth, a major power, had at most 15,000.[26] The non-citizen component of the population was made up of resident foreigners (metics) and slaves, with the latter more numerous. Around 338 BC the orator Hyperides (fragment 13) claimed that there were 150,000 slaves in Attica, but this figure is an impression: slaves outnumbered citizens.[27]

Citizenship in Athens

Only adult male Athenian citizens who completed military training as ephebes had the right to vote in Athens. The percentage of the population that participated in the government was 10% to 20% of the total number of inhabitants, but this varied from the fifth to the fourth century BC.[25] This excluded a majority of the population: slaves, freed slaves, children, women, metics (non-citizens in Athens).[28] Women had limited rights and privileges, had restricted movement in public, were segregated from the men.[29 Although legislation was not Retrospective, five years later, a gift of grain arrived from the Egyptian king to be distributed among citizens, "illegitimate" citizens were removed from registers.[32]

Citizenship applied to both individuals and their descendants. It could also be granted by the assembly and was sometimes given to large groups (e.g., Plataeans in 427 BC and Samians in 405 BC). However, by the 4th century, citizenship was given only to individuals and by a special vote with a quorum of 6,000. This was done as a reward for service to the state. In the course of a century, the number of citizenships so granted was in the hundreds.[33]

Women in Athens

With participation in Athenian Democracy only being available to adult male Athenian citizens, women were left out of government and public roles. Even in the case of citizenry, the term was rarely used in reference to women. Rather, women were often referred to as an astē which meant 'a woman belonging to the city' or Attikē gunē which meant 'an Attic woman/wife.' Even the term Athenian was largely reserved for just male citizens.[34] Before Pericles' law that decreed citizenship to be restricted to children of both Athenian men and women, the polis did not register women as citizens or keep any form of registration for them which resulted in many court cases of witnesses proving that women were wives of Athenian men.[34]

In addition to being barred from any form of formal participation in government, women were also largely left out of public discussions and speeches with orators going as far as leaving out the names of wives and daughters of citizens or finding round about ways of referring to them. Pushed out of the public sphere, women's role was confined to working in the home and being subservient to her male guardian whether that be a father or husband.

In the realm of Athenian men's rationalization, part of the reasons for excluding women from politics came from widely held views that women were more sexual, and intellectually handicapped. Athenian men believed that women had a higher sex drive and consequentially if given free range to engage in society would be more promiscuous.

With this in mind, they feared that women may engage in affairs and have sons out of wedlock which would jeopardize the Athenian system of property and inheritance between heirs as well as the citizenry of potential children if their parentage was called into question.[34] In terms of intelligence, Athenian men believed that women were less intelligent than men and therefore, similarly to barbarians and slaves of the time, were considered to be incapable of effectively participating and contributing to public discourse on political issues and affairs. These rationales, as well as the barring women from fighting in battle, another requirement of citizens, meant that in the eyes of Athenian men, by nature, women were not meant to be allowed citizenship.

While barred from voting and citizenship, women could practice religion.[34]

Main bodies of government

Athens has had many different constitutions under its different leaders. Some of the history of Athens' reforms as well a collection of constitutions from other Ancient Greek city-states was compiled and synthesized into an all-encompassing constitution created by Aristotle or one of his students called the *Constitution of the Athenians.*[35] The *Constitution of the Athenians* provides a run-down of the structure of Athens' government and its processes.

There were three political bodies where citizens gathered in numbers running into the hundreds or thousands. These are the assembly (in some cases with a quorum of 6,000), the council of 500 (*boule*), and the courts (a minimum of 200 people, on some occasions up to 6,000). Of these three bodies, the assembly and the courts were the true sites of power – courts, unlike the assembly, were never called the *demos* ('the people'), as they were manned by just those citizens over thirty. Crucially, citizens voting in both were not subject to review and prosecution, as were council members and all other officeholders.

In the 5th century BC, there is often a record of the assembly sitting as a court of judgment itself for trials of political importance and it is not a coincidence that 6,000 is the number both for the full quorum for the assembly and for the annual pool from which jurors were picked for particular trials. By the mid-4th century, however, the assembly's judicial functions were largely curtailed, though it always kept a role in the initiation of various kinds of political trial.

Ecclesia

Events of Athenian democracy were meetings of the assembly (ἐκκλησία, *ekklesía*).

Unlike a parliament, the assembly's members were not elected but attended by right when they chose. Greek democracy created at Athens was direct, rather than representative: any adult male citizen over the age of 20 could take part.[36] The officials of democracy were in part elected by the Assembly and in large part chosen by lottery in a process called sortition.

The assembly had four main functions: it made executive pronouncements (decrees, such as deciding to go to war or granting citizenship to a foreigner), elected some officials, legislated, and tried political crimes. As the system evolved, the last function was shifted to the law courts. The standard format was that of speakers making speeches for and against a position, followed by a general vote (usually by show of hands) of yes or no.

Though there might be blocs of opinion, sometimes enduring, on important matters, there were no political parties and likewise no government or opposition (as in the Westminster system). Voting was by simple majority. In the 5th century at least, there were scarcely any limits on the power exercised by the assembly. If the assembly broke the law, the only thing that might happen is it would punish those who had made the proposal that it had agreed to. If a mistake had been made, from the assembly's viewpoint it could only be it was misled.[37]

As usual in ancient democracies, one had to physically attend a gathering to vote. Military service or distance prevented exercise of citizenship. Voting was by show of hands (χειροτονία, *kheirotonia*, 'arm stretching') with officials judging the outcome by sight. This could cause problems when it became too dark to see properly. However, any member could demand officials issue a recount.[38] For a small category of votes, a quorum of 6,000 was required, principally grants of citizenship, and here small colored stones were used, white for yes and black for no. At the end of the session, each voter tossed one of these into a large clay jar which was afterwards cracked open for the counting of the ballots. Ostracism required the voters to scratch names onto pieces of broken pottery, though this did not occur within the assembly as such.

In the 5th century BC, there were 10 fixed assembly meetings per year, one in each of the ten state months, with other meetings called as needed. In the following century, the meetings were set to forty a year, with four in each state month. One of these was now called the main meeting, *kyria ekklesia*. Additional meetings might still be called, especially as up until 355 BC there were political trials that were conducted in the assembly, rather than in court.

The assembly meetings did not occur at fixed intervals, as they had to avoid clashing with the annual festivals that followed the lunar calendar. There was also a tendency for the four meetings to be toward the end of a state month.[39]

Attendance at the assembly was not always voluntary. In the 5th century, public slaves forming a cordon with a red-stained rope herded citizens into the assembly meeting place (Pnyx), with a fine being imposed on those who got the red on their clothes.[40] After the restoration of the democracy in 403 BC, pay for assembly attendance was introduced. This promoted a new enthusiasm for assembly meetings. Only the first 6,000 to arrive were admitted and paid, with the red rope used to keep latecomers at bay.[41]

The Boule

In 594 BC, Solon created a boule of 400 to guide the work of the assembly.[42] After the reforms of Cleisthenes, the Athenian Boule was expanded to 500, elected by lot every year. Each of Cleisthenes's 10 tribes provided 50 councilors at least 30 years old. The Boule's roles in public affairs included finance, maintaining military's cavalry and fleet of ships, advising the generals, approving newly elected magistrates, and receiving ambassadors. Most importantly, the Boule would draft *probouleumata*, or deliberations for Ecclesia to discuss and approve. In emergencies, the Ecclesia would grant special powers to the Boule.[43]

Cleisthenes restricted the Boule's membership to zeugitai status (and above) because these classes' financial interests gave them an incentive towards effective governance. A member had to be approved by his deme, each of which would have an incentive to select those with experience in local politics and the greatest likelihood at effective participation in government.[44] The members from each of the ten tribes in the Boule took turns to act as a standing committee (the *prytaneis*) of the Boule for a period of thirty-six days. All fifty members of the prytaneis on duty were housed and fed in the tholos of the *Prytaneion*, a building adjacent to the *bouleuterion*, where the boule met. A chairman for each tribe was chosen by lot each day and required to stay in the tholos for the next 24 hours, presiding over the Boule and Assembly.[45]

The boule also served as an executive committee for the assembly and oversaw the activities of certain other magistrates. The boule coordinated the activities of the various boards and magistrates that carried out the administrative functions of Athens and provided from its own membership randomly selected boards of ten responsible for areas ranging from naval affairs to religious observances.[46]

Altogether, the boule was responsible for a great portion of the administration of the state, but was granted little latitude for initiative; the boule's control over policy was executed in its probouleutic, rather than its executive function; in the former, it prepared measures for deliberation by the assembly, in the latter, it executed wishes of the assembly.[47]

Courts (Dikasteria)

Athens had an elaborate legal system centered on full citizen rights (see *atimia*). The age limit of 30 or older, the same as that for office holders but ten years older than that required for participation in the assembly, gave courts a certain standing in relation to the assembly. Jurors were required to be under oath, which was not required for attendance at the assembly. The authority exercised by courts had the same basis as the assembly: both were regarded as expressing the direct will of the people. Unlike office holders, who could be impeached and prosecuted for misconduct, the jurors could not be censured, for they, in effect, were the people and no authority could be higher than that. A corollary of this was at least acclaimed by defendants, if a court had made an unjust decision, it must have been because it had been misled by a litigant.[48]

Essentially there were two grades of a suit, a smaller kind known as *dike* or private suit, and a larger kind known as *graphe* or public suit. For private suits, the minimum jury size was 200 (increased to 401 if a sum of over 1,000 drachmas was at issue), for public suits 501. Under Cleisthenes's reforms, juries were selected by lot from a panel of 600 jurors, there being 600 jurors from each of the ten tribes of Athens, making a jury pool of 6,000 in total.[49] For particularly important public suits the jury could be increased by adding in extra allotments of 500. 1,000 and 1,500 are regularly encountered as jury sizes and on at least one occasion, the first time a new kind of case was brought to court (see *graphē paranómōn*), all 6,000 members of the jury pool may have attended to one case.[50]

The cases were put by the litigants themselves in the form of an exchange of single speeches timed by a water clock or *clepsydra*, first prosecutor then defendant. In a public suit the litigants each had three hours to speak, much less in private suits (though here it was in proportion to the amount of money at stake). Decisions were made by voting without any time set aside for deliberation. Jurors did talk informally amongst themselves during the voting procedure and juries could be rowdy, shouting out their disapproval or disbelief of things said by the litigants. This may have had some role building consensus. The jury could only cast a 'yes' or 'no' vote as to guilt and sentence of the defendant.

For private suits only the victims or their families could prosecute, for public suits anyone (*ho boulomenos*, 'whoever wants to' i.e., any citizen with full citizen rights) could bring a case since issues in major suits were regarded as affecting the community as a whole.

Justice was rapid: a case could last no longer than one day, to be completed by the time the sun set.[51] Some convictions triggered an automatic penalty, but where this was not the case the litigants proposed a penalty for the convicted defendant and the jury chose between them in a further vote,[52] with no appeal. There was a mechanism for prosecuting the witnesses of a successful prosecutor, which appeared to lead to the undoing of the earlier verdict. Payment for jurors began around 462 BC and is ascribed to Pericles, a feature described by Aristotle as fundamental to radical democracy (*Politics* 1294a37). Pay was raised from two to three obols by Cleon early in the Peloponnesian war; the original amount is not known. Notably, this was introduced more than fifty years before payment for attendance at assembly meetings. Running the courts was a major expense of the Athenian state and there were moments of financial crisis in the 4th century when courts, at least for private suits, had to be suspended.[53] The system showed marked anti-professionalism. No judges presided over the courts, nor did anyone give legal direction to the jurors. Magistrates had only an administrative function and were laymen. Most of the annual magistracies in Athens could only be held once in a lifetime. There were no lawyers; litigants acted solely in their capacity as citizens. Professionalism tended to disguise itself; it was possible to pay for the services of a speechwriter or logographer, but this may not have been advertised in court. Jurors would likely be more impressed if it seemed litigants were speaking for themselves.[54]

Shifting balance between assembly and courts

As the system evolved, the courts (that is, citizens under another guise) intruded upon the power of the assembly. Starting in 355 BC, political trials were no longer held in the assembly, but only in a court. In 416 BC, the *graphē paranómōn* ('indictment against measures contrary to the laws') was introduced. Under this, anything passed or proposed by the assembly could be put on hold for review before a jury – which might annul it and punish the proposer as well.

Remarkably, it seems that blocking and then successfully reviewing a measure was enough to validate it without needing the assembly to vote on it. For example, two men have clashed in the assembly about a proposal put by one of them; it passes, and now the two of them go to court with the loser in the assembly prosecuting both the law and its proposer. The quantity of these suits was enormous. The courts became in effect a kind of upper house.

In the 5th century, there were no procedural differences between an executive decree and a law. The assembly passed both. Beginning in 403 BC, they were set sharply apart. Thereafter, lawmaking transitioned out of the assembly, into special panels of citizens drawn from the annual jury pool of 6,000. These were known as the *nomothetai* (νομοθέται, 'the lawmakers').[55]

Citizen-initiator

The institutions sketched above – assembly, officeholders, council, courts – are incomplete without the figure that drove the whole system, *Ho boulomenos* ('he who wishes', or 'anyone who wishes'). This expression encapsulated the right of citizens to take the initiative to stand to speak in the assembly, to initiate a public lawsuit (one held to affect the political community as a whole), to propose a law before lawmakers, or to approach council with suggestions.

Unlike officeholders, the citizen initiator was not voted on before taking office or automatically reviewed after stepping down; these institutions had no set tenure and might last only a moment. However, stepping forward was risky. If another citizen chose, a public figure could be called to account for their actions and punished. In situations involving a public figure, the initiator was referred to as a *kategoros* ('accuser'), a term used in cases involving homicide, rather than *ho diokon* ('the one who pursues').[56]

Thucydides said that Pericles characterized Athenians as being very well-informed on politics:

> We do not say that a man who takes no interest in politics is a man who minds his own business; we say that he has no business here at all.[57]

The word *idiot* originally meant "private citizen"; in combination with its more recent meaning of "foolish person", sometimes used by modern commentators to demonstrate that the ancient Athenians considered those who did not participate in politics as foolish.[58][59][60] History does not support this interpretation.[61][62]

Although, voters under Athenian democracy were allowed the same opportunity to voice their opinion and to sway the discussion, they were not always successful, and, often, the minority was forced to vote in favor of a motion with which they did not agree.[63]

Archons and the Areopagus

Just before the reforms of Solon in the 7th century BC, Athens was governed by a few archons (three, then later nine) and the council of the Areopagus, which was composed of members of powerful noble families. While there seems to have also been a type of citizen assembly (presumably of the hoplite class), the archons and the body of the Areopagus ran the state and the mass of people had no say in government at all before these reforms.[64] Solon's reforms allowed the archons to come from some of the higher propertied classes and not only from the aristocratic families. Since the Areopagus was made up of ex-archons, this would eventually mean weakening the hold of the nobles there as well. Even with Solon's creation of the citizen's assembly, the Archons and Areopagus still wielded a great deal of power.[65]

The reforms of Cleisthenes meant that the archons were elected by the Assembly, but were still selected from the upper classes.[66] The Areopagus kept power as 'Guardian of the Laws', which meant it could veto actions deemed unconstitutional, this worked in practice.[67] Ephialtes, and later Pericles, stripped the Areopagus of its role in supervising and controlling the other institutions, dramatically reducing its power. In the play *The Eumenides*, performed in 458, Aeschylus, himself a noble, portrays the Areopagus as a court established by Athena herself, an apparent attempt to preserve the dignity of the Areopagus in the face of its disempowerment.[17]

Officeholders

Approximately 1,100 citizens (including the members of the council of 500) held office each year. They were chosen by lot, with a much smaller (and more prestigious) group of about 100 elected. Neither was compulsory; individuals had to nominate themselves for both selection methods. Those chosen by lot were citizens acting without particular expertise. This was almost inevitable since, with the notable exception of the generals (strategoi), each office had restrictive term limits. For example, a citizen could only be a member of the Boule in two non-consecutive years in their life.[68] In addition, there were some limitations on who could hold office. Age restrictions were in place with thirty years as a minimum, rendering about a third of the adult citizen body ineligible at any one time. An unknown proportion of citizens were also subject to disenfranchisement (atimia), excluding some of them permanently and others temporarily (depending on the type). Furthermore, all citizens selected were reviewed before taking up office (*dokimasia*) at which time they might be disqualified.

While citizens voting in the assembly were free of review or punishment, those same citizens, when holding an office *served* the people and could be punished very severely. In addition to being subject to review prior to holding office, officeholders were also subject to an examination after leaving office (*euthunai*, 'straightenings' or 'submission of accounts') to review their performance. Both of these processes were in most cases brief and formulaic, but they opened up the possibility of a contest before a jury court if some citizen wanted to take a matter up.[69] In the case of scrutiny going to trial, there was the risk for the former officeholder to suffer severe penalties. Even during his period of office, an officeholder could be impeached and removed from office. In each of the ten yearly "main meetings" (*kuriai ekklesiai*), the question was explicitly raised in the assembly agenda: were office holders performing their duties correctly?

Citizens active as officeholders served in a different capacity from when they voted in the assembly or served as jurors. By and large, the power exercised by these officials was routine administration and quite limited. These officeholders were the agents of the people, not their representatives, so their role was that of administration, rather than governing. The powers of officials were precisely defined and their capacity for initiative limited. When it came to penal sanctions, no officeholder could impose a fine over fifty drachmas. Anything higher had to go before a court. Competence does not seem to have been the main issue, but rather, at least in the 4th century BC, whether they were loyal democrats or had oligarchic tendencies. Part of the ethos of democracy, rather, was the building of general competence by ongoing involvement. In the 5th century setup, the ten annually elected generals were often very prominent, but for those who had power, it lay primarily in their frequent speeches and in the respect accorded them in the assembly, rather than their vested powers.

Selection by lot / *Sortition*

The allotment of an individual was based on citizenship, rather than merit or any form of personal popularity which could be bought. Allotment was seen to prevent the corrupt purchase of votes, and it gave citizens political equality, as all had an equal chance of obtaining government office. This also acted as a check against demagoguery, though this check was imperfect and did not prevent elections from involving pandering to voters. The random assignment of responsibility to individuals who may or may not be competent has obvious risks, but the system included features meant to mitigate potential problems. Athenians selected for office served as teams (boards, panels). In a group, one person is more likely to know the right way to do things and those that do not may learn from those that do.

During the period of holding a particular office, everyone on the team would be observing everybody else as a sort of check. However, there were officials, such as the nine archons, who while seemingly a board conducted very different functions from each other.

No office appointed by lot could be held twice by the same individual. The only exception was the boule or council of 500. In this case, simply by demographic necessity, an individual could serve twice in a lifetime. This principle extended down to the secretaries and undersecretaries who served as assistants to magistrates such as the archons. To the Athenians, it seems what had to be guarded against was not incompetence but any tendency to use the office to accumulate power.[71]

The representativeness of the Athenian offices (councils, magistrates, and juries) selected by lot was mathematically examined by Andranik Tangian, who confirmed the validity of this method of appointment, as well as the ineffectiveness of democracy during times of political instability.[72][73]

Elections

During an Athenian election, approximately one hundred officials out of a thousand were elected rather than chosen by lot. There were two main categories in this group: those required to handle large sums of money, and the 10 generals, the *strategoi*. One reason financial officials were elected was that money embezzled could be recovered from their estates; election in general strongly favoured the rich, in this case, wealth was a prerequisite.

Generals were elected not only because their role required expert knowledge, but also because they needed to be people with experience and contacts in the wider Greek world where wars were fought. In the 5th century BC, principally as seen through the figure of Pericles, the generals could be among the most powerful people in the polis. Yet in the case of Pericles, it is wrong to see his power as coming from his long series of annual generalships (each year along with nine others). His officeholding was rather an expression and a result of the influence he wielded. That influence was based on his relationship with the assembly, a relation that in the first instance lay simply in the right of any citizen to stand and speak before the people. Under the 4th century version of democracy, the roles of general and of key political speaker in the assembly tended to be filled by different people. In part, this was a consequence of the increasingly specialized forms of warfare practiced in the later period.

Elected officials, were subject to review before holding office and scrutiny after office. They could also be removed from office at any time that the assembly met. There was a death penalty for "inadequate performance" while in office.[74]

Criticism

Athenian democracy has had many critics, both ancient and modern. Greek critics of Athenian democracy include Thucydides the general historian, Aristophanes the playwright, Plato the pupil of Socrates, Aristotle the pupil of Plato, and a writer known as the Old Oligarch. While modern critics are more likely to find fault with the restrictive qualifications for political involvement, these ancients viewed democracy as being too inclusive. For them, the common people were not necessarily the right people to rule and were likely to make huge mistakes.[73] According to Samons:

> The modern desire to look to Athens for lessons or encouragement for modern thought, government, or society must confront this strange paradox: the people that gave rise to and practiced ancient democracy left us almost nothing but criticism of this form of regime (on a philosophical or theoretical level). And what is more, the actual history of Athens in the period of its democratic government is marked by numerous failures, mistakes, and misdeeds—most infamously, the execution of Socrates—that would seem to discredit the ubiquitous modern idea that democracy leads to good government.[75]

Thucydides, from his aristocratic and historical viewpoint, reasoned that a serious flaw in democratic government was that the common people were often much too credulous about even contemporary facts to rule justly, in contrast to his own critical-historical approach to history. For example, he points to errors regarding Sparta; Athenians erroneously believed Sparta's kings each had two votes in council and there existed a Spartan battalion called Pitanate *lochos*. To Thucydides, carelessness was peoples' "preference for ready-made accounts".[76]

Plato and Aristotle criticized democratic rule as a numerically preponderant poor tyrannizing the rich. Instead of seeing it as a fair system under which everyone has equal rights, they regarded it as manifestly unjust. Aristotle categorized this as the difference between 'arithmetic' and 'geometric' (proportional) equality.[77][73]

To ancient detractors, rule by the *demos* was reckless and arbitrary. Examples:

1. In 406 BC, after years of defeats in the wake of the annihilation of their vast invasion force in Sicily, the Athenians at last won a naval victory at Arginusae over the Spartans. After the battle, a storm arose and the generals in command failed to collect survivors. The Athenians tried and sentenced six of the eight generals to death.

2. Technically, it was illegal, as the generals were tried and sentenced together, rather than one by one as Athenian law required. Socrates happened to be the citizen presiding over the assembly that day and refused to cooperate (though to little effect) and stood against the idea that it was outrageous for the people to be unable to do whatever they wanted. In addition to this unlawful injustice, the *demos* later on regretted the decision and decided that they had been misled. Those charged with misleading the *demos* were put on trial, including the author of the motion to try the generals together.[78]
3. In 399 BC, Socrates himself was put on trial and executed for "corrupting the young and believing in strange gods". His death gave Europe one of the first intellectual martyrs still recorded, but guaranteed democracy an eternity of bad press at the hands of his disciple and enemy to democracy, Plato. From Socrates' arguments at his trial, Loren Samons writes, "It follows, of course, that any majority—including the majority of jurors—is unlikely to choose rightly." However, some might argue, Athens is the only state that can claim to have produced Socrates. Surely, some might continue, we may simply write off events such as Socrates' execution as examples of the Athenians' failure to realize fully the meaning and potential of their own democracy."[79]
4. While Plato blamed democracy for killing Socrates, his criticisms *demos* were extensive. Many of his writings were democracy alternatives. His books *The Republic*, *The Statesman*, and *Laws* argued against democratic rule and in favour of a much narrower form of government:

   > "Organization of the city must be confided to those who possess knowledge, who alone can enable their fellow-citizens to attain virtue, and therefore excellence, by means of education."[80]

5. Whether the democratic failures should be seen as systemic, or as a product of the extreme conditions of the Peloponnesian war, there does seem to have been a move toward correction.[81] A new version of democracy was established in 403 BC, but it can be linked with both earlier and subsequent reforms (graphē paranómōn 416 BC; end of assembly trials 355 BC). For instance, the system of *nomothesia* was introduced. In this:

   > A new law might be proposed by any citizen. Any proposal to modify an existing law had to be accompanied by a proposed replacement law. The citizen making the proposal had to publish it [in] advance: publication consisted of writing the proposal on a whitened board located next to the statues of the Eponymous Heroes in the agora. The proposal would be considered by the Council and would be placed on the agenda of the Assembly in the form of a motion. If the Assembly voted in favor of the proposed change, the proposal would be referred for further consideration by a group of citizens called nomothetai (literally "establishers of the law").[25]

Increasingly, responsibility was shifted from the assembly to the courts, with laws being made by jurors and all assembly decisions becoming reviewable by courts. That is to say, the mass meeting of all citizens lost some ground to gatherings of a thousand or so which were under oath, and with more time to focus on just one matter (though never more than a day). One downside to this change was that the new democracy was less capable of responding quickly in times where quick, decisive action was needed.

Another criticism is to notice the disquieting links between democracy and several less than appealing features of Athenian life. Although democracy predated Athenian imperialism by over thirty years, they are sometimes associated with each other. For much of the 5th century at least, democracy fed off an empire of subject states. Thucydides the son of Milesias (not the historian), an aristocrat, stood in opposition to these policies, and was ostracised in 443 BC.

At times, the imperialist democracy acted with extreme brutality, as in the decision to execute the entire male population of Melos and sell off its women and children simply for refusing to become subjects of Athens. The common people were numerically dominant in the navy, which they used to pursue their own interests in the form of work as rowers and in the hundreds of overseas administrative positions. Furthermore, they used the income from empire to fund payment for officeholding. This is the position set out by the anti-democratic pamphlet known whose anonymous author is often called the Old Oligarch. This writer (also called pseudo-Xenophon) produced several comments critical of democracy, such as:[82]

1. Democratic rule acts for the benefit of smaller self-interested factions, rather than the entire polis.
2. Collectivizing political responsibility lends itself to both dishonest practices and scapegoating individuals when measures become unpopular.
3. Via inclusivity, opponents are naturally included within democratic framework, thus democracy itself will generate few opponents, despite its flaws.
4. A democratic Athens with an imperial policy will spread the desire for democracy outside of the polis.
5. The democratic government depends on the control of resources, which requires military power and material exploitation.
6. Values of freedom of equality include non-citizens more than they should.
7. By blurring the distinction between the natural and political world, democracy leads the powerful to act immorally and outside their own best interest.

Aristotle also wrote about what he considered a better form of government than democracy. Rather than any citizen partaking with an equal share in the rule, he thought those who were more virtuous should have greater power in governance.[83] A case can be made that discriminatory lines came to be drawn more sharply under Athenian democracy than before or elsewhere, in relation to women and slaves, as well as in the line between citizens and non-citizens. By so strongly validating one role, that of the male citizen, it is argued democracy compromised
the status of those who did not share it.

- Originally, a male would be a citizen if his father were a citizen, Under Pericles, in 450 BC, restrictions were tightened so that a citizen had to be born to an Athenian father and an Athenian mother. So *Metroxenoi*, those with foreign mothers, were now to be excluded. These mixed marriages were heavily penalized by the time of Demosthenes. Many Athenians prominent earlier in the century would have lost citizenship had this law applied:

  > Cleisthenes, the founder of democracy, had a non-Athenian mother, mothers of Cimon and Themistocles were Thracian.[84]

- Likewise, status of women seems lower in Athens than in many Greek cities. In Sparta, women competed in public exercise –in Aristophanes' *Lysistrata* the Athenian women admire the tanned, muscular bodies of their Spartan counterparts – and women could own property in their own right, as they could not at Athens. Misogyny was by no means an Athenian invention, but it has been claimed that Athens had worse misogyny than other states at the time.[85]
- Slavery was more widespread at Athens than in other Greek cities. Indeed, the extensive use of imported non-Greeks ("barbarians") as chattel slaves seems to have been an Athenian development. This triggers the paradoxical question: Was democracy "based on" slavery? It does seem clear that possession of slaves allowed even poorer Athenians — owning a few slaves was by no means equated with wealth — to devote more of their time to political life.[86] But whether democracy depended on this extra time is impossible to say. The breadth of slave ownership also meant that the leisure of the rich (the small minority who were actually free of the need to work) rested less than it would have on the exploitation of their less well-off fellow citizens. Working for wages was clearly regarded as subjection to the will of another, but at least debt servitude had been abolished at Athens (under the reforms of Solon at the start of the 6th century BC). Allowing a new kind of equality among citizens opened the way to democracy, which in turn called for a new means, chattel slavery, to equalize the availability of leisure at least partially between rich and poor. In absence of reliable statistics, these connections remain speculative.

- However, as Cornelius Castoriadis pointed out, other societies also kept slaves but did not develop democracy. Even with slavery, it is speculated that Athenian fathers had originally been able to register offspring conceived with slave women for citizenship.[84]

Since the 6th century, the Athenian version of democracy has been seen by one group as a goal yet to be achieved by modern societies. They want representative democracy to be added to or even replaced by direct democracy in the Athenian way, perhaps by utilizing electronic democracy. Another group, on the other hand, considers that, since many Athenians were not allowed to participate in its government, Athens was not a democracy at all. "Comparisons with Athens will continue to be made as long as societies keep striving to realize democracy under modern conditions and their successes and failures are discussed."[87]

Greek philosopher and Takis Fotopoulos has argued that "the final failure, of Athenian democracy was not due, as it is usually asserted by its critics, to the innate contradictions of democracy itself but, on the contrary, to the fact that the Athenian democracy never matured to become an inclusive democracy. This cannot be adequately explained by simply referring to the immature 'objective' conditions, the low development of productive forces and so on—important as may be—because the same conditions prevailed at that time in many places all over the Mediterranean, let alone Greece, but democracy flourished only in Athens" .[88]

Legacy

Since the middle of the 20th century, most countries have claimed to be democratic, regardless of the actual composition of their governments. Yet after the demise of Athenian democracy few looked upon it as a good form of government. No legitimation of that rule was formulated to counter the negative accounts of Plato and Aristotle, who saw it as the rule of the poor, who plundered the rich. Democracy came to be viewed as a "collective tyranny". "Well into the 18th century democracy was consistently condemned." Sometimes, mixed constitutions evolved with democratic elements, but "it did not mean self-rule by citizens".[89] It would be misleading to say that the tradition of Athenian democracy was an important part of the 18th-century revolutionaries' intellectual background. The classical example that inspired the American and French revolutionaries, as well as English radicals, was Rome rather than Greece, in the age of Cicero and Caesar, Rome was a republic but not a democracy. Thus, the Founding Fathers of the United States who met in Philadelphia in 1787 did not set up a Council of the Areopagos, but a Senate, meeting in the Capitol.[90]

Several German philosophers took delight in what they saw as the fullness of life in ancient Athens, not long afterwards "English liberals put forward a new argument in favor of the Athenians". In opposition, Samuel Johnson worried about ignorance of democratic decision-making, but "Macaulay and John Stuart Mill and George Grote saw the great strength of Athenian democracy in the high level of cultivation citizens enjoyed, and called for improvements in the education system of Britain that would provide a parallel to that of the ancient Athenians".[91]

George Grote claimed in his *History of Greece* (1846–1856) that "Athenian democracy was neither the tyranny of the poor, nor the rule of the mob". He argued that only by giving every citizen the vote would people ensure that the state would be run in the general interest. Given the many dramatic similarities between ancient demokratia and the design and operation of democracy in 21st Century, it is unfortunate to note a disturbing trend away from any description of democracy, and modern society is trending back sharply toward a DARK AGES scenario. As you continue to read, this point should be made clear. Further, it is beyond adamant that key professional sectors recognize this problem and become active in the corrections. Our Teachers, Professors, Preachers, and Politicians must recognize the problem and apply the knowledge herein to begin correction.

WHY DID GREEK DEMOCRACY FAIL

United we stand, and divided we fall. The many Greek city/states (possibly 1000) never united. Given the massive attack staged by Persia, only Sparta and Athens joined together to defeat Persia, which was the most powerful military in existence at that time. Athenians were even prosecuted for their failure to participate in the battle as was law. Barring some future translation proves this book in error, "divided they ultimately fell. Equally true in ancient Rome, the corruption and money factor continued to play a role in politics and government. Greece introduced the fact that Aristocracy and their kin can be blocked from government participation. However, they allowed them to corrupt anyway.

We are taught in school that in Greece the people introduced legislation and voted on all things. Your reading of this chapter alone makes it clear that is not correct. Only native men who were citizens and had completed military duty and had not been barred were allowed to vote. Upper class typically controlled what legislation was introduced.

Greek democracy was far ahead of its time. Had they united with their cousin Alexander the Great, they might have been the major power on earth today.

References and sources

1. Robinson, Eric W. (1997). First Democracies: Early Popular Government Outside Athens. Historia - Einzelschriften. Stuttgart, Germany: Franz Steiner Verlag. ISBN 978-3515069519.
2. Robinson, Eric W. (2011). Democracy beyond Athens: Government in the Greek Classical Age. Cambridge, England: Cambridge Uni Press. ISBN 978-0521843317.
3. Josiah Ober, The Rise, and Fall of Classical Greece (2015) Princeton U Press, USA.
4. Thorley, John (2005). Athenian Democracy. Lancaster Pamphlets in Ancient History. Routledge. p. 74. ISBN 978-1-13-479335-8.
5. "Ancient Greek civilization - reforms of Cleisthenes". Encyclopedia Britannica. 3/10/21
6. Raaflaub, Kurt A. (2007). "The Breakthrough of Demokratia in Mid-Fifth-Century Athens". In Raaflaub, Kurt A.; Ober, Josiah; Wallace, Robert (eds.). Origins of Democracy in Ancient Greece. Berkeley: University of California Press. p. 112.
7. Xenophon, Anabasis 4.4.15.
8. Clarke, PB. - Foweraker, Encyclopedia Democratic Thought. Routledge, 2003, p. 196.
9. Thorley, J., Athenian Democracy, Routledge, 2005, p.10.
10. Farrar, C., The Origins of Democratic Thinking: The Invention of Politics in Classical Athens, CUP Archive, 8/25/89, p.7.
11. "Draconian laws | Definition & Facts". Encyclopedia Britannica. Retr 5 May 2021.
12. Thorley, John (2004). Athenian democracy (2nd ed.). London, New York: Routledge. ISBN 0-203-62256-1. OCLC 174145266.
13. Encyclopædia Britannica, Areopagus.
14. "Solon's laws | Greek history". Encyclopedia Britannica. Retrieved 5 May 2021.
15. Farrar, C., The Origins of Democratic Thinking: The Invention of Politics in Classical Athens, CUP Archive, 8/25/89, p.21.
16. Thorley, J., Athenian Democracy, Routledge, 2005, p.25.
17. Thorley, J., Athenian Democracy, Routledge, 2005, pp. 55–56
18. Blackwell, Christopher. "The Development of Athenian Democracy". Dēmos: Classical Athenian Democracy. Stoa. Retrieved 4 May 2016.
19. "The Final End of Athenian Democracy".
20. Habicht, C., Athens from Alexander to Antony, Harvard Uni Press, 1997, p. 42.
21. Green, P., Alexander to Actium: Historical Evolution, Hellenistic Age, UCal Press, 1993, p.29.
22. A Companion to Greek Studies, CUP Archive, p. 447.
23. Cartledge, P, Garnsey, P. and Gruen, ES., Hellenistic Constructs: Essays in Culture, History, Historiography, University of California Press, 1997, Ch. 5.
24. Habicht, passim
25. Rothchild, JA., Intro to Athenian Democracy of the Fifth and Fourth Centuries BCE.
26. Dixon, MD., Late Classical Early Hellenistic Corinth: 338–196 BC, Routledge, 2014, p. 44.
27. Kamen, D., Status in Classical Athens, Princeton University Press, 2013 p. 9.
28. agathe.gr: The Unenfranchised II – Slaves and Resident Aliens
29. agathe.gr: The Unenfranchised I – Women
30. Lape, Susan (2010). Race and citizen identity in the classical Athenian democracy. Cambridge: Cambridge University Press. ISBN 978-0-511-67676-5. OCLC 798549142.
31. Thorley, J., Athenian Democracy, Routledge, 2005, p.59.
32. Cohen D. and Gagarin, M., The Cambridge Companion to Ancient Greek Law Cambridge University Press, 2005, p. 278.
33. Sinclair, RK., Democracy Participation in Athens, Cambridge U Press, 30 Aug 1991, pp. 25–
34. Pritchard, David (2014). "The Position of Attic Women in Democratic Athens" (PDF). Greece and Rome. **61.2**.

35. "Internet Classics Archive | Athenian Constitution by Aristotle". classics.mit.edu. Retr 5/5/21
36. Thorley, J., Athenian Democracy, Routledge, 2005, p.32.
37. Thorley, J., Athenian Democracy, Routledge, 2005, p.57.
38. Thorley, J., Athenian Democracy, Routledge, 2005, p 33–34.
39. Manville, PB., Origins of Citizenship in Ancient Athens, Princeton U Press, 2014 p. 182.
40. Aristophanes Acharnians 17–22.
41. Aristoph. Ekklesiazousai 378-9
42. Terry Buckley, Aspects of Greek History: A Source-Based Approach, Routledge, 2006, p. 98.
43. "Boule: ancient Greek council". Encyclopædia Britannica.
44. Thorley, J., Athenian Democracy, Routledge, 2005, pp. 31–32
45. Thorley, J., Athenian Democracy, Routledge, 2005, pp. 30–31.
46. Hignett, History of the Athenian Constitution, 238
47. Hignett, History of the Athenian Constitution, 241
48. Dover, KJ., Greek Popular Morality, Time of Plato, Aristotle, Hackett Publishing, 1994,p.23.
49. Thorley, J., Athenian Democracy, Routledge, 2005, pp. 36–38.
50. MacDowell, DM., The Law in Classical Athens, Cornell University Press, 1978, p.36.
51. Bertoch, MJ., The Greeks had a jury for it, ABA Journal, October 1971, Vol. 57, p.1013.
52. Arnason, JP., Raaflaub, KA. and Wagner, P., Greek Polis, Invention of Democracy: A Politico-cultural Transformation and Its Interpretations, John Wiley & Sons, 2013' p. 167.
53. Rhodes, History Classical Greek World: 478 – 323 BC, John Wiley & Sons, 2011, p. 235.
54. MacDowell, DM., The Law in Classical Athens, Cornell Uni Press, 1978, p.250.
55. Thorley, J., Athenian Democracy, Routledge, 2005, p.60.
56. Cohen D. and Gagarin, M., The Cambridge Companion to Ancient Greek Law Cambridge University Press, 2005, p. 130.
57. "Funeral Oration", Thucydides II.40, trans. Rex Warner (1954).
58. Goldhill, S., 2004, The Good Citizen, in Love, Sex & Tragedy: Why Classics Matters. John Murray, London, 179-94.
59. .Goldhill, S., 2004, The Good Citizen, in Love, Sex & Tragedy: Why Classics Matters. John Murray, London, 179-94
60. Parker, Walter C. (Jan 2005). "Teaching Against Idiocy". Phi Delta Kappan. **86** (5): 344. doi:10.1177/003172170508600504. S2CID 144893136. ERIC EJ709337.
61. Sparkes, A.W. (1988). "Idiots, Ancient and Modern". Australian Journal of Political Science. **23** (1): 101–102. doi:10.1080/00323268808402051.
62. see Etymology
63. Benn, Stanley (2006). "Democracy". In Borchert, Donald M. (ed.). Encyclopedia of Philosophy. Vol. 2 (2nd ed.). Detroit: Macmillan Reference USA. pp. 699–703
64. Thorley, J., Athenian Democracy, Routledge, 2005, pp. 8–9.
65. Sinclair, RK., Democracy Participation in Athens, Cambridge U Press, 30 Aug 1991, pp. 1–2.
66. Encyclopædia Britannica: archon
67. Thorley, J., Athenian Democracy, Routledge, 2005, p. 55.
68. Thorley, J., Athenian Democracy, Routledge, 2005, p.29.
69. Thorley, J., Athenian Democracy, Routledge, 2005, pp. 42–43.
70. Samons, L., What's Wrong with Democracy? From Athenian Practice to American Worship, U Cal Press, 2004, pp. 44–45.
71. Raaflaub, Kurt A., Ober, Josiah and Wallace Robert W., Origins of Democracy in Ancient Greece, U Cal Press, 2007 p. 182.
72. Tangian, Andranik (2008). "A mathematical model of Athenian democracy". Social Choice and Welfare. **31** (4): 537–572. doi:10.1007/s00355-008-0295-y. S2CID 7112590.
73. Tangian, Andranik (2020). Chapter 1 Athenian democracy, Chapter 6 Direct democracy. Analytical theory of democracy. Vols. 1 and 2. Studies in Choice and Welfare. Cham, Switz: Springer. pp. 3–43, 263–315. doi:10.1007/978-3-030-39691-6. ISBN 978-3-030-39690-9.

74. Cartledge, Paul (July 2006). "Ostracism: selection and de-selection in ancient Greece" History & Policy. United Kingdom: History & Policy. Arch 16 April 2010. Retr 9 Dec 2010.
75. Samons, L., What's Wrong with Democracy? From Athenian Practice to American Worship, U California Press, 2004, p. 6.
76. Ober, J., Political Dissent in Democratic Athens: Intellectual Critics of Popular Rule, Princeton U, 2001, pp. 54 & 78–79.
77. Kagan, D. (2013). Fall of Athenian Empire. Cornell U Press. p. 108. ISBN 9780801467264.
78. Hobden, F. and Tuplin, C., Xenophon: Ethical Principles Historical Enquiry, BRILL, 2012, pp. 196–199.
79. Samons, L., What's Wrong with Democracy? From Athenian Practice to American Worship, University of California Press, 2004, p. 12 & 195.
80. Beck,H.,Companion to Ancient Greek Government, John Wiley&Sons, 2013 p. 103
81. Adamidis, Vasileios (2019). "Manifestations of Populism in late 5th Century Athens". New Studies History and Law: 11–28.
82. Ober, J., Political Dissent in Democratic Athens: Intellectual Critics of Popular Rule, Princeton University Press, 2001, p. 43.
83. Beck, H., companion to Ancient Greek Government, John Wiley&Sons, 2013, p.107.
84. Hansen, MH., The Athenian Democracy in the Age of Demosthenes: Structure, Principles, and Ideology, University of Oklahoma Press, 1991, p.53.
85. Just, R., Women in Athenian Law and Life, Routledge, 2008, p. 15.
86. Rodriguez, Historical Encyclopedia World Slavery, Vol 7, ABC-CLIO, 1997, pp. 312–314.
87. Grafton, A., Most, GA. and Settis, S., Classical Tradition, Harvard U Press, 2010, .259.
88. Fotopoulos Takis, Towards An Inclusive Democracy, Cassell/Continuum, 1997, p.194"
89. Grafton, A., Most, G. and Settis, S., Classical Tradition, Harvard Press, 2010, pp. 256–259.
90. Hansen, M.H., The Tradition of Ancient Greek Democracy and Its Importance for Modern Democracy, Kgl. Danske Videnskabernes Selskab, 2005, p. 10.
91. Roberts, J., in Euben, J.P., et al., Athenian Political Thought and the Reconstruction of American Democracy', Cornell University Press, 1994, p. 96.

Sources

- Habicht, Christian (1997). Athens from Alexander to Antony. Harvard. ISBN 0-674-05111-4.
- Hansen, M. (1987) Athenian Democracy age of Demosthenes. Oxford. ISBN978-0-8061-3143-6
- Hignett, Charles (1962). A History of the Athenian Constitution. Oxford. ISBN 0-19-814213-7.
- Manville, B.; Ober, Josiah (2003). A company of citizens: what the world's first democracy teaches leaders about creating great organizations. Boston.
- Meier C. 1998, Athens: portrait of the city in its Golden Age (translated by R. and R. Kimber). NY
- Ober, Josiah (1989). Mass and Elite in Democratic Athens: Rhetoric, Ideology, and the Power of the People. Princeton.
- Ober, Josiah; Hendrick, C. (1996). Demokratia: a conversation on democracies, ancient and modern. Princeton.
- Rhodes, P.J. (2004). Athenian democracy. Edinburgh.
- Sinclair, R. K. (1988). Democracy and Participation in Athens. Cambridge University *Press*.

ROMAN ELECTIONS

Elections in the Roman Republic were an essential part of its governance, with participation only being afforded to Roman citizens. Scholars agree voting was a practice in ancient Rome for 500 years, therefore commencing between 500-400 BC. Documentation has not been discovered that provides a precise beginning date. Upper-class interests, centered in the urban political environment of cities, often trumped the concerns of the diverse and disunified lower class; while at times, those already in power would pre-select candidates for office, reducing the value of voters' input.[1] The candidates themselves at first remained distant from voters and refrained from public presentations (in fact, formal speech-making was at one point forbidden in an effort to focus on the policies rather than the charisma of the candidate),[2] but they later made up for time lost with habitual bribery, coercion, and empty promises. As the practice of electoral campaigning grew in use and extent, the pool of candidates was no longer limited to a select group with riches and high birth. Instead, many more ordinary citizens had a chance to run for office, allowing for more equal representation in key government decisions.

In the Roman Republic, citizens would elect officeholders annually. Popular elections for high office were largely undermined and then brought to an end by Augustus (27 BC - 14 AD), the first Roman emperor (earlier known as Octavian). However, Roman elections continued at the local level.

Elections were a central element to the history and politics of Rome for some 500 years, and the major historians such as Livy and Plutarch make frequent references to them. No comprehensive account exists on how elections worked.[3] Historians reconstructed details from scattered accounts from different eras, but much is still uncertain and there is scholarly debate over several elements.

Historian Sallust gives a valuable account of Marius' campaign of 107 BC in the *Jugurthine War.* The most important sources are writings by Cicero. While his major works are on elections, his daily life was immersed in late Republican politics, and his surviving letters and orations are most valuable. Two important ones are *Pro Murena* and *Pro Plancio*, both legal speeches to defend candidates accused of bribery.[4] The most comprehensive source is the *Commentariolum Petitionis* (*Little Handbook on Electioneering*) by Quintus Tullius Cicero. It is a how-to guide on running for consul, written by Quintus for his brother's campaign in 64 BCE. There are many doubts as to its authenticity, accepted by some as authentic, others date it a century later to an author who would not have direct knowledge of election realities.[5]

Legislative assemblies of the Roman Republic

At the origin of the Republic, the only elected positions were the two consuls; over the course of the Republic new public offices were added, and by the end of the Republic 44 public offices were elected. All were elected to one-year terms except the censor, whose term covered five years. The only public offices which were not elected were dictator and his deputy the Master of Horse, appointed, in emergency circumstances.[6] Candidates were elected by assemblies. Centuriate Assembly elected the highest offices of consul, praetor, and censor. This assembly divided adult male citizens in 193 centuries.[7] Its organization was descended from that of the Roman Army, and the centuries were organized into tiers rank and property with cavalry equites at the top and unarmed and unpropertied at the bottom.

Quaestors, and curule aediles were elected by the Tribal Assembly, while tribunes and plebeian aediles were elected by Plebeian Council.[8] These were divided into 35 tribes, (geographical units). The membership of the two is almost identical, the only difference is that patricians were excluded from Plebeian Council. For the Centuriate, voting was in descending order by status and wealth.

The first property class would divide itself first into their 35 tribes and then split each tribe by age forming the *iuniores* (juniors) and the *seniores* (seniors). This would form 70 centuries, each with a vote. The *iuniores* would vote first, and one of them would be chosen by lot. This group, known as the *centuria praerogativa*, would be first to vote, and it would have its results announced before every other century voted. Cicero put great weight on the ability of this first announced result to sway voters.[9] After *centuria praerogativa* voted, 34 *iuniores* would have their results announced simultaneously. Next, the 35 seniors and the 18 equites cast ballots. The first property class and the equites combined for 98 votes, and if they were unanimous a candidate would be declared elected. If no majority was reached, balloting continued to lower classes.

Tribal Assembly did not have a similar order of precedence. Each of the 35 tribes voted simultaneously. The results were counted and announced in an order determined by lot. Once a candidate had reached a majority of 18 tribes, counting would stop.

Voting itself was originally oral and initiated via a magistrate's call for a public meeting. Candidates would stand for the electorate, without having prepared any sort of formal speech, and voters would separate to different sections of the saepta (a large unroofed wooden structure with 35 divisions) according to tribe.

Each division connected to the magistrate's tribunal by a pons (plank) over which the voters would pass to cast their ballots. Each compartment had their votes taken individually and then given to tabulators on the tribunal. Until 139 BC, citizens cast their votes verbally by stating a candidate's name, *rogatores* (tabulators) marked off the votes on wax tablets.

The *lex Gabinia tabellaria* of 139 BC introduced the secret ballot, where each voter wrote the initials of the desired candidate on a small wax tablet to be placed in a box known as the *cista* at the exit of each of the *pontes.*[10] To prevent dishonesty, poll watchers guarded the ballot boxes, and the official tabulators, now called custodes, counted the votes. The process of voting itself occurred either in the capital's forum before the temple of Castor and Pollux or before the Rostra, limited space prevented all the tribes from voting at once.[11]

Campaigning would begin when election day was announced by the magistrate in charge of elections. In 98 BCE the *Lex Caecilia Didia* set the campaign length between 17 and 25 days.[3]

A core campaign activity was canvassing in the Forum. The candidate would walk to the forum surrounded by supporters, to meet another cluster of allies in the Forum. At the forum, the candidate would shake hands with voters. Whispering into the ear of some candidates would be a *nomenclator*, a slave who had been trained to memorize names of all the voters, so that the candidate could greet them by name.[12] The candidate would wear an especially whitened toga, known as the *toga candida*. It is from this term that we get the modern word candidate.[12] Some candidates may have canvassed to rural markets around Rome once those outside the city were allowed to vote.

Political rallies were not permitted in Roman elections. To attract voters, candidates instead held banquets and gave away free tickets to the games. To pay for these either a candidate had to be wealthy or rely on sponsorship of wealthy friends. There are cases of people going ruinously into debt to fund campaigns. There were no attempts to restrict who could donate, several laws passed to limit candidate spending.[13]

Development of Candidacy

Public voting in Rome was originally a process that did not allow for a true choice from the people. After the Senate prepared a list of candidates, it was the magistrate that narrowed the list to the two candidates that could contend for the nomination. Later on, in Roman Republic a practice called *professio* was established, in which potential candidates started to "profess to the magistrate"[2] their wish to be nominated for candidacy. This led to the nominated candidates publicly advertising their aspirations to office and "[conducting] their own canvass,"[14] clearly campaigning with the idea of voters' choice in mind.

Still, the power of people could be limited, as there were a few instances in 201 BC and 169 BC when candidates became elected just a day after they declared themselves a candidate, which would of course allow no real time for the people to be aware of, much less vote for, last-minute choices. In the later century, more concrete rules were established regarding the behavior and canvassing of candidates.[2] These laws kept people from declaring candidacy the day before election, requiring the profession to be made before a set date.

Campaigning strategies

Politicians running for a position of power in the Roman Republic followed campaigning strategies similar to those used by modern politicians. In a contemporary letter written to consul candidate Marcus Cicero by his brother, Quintus, during Marcus' campaign, Quintus wrote on the various campaigning strategies that would help Marcus be elected. One of the most important tips Quintus emphasized was that Marcus should create friendships with men of higher status because these were the men that had the most influence. In addition to creating relationships with the wealthy, Quintus also advised Marcus to "remind everyone in your debt that they should repay you with their support." To have a chance to be elected, politicians needed to recall any favors owed them because they needed all the support they could receive.

Furthermore, in a similar fashion to modern politics, politicians in the Roman Republic needed to please everyone, whether making promises they knew they could not keep or simply being very polite. In Marcus's response to his brother, he noted that "people would prefer a gracious lie than an outright refusal."[15] All that mattered was that the politician kept everyone happy, even if that meant lying to supporters. In addition to flattery and favor-trading, politicians would even resort to ad hominem tactics; one can find inscribed on walls in Pompeii numerous attacks on the character or constituency of those opponents running for office. Some clever candidates apparently scrawled derisive messages implying that only unsavory characters such as "the sneak thieves... the whole company of late drinkers [and] late risers" supported the opposing candidate.[16

Corruption *Ambitus*

Since most voters saw elections as irrelevant to their own lives, many candidates resorted to bribery to convince the people to cast votes. Bribery became such a commonplace practice in the later Republic that it was seen as a normal part of the political process and ranged from the blatant promising of money to simply hosting games and entertaining people.

During mid-second century, Polybius noted the prohibition of bribery, but this proved to be useless as it continued to be prominent in elections and was very difficult to differentiate between bribery and the patronage system.[17][18] Some evidence suggests that as the dominance of the practice grew, the number of men who gained consulship without any consulates in his family grew as well. Political office, then, was no longer restricted to those of noble birth, and the Republic began to transition from an aristocratic government to more oligarchic in nature.

Some sources assert that the money gained from bribes actually helped common voters afford the cost of voting.[19] In fact, the biggest target of corruption was poorer citizens, revealing that voters still had considerable influence in the outcome of elections.[17] Consequences of corruption caused a lack of faith in the constitution and political process, and to civil war.[18]

Corruption posed the greatest problem in the later Republic when the lucrative benefits of high office led to more competitive elections. Candidates were frequently accused of breaking the laws restricting spending, and directly bribing voters. Electoral crimes were known as *ambitus*, and there was a long series of laws passed trying to eliminate it, seemingly to little effect. In the consular election of 59 BCE, both Julius Caesar and his rival Bibulus committed to large bribes. In the election of 54 BCE two candidates promised the vast sum of 10 million sesterces to the *centuria praerogativa* for its vote.[20]

Representation and electorate

Roman Republic elections were often characterized by tension between patricians and the plebeians and, as modern scholarship has shown, dominated by oligarchic elite. The Tribal Council on its surface was equitable, but actually worked in favor of elites who had the resources to travel to the city to participate in the election. The Roman system of clients and patronage also ensured votes of the lower classes were tied to an elite.[21] While voting was more open, running for office was more restricted. Candidates had more stringent property tests and required ten years of military service. Throughout the history of the Republic, winning office was dominated by elite families.[6] The plebeian group, consisting of rural farmers, gained greater political representation slowly over time. By the middle of the 5th century BCE, the plebeians had gained enough power that an assembly of them called the Concilium (a consolidation of a number of other disjointed plebeian assemblies) was able to elect ten tribunes, or representatives, annually. The Concilium was notable as it was the first to represent all plebeians, not just those in the city.[22] It was one of few assemblies of its time to employ group voting, in which each tribe agreed on a single vote to cast, similar to the United States electoral college and processes of English Parliament.[23]

When it came to electing officials and magistrates higher up, that responsibility still lay with the Centuriate Assembly, which was for the most part controlled by patrician interests. Eventually, that too changed to include the votes of more than 35 countryside plebeian tribes.[24] Once the lower class had greater political representation, there came a greater opportunity for them to ascend the political and social ladder, making "rule by the people" attainable.[25]

Electorate and turnout

Voting for offices was open to all full Roman citizens, except women, slaves and those living outside Rome. The *Lex Julia* of 90 BCE extending voting rights to citizens across Italy expanded the franchise. By the census of 70 BCE, there were 910,000 possible electors.[26]

One unknown is how the Romans kept track of who was eligible to vote. One possibility is that as voters gathered as a tribe the members would be well known enough to each other so that an outsider could be spotted, but as the populations grew this would have been difficult. Historians have proposed that a central voters list was kept or that citizens were given some form of voter identification, no archaeological evidence survives for either.[10]

Another debated issue is turnout. No contemporary source indicates how many cast ballots in an election. One approximate number is the size of the voting area. As consul, Julius Caesar began construction of a structure on the Campus Martius to hold the voters while voting. The size of the structure, if completely filled with voters, could have held between 30,000 and 70,000 people. This is almost certainly a high estimate, as open spaces for conducting polling itself would at the least have been required. Cicero mentions in one work that voting for a single consul in 45 BCE took 5 hours, with the equites and first and second classes voting. From what we know of voting, historians have estimated that between 6,000 and 16,800 could have voted in that election. With an electorate of 910,000, generous guesses put turnout below 10%.[26]

End of elections

The reign of Caesar Augustus saw the final decline of democratic elections in Rome. Augustus undermined and lessened significance of the election results, eventually eliminating elections entirely. He also diminished the importance of the offices themselves - the senate was full of his supporters, so candidacy was based on flattery and not on merit since he could nominate senators freely and essentially controlled all membership.[27]

Augustus had extensive influence over the magistrates as well; he was given the power to grant commendation to candidates for office, which became a guarantee of winning the election.[27]

Augustus later eliminated direct election entirely, establishing designation by a group of senators and equites. Citizens were still allowed to elect municipal officers, but filling higher-level posts was left to those in power. There is evidence that elections continued at the municipal level for some time outside of Rome. The remains of Pompeii had graffiti inscriptions lauding one candidate or another, indicating contested elections are still underway in 79 CE.[28]

1. Adcock 1964, pp. 19-35.
2. Staveley 1972, p. 148.
3. Vishnia 2012, p. 106
4. Yakobson 1999, p. 20
5. Vishnia 2012, p. 108
6. Vishnia 2012, p. 105
7. Tatum, Jeffrey. "Elections in Rome". Jstor.org.
8. Taylor 1966, p. 4
9. Vishnia 2012, p. 123
10. Staveley 1972, p. 159.
11. Best 1974, 428-38.
12. Vishnia 2012, p. 112
13. Vishnia 2012, p. 111
14. Staveley 1972, 146.
15. Cicero & Carville 2012, pp. 18–28
16. Inscriptions from houses in Pompeii, 79 AD. See Davis 1912–13), pp. 260-265.
17. Yakobson 2012
18. Lintott 1990, pp. 1-16.
19. Roper 2013, pp. 37-61.
20. Vishnia 2012, p. 139
21. Yakobson 1999, p. 9
22. Adcock 1964, p. 30.
23. Staveley 1972, pp. 122, 133.
24. Adcock 1964, pp. 32, 34.
25. Adcock 1964, p. 31.
26. Vishnia 2012, p. 125
27. Adcock 1964, p. 76
28. Staveley 1972, p.

224. Sources:

- Adcock, F.E. (1964). Roman political ideas and practice. Ann Arbor: U of Mich Press ISBN 978-0-472-06088-7.
- Cicero, Quintus Tullius; Carville, James (2012). "Campaign Tips from Cicero: Art of Politics, From Tiber to Potomac". Foreign Affairs. Council on Foreign Relations. 91 (3): 18–28. JSTOR 23217963.
- Best, Edward E. (1974). "Literacy and Roman Voting". Historia: Zeitschrift für Alte Geschichte. **23** (4): 428–38. JSTOR 4435413.
- Lintott, Andrew (1990). "Electoral Bribery in The Roman Republic". Journal of Roman Studies. **80**: 1–16. doi:10.2307/300277.
- Roper, Brian S. (2013). "Democracy Suppressed: Roman Republic and Empire". history of democracy: Marxist interpretation. London: Pluto Press. pp. 37–61. ISBN 978-0745331898. JSTOR j.ctt183p7kp.6.
- Staveley, E. S. (1972). Greek-Roman voting and elections. Ithaca, N.Y.: Cornell U Press. ISBN 978-0801406935.
- Taylor, Lily Ross (1990). Roman voting assemblies from the Hannibalic War to the dictatorship of Caesar (1st ed.). Ann Arbor, Michigan: University of Michigan Press. ISBN 0-472-08125-X.
- Vishnia, Rachel Feig (2012). Roman elections in the age of Cicero: society, government, and voting. New York: Routledge. ISBN 978-0415879699.
- Yakobson, Alexander (1999). Elections and electioneering in Rome: a study in the political system of the late republic. Stuttgart: Steiner. ISBN 978-3515074810.
- Yakobson, Alexander (2012). "Elections, Roman". In Bagnall, Roger S. (ed.). The Encyclopedia of Ancient History. Malden, MA: Wiley-Blackwell. ISBN 978-1405179355.

CHAPTER 20. LEGAL EXPERTS SPEAK AGAINST TRUMP TRIALS

Turley says it would be 'absurd' to send 'elderly, first offender' Trump to jail by Nick Robertson - 06/10/24 10:49 PM ET

Legal expert Jonathan Turley said Monday that it would be "absurd" if former President Trump were sentenced to jail for his conviction on felony charges, predicting that he would instead get off with a lighter punishment.

Trump was convicted early this month of 34 counts of falsifying business documents in a case where prosecutors argued he illegally covered up hush money payments made to hide a past affair and influence the 2016 election.

Sentencing is scheduled for July 11, four days before the Republican National Convention begins. He has appealed, though the sentencing will go on as scheduled. The former president could face up to four years in prison, though Turley argued that is not likely.

"Trump came fully baked, in the view of many people, jurors and judge. People have this idea of who Trump is. They either love him, or they hate him," Turley said in a Fox News interview with Neil Cavuto. "I've never met anyone in the middle of those two camps. And so, I don't think that the needle is going to move much here."

"But it also would be absurd to send him to jail," he continued. "He is an elderly first offender, nonviolent crime, and a controversial prosecution. This whole case could be overturned on appeal. I think that Judge Merchan would be considerably outside the navigational beacons to send him to even a day in jail."

Trump sat for a probation interview earlier Monday, as is standard procedure. Though court officials made an exception to the rule for the former president, allowing him to attend virtually.

Turley added that he thought Judge Juan Merchan was somewhat biased in his court rulings towards prosecutors, so he wouldn't be surprised by any outcome.

"There's a lot of pressure. When I came out of that courtroom after the verdict, it was like the Roman games. People were static, to a point that it was difficult to watch," Turley said. "People were dancing in the streets. That's the environment around this courthouse."

"And there were other people who were in deep, you know, agony and sorrow," he continued. "It was a picture of the United States, and it was not necessarily a good one. I mean, I stood there for a second and took it in, because it was such a bizarre, bifurcated scene."

Fox News' Jonathan Turley Goes Off on 'Absurd' NY-Trump Case: 'The More Cases Against Trump, the Less Justice We Receive as a People' Isaac Schorr Apr 15th, 2024, 12:16 pm

Fox News legal analyst Jonathan Turley argued that the more cases are brought against Donald Trump by prosecutors, "the less justice we receive as a people" while inveighing against the "absurd" trial that began in New York on Monday.

"Jonathan, you wrote about Cicero saying, 'the more laws, the less justice,' and you see the same here. How so?" Inquired America's Newsroom host Dana Perino.

"Well, the more cases against Trump, the less justice we receive as a people. You know, the opponents of Trump would have been far better off with just one case, the Mar-a-Lago case. That's based on real law, real precedent, and one can disagree with the interpretations. But it's not a reach in the sense of this case," began Turley. "This case is, creating something, it's creating a criminal code just for Trump. You know, you have a misdemeanor whose time has expired, the statute limitations ran out, and it was revived in this rather curious way. He's effectively arguing that Trump was filing false business records through his counsel to hide a federal crime. But it isn't a federal crime, this wasn't a campaign contribution." "None of that appears to matter, and that's why a lot of us are looking at this and recoiling. This is not how law is supposed to be."

"New Yorkers appear to like it this way. They elected [New York Attorney General Letitia James, who ran on bagging Trump for anything, didn't even mention what. And they now are lionizing this district attorney who's putting together what many of us consider to be an absurd indictment," concluded Turley.

Trump's trial began in New York on Monday morning. He is also staring at two federal criminal trials, as well as another one in Georgia.

https://www.mediaite.com/tv/fox-news-jonathan-turley-goes-off-on-absurd-ny-trump-case-the-more-cases-against-trump-the-less-justice-we-receive-as-a-people/

Jonathan Turley Says Bragg's Case Against Trump Is 'Collapsing' After Witness Testimony   Jason Cohen | April 26, 2024

George Washington University law professor Jonathan Turley on Friday said the prosecution's case against former President Donald Trump is failing as a key witness is benefiting the defense.

Trump is on trial facing 34 felony counts of allegedly falsifying business records in relation to a $130,000 payment to porn star Stormy Daniels ahead of the 2016 election. The prosecution's first witness, former National Enquirer publisher David Pecker, was helpful to Trump as prosecution made mistakes that the defense capitalized on during cross-exam, Turley asserted on Fox News' "Outnumbered."

"It's a breakdown in the courtroom. They have a witness that is disassembling in front of them," Turley said. "The prosecution never revealed to the jury in the direct that Pecker had actually killed stories for other celebrities, that he had been working on stories two decades before the election with Trump that he was suppressing. And now it's only getting worse. Yesterday was really bad In terms of the cross-examination for the prosecution."

"Today is much worse. I mean, here Pecker is saying that Trump didn't want to purchase the story. Yesterday when he asked him about reimbursing [former Trump lawyer Michael] Cohen, he said he didn't know anything about that."

Pecker has testified about former Trump attorney Michael Cohen and the former president allegedly purchasing former playboy model Karen McDougal's story of an alleged affair from the outlet, one of three instances the prosecution argues reveal an unlawful "conspiracy" to influence the 2016 election.

"I think the defense is doing a very good job, but I have to say that this is collapsing on its own weight," he added. "You just have to stand back and let it fall. Just asking simple questions that the jury would want to know has left serious damage to the prosecution. These are not strange tangential questions; these are questions you would've expected the prosecution to ask as just the completion of their line of questioning. Like was Donald Trump the only one you did this for, when did you start to do this?"

Despite Pecker's testimony not damaging Trump, former federal prosecutor Andy McCarthy on Friday suggested Judge Juan Merchan's friendliness toward District Attorney Alvin Bragg could lead to jury bias against the former president.

"It's one thing to be watching the trial through the media, if you are watching it on our channel, you hear me. You hear [Fox News legal editor] Kerri Kupec [Urbahn], you hear Jonathan Turley talk about the weaknesses of the case," McCarthy said.

"The jury is not getting that filter. The jury is getting the district attorney's version of events and taking its cues from a judge who has been very friendly to the district attorney. So, if you're watching with legal commentary, you know they're not really proving a conspiracy in there and don't really have federal campaign finance in there. But I don't know that the jury knows that." https://www.dailysignal.com/2024/04/26/jonathan-turley-says-braggs-case- against-trump-is-collapsing-after-witness-testimony/

ALAN DERSHOWITZ WORLDWIDE LEGAL SCHOLAR COMMENTS ON VARIOUS TRUMP CASES
https://www.foxnews.com/media/alan-dershowitz-rips-tyrant-judge-outrageous-rulings-trump-trial-never-seen-spectacle

Legal expert Alan Dershowitz called out Judge Merchan for "outrageous" rulings in the New York criminal trial against former President Trump, arguing the case should be broadcast on television so Americans can see the "spectacle." On "The Brian Kilmeade Show," Tuesday, Dershowitz called Merchan a "tyrant" after he threatened to strike the testimony of Bob Costello, the defense's main witness, an act that Dershowitz argued would have violated the Sixth Amendment.

ALAN DERSHOWITZ: I've been in courthouses in every part of the world and in China, in Russia, in Ukraine, in Israel. I've been all over. I've never seen a spectacle like this. And that's why it should have been on television, so the American public could see how outrageous this judge is. And CNN just does his bidding. CNN lies, lies through their teeth about what happened in court yesterday between Judge Merchan and Bob Costello. Costello testifies, Merchan rules against him at every point, keeps out his testimony, makes outrageous rulings that any first-year student taking evidence would know was wrong.

And Bob Costello does what I did: He rolled his eyes. And I rolled my eyes, I said, I couldn't believe the judge was making these rulings. And the judge, thinking he's a tyrant, clears the courtroom, throws out everybody from the media. For some reason, they allowed me to stay, and I watched as the judge berated him. And the judge said something I have never seen in a courtroom in my history, 60 years. He threatened to strike the testimony of the main witness for the defendant because of punishment of the witness for staring at the judge. Can you imagine the violation of the Sixth Amendment? The Sixth Amendment allows any defendant to confront witnesses and to present evidence in his defense. Can you imagine if this judge had actually struck the testimony of Bob Costello? It would result in an automatic mistrial, new trial, and a verdict against the prosecution. The judge was bluffing.

He ought to be disciplined for making that threat because the threat was an idle threat. He obviously didn't act on it. ...

You can't throw out a witness's testimony and punish the defendant that way. It's just an outrageous threat. And we didn't see it because television is not allowed in the courtroom. ... They just won't allow the American public to watch this trial, and I don't blame them. If I were the judge, I would never want this trial to be on television because he's behaved so outrageously.

JONATHAN TURLEY
https://apnews.com/article/trump-trial-experts-mccarthy-turley-556f3eeb724c8bd11b26369f66620627

McCarthy once prosecuted terrorism cases in the U.S. attorney's office in New York's Southern District and represented Rudolph Giuliani. Turley is a professor at George Washington University's law school and founded the Project for Older Prisoners, which helps seek release of geriatric prison inmates.

Writing about the trial in the National Review, McCarthy said "Trump ought to be acquitted for the simplest of reasons: Prosecutors can't prove their case." He criticized prosecution witness and former Trump attorney Cohen on the air, saying Cohen's dishonesty and bias against Trump will be jury problems to overcome.

Turley, speaking to Fox's Jesse Watters last week, called Cohen "the most compromised, unbelievable witness in the history of the federal legal system." On another Fox appearance, Turley said judge Merchan, shouldn't even give the case to the jury. I think this case is gone," Turley said. "They didn't state basis for a crime."

CHAPTER 21. STATES ACTIONS TO IMPROVE ELECTION INTEGRITY

What are the states' actions to be sure our elections work!

GEORGIA

https://www.npr.org/2024/08/07/g-s1-15750/georgia-election-board-counties-investigate-elections

Georgia election board says counties can do more to investigate results. August 7, 20241:11 AM ET By The Associated Press

ATLANTA — Georgia's State Election Board voted Tuesday to require county election officials to make a "reasonable inquiry" before certifying election results to the state, signaling that fights about approving election results could intensify in the South's battleground.

Supporters say the measure is needed because election boards must swear results are accurate and need to adequately assure themselves that the totals are correct before doing so.

"Why one would not want to assume there is some oversight?" asked State Election Board member Janice Johnston, who was appointed the panel by the state Republican Party. "It's the duty of the board to provide some oversight, in a fair way, in a reasonable way."

But opponents of the rule say it's an invitation to create post-election chaos and that the board is defying state law that says that county officials "shall certify" results, as well as more than a century of court precedent finding county officials have little wiggle room.

"The proposed rule changes will give authority to local election officials to halt the counting of votes and slow down, or even outright refuse certification if they contend there are any irregularities, essentially making the certification of election results discretionary," said House Minority Whip Sam Park, a Democrat from Lawrenceville. "The key word there is discretionary. This would give partisan county board of elections personal control over election results, allowing them to uphold certifying the election if they disagree with the results."

The rule will take effect after 20 days, although it could be challenged in court. It's yet another battle over what "had been an afterthought" with state and local boards certifying results.

https://www.democracydocket.com/news-alerts/right-wing-activists-sue-fulton-county-georgia-election-board-over-voter-challenges/

Right-Wing Activists Sue Fulton County, Georgia Election Board Over Voter Challenges. By Crystal Hill August 29, 2024

Two right-wing activists who've challenged the status of thousands of voters in Georgia are suing Fulton County election officials over what they describe as a failure to properly maintain the county's voter rolls and respond to voter challenges.

The lawsuit filed Wednesday against Fulton County Department of Registration and Elections and Secretary of State Brad Raffensperger alleges the county "does not maintain, nor does it attempt to maintain, accurate voter rolls."

In Wednesday's complaint, a Republican plaintiff, Jason Frazier, claims he submitted a voter challenge on Aug. 4 that contested status of electors no longer eligible to vote in Fulton County. Such challenges are allowed under Georgia law.

Frazier said his challenge required the Fulton County board to provide him notice of a hearing within ten days of the challenge. "But as of the date of this filing, the (county) continues to violate its obligation."

The complaint argues the county is violating the National Voter Registration Act (NVRA) and state law by failing to conduct routine voter list maintenance and not responding to his challenge.

Also at issue is a provision in the NVRA that requires states to complete any program used to systematically remove the names of ineligible voters from the official list of eligible voters no later than 90 days prior to a primary election or general election for federal office.

Plaintiffs say the state is relying on federal law as the basis for refusing to remove voters identified by challengers, even though NVRA is referring to removal of voters through an official state-run system.

"In other words, Raffensperger falsely advised and/or instructed that federal law (NVRA) prohibits county election officials in Fulton and throughout Georgia's 159 counties from removing voters within 90 days of a federal election if ineligible voters identified by … challenge were found ineligible," the complaint said."

Raffensperger is a defendant in another pending lawsuit brought in July from pro-voting groups over Senate Bill 189, which made it easier for a Georgia resident to challenge another resident's voter eligibility. Republican Gov. Brian Kemp signed the law in May.

Frazier and his co-plaintiff are asking a federal district court to declare that the county violated state and federal law and compel them to remove ineligible voters from the rolls before the Nov. 5 election. They're also asking the court to reinstate any voter challenges that were denied based on the 90-day rule.

TEXAS

https://www.votebeat.org/texas/2024/08/27/governor-greg-abbott-voter-roll-cleanup-suspense-list-noncitizens/

Abbott says a million names have been deleted from Texas voter rolls. What does that number mean? Most were people who died or moved out of state, but the governor also highlighted some who were flagged as noncitizens.

By Juan Salinas II and Natalia Contreras
| August 27, 2024, 3:35pm CDT

Update, Aug. 28: In response to Abbott's press release, a coalition of watchdog and voting rights groups in a letter Wednesday asked Texas Secretary of State Jane Nelson whether Texas has been removing voters from its rolls within the 90-day period before an election, which would be a violation of federal law.

The groups, which include ACLU, Texas Civil Rights Project, and the Campaign Legal Center said some of the 6,500 potential noncitizens Abbott highlighted in his press release could have been mistakenly flagged. "We are alarmed by the large number of voters removed, indicating eligible Texas voters have likely been erroneously identified as noncitizens and purged from the rolls," they said in a letter, which requested documents from Secretary of State.

Texas Gov. Greg Abbott announced on Monday that the state has removed roughly a million people from its voter rolls since he signed a legislative overhaul of election laws in 2021.

"Illegal voting in Texas will never be tolerated. We will continue to safeguard Texans' sacred right to vote while also aggressively protecting our elections from illegal voting," he said.

Election experts point out that both federal and state law already required voter roll maintenance, and the governor's framing of this routine process as a protection against illegal voting could be used to undermine trust in elections. The National Voter Registration Act of 1993 already governs how states should keep their registration rolls accurate and up-to-date, and also includes protections to avoid inadvertent removal of properly registered voters.

"Year after year, people are taken off the voting rolls for all manner of innocuous reasons," said Sarah Xiyi Chen, an attorney at the Texas Civil Rights Project. Neither the governor nor the Secretary of State's Office responded to requests for comment.

Removal of 'noncitizens' raises questions

The majority of voters removed from the rolls were taken off because they died, failed to respond to notices from election officials, or moved out of Texas. Abbott's press release also said more than 6,000 voters were removed after being convicted of a felony.

The total Abbott cited includes more than 463,000 who were taken off after being placed on what is known as the suspense list. Such voters are removed after the registrar receives information they have moved. If the voters do not update their information and do not vote for two election cycles, they're removed from the rolls. In addition, the governor stressed that more than 6,500 "noncitizens" who shouldn't have been registered were removed, and approximately 1,930 of those had a voting history.

Voter watchdogs such as Alice Clapman, senior counsel at the Brennan Center's Voting Rights Program, said they want to know more about those voters, because Texas has wrongly flagged people as noncitizens before.

Flagging legal voters as noncitizens can occur when outdated information is obtained from naturalized citizens or if you mistakenly check the wrong box at DMV, Clapman said.

In 2019, Texas officials flagged 95,000 voters they identified as "noncitizens" and accused broadly of voter fraud. After review, it turned out that many of the people identified on the rolls were naturalized citizens. The scandal resulted in the secretary of state resigning. The state abandoned the effort after numerous lawsuits, which resulted in the state setting new guidelines for voter roll clean-ups.

OHIO

https://apnews.com/article/election-2024-ohio-voter-rolls-395d9a1ad811ea9a710e93f1dca06f6f

Ohio launches effort to clean up voter rolls ahead of November's presidential election

By JULIE CARR SMYTH   Updated 4:52 PM CDT, May 2, 2024

COLUMBUS, Ohio (AP) — Ohio's Republican Secretary of State Frank LaRose directed county election directors on Thursday to begin a "routine but enhanced" hunt through the voter rolls ahead of November's election, in an effort to remove inactive registrations.

"Every state is required to have an ongoing process to verify the accuracy of its voter rolls, but Ohio has the most advanced and effective protocols in the nation," LaRose said in announcing the directive. "This work is not only critical to keeping our elections honest, but it's also essential to making sure election officials can properly plan for the right number of ballots, voting machines, polling places and poll workers."

The list maintenance effort will target four specific areas:

1. Changes of address. These are registrations that appear to be inactive because of a change of address registered with the U.S. Postal Service that the voter has failed to confirm to their local elections board. The listings are flagged for removal after four consecutive years of voter inactivity.
2. Past due removals. These are records previously flagged for removal after the required four-year waiting period, and identified through a data integrity investigation conducted by LaRose's Office of Data Analytics and Archive as remaining in the system.
3. Returned acknowledgements. These are new registrations that counties acknowledged with an informational postcard that was returned as undeliverable. By law, these registrations are placed in "confirmation" status, which sets them up to be purged barring eligible voter activity.
4. BMV mismatches. These are registrations that don't match certain details a person provided to the Ohio Bureau of Motor Vehicles, such as their name, birth date, Social Security number or driver's license number. This process can flag registrations for voters who died.

All registrations deemed inactive and legally qualified for removal will be listed for public review on a Registration Readiness roster posted for public review to the Ohio Secretary of State's website. This provides one final opportunity for voters and voting rights to prevent deletion.

SEVEN STATES INITIATIVE
https://www.democracydocket.com/analysis/in-seven-states-removing-voters-from-the-rolls-just-got-easier/

Arizona

Arizona Republicans enacted two laws related to voter purges — one in 2021 and the other earlier this year. The first was included in a budget bill with a hodgepodge of policy changes and would have required the Arizona secretary of state to allow any individual or organization designated by the Legislature to access the state's voter rolls. If this individual or organization deems any registration on the rolls as ineligible, election officials are required to remove it — without providing notice to the voter. This bill, however, was ultimately struck down by the state Supreme Court for violating the state constitution.

The second law is House Bill 2243, which Gov. Doug Ducey (R) signed into law in July — despite vetoing an almost identical bill this year. The law requires county recorders to cancel registrations if they receive information suggesting the voter is not qualified to vote due to non-citizenship, change of address or death. When Ducey vetoed the earlier bill, he said the requirement "is vague and lacks any guidance for how a county recorder would confirm" a voter's qualifications. He also suggested that "bad actors" could use the bill to "falsely allege a voter is not a qualified elector." While a spokesperson for Ducey said changes to the bill met his concerns, voting rights groups fear the bill's lack of safeguards will block Arizona citizens from being able to vote.

Florida

Florida's new Senate Bill 524, which Gov. Ron DeSantis (R) signed into law in April, received most of its attention for creating a new special force to investigate election crimes. But it also included a myriad of other voting restrictions, such as provisions related to list maintenance. S.B. 524 increases the frequency of removals and requires elections officials to use data from other government agencies to identify ineligible voters, including potential noncitizens. The law also makes it harder for voters to reactivate their registrations — previously, voters had to update their registrations or vote to reactivate them. Now, they have to confirm their residential addresses to remain on the rolls.

Iowa

Iowa's Senate File 413, one of a pair of comprehensive voter suppression laws enacted last year, increases the risk of Iowans having their registrations canceled. Previously, Iowa voters could be placed on the inactive voter list if they did not vote in two successive general elections. S.F. 413 accelerates this process, marking any voter who doesn't vote in a single election as inactive and kickstarting a process that could end in their removal from the voter rolls simply because they chose not to vote for whatever reason.

Kentucky

In April 2021, Kentucky Gov. Andy Beshear (D) signed a bipartisan voting bill into law that made several key reforms to Kentucky elections, like early voting, drop boxes and voting centers. But the bill also included some provisions that could risk voter purges — the law requires registrations to be deleted within five days of receiving a notice that they registered in a new jurisdiction like another state. The law doesn't require voters be notified in case the information is wrong or there are mistakes, leaving voters no recourse to prevent their registrations being canceled.

Mississippi

Mississippi's House Bill 1510, signed into law by Gov. Tate Reeves (R) in April, imposes a documentary proof of citizenship requirement on new voters. Like a similar law in Arizona, the requirement is likely to violate federal law. The law also requires election officials to crosscheck databases to see if voters are noncitizens. If flagged, voters have to prove their citizenship within 30 days or else they will be removed. Since citizenship databases are unreliable and often inaccurate, the law could result in the purging of actual citizens — particularly naturalized ones — from the voter rolls.

Texas

While Texas' omnibus voter suppression law, Senate Bill 1, has gotten a lot of attention, you might not have heard of its voter purge provisions. S.B. 1 increases the frequency of purges, requires the removal of voters thought to be noncitizens without notice and imposes penalties on election officials if they don't comply.

As one of the plaintiffs in the lawsuits challenging S.B. 1 notes, if officials aren't careful in their efforts, "eligible voters may be purged from the voter register," an impact that will have "a disparate impact on Latino voters."

Utah

Utah's House Bill 12, signed into law in February 2021, modifies the state's procedures for removing deceased voters from the polls. The law requires county clerks to cross-reference all death certificates and remove voter registrations within 10 days. But since the law doesn't require any notice to voters, or require auditing for accuracy, it increases risk that officials will remove the wrong names by mistake.

Florida

https://www.wmnf.org/almost-1-million-florida-voters-declared-inactive-after-law-purging-voter-lists/

Almost 1 million Florida voters declared inactive after law purging voter lists
Posted on January 3, 2024, by Chris Young

Nearly 1 million registered voters have been dropped from Florida's active voter rolls since 2022, and 2023 law might have something to do with this. Senate Bill 7050 toughened requirements for maintaining lists of voters, and added severe restrictions to third-party voter registration and mail-in voting. This led to the considerable number of registered voters being dropped from active voter rolls, according to the news site Florida Bulldog.

Some argued that the law was voter suppression. The League of Women Voters of Florida sued last year, saying the new restrictions are overbroad, vague, and violate the First Amendment.

However, In Hillsborough County, Supervisor of Elections Craig Latimer says its making voter lists more efficient.

"What we're seeing is that these people basically weren't here. They weren't living here anymore; they had moved on. Nobody thinks the very first thing they're going to do when they move is inform the Supervisor of Elections." He says just because voters are declared inactive, doesn't mean they can't vote.

"It means they're going to stay in that inactive status through two general elections. If they do nothing, then they'll be removed. But anytime during those two general elections, they can walk in and vote, they can request a vote by mail ballot if they sign a petition, any action at all will move them back active again."

Latimer encourages voters to keep their information up to date.

Michigan

https://www.votebeat.org/michigan/2023/3/16/23643866/voter-registration-list-maintenance-jocelyn-benson/

Before canceling 100,000 voter registrations, Michigan officials call on community groups and clerks to double-check their lists.

As Michigan election officials prepare to remove nearly 100,000 potentially ineligible voters as part of its periodic cleanup of registration rolls, they are turning to local clerks and community groups to check their work and ensure no eligible voters are improperly removed.

Clerks and other election officials have been scouring Social Security death records and local obituaries to ensure that people flagged as deceased are truly dead.

Meanwhile, local community groups that the secretary of state's office refers to as "democracy partners," including Pontiac-based Oakland Forward, are inspecting the lists of voters to potentially be removed to see if any neighbors or familiar names are incorrectly flagged as having moved away.

"We are trying to make sure that as many people as possible actually stay on the voting rolls and [understand] that they need to update their registration," said Kermit Williams, the executive director of Oakland Forward, a nonprofit community organization that's part of the Promote the Vote coalition of organizations.

Williams said he and 12 staffers will be inspecting the rolls. Staff members and volunteers will then canvass neighborhoods in person in Oakland County to alert residents that they are on the list for removal. They will also help them contact the local clerk or secretary of the state's office to update registration and avoid removal from voter rolls.

Oakland Forward is also contacting inactive voters and asking them to visit the state's voter registration website to make sure their registration is up-to-date and prevent themselves from being flagged for cancellation in the future.

"We want to make sure not only is it accurate, but we want to make sure that it's not disproportionately affecting people in front of this presidential election," Williams said. "It's going to be very critical to make sure that everybody who wants to cast a vote can vote."

Election officials at the Michigan secretary of state's office and the Bureau of Elections say removing voters who don't belong on the rolls — officially called the Qualified Voter File — is part of their federally mandated efforts to prevent fraudulent voting by making sure the file is clear of deceased voters or those who moved out of state.

Out of Michigan's 8.2 million registered voters, nearly 100,000 registrations are up for cancellation. They include voters no longer living at addresses where registered or those who have surrendered their Michigan driver's license to another state. In such cases, officials received returned mail or other information giving them reason to believe the individual moved.

Arizona

https://azmirror.com/briefs/republicans-sue-to-purge-at-least-500000-people-from-arizonas-voter-rolls/

Republicans sue to purge 500,000 people from Arizona's voter rolls.
Bye: Emily Holshouser - June 10, 2024, 10:42 am

Leaders of the Arizona Republican Party and a conservative dark money group have filed a lawsuit alleging the state has not kept an accurate count of registered voters and asking a court to force elections officials to purge 500,000 Arizonans from the voter rolls.

The lawsuit claims the state's list of registered voters contains up to 1.27 million voters who have either died or moved out of state, violating National Voter Registration Act. Four counties in Arizona have more registered voters than total voting-age citizens, the group's suit says — Apache, La Paz, Navajo, and Santa Cruz. The suit uses 2022 voter registration figures and data from U.S. Census.

The suit was filed by Scot Mussi, president of the Arizona Free Enterprise Club; Arizona GOP chair Gina Swoboda; and Steve Gaynor, who unsuccessfully ran for the Republican nomination for Arizona secretary of state in 2018.

"Election integrity is a serious issue," said Mussi in a written statement announcing the lawsuit. "Ensuring Arizonans have faith in the integrity of our election system and representative government starts with clean voter rolls that leave no doubts about who is able to cast a ballot.

The Arizona Free Enterprise Club, a 501(c)(4) nonprofit that advocates for conservative policies and spends to help Republican candidates win, has filed multiple lawsuits against Fontes. One from October 2023 attempted to block the use of ballot boxes in the state, while another filed in February sought to defend ballot box monitoring.

CHAPTER 22. CICERO OF ROME

FIRST EXAMPLE DEPICTING MODERN EFFECTIVE POLITICIAN
(Chapter 38 DEMOKRATIA TO DEMOCRACY, THE REQUIEM)

Cicero is one of the unsung heroes of ancient democracy. He ranks as one of the most accomplished academics and leaders in the history of Rome. A contemporary of Julius Caesar, Cicero worked strongly to protect the Republic type of government followed by Rome of that day, and Cicero was ultimately executed. Reaching the highest level of leadership, Julius Caesar asks Cicero to join his four-man triumvirate, and Cicero was so convinced Caesar was a danger to the Roman Republic, he refused to join, stating “it will be the end of the Republic.” You will witness Cicero going to his execution, likely upon manufactured charges that violate ex post facto, due to the Cicero attempt to protect democratic Rome. The world today needs to find more committed leaders who have the strong beliefs of Cicero.

Cicero grew up in a time of civil unrest and war. His social class and loyalty to the Republic ensured that he would "command the support and confidence of the people as well as the Italian middle classes". The *optimates* faction never truly accepted Cicero, and this undermined his efforts to reform the Republic while preserving the constitution. Nevertheless, he successfully ascended the *cursus honorum*, holding each magistracy at or near the youngest possible age. He was then elected consul at age 42.

Dates of the Three forms of Roman Government

750 BC to 510 BC	Roman Kingdom
510 BC to 28 BC	Roman Republic (Democracy)
28 BC to 1453 AD	Roman Empire

Consulship

Cicero, seizing the opportunity, was elected consul for the year 63 BC; (1 year term limits) he was elected with the support of every unit of the centuriate assembly, and the leaders of municipalities throughout post–Social War Italy.[2]

He began his consular year by opposing a land bill which had potential to increase corruption.[1] Cicero was active in the courts.[i] His court action prevented a return to hostility in Rome.[4] Cicero defended use of force as being authorized by the Senate.[4]

Second Catilinarian conspiracy

Most famously[3] – Cicero thwarted The Catilinarian Conspiracy to overthrow the Roman Republic, which saw Cataline winning the help of foreign armed forces, considered Treason even then. Cicero procured a *senatus consultum ultimum* (recommendation from the senate to legitimize the use of force)[3] and drove Catiline from the City. At the conclusion of Cicero's first speech, Catiline hurriedly left the Senate. Cicero delivered the second and third orations before the people, and the last one again before the Senate. By these speeches, Cicero wanted to prepare the Senate for the worst possible case; he also delivered more evidence against Catiline.[ii]

Catiline fled and left his followers behind to start the revolution from within while he assaulted the city with a small army. It is alleged Catiline attempted to involve the Allobroges, a tribe of Transalpine Gaul, but Cicero seized evidence and forced them to confess in front of the senate.[iii] Martial law was in effect. At first Silanus spoke for the "extreme penalty" for conspirators; many were swayed by Caesar, who decried the precedent and argued in favor of life imprisonment. Cato the Younger rose in defense of the death penalty and the entire Senate finally agreed on the matter and they were executed.

Cicero received the honorific "*pater patriae*" for his efforts to suppress the conspiracy but lived in fear of trial or exile for having put Roman citizens to death without trial. While the *senatus consultum ultimum* gave legitimacy to the use of force, Cicero argued that Catiline's conspiracy, by virtue of its treason, made the conspirators enemies of the state and forfeited the protections intrinsically possessed by Roman citizens.[4] The consuls moved decisively to defeat Catiline.[iv] After suppression of the conspiracy, Cicero was exiled from Italy, then allowed back. He claimed the republic would be restored along with him.[v] Cicero,
promoted the status quo so as to return to the Republic.[vi]

Shortly after completing his consulship, in late 62 BC, Cicero purchased a large townhouse on the Palatine Hill,[vii] which he proudly boasted was in sight of nearly the whole city, and the Roman Forum.[viii]

Exile and return

In 60 BC, Julius Caesar invited Cicero to be the fourth member, with Pompey and Crassus, called the First Triumvirate. Cicero refused because he suspected it would undermine the Republic.[ix]

During Caesar's consulship, 59 BC, the triumvirate had achieved many goals.[x] Then turned on Cicero in 59 BC by threatening exile to anyone who executed a Roman citizen without a trial. Cicero, having executed members of the Catiline conspiracy four years previously, 63 BC, without a trial, was the intended target (EX POST FACTO).[xi] Cicero argued the *senatus consultum ultimum* indemnified him, and sought support of senators and consuls.[xii] (Opening paragraphs make clear Cicero had the consent and near unanimous support to execute the treasoners, now, Julius Caesar seeks to destroy Cicero. Caesar will apply a new law to Cicero, a clear violation of EX POST FACTO intent.)

Clodius' gangs dogged him, hurling abuse, stones and even excrement. Everyone seemed to have abandoned Cicero.[xiii]

Cicero went into exile.[xiv] He arrived at Thessalonica, in May 58 BC.[xv][xvi][xvii] In his absence, Clodius, confiscated and purchased part of the Cicero property to extend his own.[11] After demolishing Cicero's house, Clodius symbolically erected a temple of Liberty.[ ]

Cicero wrote to Atticus: My afflictions surpass any you ever heard of earlier".[79] Titus Annius Milo, intervened on behalf of Pompey who wanted Cicero as a client,[17] and the senate voted to recall Cicero from exile. Cicero returned to Italy on 5 August 57 BC.[xix] He was greeted by a cheering crowd.[xx] Cicero convinced the College of Pontiffs to rule the consecration of his land was invalid, thereby allowing him to regain his property and rebuild on the Palatine.[xxi][xxii]

Cicero tried to re-enter politics,[17] but his attempts to attack portions of Caesar's legislation were unsuccessful[16] and encouraged Caesar to re-solidify his political alliance with Pompey and Crassus.[xxiii] The conference at Luca in 56 BC left the three-man alliance in domination of the republic's politics; this forced Cicero to recant and support the triumvirate.[xxiv] He also delivered a speech 'On the consular provinces'[27] which checked an attempt by Caesar's enemies to strip him of provinces in Gaul.[xxv] After this, Cicero concentrated on literary works.[xxvi]

Governorship of Cilicia

In 51 BC Cicero accepted promagistracy in Cilicia for the year;[xxvii][xxviii] and as proconsul of Cilicia from May 51 BC.[30] In 53 BC Crassus had been defeated by the Parthians at the Battle of Carrhae. This opened the Roman East for a Parthian invasion. Cicero discovered that a great amount of property had been embezzled and did his utmost to restore it. Thus, he greatly improved the cities.[xxix]

He retained the civil rights of, and exempted from penalties, the men who gave property back.[xxx] Extreme frugality made him popular.[xxxi]

Cicero received information the Parthians had crossed the Euphrates, ravaged the Syrian countryside, besieged Cassius in Antioch.[xxxii] Cicero marched with two understrength legions and defeated them near Antigonea.[ ] Another large troop of Parthian horsemen was defeated by Cicero's cavalry. (The Parthian horsemen were an enemy Rome historically had been unable to defeat).

Julius Caesar's civil war

The struggle between Pompey and Caesar grew more intense in 50 BC. Cicero arrived in Rome on 4 January 49 BC.[38] Cicero favored Pompey, as a defender of Republican tradition, but avoided alienating Caesar.[xxxiv] When Caesar invaded Italy in 49 BC, Cicero fled Rome. Caesar, seeking an endorsement courted Cicero's favor, but Cicero slipped out of Italy and to Illyria, to meet Pompey.[xxxv] Cicero traveled with the Pompeian forces to Pharsalus in 48 BC.[ ] After Caesar's victory at the Battle of Pharsalus, Cicero refused to continue the war. He returned to Rome, in 47 BC. Caesar pardoned Cicero.

Cicero was surprised by the Ides of March, 44 BC. Not included in the conspiracy, Brutus called out Cicero's name, asking him to restore the republic.

Opposition to Marc Antony and Death

Cicero and Antony became the two leading men in Rome. Relations worsened after Cicero claimed Antony was taking liberties interpreting Caesar's wishes. He attacked Antony in speeches called Philippics, (Demosthenes's denunciations of Philip II of Macedon). Cicero's popularity was unrivalled.

Cicero urged and Senate declared Antony an enemy of the state, yet Antony would reverse the issue, by execution of Cicero.

Cicero was one of the most viciously hunted among the proscribed. He was viewed with sympathy by the public and many people refused to report they had seen him. He was executed on 7 December 43 BC enroute to Macedonia. Cicero's own slaves said they had not seen him.

He bowed to his captors, leaning his head out of the litter in a gladiatorial gesture to ease the task. According to Plutarch, Herennius first slew him, then cut off his head.

1. Wiedemann 1994, p. 44.
2. Cicero, Marcus Tullius, Selected Works, Penguin Books Ltd, Great Britain, 1971.
3. Cicero, In Catilinam 3.2 (at the Perseus Project); Sallust, Bellum Catilinae 40–45 (at Lacus Curtius); Plutarch, Cicero 18.4.
4. Wiedemann 1994, p. 46
5. Clayton, Ed "Cicero (106–43 BC)". Internet Encyclopedia of Philosophy. Retr 21 Oct 2013.
6. Arthur D. Kahn (2000)[1986]. Education Julius Caesar. iUniverse.com, Inc. pp. 149–75

7. Wiedemann 1994, p. 47.
8. Steven M. Cerutti (1997). "The Location of the Houses of Cicero and Clodius and the Porticus Catuli on the Palatine Hill". Vol. 118, no. 3. American Journal of Philology. p. 417.
9. Rawson, Elizabeth (1984). "Cicero Historian and Antiquarian". Journal of Roman Studies.
10. Wiedemann 1994, p. 51.
11. Wiedemann 1994, p. 50.
12. Holland, Tom (2003). Rubicon: Triumph and Tragedy in Roman Republic. pp. 237–39 Abacus. ISBN 978-0-349-11563-4.
13. Tom Holland, Rubicon, pp. 238–39.
14. Wiedemann 1994, p. 50.
15. Haskell, H.J.: This was Cicero, (1964) p. 200
16. Haskell, H.J.: This was Cicero, (1964) p. 201
17. Plutarch Penguins Classics English translation by Rex Warner, Fall of the Roman Republic, Six Lives by Plutarch: Marius, Sulla, Crassus, Pompey, Caesar, Cicero 32 (Penguin Books, 1958; with Introduction and notes by Robin Seager, 1972)
18. Anthony Everitt (2003). Cicero. Random House. p. 145. ISBN 9780375758959
19. Cicero, Samtliga brev/Collected letters (in a Swedish translation)
20. Haskell. H.J.: This was Cicero, p. 204
21. Anthony Everitt (2003). Cicero. Random House. p. 165. ISBN 9780375758959.
22. Cicero. De Domo Sua. perseus.tufts.edu.
23. Wiedemann 1994, p. 52.
24. Wiedemann 1994, p. 53.
25. John Leach, Pompey the Great, p. 144.
26. Grant, M: "Cicero: Selected Works", p. 67
27. Wiedemann 1994, p. 59.
28. Everitt, A. "Cicero: Life and Times of Rome's Greatest Politician" (2001), pp. 186–88
29. Alfred John Church, Roman Life in Days of Cicero, (Kindle edition), ch. XIII., loc. 1834
30. Church, loc. 1871
31. Church, loc. 1834
32. Church, loc. 1845; Gareth C. Sampson, The defeat of Rome, Crassus, Carrhae & the invasion of the East, pp. 155–58; Cicero, Letters to friends, 15.3.1.
33. Gareth C. Sampson, defeat of Rome, Crassus, Carrhae & the invasion of the East, p.159; Cicero, Letters to friends, 2.10.2.
34. Church, loc. 1855
35. Wiedemann 1994, p. 62.
36. Church, ibid
37. Plutarch, The Life of Cicero, 36.
38. Plutarch. "Life of Caesar". University of Chicago. p. 575. It was Cicero who proposed the first honours for [Caesar] in the senate, and their magnitude was, after all, not too great for a man;.
39. Everitt, Anthony: Cicero p. 215.

In the WEIGHT OF THE EVIDENCE existing against those who would prosecute Cicero, we can see precisely the same empirical intent of those who would prosecute Trump.

The sheer litany of cases against the very popular former President Donald J. Trump looks very nearly like a precursor of the very same punishment that ultimately executed Cicero, possibly the most popular Presidential figure in the democratic Roman Republic.

CHAPTER 23. EXECUTIVE BRANCH AND IMMUNITY

https://constitution.congress.gov/browse/article-2/section-1

We return to US CONSTITUTION ANNOTATED. It is crucial that everyone understand the totality by which our Constitution provides Executive Branch and Presidential authority to act and function, as he is essential to the free flow of democracy and our safety and daily lives.

Article II Executive Branch Section 1
Function and Selection Clause President's Role

- The executive Power shall be vested in a President of the United States of America. He shall hold his Office during the Term of four Years, and, together with the Vice President, chosen for the same Term, be elected, as follows:
- Art II.S1.C1.1 Overview of Executive Vesting Clause
- Art II.S1.C1.2 Historical Background on Executive Vesting Clause
- Art II.S1.C1.3 Early Perspectives on Executive Power
- Art II.S1.C1.4 The President's Powers, Myers, and Seila
- Art II.S1.C1.5 The President's Powers and Youngstown Framework
- Art II.S1.C1.6 Separation of Powers, Executive Branch Functions
- Art II.S1.C1.7 Major Questions Doctrine and Admin Agencies
- Art II.S1.C1.8 President's Foreign Affairs Power, Curtiss-Wright, Zivotofsky
- Art II.S1.C1.9 Term of the

President Clause 2 Electors

- Each State shall appoint, in such Manner as the Legislature thereof may direct, a Number of Electors, equal to the whole Number of Senators and Representatives to which the State may be entitled in the Congress: but no Senator or Representative, or Person holding an Office of Trust or Profit under the United States, shall be appointed an Elector.
- Art II.S1.C2.1 Overview of Electors Appointment Clause
- Art II.S1.C2.2 Historical Background on Electors Appointments
- Art II.S1.C2.3 State Discretion Over Selection of Electors
- Art II.S1.C2.4 Legal Status of Electors
- Art II.S1.C2.5 Discretion of Electors to Choose a President
- Art II.S1.C8.1 Oath of Office for the Presidency

Art II.S1.C8.1 Oath of Office for the Presidency

Before he enter on the Execution of his Office, he shall take the following Oath or Affirmation:–I do solemnly swear (or affirm) that I will faithfully execute the Office of President of the US, and will to the best of my Ability, preserve, protect, and defend the Constitution of the US.

What is the time relationship between a President's assumption of office and his taking the oath? Apparently, the former comes first, this answer appearing to be the assumption of the language of the clause. The Second Congress assumed President George Washington took office on March 4, 1789,[1] although he took the oath on April 30.

That the oath the President is required to take might be considered to add anything to the powers of the President, because of his obligation to preserve, protect and defend the Constitution, might appear to be rather a fanciful idea. **But in President Andrew Jackson's message** announcing his veto of the act renewing the Bank of the United States there is language which suggests the President has the right to refuse to enforce both statutes and judicial decisions on his own independent decision they were unwarranted by the Constitution.[2] The idea next turned up in a message by **President Abraham Lincoln** justifying his suspension of writ of habeas corpus without obtaining congressional authorization.[3] And counsel to **President Andrew Johnson** during his impeachment trial adverted to the theory, but only in passing.[4] Beyond these isolated instances, it does not appear to be seriously contended that the oath adds anything to the President's powers.

1. 1Act of March 1, 1792, 1 Stat. 239, § 12.
2. 22 MESSAGES AND PAPERS OF THE PRESIDENTS 576 (J. Richardson ed. 1896). Chief Justice Roger Taney, who as a member of Jackson's Cabinet had drafted the message, later repudiated this possible reading of the message. 2 C. WARREN, THE SUPREME COURT IN UNITED STATES HISTORY 223–224 (1926).
3. 36 MESSAGES AND PAPERS OF THE PRESIDENTS, supra note 2, at 25.
4. 42 TRIAL OF ANDREW JOHNSON 200, 293, 296 (1868).

Art II.S1.C1.1 Overview of Executive Vesting Clause

The executive Power shall be vested in a President of the United States of America. He shall hold his Office during Term of four Years, together with the Vice President, chosen for same Term, be elected, as follows:

Under Article II, Section 1, Clause 1, the executive power is vested in a single person—the President of the United States. The nature and extent of the executive power is less clear.[1] Article II identifies exclusive powers of the President, including the President's authority as Commander in Chief and the power to pardon;[2] powers the President shares with the Senate, including the appointments and treaty-making powers;[3] and the President's duties, most important of which is the duty to **take Care** that the Laws be faithfully executed.[4]

Moreover, the Supreme Court has recognized that because no single person could fulfill that responsibility, the Take Care Clause implicitly provides the President with authority to supervise subordinate officers assisting with this responsibility.[5] Likewise, Article I provides the President a role in the legislative process, including authority to veto legislation, subject to potential override by a two-thirds vote of both Houses of Congress.[6]

It is less clear from the Constitution whether executive powers expressly identified in the Constitution are exclusive or illustrative. Whereas Article I Legislative Vesting Clause provides All legislative powers granted shall be vested in Congress,[7] thereby distinguishing the powers granted by states from those they retained, the Article II Executive Vesting Clause does not limit the executive Power in any way.[8] Consequently, since the earliest days of the Republic, the parameters of the executive power and, in particular, what implicit or residual powers such executive power encompasses have been the subject of debate.

9. U.S. CONST. art. II, § 1, cl. 1.
10. Id. art. II, § 2, cl. 1. See ArtII.S2.C1.1.1 Historical Background, Commander in Chief Clause.
11. Id. art. II, § 2, cl. 2. See ArtII.S2.C1.3.1 Overview of Pardon Power.
12. Id. art. II, § 3. See ArtII.S3.3.1 Overview of Take Care Clause.
13. Seila Law LLC v. Consumer Fin. Protection Bureau, No. 19-7, slip op. at 2 (U.S. 6/29/20). See also Free Enter. Fund v. Pub. Co. Acct. Oversight Bd., 561 U.S. 477, 492–93 (2010).
14. U.S. CONST. art. I, § 7, cl. 2. See ArtI.S7.C2.1 Overview Presidential Approval /Veto of Bills.
15. Id. art. I, § 1, cl. 1 See ArtI.S1.1 Overview of Legislative Vesting Clause.
16. Id. art. II, § 1, cl. 1.

Art II.S1.C1.2 Historical Background on Executive Vesting Clause

The executive Power shall be vested in a President of the United States of America. He shall hold his Office during the Term of four Years, and, together with the Vice President, chosen for the same Term, be elected, as follows:

The nature of the presidency ranked among the most important issues the Framers considered at the Constitutional Convention.[1] Reacting to how royal governors had exercised their powers, the framers of the state constitutions had created weak executives and strong legislatures. Likewise, the Articles of Confederation vested the national government's powers in a unicameral congress.[2] Experience during the period the Articles of Confederation had been in effect, had demonstrated to the delegates that an unfettered legislature, like an uncurbed executive, posed disadvantages, and that a legislature could not confer many advantages of a reasonably strong executive.[3]

The Framers considered several ways to organize the Executive Branch, including plural executives, selection of the executive or executives by Congress, and whether the executive should be advised by a council.

The constitution of the State of New York, which provided for a Governor who was largely independent of the state legislature, offered one possible template for the Framers. Under New York's constitution, the Governor was directly elected by the people for three-year terms and eligible for re-election indefinitely. Because the state legislature did not select the Governor, the Governor was less beholden to it. Except with regard to appointments and vetoes, the Governor's decisions were unencumbered by a council. The Governor was also in charge of the militia, possessed the power to pardon, and was responsible for ensuring that the laws were faithfully executed.[4]

The Virginia Plan offered an alternative structure to that of the New York constitution. Under the Virginia Plan, the legislature would select the executive but would not be able to change the executive's salary during the executive's term in office. In addition, the executive would be ineligible for re-election, thereby reducing any incentive the executive might have to be overly deferential to the legislature. The Virginia Plan also provided for a council of revision, which included the executive, that could negate national and state legislation. The Virginia Plan provided that the executive power was the power to execute the national laws and to enjoy the Executive rights vested in Congress by the Confederation, but it left open whether the executive would be a single or plural position.[5]

When the executive portion of the Virginia Plan was considered on June 1, 1787, James Wilson of Pennsylvania moved that the executive should consist of a single person.[6] In the course of his remarks, Wilson argued for a strong executive, directly elected by the people so that the executive would not be dependent on Congress or state legislatures. Wilson further proposed that the executive be eligible for reelection and granted power to negate legislation with the concurrence of a council of revision.[7] The vote on Wilson's motion was postponed until the method of selection, term, and mode of removal of, and powers to be conferred on the executive had been considered and approved.[8]

Ultimately, the Framers decided on a single executive and did not provide for an executive council, which would have participated in exercising the executive's veto, appointments, and treaty-making powers.[9] Instead, the Framers granted the Senate power to advise and consent on appointments and treaties[10] and gave the President power to require the principal Officer in each of the executive Departments to provide their Opinion, in writing on any Subject relating to the Duties of their respective Offices.[11]

The Committee of Detail reported draft language providing the executive be designated the President of the United States,[12] which the Convention accepted without discussion.[13] The same clause also provided that the President's title be His Excellency,[14] and, while this language was accepted without discussion,[15] the Committee of Style and Arrangement subsequently omitted it from the final text.[16]

1. The background and action of the Convention is comprehensively examined in Charles Thach, Creation of the Presidency 1775–1789 (1923). See also John Hart, The American Presidency in Action 1789 (1948).
2. 3 Joseph Story, Commentaries on the Constitution of the US § 1407 (1833) (Under the confederation there was no national executive. The powers of national government were vested in congress, consisting of a single body; authorized to appoint a committee of the states, composed of one delegate from every state, to sit in the recess, and to delegate such of their own powers, not requiring consent of nine states, as nine states should consent to. Want of a national executive was deemed a fatal defect of the confederation.).
3. Thach, The Creation of the Presidency, supra note 1, at 1–64.
4. Alexander Hamilton observed the similarities and differences between the President and the New York Governor. The Federalist No. 69 (Alexander Hamilton). See N.Y. Const. of 1777 arts. XVII–XIX, reprinted in 5 Francis Thorpe, The Federal and State Constitutions (1909).
5. For discussion of plans offered at Constitutional Convention and resulting debate, see Thach, Creation of the Presidency, supra note 1 at 65–91. For Virginia Plan, see 1 Records of Federal Convention of 1787 20–23 (Max Farrand ed., 1911)[hereinafter Farrand's Records].
6. Id. at 65.
7. Id. at 65–73.
8. Id. at 93.
9. The last proposal for a council voted down on September 7, 1787. 2 Farrand's Records 542.
10. See ArtII.S2.C2.1.1 Overview of President's Treaty-Making Power; ArtII.S2.C2.3.1 Overview of Appointments Clause.
11. See ArtII.S2.C1.2 Executive Departments.
12. 1 Farrand's Records, supra note 5, at 185.
13. Id. at 401.
14. Id. at 185.
15. Id. at 401.
16. Id. at 597.

Art II.S1.C1.3 Early Perspectives on Executive Power

The executive Power shall be vested in a President of the United States of America. He shall hold his Office during the Term of four Years, and, together with the Vice President, chosen for the same Term, be elected, as follows

While Article I Legislative Vesting Clause provides All legislative Powers herein granted shall be vested in a Congress,[1] thereby distinguishing the legislative powers that the states had granted to the National Government from those the states retained, the Article II Executive Vesting Clause refers only to a general executive Power, which is vested in a single person—the President.[2]

While the Constitution expressly identifies specific powers and duties that belong to the President—for example, the power to pardon and the duty to take care that the laws be faithfully enforced—the Founders differed on whether those powers were exclusive or illustrative.

The First Congress considered the parameters of the executive power and, in particular, the President's power to remove Executive Branch officers absent the consent of the Senate, the acquiescence of which is necessary for such Executive Branch officers' appointment.[3] Known as the Debate of 1789, the First Congress considered the President's removal power while it was establishing the Department of State.[4] As one commentator noted: Congress tacitly recognized the existence of unrestrained presidential removal power from 1789 to 1867, and it developed into one of the most effective instruments for control of the executive branch.[5] While Congress subsequently passed laws limiting the President's ability to remove Executive Branch officers,[6] the Supreme Court did not address such a law until 1926 in Myers v. United States.[7]

Similar questions arose with respect to the President's authority over foreign affairs.[8] After President George Washington issued a proclamation declaring the United States neutral when France and Great Britain went to war in 1793, Alexander Hamilton and James Madison took competing positions on whether President Washington had exceeded his constitutional authority. Arguing that Article II does not enumerate all executive powers,[9] Hamilton wrote:

> The enumeration [of executive powers in the Constitution] ought therefore to be considered, as intended merely to specify the principal articles implied in the definition of executive power; leaving the rest to flow from the general grant of that power, interpreted in conformity with other parts of the Constitution, and with the principles of free government.[10]
>
> Hamilton continued: The general doctrine of our Constitution is, that the executive power of the nation is vested in the President; subject only to the exceptions and qualifications, which are expressed in the instrument.[11] Rejecting Hamilton's view that the Constitution granted the President such

broad powers, Madison argued, if executive powers were unfettered, no citizen could guess at the character; the most penetrating jurist would be unable to scan the constructive prerogative.[12]

Unsurprisingly, Presidents have tended to interpret the Executive Vesting Clause's provision of executive power expansively. For example, President Thomas Jefferson justified the Louisiana Purchase based on implied executive power.[13]

1. 1U.S. Const. art. I, § 1, cl. 1 (emphasis added).
2. Id. art. II, § 1, cl. 1.
3. See David P. Currie, the Constitution in Congress: The Federalist Period 1789–1801, at 36–41 (1997) (discussing James Madison's proposal for a department of foreign affairs). In the Federalist No. 77, Alexander Hamilton commented that the Senate's consent was necessary for the President to remove an Executive Officer, stating: The consent of [the Senate] would be necessary to displace as well as to appoint.
   . . . Where a man in any station had given satisfactory evidence of his fitness for it, a new President would

be restrained from attempting a change in favor of a person more agreeable to him, by the apprehension that a discountenance of the Senate might frustrate the attempt and bring some degree of discredit upon himself. The Federalist No. 77 (Alexander Hamilton). While Congress expressly referred to the President's removal power in some legislation, e.g., Judiciary Act of 1789, ch. 20, § 27, 1 Stat. 87; Act of May 15, 1820, ch. 102, 3 Stat. 582, the Supreme Court in Myers v. United States observed Congress adopted provisions to show conformity to the legislative decision of 1789. Myers v. United States, 272 U.S. 52, 146 (1926).

4. For discussion on Debate of 1789, see ArtII.S2.C2.3.15.2 Decision of 1789 Removals in Early Republic. See Charles Thach, Creation of the Presidency 1775–1789 124–49 (1923).
5. C. Herman Pritchett, Constitutional Law of the Federal System 293 (1984). See also Act of May 15, 1820 (providing for removal of officers at pleasure of the President).
6. Tenure of Office Act of 1867, ch. 154, 14 Stat. 430 (requiring, among other things, for the President to have the Senate's consent to remove the Secretary of War and certain other department heads); Act of July 12, 1876, ch. 179, 19 State. 80, 81 (providing that Postmasters of the first, second and third classes shall be appointed by the President by and with the advice and consent of the Senate and shall hold their officers for four years unless sooner removed or suspended according to law.). See also United States v. Perkins, 116
U.S. 483 (1886). In Perkins, the Court addressed whether the Secretary of the Navy could discharge a naval cadet-engineer at will notwithstanding that the Act of August 5, 1882, provided that naval officers could not be discharged except pursuant to a court-martial. Ruling for the naval cadet-engineer, the Court stated: The head of a Department has no constitutional prerogative of appointments to offices independently of the legislation of Congress, and by such legislation he must be governed, not only in making appointments but in all that is incident thereto. Id. at 485. The Court, however, noted that it was not addressing a situation where an officer was appointed by the President with the advice and consent of the Senate. Id. (Whether or not Congress can restrict the power of removal incident to the power of appointment of those officers who are appointed by the President by and with the advice of the Senate.
7. Court discussed the President's removal power in dicta in Ex parte Hennen, 38 U.S. (39 Pet.) 230 (1839) (recognizing authority of a District Judge to remove a clerk of the court). For further discussion of the removal power, see ArtII.S2.C2.3.15.1 Overview of Removal of Executive Branch Officers .
8. See David P. Currie, Constitution in Congress: Federalist Period 1789–1801 174–82 (1997).
9. Id. See also Charles Thomas, American Neutrality 1793: A Study Cabinet Gov (1931).
10. 7 Works of Alexander Hamilton 76, 80–81 (J. C. Hamilton ed., 1851).
11. Id. (emphasis added).
12. 1 Letters and Other Writings of James Madison 621 (J.B. Lippincott & Co., 1865).
13. For discussion of the constitutionality of the Louisiana Purchase, see Everett Brown, The Constitutional History of the Louisiana Purchase, 1803–1812 (1920). For discussion of how the Jeffersonians and Federalists approached executive powers, see Leonard White, The Jeffersonians: A Study in Administrative History 1801–1829 (1951); Leonard White, The Federalists: A Study in Administrative History (1948).

Author McCarley Comments upon these statutes from US Constitution Annotated.

America's Founding Fathers were brilliant from all angles, and their brilliance is readily apparent via construction and wording of Article II, Section 1. Please note the vast majority of Article II, Section 1; is devoted to a delineation of the rules and procedures for selection of ELECTORS and responsibility of Electors following a National Election. The fact that this Section 1 concludes with the PRESIDENTIAL OATH OF OFFICE might be a prescient act of intention by our Founding Fathers, thus perfectly applicable that the OATH OF OFFICE, along with the TAKE CARE CLAUSE offer perfect Constitutional proof that Donald Trump holds immunity for his actions attempting to prevent illegal elections being certified by US Congress.

Historical instances in which Presidents "stretched authority," as some would suggest Trump stretched by his actions to correct an illegally certified election.

1. All Presidents of the United States swear or affirm an "OATH OF OFFICE" by which they swear to affirm support and defend the Constitution of the United States. Many oaths add the words, "against all enemies both foreign and domestic." This oath obligates that elected or appointed person to ensure the Constitution is obeyed, observed, and defended.
2. There is NO legal "stretch" that would allow persons identified in #1 above to ignore a violation of law. If anyone provides illegal information or legislation to #1 above, that "oath taker" would be fully expected to disallow or refuse to cooperate and to take all possible actions to prevent that situation from becoming law. IF CONGRESS AND SENATE CONCUR ON ANY ISSUE, IT BECOMES LAW. IF CONGRESS AND SENATE CONCUR ON ANY ISSUE, AND PASS THAT ISSUE TO THE PRESIDENT, AND THE ISSUE IS BESET WITH ILLEGAL ACTS OR FALSEHOOD, THAT PRESIDENT OUGHT TO AND BY RIGHT SHALL TAKE ALL ACTIONS TO ENSURE THE ACT IS REPEALED.
3. Given points #1 and #2 above, a sitting or defeated President holds full, complete, and total immunity for his actions in defense of the US Constitution, consistent with his oath of office.
4. Why would courts allow those with low mental or emotional stability to file cases against a sitting or ex-president, as is surely the point of cases filed by strippers and playboy queens?

5. Why would a prosecutor risk his job and law license by filing cases against an ex-president that are fully and unquestionably beyond his jurisdiction, as is the case with Bragg filing cases which are the unquestionable jurisdiction of IRS, SEC, Banking Regulatory, FEC. Those agencies not having filed cases surely makes those cases moot and void if filed by any other jurisdiction or purpose.
6. Why would higher courts allow cases to be filed against an ex-president when the fullest extent of all lawyers/prosecutor and judges filing cases are in the opposing party?
7. Given all but 2 Judges in the entire litany of Judges and Prosecutors acting against former President Trump are of the opposite party, we have a situation in which SCOTUS ought to toss those cases and SCOTUS should excommunicate those prosecutors and judges.
8. We have at least two cases filed against Trump in which it is proven those elected prosecutors and Attorney General actually campaigned with various slogans "TO GET TRUMP." Obviously our legal/courts system is tarnished.
9. Hanging Chad is the only contested election in US History prior to Trump/Biden.
10. This Amicus Curiae provided small briefs on other notable contested elections.

CHAPTER 24. CONSTITUTION ANNOTATED EXECUTIVE BRANCH

Many times, the word IMMUNITY is applied in the US Constitution to establishment of powers of the President and Executive Branch of The United States of America.

Sixty-Eight (68) times in the specific sections of Article II Section 3, the word immunity is applied in both Constitutional clauses along with US Supreme Court documentation of their official opinions on several court cases that came forward in which Presidential Immunity might have been an issue.

How can it be possible that so many democrat lawyers now accuse 2024 SCOTUS of constitutional destruction. Obviously, those lawyers, including the head of the New York State Bar, have zero understanding of the constitution, or else they are now confirmed liars. They were forced to pass very tough tests on our constitution in order to become a lawyer, therefore, they must understand clearly.

Article II Section 3
https://constitution.congress.gov/browse/article-2/

SECTION 3 PRESIDENTIAL POWERS TO PRESIDENTIAL IMMUNITY

ArtII.S3.5 Presidential Immunity

- Art II.S3.5.1Presidential Immunity to Suits and Official Conduct
- Art II.S3.5.2Presidential Immunity to Suits and Unofficial Conduct
- Art II.S3.5.3Qualified Immunity Doctrine
- Art II.S3.5.4Criminal Prosecution, Presidential Immunity and Former Presidents

Art II.S3.5.1 Presidential Immunity to Suits and Official Conduct

He shall from time to time give to the Congress Information of the State of the Union, and recommend to their Consideration such Measures as he shall judge necessary and expedient; he may, on extraordinary Occasions, convene both Houses, or either of them, and in Case of Disagreement between them, with Respect to the Time of Adjournment, he may adjourn them to such Time as he shall think proper; he shall receive Ambassadors and other public Ministers; he shall take Care that the Laws be faithfully executed, and shall Commission all the Officers of the United States.

In its 1867 decision Mississippi v. Johnson, the Supreme Court established that the President is largely beyond the reach of the judiciary by holding that it could not direct President Andrew Johnson in how he exercised his purely executive and political powers.[1] The Court stated, it had no jurisdiction . . . to enjoin the President in the performance of his official duties.[2]

In subsequent decisions, however, the Court made clear that Johnson does not stand for the proposition that the President is immune from judicial process. For example, in United States v. Nixon,[3] the Court held that President Richard Nixon was amenable to a subpoena to produce evidence for use in a federal criminal case. There, the President had argued that he was immune to judicial process, claiming that the independence of the Executive Branch within its own sphere insulates a President from a judicial subpoena in an ongoing criminal prosecution.[4] The Supreme Court unanimously disagreed, holding that neither the doctrine of separation of powers, nor the need for confidentiality of high-level communications, without more, can sustain an absolute, unqualified Presidential privilege of immunity from judicial process under all circumstances.[5] The Court noted that the constitutional duty of courts to do justice in criminal prosecutions was counterbalanced by the claim of presidential immunity. To accept the President's argument, the Court further reasoned, would undermine the separation of powers that was at the core of a workable government as well as gravely impair the role of the courts under Art. III.[6]

Throughout the Watergate investigation, it was unclear whether the President could be subject to criminal prosecution prior to being convicted upon impeachment.[7] The Court, however, resolved that courts may require the President to testify or produce documents in criminal proceedings.[8] This principle dates to the earliest days of the Republic, when Chief Justice John Marshall presided as the Circuit Justice for Virginia over the treason trial of Aaron Burr. In that case, Chief Justice Marshall concluded that President Thomas Jefferson could be subject to a subpoena to provide a document relevant to the trial.[9] Specifically, Chief Justice Marshall declared that, in contrast to common law privileges afforded the King of England, the President was not exempt from general provisions of the constitution, like the Sixth Amendment, which provides the defense compulsory process.[10]

Nonetheless, Chief Justice Marshall recognized that while the President could be subject to a criminal subpoena, the President could still withhold information from disclosure based on executive privilege.[11] In the two centuries since the Burr trial, the Executive Branch's practices[12] and Supreme Court rulings unequivocally and emphatically endorsed Chief Justice Marshall's position that the President was subject to federal criminal process.[13]

In its 2020 opinion in Trump v. Vance, the Court extended this precedent to state criminal proceedings, concluding that the President was not absolutely immune from state criminal subpoenas.[14]

Finally, with respect to civil liability, the Court held in Nixon v. Fitzgerald that the President is absolutely immune in actions for civil damages for all acts within the outer perimeter of his official duties.[15] The Court's close decision was premised on the President's unique position in the constitutional scheme, that is, the Court conducted a kind of 'public policy' analysis of the policies and principles that may be considered implicit in the nature of the President's office in a system structured to achieve effective government under a constitutionally mandated separation of powers.[16] Although the Constitution expressly afforded Members of Congress immunity in matters arising from speech or debate and was silent on presidential immunity, the Court nonetheless considered immunity to be a functionally mandated incident of the President's unique office, rooted in the constitutional tradition of the separation of powers and supported by our history.[17]

While the Court relied, in part, upon its practice of finding immunity for officers, such as judges, for whom the Constitution is silent, but for which a long common-law history exists, and in part upon historical evidence, which it admitted was fragmentary and ambiguous,[18] the Court focused on the fact that the President is different from all other executive officials. The President is charged with a long list of supervisory and policy responsibilities of utmost discretion and sensitivity,[19] and diversion of his energies by concerns with private lawsuits would raise unique risks to the effective functioning of government.[20] Moreover, the presidential privilege is rooted in the separation of powers doctrine, counseling courts to tread carefully before intruding. While some interests are important enough to require judicial action, the Court reasoned that merely private suit[s] for damages based on a President's official acts do not serve this broad public interest necessitating the courts to act.[21] Finally, qualified immunity would not adequately protect the President, because judicial inquiry into a functional analysis of his actions would bring with it the evil immunity it was to prevent; absolute immunity was required.[22]

1. 71 U.S. (4 Wall.) 475 (1867). The Court declined to express an opinion on whether, the President of the US may be required, by the process of this court, to perform a purely ministerial act under a positive law, or may be held amenable, in any case, otherwise than by impeachment for crime. *Id.*, at 498. *See* Franklin v. Massa, 505 U.S. 788, 825–28 (1992) (Scalia, J., concurring). In NTEU v. Nixon, 492 F.2d 587 (D.C. Cir. 1974), the court held that it could issue a writ of mandamus to compel the President to perform a ministerial act, although it said that if any other officer were available to whom the writ could run, it should be applied to him.
2. *Johnson*, 71 U.S. at 501.
3. United States v. Nixon, 418 U.S. 683 (1974)
4. *Id.* at 706.
5. 5*Id.*

6. *Id.* at 706–07. The lower courts considered the issue more fully. *In re* Grand Jury Subpoena to Richard M. Nixon, 360 F. Supp. 1, 6–10 (D.D.C. 1973) (Judge Sirica), *aff'd sub nom.*, Nixon v. Sirica, 487 F.2d 700, 708–712 (D.C. Cir. 1973) (en banc) (refusing to find President immune from process). Assessments of the subpoena of President Jefferson in the Burr trial have conflicted. United States v. Burr, 25 F. Cas. 187 (C.C.D. Va. 1807) (No. 14694). For the history, *see* Paul Freund, *Foreword: On Presidential Privilege, The Supreme Court, 1973 Term*, 88 Harv. L. Rev. 13, 23–30 (1974).
7. The Impeachment Clause provides that a party convicted upon impeachment shall nonetheless be liable for criminal proceedings. U.S. Const. art. I, § 3, cl. 7. Gouverneur Morris in the Convention and Alexander Hamilton in the *Federalist Papers* asserted that a criminal trial would follow a successful impeachment.
See 2 The Records of the Federal Convention of 1787, at 500 (Max Farrand ed., 1937); Federalist Nos. 65 & 69.
8. *See* Trump v. Vance, 591 U.S. 786 (2020) (recognizing that the public has a right to every man's evidence).
9. *See* United States v. Burr, 25 F. Cas. 30, 34 (C.C.D. Va. 1807) (No. 14,692D).
10. *See id.* (observing that while the King is born to power and can do no wrong, the President, by contrast, is of the people and subject to the law).
11. *See Burr*, 25 F. Cas. at 192.
12. *See Vance*, 591 U.S. at 797–99 (discussing historical practices of Presidents James Monroe, Ulysses S. Grant, Gerald Ford, Jimmy Carter, and William Clinton).
13. Clinton v. Jones, 520 U.S. 681, 704 (1997) (citing United States v. Nixon, 418 U.S. 683, 706 (1974)). In rejecting separation of powers challenges to claims that the President is immune from federal criminal process, the Court rejected the argument that criminal subpoenas rise to the level of constitutionally forbidden impairment of the Executive's ability to perform its constitutionally mandated functions. *Id.* at 702–03.
14. *See Vance*, 591 U.S. at 801–03 (rejecting the categorical argument that state criminal subpoenas would unduly distract the President, impose a stigma on the presidency, or result in harassment by state prosecutors). The *Vance* Court also rejected the argument that a state prosecutor should satisfy a heightened standard of need when seeking a sitting President's records. *Id.* at 808–09. More important, in *Vance*, the state prosecutor sought private presidential records, and executive privilege was not at issue. *Id.*, at 811 (Kavanaugh, J., concurring in the judgment). The Court refused to extend the heightened-need standard established in Nixon to private records, reasoning that: (1) Burr and its progeny foreclosed that argument; (2) the heightened-need standard was unnecessary to allow the President to fulfill his Article II functions; and (3) the public interest in fair and effective law enforcement favors comprehensive access to evidence. *Id.* (majority opinion).
15. Nixon v. Fitzgerald, 457 U.S. 731 (1982)
16. *Id.* at 748.
17. *Id.* at 749.
18. *Id.* at 750–52 n.31.
19. *Id.* at 750.
20. *Id.* at 751.
21. *Id.* at 754.
22. *Id.* at 755–57. Justices Byron White, William Brennan, Thurgood Marshall, and Henry Blackmun dissented. The Court reserved decision on whether Congress could expressly create a damages action against the President and abrogate immunity, *id.* at 748–49 n.27, thus appearing to disclaim that the Constitution mandated the decision; Chief Justice Warren Burger disagreed with the implication of this footnote, *id.* at 763–64 n.7 (concurring opinion), and the dissenters noted they agreed with the Chief Justice on this point. *Id.* at 770 & n.4.

Art II.S3.5.2 Presidential Immunity to Suits and Unofficial Conduct

He shall from time to time give to the Congress Information of the State of the Union, and recommend to their Consideration such Measures as he shall judge necessary and expedient; he may, on extraordinary Occasions, convene both Houses, or either of them, and in Case of Disagreement between them, with Respect to the Time of Adjournment, he may adjourn them to such Time as he shall think proper; he shall receive Ambassadors and other public Ministers; he shall take Care that the Laws be faithfully executed, and Commission all Officers of the US.

In Clinton v. Jones,[1] the Court, in a case of first impression, held that President William Clinton did not have qualified immunity from civil suit for conduct alleged to have taken place prior to his election, and therefore denied President Clinton's request to delay both the trial and discovery. The Court held that its precedents affording the President immunity from suit for his official conduct—primarily so that the President could perform his duties effectively absent fear that a particular decision might lead to personal liability—did not apply when the alleged conduct at issue had occurred before his election. Moreover, the Supreme Court observed, the separation of powers doctrine did not require a stay of all private actions against the President, as the trial court had sufficient powers to accommodate the President's schedule and his workload so as not to impede the President from performing his duties. Finally, the Court stated that allowing such suits to proceed would not generate a large volume of politically motivated harassing litigation. Congress has the power, the Court advised, if it should think necessary, to protect the President.[2].

While courts may be unable to compel the President to act or prevent him from acting, his acts, when performed, are generally subject to judicial review and disallowance. Typically, the President's subordinates, through whom he acts, may be sued pursuant to a legal fiction to enjoin committing acts that might lead to irreparable damage[3] or to compel by writ of mandamus performing a duty required by law.[4] Such suits are usually brought in the United States District Court for the District of Columbia.[5] In common law, courts may hold a subordinate executive officer personally liable for damages that resulted from any act the officer committed that was beyond his authority,[6] although he has immunity for anything, even malicious wrongdoing, that he does in performing his duties.[7]

Different rules prevail when a plaintiff sues an officer for wrongs based on a constitutional tort.[8] The Court has suggested, in sensitive areas, officers acting in the outer perimeter of duties may be accorded absolute immunity from liability.[9]

To reach such officers for acts for which they can be held responsible, courts must use the general federal question jurisdictional statute.[10]. On deleting the jurisdictional amount, see Pub. L. No. 94-574, 90 Stat. 2721 (1976); Pub. L. No. 96-486, 94 Stat. 2369 (1980). If suits are brought in state courts, they can be removed to federal district courts. 28 U.S.C. § 1442(a). See 28 U.S.C. § 1331.

1. 520 U.S. 681 (1997)
2. 457 U.S. at 749.
3. E.g., Youngstown Sheet & Tube Co. v. Sawyer, 343 U.S. 579 (1952) (suit to enjoin Secretary of Commerce to return steel mills seized by President's); Dames & Moore v. Regan, 453 U.S. 654 (1981) (suit against Secretary of Treasury to nullify presidential orders on Iranian assets). See also Noble v. Union River Logging Railroad, 147 U.S. 165 (1893); Philadelphia Co. v. Stimson, 223 U.S. 605 (1912).
4. E.g., Marbury v. Madison, 5 U.S. (1 Cr.) 137 (1803) (suit against Secretary of State to compel delivery of commissions of office); Kendall v. United States ex rel. Stokes, 37 U.S. (12 Pet.) 524 (1838) (suit against Postmaster General to compel payment of money owed under act of Congress); Decatur v. Paulding, 39 U.S. (14 Pet.) 497 (1840) (suit to compel Secretary of Navy to pay a pension).
5. This was based on the theory that the Supreme Court of the District of Columbia had inherited, via the common law of Maryland, the jurisdiction of the King's Bench over inferior jurisdictions and officers. Kendall v. US ex rel. Stokes, 37 U.S. (12 Pet.) 524, 614, 620–21 (1838). Congress has since authorized federal district courts outside the District of Columbia to entertain such suits. Act of Oct 5, 1962, Pub. L. No. 87-748, 76 Stat. 744 (codified at 28 U.S.C. § 1361).
6. E.g., Little v. Barreme, 6 U.S. (2 Cr.) 170 (1804); Bates v. Clark, 95 U.S. 204 (1877); US v. Lee, 106 U.S. 196 (1882); Virginia Coupon Cases (Poindexter v. Greenhow), 114 U.S. 270 (1885); Belknap v. Schild, 161 U.S. 10 (1896).
7. Spalding v. Vilas, 161 U.S. 483 (1896); Barr v. Matteo, 360 U.S. 564 (1959). See Westfall v. Erwin, 484 U.S. 292 (1988) (an action must be discretionary in nature as well as within the scope of employment, before a federal official is entitled to absolute immunity). Following the Westfall decision, Congress enacted the Federal Employees Liability Reform and Tort Compensation Act of 1988 (the Westfall Act), which authorized the Attorney General to certify that an employee was acting within the scope of his office or employment at the time an incident occurred that led to a lawsuit; upon certification, the employee is dismissed from the action, and the United States is substituted. As a result, sometimes the action will be dismissed against the government because the government has not waived sovereign immunity under the Federal Tort Claims Act. United States v. Smith, 499 U.S. 160 (1991) (the Westfall Act bars suit against federal employee even if sovereign immunity forecloses suit against the government). Cognizant of the temptation of the government to immunize both itself and its employee, the Court in Gutierrez de Martinez v. Lamagno, 515 U.S. 417 (1995), held that an Attorney General's certification is subject to judicial review.
8. The Supreme Court recognized an implied cause of action against officers accused of constitutional violations in Bivens v. Six Unknown Named Agents of the Federal Bureau of Narcotics, 403 U.S. 388 (1971). In Butz v. Economou, 438 U.S. 478 (1978), which concerned a Bivens action, the Court distinguished between common-law torts and constitutional torts and denied high federal officials, including cabinet secretaries, absolute immunity, in favor of the qualified immunity Congress had previously accorded high state officials under 42 U.S.C. § 1983. In Harlow v. Fitzgerald, 457 U.S. 800 (1982), the Court denied presidential aides derivative absolute presidential immunity, but it modified the rules of qualified immunity, making it more difficult to hold aides, other federal officials, state and local officials, liable for constitutional torts.
9. In Mitchell v. Forsyth, 472 U.S. 511 (1985), the Court extended qualified immunity to the Attorney General for authorizing a warrantless wiretap in a case involving domestic national security. Although the Court later held such warrantless wiretaps violated the Fourth Amendment, at the time of the Attorney General's authorization, this interpretation was not clearly established, and Harlow immunity protected officials exercising discretion on such open questions. . . .

10. Harlow v. Fitzgerald, 457 U.S. 800, 812 (1982)
11. See 28 U.S.C. § 1331. On deleting the jurisdictional amount, see Pub. L. No. 94-574, 90 Stat. 2721 (1976); Pub. L. No. 96-486, 94 Stat. 2369 (1980). If suits are brought in state courts, they can be removed to federal district courts. 28 U.S.C. § 1442(a). See 28 U.S.C. § 1331.

Art II.S3.5.3 Qualified Immunity Doctrine

He shall have Power, by and with the Advice and Consent of the Senate, to make Treaties, provided two thirds of the Senators present concur; and he shall nominate, and by and with the Advice and Consent of the Senate, shall appoint Ambassadors, other public Ministers and Consuls, Judges of the supreme Court, and all other Officers of the United States, whose Appointments are not herein otherwise provided for, and which shall be established by Law: but the Congress may by Law vest Appointment of such inferior Officers, as they think proper, in the President alone, in Courts of Law, or in the Heads of Departments.

While the courts may be unable to compel the President to act or to prevent him from acting, his acts, when performed, are in proper cases subject to judicial review and disallowance. Typically, the subordinates through whom he acts may be sued, in a form of legal fiction, to enjoin the commission of acts which might lead to irreparable damage[1] or to compel by writ of mandamus the performance of a duty definitely required by law.[2] Such suits are usually brought in the US District Court for the District of Columbia.[3] In suits under the common law, a subordinate executive officer may be held personally liable in damages for any act done in excess of authority,[4] although immunity exists for anything, even malicious wrongdoing, done in the course of his duties.[5]

Different rules prevail when such an official is sued for a constitutional tort for wrongs in violation of our basic charter,[6] although the Court has hinted in some sensitive areas officials acting in the outer perimeter of their duties may be accorded an absolute immunity from liability.[7] Jurisdiction to reach such officers for acts for which they can be held responsible must be under general federal question jurisdictional statute, which, as amended, requires no jurisdictional amount.[8]

1. E.g., Youngstown Sheet & Tube Co. v. Sawyer, 343 U.S. 579 (1952) (suit to enjoin Secretary of Commerce to return steel mills seized on President's order); Dames & Moore v. Regan, 453 U.S. 654 (1981) (suit against Secretary of Treasury to nullify presidential orders on Iranian assets). See also Noble v. Union River Logging R.R., 147 U.S. 165 (1893); Phila. Co. v. Stimson, 223 U.S. 605 (1912).
2. E.g., Marbury v. Madison, 5 U.S. (1 Cr.) 137 (1803) (suit against Secretary of State to compel delivery of commissions of office); Kendall v. United States ex rel. Stokes, 37 U.S. (12 Pet.) 524 (1838) (suit against Postmaster General to compel payment of money owed under act of Congress); Decatur v. Paulding, 39 U.S. (14 Pet.) 497 (1840) (suit to compel Secretary of Navy to pay a pension).
3. This was originally on the theory that the Supreme Court of the District of Columbia had inherited, via the common law of Maryland, the jurisdiction of the King's Bench over inferior jurisdictions and officers. Kendall v. US ex rel. Stokes, 37 U.S. (12 Pet.) 524, 614, 620–21 (1838). Congress has now authorized federal district courts outside the District of Columbia also to entertain such suits. Act of Oct 5, 1962, Pub. L. No. 87-748, 76 Stat. 744 (codified at 28 U.S.C. § 1361).

4. E.g., Little v. Barreme, 6 U.S. (2 Cr.) 170 (1804); Bates v. Clark, 95 U.S. 204 (1877); US v. Lee, 106 U.S. 196 (1882); Virginia Coupon Cases (Poindexter v. Greenhow), 114 U.S. 270 (1885); Belknap v. Schild, 161 U.S. 10 (1896).
5. Spalding v. Vilas, 161 U.S. 483 (1896); Barr v. Matteo, 360 U.S. 564 (1959). See Westfall v. Erwin, 484 U.S. 292 (1988) (action must be discretionary in nature as well as being within the scope of employment, before federal official is entitled to absolute immunity). Following the Westfall decision, Congress enacted the Federal Employees Liability Reform and Tort Compensation Act of 1988 (the Westfall Act), which authorized the Attorney General to certify that an employee was acting within the scope of his office or employment at the time of the incident out of which a suit arose; upon certification, the employee is dismissed from the action, and the United States is substituted, the Federal Tort Claims Act (FTCA) then governing the action, which means that sometimes the action must be dismissed against the government because the FTCA has not waived sovereign immunity. United States v. Smith, 499 U.S. 160 (1991) (Westfall Act bars suit against federal employee even when an exception in the FTCA bars suit against the government). Cognizant of the temptation of the government to immunize both itself and its employee, the Court in Gutierrez de Martinez v. Lamagno, 515 U.S. 417 (1995), held the AG's certification is subject to judicial review.
6. An implied cause of action against officers accused of constitutional violations was recognized in Bivens v. Six Unknown Named Agents of the Federal Bureau of Narcotics, 403 U.S. 388 (1971). In Butz v. Economou, 438 U.S. 478 (1978), a Bivens action, the Court distinguished between common-law torts and constitutional torts and denied high federal officials, including cabinet secretaries, absolute immunity, in favor of the qualified immunity previously accorded high state officials under 42 U.S.C. § 1983. In Harlow v. Fitzgerald, 457 U.S. 800 (1982), the Court denied presidential aides derivative absolute presidential immunity, but it modified the rules of qualified immunity, making it more difficult to hold such aides, other federal officials, and indeed state and local officials, liable for constitutional torts. In Mitchell v. Forsyth, 472 U.S. 511 (1985), the Court extended qualified immunity to the AG for authorizing a warrantless wiretap in a case involving domestic national security. Although the Court later held such warrantless wiretaps violated the Fourth Amendment, at the time of the AG's authorization this interpretation was not clearly established, and the Harlow immunity protected officials exercising discretion on such open questions. See also Anderson v. Creighton, 483 U.S. 635 (1987) (in an exceedingly opaque opinion, the Court extended similar qualified immunity to FBI agents who conducted a warrantless search).
7. Harlow v. Fitzgerald, 457 U.S. 800, 812 (1982).
8. See 28 U.S.C. § 1331. On deleting the jurisdictional amount, see Pub. L. No. 94-574, 90 Stat. 2721 (1976), and Pub. L. No. 96-486, 94 Stat. 2369 (1980). If such suits are brought in state courts, they can be removed to federal district courts. 28 U.S.C. § 1442(a).

Art II.S3.5.4
Criminal Prosecution, Presidential Immunity and Former Presidents

He shall have Power, by and with the Advice and Consent of the Senate, to make Treaties, provided two thirds of the Senators present concur; and he shall nominate, and by and with the Advice and Consent of the Senate, shall appoint Ambassadors, other public Ministers and Consuls, Judges of the supreme Court, and all other Officers of the United States, whose Appointments are not herein otherwise provided for, and which shall be established by Law: but the Congress may by Law vest the Appointment of such inferior Officers, as they think proper, in the President alone, in the Courts of Law, or in the Heads of Departments.

In *Trump v. United States*, the Supreme Court addressed how principles of presidential immunity apply to a criminal prosecution of a former president[1] for actions taken while in office.[2] The case concerned an indictment against former President Trump for allegedly attempting to overturn the results of the 2020 election.[3]

In evaluating President Trump's claim that he was immune from prosecution, the Supreme Court announced a three-part framework for evaluating a former president's immunity from criminal prosecution.

First, the Court held that former presidents are entitled to absolute immunity from criminal prosecution for actions within the exclusive sphere of their constitutional authority while in office.[4] Certain core presidential powers, such as granting pardons,[5] removing executive officers whom the president has appointed,[6] and discussing potential investigations and prosecutions with the Justice Department, including those concerning allegations of election crime,[7] are exclusive and preclusive—meaning the other branches of government have no constitutional power to restrict them, the Court explained.[8] For example, President Trump acted in this exclusive sphere of authority, the Court held, when he allegedly attempted to leverage the Justice Department's power and authority to convince certain States to replace their legitimate electors with Trump's fraudulent slates of electors.[9] Because the President cannot be prosecuted for conduct within his exclusive constitutional authority,[10] the Court explained, the former President is absolutely immune from prosecution for alleged conduct involving his discussions with Justice Department officials.[11]

The second facet addresses conduct that falls outside of the exclusive sphere of presidential power but still constitutes official acts the President.[12] Although not protected in the same manner as core executive powers, such official acts may still be protected by immunity, the Court reasoned, in order to safeguard the independence and effectiveness of the presidency and to enable presidents to perform their constitutional responsibilities without being overly cautious or concerned with future prosecutions.[13] Official acts are presumptively immune from criminal prosecution,[14] Supreme Court held, unless the government can show that prosecuting a former President in that instance would pose no 'dangers of intrusion on authority and functions of the Executive Branch.'[15] The Court held that President Trump's official acts included his alleged attempt to pressure the former Vice President to take certain acts in connection with certifying the electoral vote count, the Court remanded for lower courts to determine whether US could rebut the presumption immunity applied to those acts.[16]

Finally, Supreme Court held that former presidents do not have immunity for their unofficial acts.[17] The Court observed that the process of distinguishing the President's official acts from unofficial can be difficult[,][18] especially in the context of the former President's public communications on social media and in a public speech.[19] Because the official acts analysis requires a fact-specific evaluation that lower courts did not conduct, the Supreme Court remanded the case for further consideration whether certain activity qualifies as official or unofficial.[20] Id. at 28

Although Supreme Court left questions of immunity unresolved in *Trump v. United States*, it did definitively address Trump's argument that a former President can only be prosecuted after being impeached in the House and convicted in the Senate.[21] [Id. at 32-34.] Supreme Court rejected the view that impeachment is a perquisite to criminal conviction, reasoning that transforming the political process of impeachment into an essential first step in a criminal prosecution did not have support in the Constitution's text or structure of the US government.[22] [Id. at 34.]

1. Because criminal charges have never been filed against a sitting President, the Supreme Court has never considered a case addressing whether a sitting President could be prosecuted. The executive branch has expressed the view sitting Presidents enjoy absolute immunity from criminal prosecution. *See* Memorandum from Randolph D. Moss, Assistant Atty. Gen., Office of Legal Counsel, to the Atty. Gen.: A Sitting President's Amenability to Indictment and Criminal Prosecution, 24 Op. OLC 222, 222 (Oct. 16, 2000) (The indictment or criminal prosecution of a sitting President would impermissibly undermine the capacity of the executive branch to perform its constitutionally assigned functions.).
2. Trump v. United States, No. 23-939, slip op. at 1 (U.S. July 1, 2024).
3. A federal grand jury indicted President Trump on four criminal counts: (1) conspiracy to defraud the United States by overturning the election results under (18 United States Code, section 371), (2) conspiracy to obstruct an official proceeding— in this case, Congress's certification of the electoral vote (18 United States Code, section 1512(k)); (3) obstruction of, and attempt to obstruct, the certification of the electoral vote (18 United States Code, section 1512(c)(2)); and (4) conspiracy against the rights of persons to vote and to have their votes counted (18 United States Code, section 241). In *Fischer v. United States*—a different case arising out of the January 6, 2021, unrest at the U.S. Capitol issued during the same term as the Trump decision—the Supreme Court interpreted the statute on which the third count is based, 18 United States Code, section 1512(c)(2). No. 23-5572., slip op. at 1 (U.S. June 28, 2024). In *Fischer*, the Court held that charges under section 1512(c)(2) must be based on alleged impairment (or attempted impairment) of records, documents, objects, or other things used an official proceeding. *Id.* at 16. For a more detailed discussion of the charges in the Trump indictment, see Peter G. Berris, Cong. Rsch. Serv. LSB1116, Overview of the Indictment of Former President Trump Related to the 2020 Election,
4. https://crsreports.congress.gov/product/pdf/LSB/LSB11016.
5. Trump v. United States, No. 23-939, slip op. at 9.
6. *Id.* at 7-8.
7. *Id.* at 8.
8. *Id.* at 20.
9. *Id.* at 8 (quoting Youngstown Sheet & Tube Co. v. Sawyer, 343 U.S. 579, 638 (1952) (Jackson, J., concurring)). *See also id* at 19 (The Government does not dispute that the indictment's allegations regarding the Justice Department involve Trump's 'use of official power.' The allegations in fact plainly implicate Trump's 'conclusive and preclusive' authority. '[I]investigation and prosecution of crimes is a quintessentially executive function.')(citations omitted).
10. *Id.* at 19.
11. *Id.* at 21.
12. *See id.* The Court explained: The indictment's allegations that the requested investigations were 'sham[s]' or proposed for an improper purpose do not divest the President of exclusive authority over the investigative and prosecutorial functions of the Justice Department and its officials. And the President cannot be prosecuted for conduct within his exclusive constitutional authority. *Id.* (citations omitted).
13. *See id.* at 9.
14. *Id.* at 12-15.
15. *Id.* at 23, 36.
16. *Id.* at 14 (quoting Nixon v. Fitzgerald, 457 U.S. 731, 754 (1982)). *Id.* at 23-24.
17. *Id.* at 15.
18. *Id.* at 17.
19. *Id.* at 28-30.

CHAPTER 25. CLOSING ARGUMENTS

SUMMARY OF THIS BOOK OF ARGUMENTS THAT EXPOSE THE FAR-LEFT LAWFARE BY PROSECUTORS AND JUDGES ACTING AGAINST FORMER PRESIDENT DONALD TRUMP.

Amistad Project Director Phill Kline says his group collected sworn expert testimony alleging *"over 300,000 ballots are at issue in Arizona, 548,000 in Michigan, 204,000 in Georgia, and over 121,000 in Pennsylvania."* FBI requested access to their data analysis, Kline noted previously. (Chapter 7)

CLOSING ARGUMENT 1.

Three key issues in American History were far more objectionable than any allegation against Donald Trump, as indicated herein and as footnotes to all these sections of the US Constitution identifying powers of the Executive Branch:

1. President Jackson closes First Bank of the US., which destroyed the currency of the United States. While this author is a fan of Jackson, this was a big mistake that he should have repaired instead of closing.
2. President Lincoln actions during Civil War
3. Impeachment of President Andrew Johnson

Closing Argument 2 below reminds us of 68 times US Constitution actually defines and argues IMMUNITY
Closing Argument 3 below identifies Oath of Office and Take Care as applied in the cases of Jackson and Lincoln.
Closing Argument 4 outlines nearly 200 instances of murderous riots requiring troops or National Guard

CLOSING ARGUMENT 2.

Many times, the word IMMUNITY is applied in the US Constitution establishment of powers of the President and Executive Branch of The United States of America.

Sixty-Eight (68) times in the specific sections of Article II Section 3, the word immunity is applied in both Constitutional clauses along with US Supreme Court documentation of their official opinions on several court cases that came forward in which Presidential Immunity might have been an issue.

How can it be possible that so many democrat lawyers now accuse 2024 SCOTUS of constitutional destruction. Obviously, those lawyers, including the head of the New York State Bar, have zero understanding of the constitution, or else they are now confirmed liars. They were forced to pass very tough tests on our constitution in order to become a lawyer.

<u>CLOSING ARGUMENT 3</u>.

OATH OF OFFICE and TAKE CARE CLAUSE
PRESIDENT ANDREW JACKSON CLOSES 'BANK OF THE UNITED STATES
At great peril to our economic system.

PRESIDENT ABRAHAM LINCOLN SUSPENDS "WRIT OF HABEAS CORPUS"
Risking destruction of American Rule of Law

Both Jackson and Lincoln were acting in full accord with their Oath of Office along with the Take Care clause yet defied both congressional and judicial branch actions. Further, Lincoln would order closure of some 300 Newspapers and jail 3000 reporters during Civil War. These actions of both Jackson and Lincoln were a far greater true threat to America than any perceived actions of Donald Trump.

The following sections of US Constitution Annotated, will summarize the wording of US Constitution, along with key cases opined by Supreme Court of the United States, upholding Presidential Powers along with Presidential Immunity.

Article II Executive Branch
Art II.S1.C1.1 Overview of Executive Vesting Clause (Powers of the President)

The executive Power shall be vested in a President of the United States of America. He shall hold his Office during the Term of four Years, and, together with the Vice President, chosen for the same Term, be elected, as follows:

Under Article II, Section 1, Clause 1, the executive power is vested in a single person—the President of the United States. The nature and extent of executive power is less clear.[1] Article II identifies exclusive powers of the President, including President's authority as Commander in Chief and the power to pardon;[2] powers the President shares with the Senate, including the appointments and treaty-making powers;[3] and the President's duties, <u>most important of which is the duty to take Care that the Laws be faithfully executed</u>.[4] Moreover, the Supreme Court has recognized that because no single person could fulfill that responsibility, the *Take Care Clause implicitly provides the President with authority to supervise subordinate officers assisting with this responsibility*.[5] Likewise, Article I provides the President a role in the legislative process, including authority to veto legislation, subject to potential override by a two-thirds vote of both Houses of Congress.[6]

It is less clear from the text of the Constitution whether the executive powers expressly identified in the Constitution are exclusive or illustrative. Whereas the Article I Legislative Vesting Clause provides that All legislative Powers *herein granted* shall be vested in a Congress,[7] thereby distinguishing the powers granted by states from those they retained, the Article II Executive Vesting Clause does not limit the executive Power in any way.[8] Consequently, since the earliest days of the Republic, the parameters of the executive power and, in particular, what implicit or residual powers such executive power encompasses have been the subject of debate.

1U.S. Const. art. II, § 1, cl. 1.
2 *Id.* art. II, § 2, cl. 1. *See* ArtII.S2.C1.1.1 Historical Background on Commander in Chief Clause.
3 *Id.* art. II, § 2, cl. 2. *See* ArtII.S2.C1.3.1 Overview of Pardon Power.
4 *Id.* art. II, § 3. *See* ArtII.S3.3.1 Overview of Take Care Clause.
5 Seila Law LLC v. Consumer Fin. Protection Bureau, No. 19-7, slip op. at 2 (U.S. June 29, 2020). *See also* Free Enter. Fund v. Pub. Co. Acct. Oversight Bd., 561 U.S. 477, 492–93 (2010).
6 U.S. Const. art. I, § 7, cl. 2. *See* ArtI.S7.C2.1 Overview of Presidential Approval or Veto of Bills.
7 *Id.* art. I, § 1, cl. 1 (emphasis added). *See* ArtI.S1.1 Overview of Legislative Vesting Clause.
8 *Id.* art. II, § 1, cl. 1.

Art II.S1.C8.1 Oath of Office for the Presidency

Before he enter on the Execution of his Office, he shall take the following Oath or Affirmation:–I do solemnly swear (or affirm) that I will faithfully execute the Office of President of the United States, and will to the best of my Ability, preserve, protect, and defend the Constitution of the US.

What is the time relationship between a President's assumption of office and his taking the oath? Apparently, the former comes first, this answer appearing to be the assumption of the language of the clause. The Second Congress assumed that President George Washington took office on March 4, 1789,1 although he did not take the oath until the following April 30.

That the oath the President is required to take might be considered to add anything to the powers of the President, because of his obligation to preserve, protect and defend the Constitution, might appear to be rather a fanciful idea.

But in **President Andrew Jackson's** message announcing his veto of the act renewing the Bank of the United States there is language which suggests that the President has the right to refuse to enforce both statutes and judicial decisions based on his own independent decision that they were unwarranted by the Constitution.[2] The idea next turned up in a message by **President Abraham Lincoln** justifying his suspension of the writ of habeas corpus without obtaining congressional authorization.[3] And counsel to **President Andrew Johnson** during his impeachment trial adverted to the theory, but only in passing.[4] Beyond these isolated instances, it does not appear to be seriously contended that the oath adds anything to the President's powers.

1. Act of March 1, 1792, 1 Stat. 239, § 12.
2. 2 Messages and Papers of the Presidents 576 (J. Richardson ed. 1896). Chief Justice Roger Taney, who as a member of Jackson's Cabinet had drafted the message, later repudiated this possible reading of the message. 2 C. Warren, The Supreme Court in United States History 223–224 (1926).
3. 6 Messages and Papers of the Presidents, *supra* note 2, at 25.
4. 2 Trial of Andrew Johnson 200, 293, 296 (1868).

CLOSING ARGUMENT 4.

NATIONAL EMERGENCIES, EXTENT OF PRESIDENTIAL POWER (CH 19)
Murderous Riots requiring Federal Troops to overcome:

- 3 Tax Rebellions prior to 1800 required Federal Troops
- 1811-1859, 23 murderous riots required Federal Troops
- 1866-1880 (Reconstruction) 21 murderous riots required troops
- Great Railroad Strike 1877: bloody riots, 8 major railroad Cities
- 1884-1899, 17 murderous riots requiring Federal Troops
- 1900-1922, 33 riots requiring Federal Troops

INDICATES CLEAR PRESIDENTIAL IMMUNITY

CLOSING ARGUMENT 5.

In our Chapter 12, and Chapter 14, we document the massive degree of Conflict of Interest of all but two Judges and Prosecutors in the litany of false cases filed against Donald Trump. You will find evidence of 198 clear instances of Judicial Branch CONFLICT OF INTEREST against President Donald Trump.

The only correct follow-up to the many false Trump prosecutions and indictments is to disbar and remove from office for all time, any and all legal authorities acting against Trump for any purpose. The good people of these United States of America deserve far better from Judicial Branches of State and Federal government.

CLOSING ARGUMENT 6.

In 2025, now that President Trump has been strongly re-elected, we once again see a proliferation of Democrat Federal Judges attacking President Trump and his policies. As of May 2025, we already have seen democrat US Judges attempt to strike down fully 30 of President Trump's new actions. Quite clearly, these Judges have lost sight of their position within the United States Constitution. A standard of modern law deals with CONFLICT OF INTEREST. We have identified earlier 198 points of conflict of interest between the Judges who attacked Trump's attempts to correct the election of 2020. Now that he is elected once again, by an overwhelming majority, these same wayward democrat Judges continue their assault upon the US Constitution, via wayward and wrong-headed, if not criminal, treasonable, and treasonable attacks far beyond their authority as low level Judges.

CLOSING ARGUMENT 7.

We have seen the Georgia State Court System remove Fulton County chief Prosecutor Fani Willis from all Trump cases she lodged in State of Georgia. A new law in Georgia may allow Trump to recover his costs in the Georgia Case.

CLOSING ARGUMENT 8.

We have seen all the Jack Smith inspired cases to be dismissed outright, and Jack Smith has removed himself from public view.

CLOSING ARGUMENT 9.

Clear evidence herein shows us that California Senator Adam Schiff raised Over $20 million by hawking the Trump cases. Further, we see that the daughter of rookie Judge Merchan raised over $93 million for democrat political war chests by selling her fathers judicial action against Donald Trump. Where are the other courts? These should be fully separate criminal convictions.

Closing Argument 10.

Our Founding Fathers established the Judicial Branch of Government initially controlled by a Supreme Court structure. The Supreme Court was intended to establish further courts as the need would arise. The Founders did not voice a method by which Supreme Court might discipline lower level judges. Instead, they established the principle of IMPEACHMENT, to be exercised by US Congress.

It seems clear that only a few Impeachments of Judges can possibly serve as a "backstop" and possibly quickly restore normalcy to our time honored Judicial Branch of United States Government. Is it possible that Supreme Court of the United States can launch disciplinary actions more efficiently?

CLOSING ARGUMENT 11.

The "fix" for these 150 years of voting morass is underway.

- Donald Trump was re-elected President, despite the vast conflict of interest that attacked him across 4 years.
- Jack Smith has become invisible. His unit at FBI/DOJ is now shuttered.
- All boxes/documents Jack Smith removed from Mar A Lago are to be returned.
- Fanni Willis has been removed from all elements of the Trump election cases.
- A developing bill has been signed into law in Georgia that may allow Trump to recover all costs of the failed Fulton County cases lodged against Trump.
- New York Attorney General Letitia James is being investigated and sued on several fronts, stemming from her joke level attempts to "get Donald Trump."
- More action is required as an all new set of reactions to the Trump Presidency is preventing logical actions to make improvements to our Federal Government. While the vast majority of Trump actions are intended to curb fraud and corruption, some 30 US court cases have been launched by Federal Judges, acting without cognizant responsibility.

SUMMARY OF CLOSING ARGUMENTS

1. Detailed Argument #1 is documentation of 3 serious incidents of Presidential history that vastly exceed danger limits allowed to a President, making clear there has been zero danger from actions of President Trump.
2. Presidential Immunity wording and discussion appears 68 times in United States, along with US Constitution Annotated, to include the litany of SCOTUS cases opining and upholding Presidential Immunity.
3. This book solidly elaborates the "how and why" US Constitution includes Presidential OATH OF OFFICE along with THE TAKE CARE CLAUSE as a means of providing a sitting President the totality to which his Presidential actions are supported by US Constitution.
4. Argument 4 along with earlier chapters document that over 100 times in American History, sitting Presidents have found it necessary to commit military troops, along with US Marshalls, National Guard and Sheriff's, in order to quell bloody disturbances inside America. The Presidential term of Donald Trump experienced only very minor disturbances when compared with those documented in earlier chapters.
5. Closing Argument 5 makes it clear that seriously wrong-headed Judges and Prosecutors crossed any and all definition of conflict of interest in the many court cases directed at perceived actions of President Trump. These conflicts are so serious as to endanger the very fabric of Democracy. Strongest punitive legal measures must and shall be mandated to ensure such intolerable stupidity never again strikes the United States of America.
6. Federal Judges are off course. Even following re-election of Trump, we see yet another set of heavily conflicted Democrat United States Judges attacking policies of President Trump. Our Founding Fathers are not happy!
7. Fani Willis debacle continues as she is removed from all cases. Georgia law may allow Trump to recoup his exorbitant expenses in Fulton County case.
8. Jack Smith has moved into obscurity at present. His cases were dismissed.
9. Democrats have raised over $120 million campaign dollars from the case charade against Trump. Clearly, such activity should cease and desist.
10. Our Founding Fathers established a Judicial Branch of government for the express purpose of dealing with criminality. Why has our vaunted court system remained silent? Supreme Court was established and given responsibility for expanding the court system as case loads grew. Now we see SCOTUS remaining reluctant to become involved.
11. Hope flourishes as a result of preliminary wins for Donald Trump, yet already, we see yet a new wave of court actions attacking the policies of President Trump. In the case of all the new attacks, the judiciary is leading these attacks prior to cases being presented, thus the lower courts are shamefully acting beyond their assigned responsibility. All courts action against our re-elected President Trump are launched by democrat Judges. A number of states are commencing actions to bring elections under control.

" THE FRANCHISE"

HOW AND WHY

As a final closing statement, we will identify THE FRANCHISE roots. While debating The Voting Rights Act in the 1960's, and many other elections cases that came before the court, Supreme Court of the United States began to apply a term to American Voting and Elections they called "The Franchise." They make many statements related to voting, typically making reference to The Franchise. Their lingering thought is that Voting and Elections are the very fabric that holds Democracies and Democratic Republics together. Therefore, to protect The Franchise, we must constantly ensure that we make every effort to protect a free-flowing democracy exercise that returns a result in the best interest of our favorite franchise, The United States of America.

We discussed the history of Democracy in earlier chapters. The history should make clear that given the present circumstances, democracy is in great peril. Roman democracy survived 500 years; Greek democracy survived 800 years. Today in 2024 America, we approach 250 years of successful democracy, whereas the very Judicial Branch our Founding Fathers established now threatens to fully derail what has been the most successful democracy in all history. This book provides prima facie evidence that our democracy is today in a full reversal of the course mapped out by our Founding Fathers.

This book provides a relatively simple and constitutional means of removal of threats within the Judicial Branch that threatens to destroy, so that we may continue success far into the future:

Judicial restraints or IMPEACHMENT.

Chapter 26 INDEX

This extensive index has been subdivided into more specific points of interest. If not subdivided, this index would run 6 consecutive pages. The subdivisions will assist the research required to circle back and locate entries on specific issues.

SUBDIVISIONS OF THE INDEX

JUDGES / PROSECUTORS - Chapter 13

DOMINION AND SMARTMATIC

THE CO-DEFENDANTS IN TRUMP CASES ARE:

SIMILAR SMITH PROSECUTIONS, SCOTUS Overturned

CASES AGAINST DONALD TRUMP ACROSS SEVERAL STATES

IMPORTANT LOCATIONS

STATES

OTHER NAMED PEOPLE OR ISSUES

KEY UNIVERSITIES

ANCIENT HISTORY PRECEDENT

LEGAL AND GOVERNMENT TERMS

TECHNICAL/ MECHANICAL ISSUES

TRUMP DEFENSE LAWYERS THROUGHOUT, 54 REQUIRED

TRUMP DEFENSE MEMBERS NOT IN BOOK

Blanche, Bobb, Bondi, Castor, Clark, Cohn, Consovoy, Corcoran, Dhillon, DiGenova, Dillon, Dowd, Edonomou, Epshteyn, Fielding, Findling, Flood, Gaiser, Garten, Greenblatt, Habba, Halligan, Harder, Hendon, Kasowitz, Kise, McGahn, Mitchell, Passantino, Philbin, Purpura, Ray, Ross, Schoen, Scott, Sekulow, Starr, Tacopina, Toensing, Troupis, Van der Veen

INVESTIGATION TEAM IN NY CASES (in order of organization) – p. 74

The investigation and subsequent legal action were conducted by:
Kevin Wallace, Andrew Amer, Colleen K. Faherty, Alex Finkelstein, Wil Handley, Stephanie Torre, Sherief Gaber, Eric R. Haren, Louis M. Solomon, Mark Ladov, Austin Thompson, Samantha Stern, Labiba Hasan, Anushua Choudhury, Akram Hasanov, Blake Rubey, Chansoo Song, Megan Thorsfeldt, Jonathan Werberg, Hewson Chen, Paige Podolny, John Roach, Judith Vale, Ester Murdukhayeva, Dennis Fan, Cleland Welton, Daniel Magy, Eric Del Pozo, Jennifer Levy.

www.ingramcontent.com/pod-product-compliance
Lightning Source LLC
LaVergne TN
LVHW060046210926
848481LV00013B/3968